Second Edition

AMERICA'S SCENIC DRIVES

Travel Guide & Atlas

William C. Herow

Published by:
Roundabout Publications, PO Box 19235
Lenexa, KS 66285 / 800-455-2207

Please Note

Every effort has been made to make this book as complete and as accurate as possible. However, there may be mistakes both typographical and in content. Therefore, this text should be used as a general guide to the scenic byways covered. Although we regret any inconvenience caused by inaccurate information, the author and Roundabout Publications shall have neither liability nor responsibility to any person or entity with respect to any loss or damage caused, or alleged to be caused, directly or indirectly by the information contained in this book.

 Published by: Roundabout Publications, P.O. Box 19235, Lenexa, Kansas 66285, Phone: 800-455-2207

Library of Congress Catalog Card Number: 00-132061

ISBN: 1-885464-29-0

Publisher's Cataloging-in-Publications
(Provided by Quality Books, Inc.)

Herow, William C.
America's scenic drives : travel guide & atlas / William C. Herow. -- 2nd ed.
p. cm.
Includes index.
LCCN: 00-132061
ISBN: 1-885464-29-0

1. Scenic byways--United States--Guidebooks.
2. Scenic byways--United States--Atlases.
3. Automobile travel--United States--Guidebooks
4. Automobile travel--United States--Atlases
5. United States--Guidebooks. I. Title.

E158.H47 2000 917.304'929
QBI00-338

Contents

Introduction

America's Best

America is linked by a vast network of nearly four million miles of roads. Most are not four lanes of concrete carrying fast-moving vehicles. They're roads that twist and turn, conforming to the path dictated by the river flowing alongside. They cut a path through canyons, dense forests, and mountains. They'll take you to fishing holes and small towns. They are roads that take you through the heart of America, the best she has to offer! Consider this your invitation to get off the fast lane and experience the America we're proud to call home.

About The Scenic Drives

On January 28, 1985, President Ronald Reagan established the President's Commission on Americans Outdoors. The Commission reviewed public and private outdoor recreational opportunities and made recommendations to ensure the future availability of outdoor recreation to the American people. Results of the study found that 43% of American adults identified driving for pleasure as a favorite leisure pursuit, second only to walking. In response to these findings, scenic byway programs were born.

National Forest Scenic Byways

In 1988 the U.S. Forest Service (USFS) began designating routes as National Forest Scenic Byways. The Forest Service manages more than 190 million acres of public land in 156 forests. Officially designated byways represent the best of the 100,000 miles of roads running through the national forests. These byways are represented throughout the book by the symbol shown.

BLM Back Country Byways

The Bureau of Land Management manages more than 270 million acres of public land, over 40 percent of all federal land. Their Back Country Byways program started in 1989 and provides a unique opportunity for traveling the more remote areas and back roads of America.

When traveling through remote areas, it is always a good idea to be prepared for your journey. Carry plenty of water for you and your vehicle's radiator. Be sure to start each trip with enough gasoline to drive the entire route. It is also a good idea to have a spare tire, jack, shovel, blanket, and tools for emergency road repairs. Many of these byways become impassable during winter or after periods of heavy rain. Inquire locally about road conditions and any vehicle limitations before attempting to travel the route.

Back Country Byways are classified into four types that determine the level of difficulty, road surface, and type of vehicle required. Listed below are descriptions of each classification.

Type I - Roads that are paved or have an all-weather surface and have grades that are negotiable by a normal touring car. These roads are usually narrow, slow speed, secondary roads. The symbol shown on the left is used throughout the book to indicate this type of byway.

Type II - These roads require a high-clearance vehicle such as a truck or four-wheel drive. They are usually unpaved but may have some type of surfacing. Grades, curves, and road surface are such that they can be negotiated with a two-wheel drive, high-clearance vehicle without undue difficulty. The symbol shown is used to indicate this type of byway.

Type III - These are roads that require a four-wheel drive vehicle or other specialized vehicle such as a dirt bike or all-terrain vehicle (ATV). These roads are usually not surfaced, but are managed to provide for safety considerations and resource protection needs. They have grades, tread surfaces, and other characteristics that require specialized vehicles to negotiate. The symbol to the left is used to indicate this type of byway.

Type IV - These are trails managed specifically to accommodate dirt bikes, mountain bikes, snowmobiles, or all-terrain vehicles. They are usually single-track trails. The symbol shown is used to indicate this type of byway.

National Scenic Byways & All-American Roads

The National Scenic Byways Program was established under the Intermodal Surface Transportation Efficiency Act of 1991 (ISTEA). The Scenic Byways Advisory Committee, working with the Federal Highway Administration, recommended that the program designate a system of National Scenic Byways and All-American Roads.

National Scenic Byways are chosen by the Secretary of Transportation for their scenic, historic, natural, cultural, recreational, or archaeological qualities. All-American Roads are chosen for the same qualities but are considered to be the "best of the best." These scenic byways represent the finest examples of scenic drives in America, making them "destinations unto themselves." The symbols shown indicate these types of byways. The first represents National Scenic Byways; the three-starred icon represents All-American Roads.

National Parkways

The National Park Service has designated four routes as National Parkways. Initial efforts for funding Parkways began as early as 1930. Today, these ribbons of land flanking the designated roadways offer an opportunity for a leisurely drive through areas of scenic and historical interest.

About This Book

This book provides you with a wealth of information on traveling America's scenic drives. You will find the information is presented in the same general format for each byway. The first paragraph provides information on the location, roads followed, any vehicle limitations, and travel season. That is followed by a description of the route, which is followed by sources for additional information on the byway and attractions found along the route.

Some byways include special lodging information. These are businesses that have extended a special welcome to byway travelers. The lodging establishments supplied us with information and a description of their location to help you plan and enjoy your scenic byway adventure. At the end of each lodging description is a row of icons to identify the facilities and services offered. A brief description of each icon is listed below. We would like to thank all the participating locations for providing you the opportunity to receive more enjoyment from the scenic drives. Please show your appreciation for their support by paying them a visit next time you are in their town.

- Wheelchair Access
- Exercise Room
- Sauna
- Swimming Pool
- Indoor Swimming Pool
- In-room Phones
- Movies / Cable
- Fireplaces
- Air Conditioning
- Restaurant
- Lounge
- Near Shopping
- Near Skiing
- Near Golf
- Near Fishing / Boating
- Near Hospital
- Near Airport
- Near Mass Transit
- Kitchen / Kitchenettes
- Pets Allowed
- Playground
- Laundry Facilities / Services
- Non-smoking Rooms
- Room Service
- Credit Cards Accepted
- Full or Continental Breakfast

Helpful Tips

As you drive these scenic byways, you may come across sites that seem to beg for closer examination. Many buildings or other attractions may be located on private property. Please respect the rights of landowners and obtain their permission before inspecting any sites of interest to you. Some byways will take you to sites of historic or archaeological significance, such as ancient Indian pictographs. Please enjoy the site and leave it undisturbed so others may enjoy it. Take only pictures and leave only footprints!

When you find yourself on a scenic byway that is a one-lane mountain pass road, remember the rule of courtesy gives the right of way to uphill traffic. Always use caution when approaching blind turns and be prepared for another vehicle around the bend.

ALABAMA

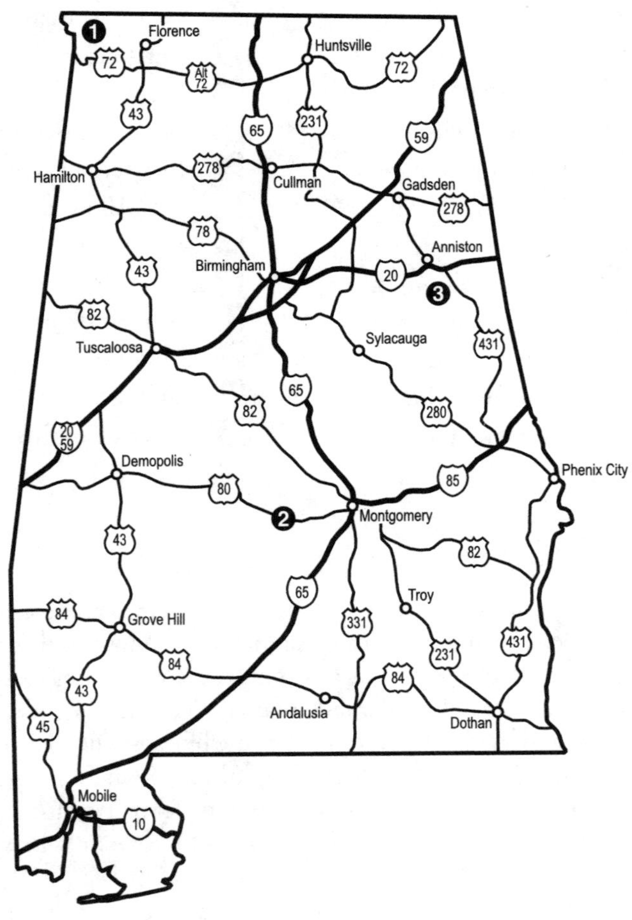

1
Florence
Huntsville
72
Alt 72
72
43
65
231
59
Hamilton
278
Cullman
Gadsden
278
78
Anniston
43
Birmingham
20
3
82
Sylacauga
431
Tuscaloosa
65
82
280
20 59
Demopolis
Phenix City
85
80
2
Montgomery
43
82
65
Troy
84
Grove Hill
331
431
231
84
84
43
Andalusia
Dothan
45
Mobile
10

Natchez Trace Parkway

Tennessee section see page 272 / Mississippi portion see page 150

This historic route generally follows the old Indian trace, or trail, between Nashville, Tennessee and Natchez, Mississippi. This portion of the byway cuts across northwestern Alabama for 33 miles. The parkway is a two-lane paved road suitable for all types of vehicles and is open year-round.

Once trekked by Indians and trampled into a rough road by traders, trappers, and missionaries, the Natchez Trace Parkway is now a scenic 445-mile route traveling from Natchez, Mississippi to Nashville, Tennessee. In the late 1700s and early 1800s, "Kaintucks," as the river merchants were called, would float downriver on flatboats loaded with their merchandise to be sold in New Orleans. Since there wasn't any practical way to return by river, the boats were dismantled and the lumber sold. The Natchez Trace would be the only pathway home.

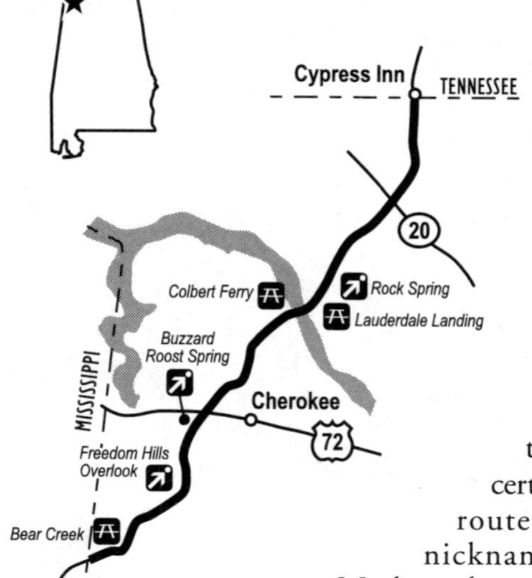

At that time, the Trace was a dangerous path to take. Travelers waded through swamps and swam streams and fended off attacks by wild animals and poisonous snakes. It was also necessary to keep an eye open for murderous bandits and Indian attacks. The terrain of the trace was rough, too. A broken leg of a lone traveler would often mean certain death. The dangers of the route earned the Trace the nickname "Devil's Backbone." Modern-day travelers don't have these dangers to face as they travel this historic route.

The Alabama portion of the Trace offers a variety of outdoor activities. Bear Creek, near the Mississippi state line, has picnic facilities and access to the creek for canoeing. Colbert Ferry, on the banks of the Tennessee River, has a picnic area, restrooms, telephone, and boat ramp. A ranger station is also located here, where George Colbert once operated a stand and ferry. Mr. Colbert is reported to have once charged Andrew Jackson $75,000 to ferry his army across the river. Lauderdale Landing is also a nice spot for a picnic.

A steep quarter-mile trail in Freedom Hills Overlook will take you to the highest point of the parkway in Alabama. Also worth stopping for is the Buzzard Roost Spring area. An exhibit here tells the story of Levi Colbert, a Chickasaw chief who owned a nearby stand. A short trail leads to the spring. A nature trail follows Colbert Creek at the Rock Spring area, milepost 330, and will take about 20 minutes to complete.

Information: National Park Service, Natchez Trace Pkwy, 2680 Natchez Trace Pkwy, Tupelo MS 38804 / 662-680-4025. Traveler Information: 800-305-7417.

Selma to Montgomery March Byway

This scenic byway is in central Alabama and travels between the cities of Selma and Montgomery. The 43-mile byway follows US 80, a four-lane divided highway suitable for travel by all types of vehicles. The byway is open year-round.

The Selma to Montgomery March Byway is more than a scenic drive, it celebrates one of the major historic events in 20th century American

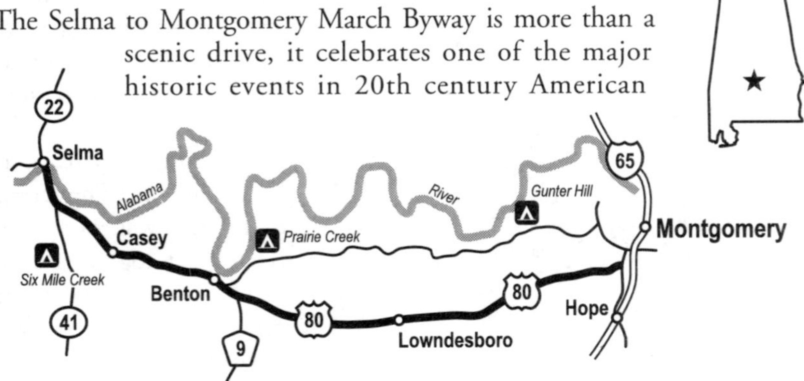

history. The Selma to Montgomery march represents two fundamental ideals of the American people—democratic equality and nonviolent protest. It is also recognized as a catalyst for passage of the Voting Rights Act of 1965.

On March 7, 1965, more than 500 African-Americans determined to march arrived at Brown Chapel A.M.E. Church in Selma. Early that afternoon the marchers left the church. When they reached the Edmund Pettus Bridge, the marchers could see state troopers waiting on the other side. The troopers blocked the road just outside the city limits of Selma. The commander of the troopers declared that the march was unlawful and ordered the marchers to disperse. When they did not move, the troopers began to move toward the marchers and pushed them back with their billy clubs. Then suddenly, the troopers attacked by firing tear gas and striking marchers with their clubs. The two hospitals in Selma that admitted blacks reported 65 injuries from the attack. Footage of the attack was broadcast that evening on network television, outraging much of the Nation. Dr. Martin Luther King, Jr. urged clergy nationwide to come to Selma to join in a minister's march the following Tuesday.

On Tuesday, March 10, 1965, King and the group of ministers marched only to the site of the attack. When the ministers reached the line of troopers, they offered prayers and then turned around.

At about 1:15 p.m. on Sunday, March 21, about 3,000 marchers once again began the march to Montgomery. This time they had the protection of the National Guard. It was in Lowndes County that the march size was reduced to 300 and the road narrowed to two lanes. It was also in Lowndes that Stokely Carmichael began to speak to the African-Americans about registering to vote. On March 25, the marchers arrived at the state capitol in Montgomery where a platform had been erected for King and others to speak. The largest civil rights march ever to take place in the South had finally reached its destination.

Recreational opportunities are limited directly along the scenic byway, however, camping facilities can be found at Six Mile Creek on Dannelly Reservoir, and at Prairie Creek and Gunter Hill on Woodruff Lake. These Corps of Engineers projects also offer picnicking, swimming, boating, and fishing.

Information: Selma-Dallas County C of C, 513 Lauderdale St, Selma AL 36702 / 334-875-7241; 800-45-Selma.

Talladega Scenic Drive

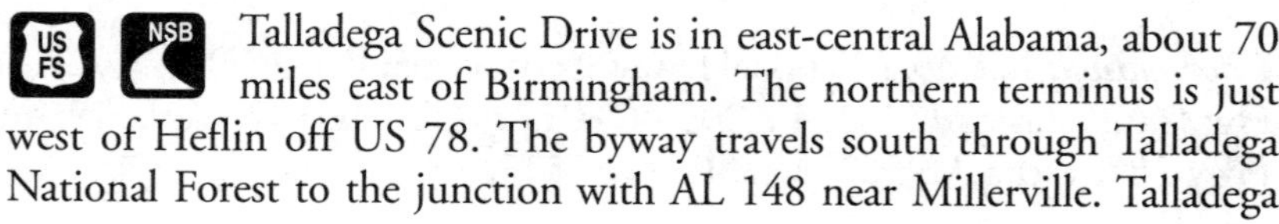

Talladega Scenic Drive is in east-central Alabama, about 70 miles east of Birmingham. The northern terminus is just west of Heflin off US 78. The byway travels south through Talladega National Forest to the junction with AL 148 near Millerville. Talladega

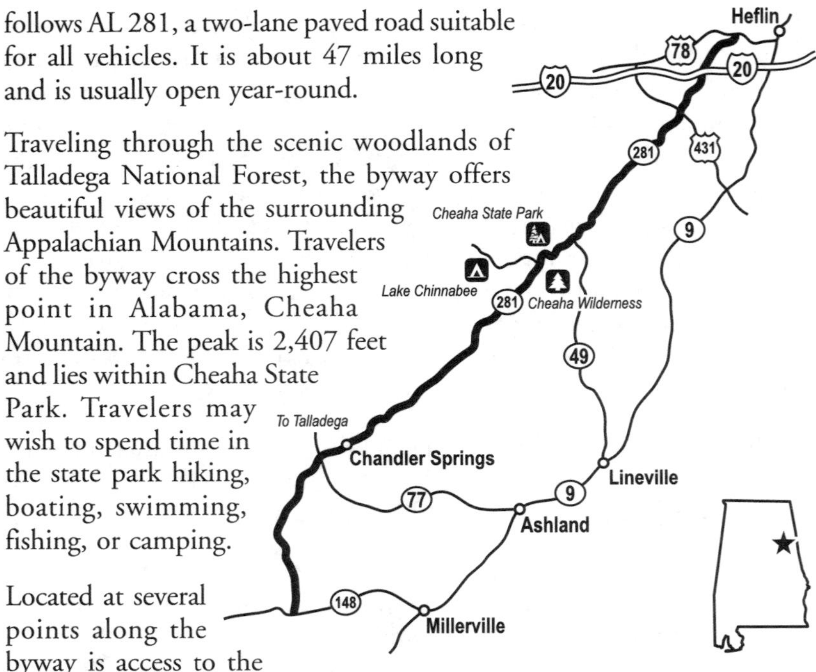

follows AL 281, a two-lane paved road suitable for all vehicles. It is about 47 miles long and is usually open year-round.

Traveling through the scenic woodlands of Talladega National Forest, the byway offers beautiful views of the surrounding Appalachian Mountains. Travelers of the byway cross the highest point in Alabama, Cheaha Mountain. The peak is 2,407 feet and lies within Cheaha State Park. Travelers may wish to spend time in the state park hiking, boating, swimming, fishing, or camping.

Located at several points along the byway is access to the Pinhoti National Recreation Trail. Also available to hikers and equestrians is Cheaha Wilderness, south of the state park. The wilderness is also open to hunting, fishing, and primitive camping. Motorized vehicles and bicycles are prohibited.

Talladega National Forest has many developed recreation areas. There are two designated for off-road vehicle use: Ivory Mountain and Kentuck Mountain. Coleman Lake, Lake Chinnabee, and Pine Glen Recreation Areas provide opportunities for camping, picnicking, fishing, hiking, and hunting.

Wildlife is abundant in the area. Careful observers may catch glimpses of white-tailed deer wandering through the forest. The bald eagle can also occasionally be seen soaring overhead. Other forms of wildlife include bobwhite quail, gray and fox squirrel, turkey, rabbit, opossum, and various waterfowl.

Information: Talladega National Forest, Shoal Creek Ranger District, 2309 Hwy 46, Helfin AL 36264 / 205-463-2272. Cheaha State Park, 19644 Hwy 281, Delta AL 36258 / 205-488-5111.

Alaska

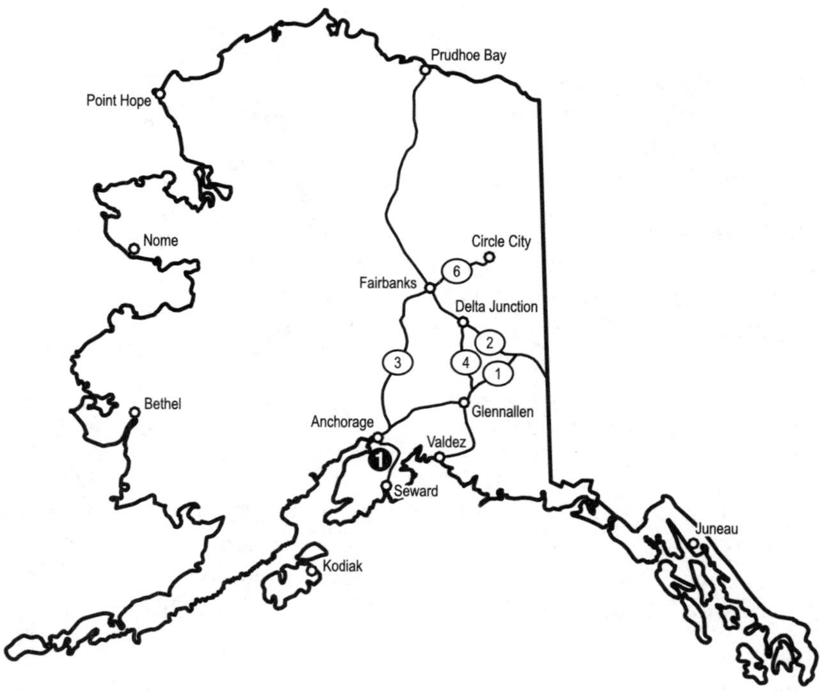

Seward Highway

Seward Highway is in south-central Alaska on the Cook Inlet. The byway begins in the city of Anchorage and travels south through the Chugach National Forest to the community of Seward. The scenic drive follows AK 1 and AK 9, which are two-lane paved roads. The roads are suitable for all types of vehicles although some sections are narrow and winding. Seward Highway is 127 miles long and is usually open year-round. Winter driving conditions may be hazardous. Snow avalanches can temporarily close sections of the highway.

Seward Highway ties Alaska's metropolitan center with the port of Seward on Resurrection Bay. From Anchorage the byway follows the shores of Turnagain Arm as it travels through Chugach State Park. After passing through Girdwood, the byway enters the beautiful scenery of the Chugach National Forest.

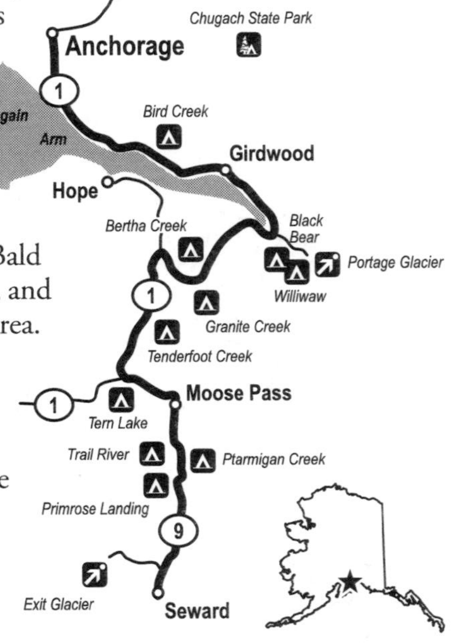

The byway offers spectacular scenery and a variety of wildlife all along its 127 miles. Beluga whales are occasionally seen rolling at the surface of the Turnagain Arm as they chase salmon and searun smelt. Dall sheep can sometimes be seen as they scale the rugged mountain sides. Bald eagles, moose, bear, mountain goat, and a variety of birds also inhabit the area.

Tracks of the Alaska Railroad are visible as you travel along the Turnagain Arm. This railroad was completed in 1923 and linked the port of Seward to the gold fields. Today, the Alaska Railroad operates various scenic train rides from May through September.

Seward Highway gives the byway traveler an opportunity to view glaciers close-up. Portage Glacier lies at the end of Turnagain Arm and is one of Alaska's most visited recreation sites. Exit Glacier, outside of Seward in the Kenai Fjords National Park, is also a great place to experience a glacier firsthand.

Information: Alaska Division of Tourism, 333 Willoughby Ave, State Office Bldg - 9th Fl, PO Box 11081, Juneau AK 99811-0801 / 907-465-2012, 888-256-6784. Chugach National Forest, 3301 C St, Anchorage AK 99503 / 907-271-2500. Chugach State Park, HC 52 Box 8999, Indian AK 99540 / 907-345-5014. Alaska Railroad Corporation, Passenger Services, P.O. Box 107500, Anchorage AK 99510 / 907-265-2494, 800-544-0552.

Lodging Invitation

The Taroka Inn Motel
235 3rd Avenue
P.O. Box 2448
Seward, AK 99664

Phone: 907-224-8975

Clean units with equipped kitchens, private bathrooms, in-room phones, and queen beds. Can accommodate one to nine persons. Conveniently located one block from Alaska Sealife Center. Great Rates! Please call for brochure or reservations.

Arizona

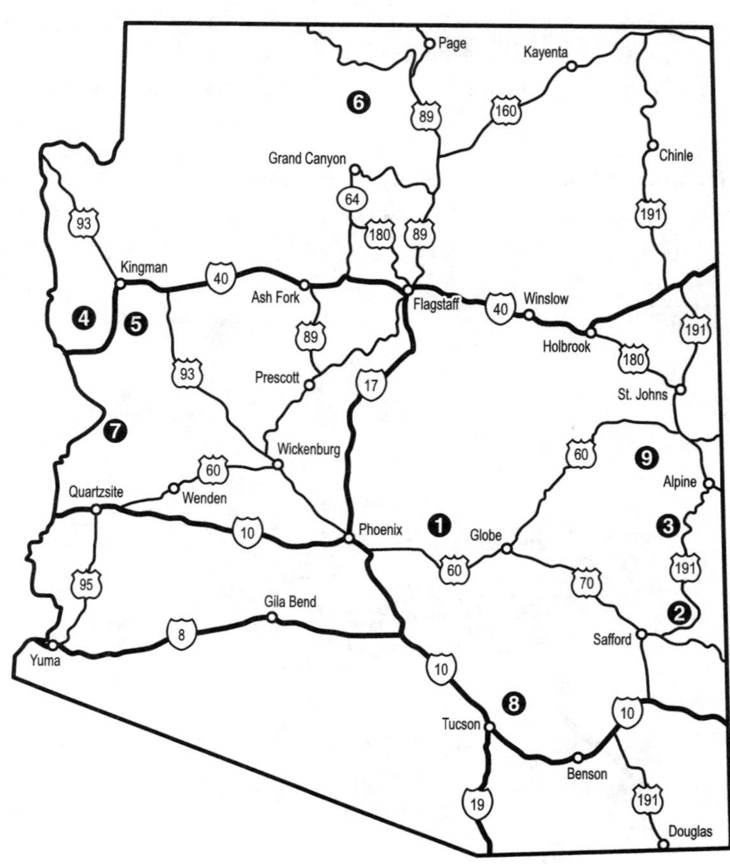

Page
Kayenta
6
89
160
Grand Canyon
Chinle
64
93
180
89
191
Kingman
40
Ash Fork
Flagstaff
40
Winslow
4
5
89
Holbrook
191
93
Prescott
17
180
St. Johns
7
Wickenburg
60
9
60
Alpine
Quartzsite
Wenden
10
Phoenix
1
Globe
3
60
191
95
70
Gila Bend
2
Safford
8
Yuma
10
8
Tucson
10
Benson
19
191
Douglas

Apache Trail

US FS Apache Trail is located in central Arizona, east of Phoenix. The byway begins in Apache Junction off US 60. The scenic drive follows AZ 88 northeast to the community of Roosevelt on Theodore Roosevelt Lake. Apache Trail is 46 miles long and is usually open year-round. Portions of the route are subject to closure due to heavy rain. The byway travels over dirt and paved roads with many sharp curves and an occasional narrow stretch. Vehicles pulling trailers are discouraged from traveling the section from Tortilla Flat to Roosevelt, especially over Fish Creek Hill.

The Apache Trail winds through some of the most awe-inspiring country in Arizona as it crosses Tonto National Forest. The scenic drive is bordered on the north by Canyon, Apache, and Roosevelt Lakes, and on the south by the rugged Superstition Mountains. At Fish Creek Hill, perhaps the most impressive part of Apache Trail, the road is primarily one-way and drops 1,000 feet in elevation over a 15 to 17 percent grade. Views of the Walls of Fish Creek Gorge are simply fantastic from this area.

Tonto National Forest covers nearly three million acres of rugged, scenic landscape ranging from cactus-studded desert to pine-covered mountains. Seven wilderness areas encompassing 589,000 acres are found within the

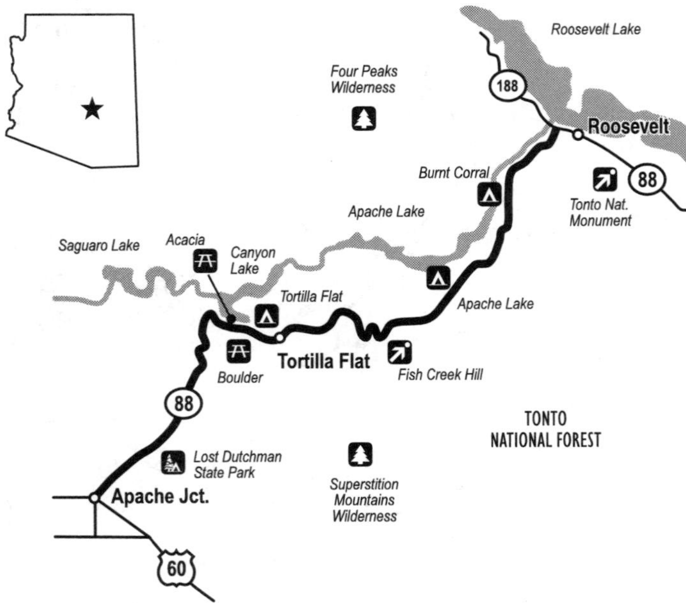

national forest. Two wilderness areas are located next to the byway: Four Peaks Wilderness and Superstition Wilderness. Hiking trails can be accessed along the drive that lure you into the Superstition Wilderness.

There are several Forest Service recreation areas along or near the byway. Acacia and Boulder offer picnic facilities; a swimming beach is in Acacia. Tortilla Flat Campground has 77 RV and tent sites; all have water and sewage hookups but no electricity. Near the byway's eastern end is the Burnt Corral Campground. It has 79 RV and tent campsites and is open all year. There is a 22-foot RV length limit at both campgrounds.

Lost Dutchman State Park is five miles northeast of Apache Junction. The nearly 300-acre park offers a 35-site campground with restrooms, showers, and sanitary disposal station. There are many desert interpretive trails here. It is also a good place to access the Superstition Wilderness.

Information: Tonto National Forest, PO Box 5348, Phoenix AZ 85010 / 602-225-5200. Lost Dutchman State Park, 6109 N Apache Trail, Apache Junction AZ 85219 / 602-982-4485.

Black Hills

BLM 2 The Black Hills Back Country Byway is in southeast Arizona, east of Safford near the New Mexico border. Eastern access is south of Clifton off US 191 (milepost 160). The byway travels southwest back to US 191 (milepost 139) near US 70 and Safford.

Black Hills is a 21-mile drive along the Old Safford-Clifton Road, an unpaved, narrow, and winding road. The byway is generally open year-round although sections may become impassable during and after heavy rain. Travelers should not attempt to drive the byway if pulling a trailer or in an RV longer than 20 feet. Motorhomes and trailers can be left at parking areas located on each end of the byway.

The Black Hills Back Country Byway passes through the historical territory of the Chiricahua and Western Apache, who arrived in southeast Arizona around 1600. Some Apaches used the area as a local travel route and hideout prior to the surrender of Geronimo in 1886. In 1540, Coronado passed through the area as he led Spanish conquistadors in search of gold and the Seven Cities of Cibola.

Each end of the byway begins in a desert shrub plant community and travels up through bands of desert grassland and then higher into stands of juniper, pinyon pine, and oaks. The Gila Box Riparian National Conservation Area preserves 21,000 acres of scenic desert canyons surrounding perennial rivers and creeks. The byway crosses the conservation area near the Old Safford Bridge.

Near the byway's western end are rock piles marking prisoner grave sites. This road was originally built by prisoners between 1914 and 1920. In 1916, a prisoner was killed by a guard while attempting to escape.

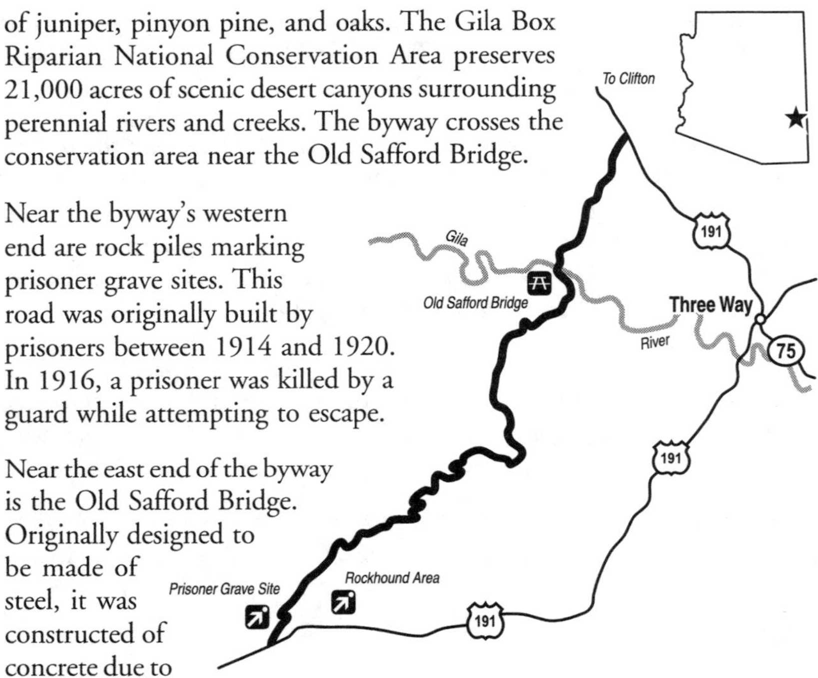

Near the east end of the byway is the Old Safford Bridge. Originally designed to be made of steel, it was constructed of concrete due to limits on the use of steel during World War I. The bridge was completed in 1918 and is on the National Register of Historic Places. Picnic areas at each end of the bridge serve as launch points for those interested in floating the Gila River.

Recreation along the byway is diverse and plentiful. Many primitive side roads invite off-road-vehicle users and challenges the experienced mountain biker. Rock collectors will want to visit the Black Hills Rockhound Area near the byway's western end. Anglers may wish to spend some time fishing in the Gila River. In early spring, snowmelt enables rafts, kayaks, and canoes to float through the Gila Box to Bonita Creek, 19 miles downstream.

Information: BLM-Safford Field Office, 711 S 14th Ave, Safford AZ 85546 / 520-348-4400.

Coronado Trail

US FS Coronado Trail is in east-central Arizona, northeast of Safford. The southern access is in Morenci. The byway parallels the Arizona-New Mexico border as it travels north to Springerville.

The 123-mile route follows US 180 and US 191, which are two-lane paved roads. Sharp curves and steep drop-offs exist along several sections of narrow road with no guardrails. The byway is not recommended for vehicles towing a trailer or RVs over 20 feet long. Temporary closure is possible during winter, otherwise the route is open year-round.

Coronado Trail travels through steep canyons and across high rolling mountains with beautiful views of lakes and meadows. The byway crosses the Apache-Sitgreaves National Forests, which have the largest stand of ponderosa pine in the nation. Two wilderness areas are adjacent to the byway: 5,200-acre Escudilla Wilderness and 11,080-acre Bear Wallow Wilderness. Numerous trails along the byway provide access to these pristine wilderness areas.

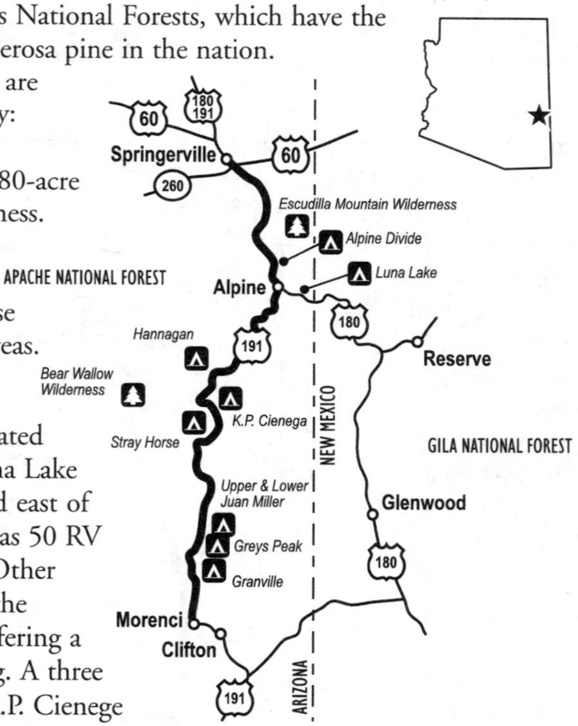

Several Forest Sevice campgrounds are located along the byway. Luna Lake Campground, located east of Alpine off US 180, has 50 RV and tent campsites. Other campgrounds along the byway are smaller, offering a more secluded setting. A three mile hiking trail at K.P. Cienege Campground leads to a scenic waterfall on K.P. Creek.

Information: Apache-Sitgreaves National Forests, PO Box 640, Springerville AZ 85938 / 520-333-4301.

Historic Route 66

BLM 1

Historic Route 66 is located in western Arizona, just south of Kingman. The byway begins in McConnico off I-40 and travels southwest to Topock, returning to I-40.

The 48-mile drive follows a paved, two-lane road suitable for most vehicles. There are sharp curves along this route; it is not recommended for vehicles over 40 feet. The byway is usually passable all year.

The Black Mountains region of the original Route 66 is preserved here along this scenic drive. There are famous sites to be discovered or revisited, including the Sitgreaves Pass tri-state overlook, which provides a spectacular view into the states of California, Nevada, and Arizona. Also along this back country byway is the vintage Cool Springs Gas Station, which was in operation during the 1930s. Please note that the remains of the stone structure are on private property, take only pictures.

Building foundations, rock formations, and mine shafts are all that remain of the once bustling gold mining community of Gold Road Townsite. In its heyday, thousands of people inhabited the area. The former townsite is privately owned, please respect the property owner's rights!

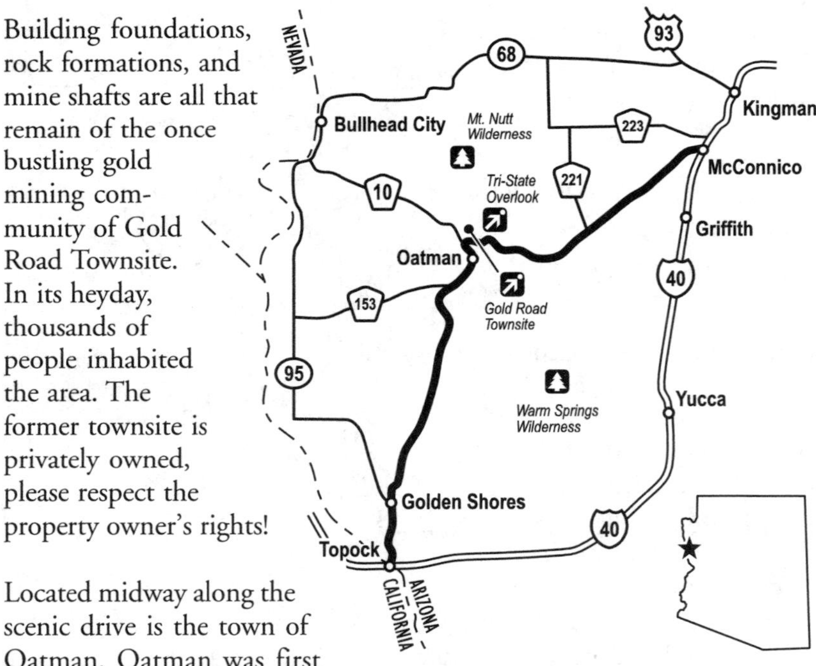

Located midway along the scenic drive is the town of Oatman. Oatman was first settled in the late 1880s and once claimed a bustling population of 8,000. It is famous for the Oatman Hotel, the honeymoon hideaway of Clark Gable and Carole Lombard. The hotel is now a museum. Among the town's other attractions are wild burros, which freely wander through the streets.

Mount Nutt Wilderness lies to the north of the byway and Warm Springs Wilderness to the south. These wilderness areas are an invitation for hiking, backpacking, and horseback

Information: BLM-Barstow Field Office, 2601 Barstow Rd, Barstow CA 92311 / 760-252-6000.

Lodging Invitation

Kingman KOA
3820 N. Roosevelt
Kingman, AZ 86401

Phone: 800-562-3991
520-757-4397
Fax: 520-757-1580

Quiet tree shaded area away from freeway noise. Large pull-thru sites, Kamping Kabins, and tent area. Swimming pool • mini golf • convenience & gift store • hot showers • game room • laundry facilities • cable TV. East bound travelers take exit 51 off I-40, Stockton Hill Road, go north ½ mile to Airway and turn right to Roosevelt. West bound travelers take exit 53 off I-40 and proceed north to Airway. Highway 93 rejoins with I-40.

Travelodge
3275 E. Andy Devine
Kingman, AZ 86401

Phone: 520-757-1188
Fax: 520-757-1010

Travelodge offers travelers 65 beautiful rooms, queen size beds and cable TV with remote. Non-smoking rooms • heated pool • bus/RV parking • laundry facilities on premises. Only ½ block from shopping center, walking distance to restaurants, convenient store and gas. Only 4 miles to airport and ½ mile to Big Park. From I-40 take exit 53 onto Andy Devine, turn left.riding. Back country camping is permitted nearly anywhere within the wilderness. A number of rough, unmarked side roads along the byway serve as access points to the areas. There are no maintained trails; travel is cross-country.

Hualapai Mountains

BLM 1 BLM 2 Hualapai Mountains Back Country Byway is located in western Arizona, near Kingman. The byway's northern access is at the corner of Stockton Hill Road and Andy Devine Avenue in Kingman. The byway can also be accessed from the south off I-40 near Yucca.

Travelling from the northern access point, the byway is divided into four road type segments. The first segment is Hualapai Mountain Road, 13 miles of paved two-lane road suitable for passenger cars. The next segment of road is mostly one-lane with an unpaved surface that can be negotiated by passenger cars when the road is dry and free of ice. This segment is approximately four miles in length. The third segment is 21 miles of unpaved single-lane road that requires a high-clearance or four-wheel-drive vehicle. The final segment is 12 miles of unimproved two-lane dirt road that is suitable for passenger cars from Boriana Mine to its terminus at I-40. Hualapai Mountains Back Country Byway is 50 miles long. You may want to inquire locally about the current road conditions before traveling the byway.

Hualapai Mountains Back Country Byway crosses a diverse landscape, from the open Mojave Desert near Kingman, up through foothills covered in pinyon pine and juniper, to an oak and ponderosa pine forest. Travelers begin at an elevation of 3,500 feet and climb to 6,500 feet in the Hualapai Mountains. Descending from the crest, travelers are given breathtaking views of pinyon and juniper woodland extending into the desert vegetation below.

Wildlife observation opportunities are plentiful, as the area is home to more than 80 species of birds, including hawks, owls, whippoorwills, and hummingbirds. Mule deer and elk also inhabit the area and share the region with coyotes and bobcats, among other wildlife.

Recreation along the byway is in the form of hiking, backpacking, off-road vehicle pursuits, and camping. The very popular 2,320-acre Hualapai Mountain County Park offers emergency first aid, campgrounds, water, hiking trails, rental cabins, and picnicking facilities. A smaller, less developed recreation site is managed by the BLM, the Wild Cow Springs Campground. The recreation area is only partially developed but provides camping and restroom facilities, grills, fire pits, and picnic tables. No potable water is available. The campground has 20 RV and tent sites. There is an RV length limit of 20 feet. The campground is generally open May through October.

Information: BLM-Kingman Field Office, 2475 Beverly Ave, Kingman AZ 86401 / 520-692-4400.

Lodging Invitation

Kingman KOA	Phone:	800-562-3991
3820 N. Roosevelt		520-757-4397
Kingman, AZ 86401	Fax:	520-757-1580

Quiet tree shaded area away from freeway noise. Large pull-thru sites, Kamping Kabins, and tent area. Swimming pool • mini golf • convenience & gift store • hot showers • game room • laundry facilities • cable TV. East bound travelers take exit 51 off I-40, Stockton Hill Road, go north ½ mile to Airway and turn right to Roosevelt. West bound travelers take exit 53 off I-40 and proceed north to Airway. Highway 93 rejoins with I-40.

Travelodge
3275 E. Andy Devine
Kingman, AZ 86401

Phone: 520-757-1188
Fax: 520-757-1010

Travelodge offers travelers 65 beautiful rooms, queen size beds and cable TV with remote. Non-smoking rooms • heated pool • bus/RV parking • laundry facilities on premises. Only ½ block from shopping center, walking distance to restaurants, convenient store and gas. Only 4 miles to airport and ½ mile to Big Park. From I-40 take exit 53 onto Andy Devine, turn left.riding. Back country camping is permitted nearly anywhere within the wilderness. A number of rough, unmarked side roads along the byway serve as access points to the areas. There are no maintained trails; travel is cross-country.

Kaibab Plateau - North Rim Parkway

US FS NSB The Kaibab Plateau - North Rim Parkway is in north-central Arizona about 35 miles south of the Utah/Arizona border. The northern access is in Jacob Lake off US Alternate 89, about 30 miles southeast of Fredonia. The byway travels south to North Rim in Grand Canyon National Park.

The 44-mile route follows AZ 67, a paved, two-lane road suitable for all vehicles. The road ends in North Rim; you'll need to retrace the route back to Jacob Lake. Due to heavy winter snow, the byway is usually closed from mid to late November through mid-May.

This scenic byway crosses the high-elevation plateau known as the Kaibab Plateau through dense forests of pine, fir, and aspen. Piute Indians call this high plateau "the mountain lying down" or "Kaibab." The byway crosses the Kaibab National Forest and ends at the northern rim of the spectacular Grand Canyon National Park.

Recreation opportunities abound in the Kaibab National Forest. Those interested in hiking, backpacking, or horseback riding will have access to two wilderness areas. Saddle Mountain Wilderness lies to the west; Kanab Creek Wilderness to the southeast. Although the byway is closed during winter, the national forest remains open to winter sport enthusiasts. Snowpacked national forest roads provide excellent opportunities for snowmobiling and cross-country skiing.

There are three developed campgrounds along or near the byway: Jacob Lake, Indian Hollow, and Demotte. Jacob Lake Campground sits at an elevation of 7,900 feet and has 53 sites with tables, cooking grills, and water. Demotte Campground has 20 campsites; Indian Hollow has three. Camping is not restricted, however, to the developed campgrounds. If you prefer solitude and privacy, you may camp nearly anywhere within the forest boundary. Some of the more popular and accessible primitive camping areas are shown on the map.

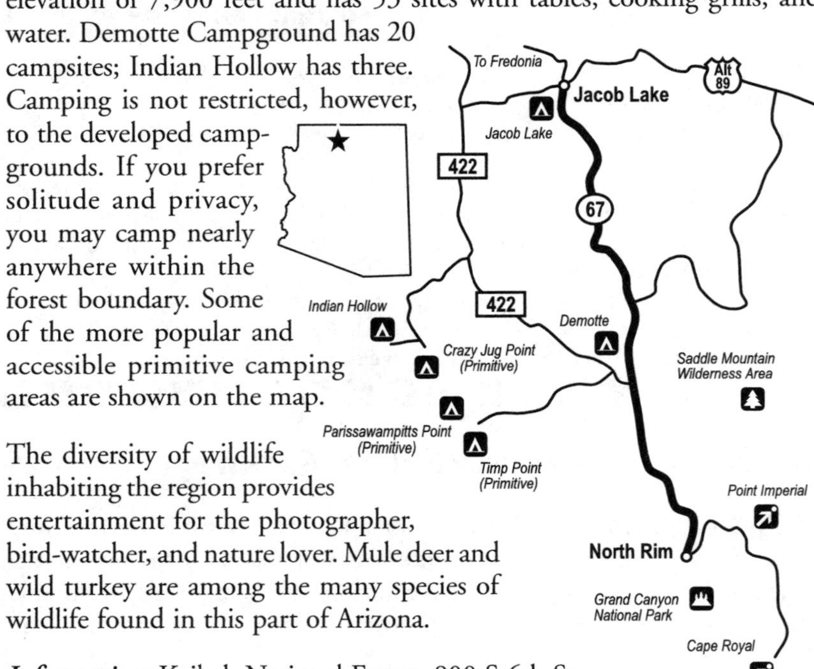

The diversity of wildlife inhabiting the region provides entertainment for the photographer, bird-watcher, and nature lover. Mule deer and wild turkey are among the many species of wildlife found in this part of Arizona.

Information: Kaibab National Forest, 800 S 6th St, Williams AZ 86046 / 520-635-8200. Grand Canyon National Park, P.O. Box 129, Grand Canyon AZ 86023 / 520-638-7888.

Parker Dam Road

BLM 1 Parker Dam Road is in southeast California and west-central Arizona on the banks of the Colorado River. On the California side, the byway travels between Earp and Parker Dam. Earp is on CA 62 about 50 miles north of Blythe. The Arizona side travels between Parker and Lake Havasu City. Lake Havasu City is approximately 60 miles south of Kingman.

The California side of the byway is the officially designated portion. As its name implies, the scenic drive follows Parker Dam Road, which is a two-lane paved road safe for travel by all types of vehicles. The Arizona side also follows a two-lane pave road, AZ 95. Both roads generally remain open year-round. Eleven miles of this 55-mile route is designated a Type I Back Country Byway.

Parker Dam Road follows alongside the Colorado River through an area commonly referred to as the Parker Strip. The byway passes through the wide river valley with views of surrounding mountains. There are hiking trails along the byway that will take you into the mountains. Anglers will find bass, bluegill, and catfish in the river and Lake Havasu. There are two areas for those that enjoy off-road vehicle activities: Copper Basin Dunes and Crossroads.

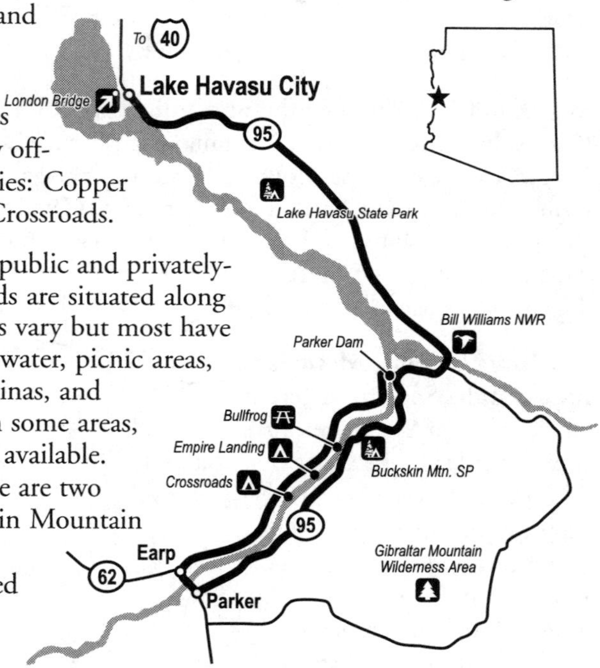

A large number of public and privately-owned campgrounds are situated along the byway. Facilities vary but most have hookups, drinking water, picnic areas, gasoline, food, marinas, and swimming areas. In some areas, golf course are also available. On the Arizona side are two state parks: Buckskin Mountain and Lake Havasu. Both have developed campgrounds with hookups. Some campsites at both state parks are only accessible by boat.

On the Arizona side in Lake Havasu City is the famous bridge that once spanned the Thames River in London, England. The London Bridge, built in 1825, was put up for sale in 1967 after engineers discovered the structure was slowly sinking into the river and could no longer handle busy city traffic. Robert McCulloch purchased the bridge for over two million dollars, dismantled it block by block, and had it shipped to California. From there, it was trucked to its present location and reassembled over a three-year period. It now stretches across the water to Lake Havasu's largest island. An English Tudor village is located on the east end of the bridge.

Information: BLM-Lake Havasu Field Office, 2610 Sweetwater Ave, Lake Havasu City AZ 86406 / 520-505-1200. Lake Havasu State Park, P.O. Box 1990, Lake Havasu City AZ 86405 / 520-855-1223. Buckskin Mountain State Park, 54751 Hwy 95, Parker AZ 85344 / 520-667-3231.

Sky Island

The Sky Island Scenic Byway is located in southern Arizona. The byway begins near the eastern city limits of Tucson and travels north to Summerhaven. Sky Island is reached from I-10 by following Grant Road east to the Catalina Highway.

Sky Island is 30 miles long and follows Catalina Highway through Coronado National Forest. Catalina Highway is also known as General Hitchcock Highway or Mount Lemmon Highway. The byway officially terminates near the village of Summerhaven. Catalina Highway is a two-lane paved road. It twists and turns as it climbs in elevation, with turns becoming more severe as elevation increases. The byway is usually open all year.

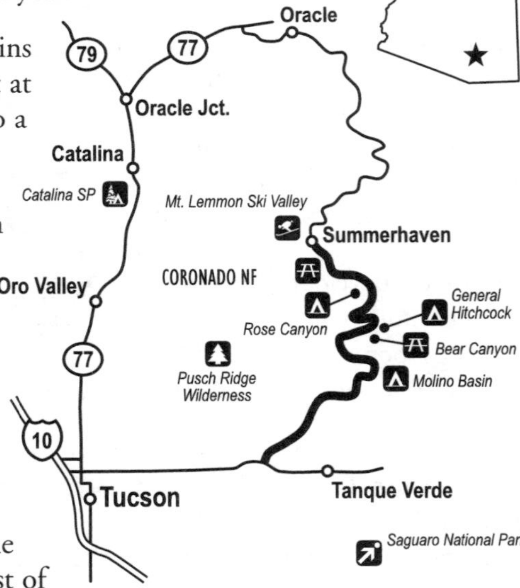

The Santa Catalina Mountains rise from the Sonoran desert at an elevation of 2,500 feet, to a mixed conifer forest above 9,000 feet. Travelers begin their journey in the Sonoran desert scrub, dotted with mesquite and palo verde trees in low lying areas and cacti braced upon the steep rocky mountain side and canyon walls. As you climb into the mountains, the desert gives way to oak and cypress trees. Farther into the mountains, you enter a forest of juniper, mixed conifers, and ponderosa pine. Portions of the forest are preserved in the Pusch Ridge Wilderness.

Nearly three miles from the forest boundary, visitors reach the first vista point, Babat Duag, Tohono O'odham for "frog mountain." From here you can gaze upon the Tucson Basin and the many mountain peaks that rise sharply above the desert floor. This vista point is popular with visitors in the evening that watch the sun set behind the Tucson Mountains.

Coronado National Forest has many developed recreation areas for camping and picnicking. The first campground you come to is Molino

Basin, which has nearly 50 RV and tent sites. Hikers can access the Arizona Trail from this area. General Hitchcock campground is nestled in the oak woodlands of the upper reaches of Bear Canyon and has 13 tent sites. Rose Canyon is a popular recreation area with a 74-site campground and seven-acre lake that is stocked with trout. Molino Basin and Rose Canyon campgrounds have an RV length limit of 22 feet.

Information: Coronado National Forest, 300 W Congress St, Tucson AZ 85701 / 520-670-4552.

White Mountain Scenic Highway

US FS White Mountains Scenic Highway is in east-central Arizona, approximately 170 miles east of Phoenix. The southwest access is in Whiteriver in Fort Apache Indian Reservation. From Whiteriver, the byway travels north to McNary and then east to the junction of US 180/191, north of Alpine.

The 123-mile scenic drive follows Arizona Highways 73, 260, 261, 273, and 373 and Forest Service Roads 87 and 249. This series of connecting roads follow a combination of two-lane paved and gravel-surfaced roads that are suitable for all vehicles. Arizona Highways 73 and 260 are usually open year-round. The remaining roads are subject to closure in the winter.

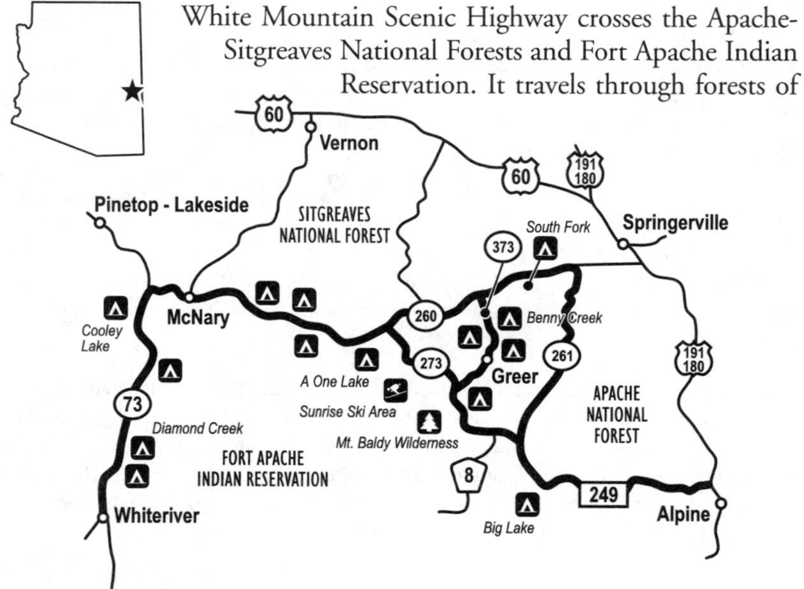

White Mountain Scenic Highway crosses the Apache-Sitgreaves National Forests and Fort Apache Indian Reservation. It travels through forests of pinyon, juniper, and ponderosa pine. Recreation activities within the reservation require a tribal permit. Permits are available in Whiteriver at the Game and Fish Office.

Several lakes and streams offer excellent opportunities for catching trout. Some lakes are too shallow for fish survival, but are deep enough for canoes or rowboats. Because of their small size, most lakes have restrictions on horsepower for boat motors.

Hiking opportunities range from short nature walks to longer back country hikes. Over 800 miles of trail exist within the national forests. Two trails form a 28-mile loop between Greer and Mount Baldy. Each trail is 14 miles long. Portions of both pass through 7,000-acre Mount Baldy Wilderness and are heavily used. Mount Baldy lies within the Indian reservation and should not be entered without first contacting tribal headquarter.

Information: Apache-Sitgreaves National Forest, PO Box 640, Springerville AZ 85938 / 520-333-4301.

Lodging Invitation

Bonanza Motel	Phone:	520-367-4440
858 E. White Mtn. Blvd.		888-577-4440
Pinetop, AZ 85935		

A beautiful location surrounded by large Ponderosa Pine trees, the Bonanza Motel offers travelers spacious rooms and friendly service with reasonable rates. Your stay includes free coffee, tea and hot chocolate on weekends. Nearby outdoor recreational activities are abundant in the Sitgreaves and Apache National Forests.

White Mountain Lodge	Phone:	520-735-7568
140 Main St.	Fax:	520-735-7498
P.O. Box 143	Internet:	www.wmonline.com/wmlodge
Greer, AZ 85927		

Enjoy a stay in this charming 1892 country home on the banks of the Little Colorado River in the hamlet of Greer — at 8,500 feet in the heart of Arizona's beautiful White Mountain recreation area. Remodeled in 1993-95, all rooms are individually decorated and include private baths and king or queen size beds. Full housekeeping cabins are also available. Your stay includes full breakfast with homebaked goods, and the cookie jar is always full. You can also enjoy great hiking and horseback riding.

ARKANSAS

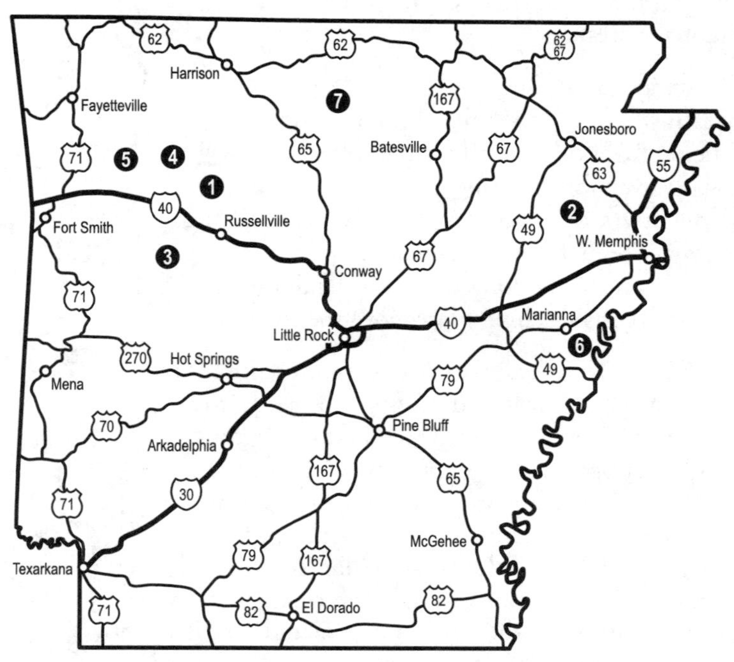

62
62
62
67
Harrison
7
167
Fayetteville
Jonesboro
71
5
4
65
Batesville
67
63
55
1
40
2
Fort Smith
Russellville
49
W. Memphis
3
67
Conway
71
40
Marianna
Little Rock
6
270
Hot Springs
Mena
79
49
70
Pine Bluff
Arkadelphia
167
65
30
71
McGehee
79
167
Texarkana
82
El Dorado
82
71

Arkansas Highway 7

Arkansas Highway 7 travels across western Arkansas between Harrison and Hot Springs. The 160-mile scenic drive follows AR 7, which is a two-lane paved road suitable for all types of vehicles. Arkansas Highway 7 usually remains open year-round.

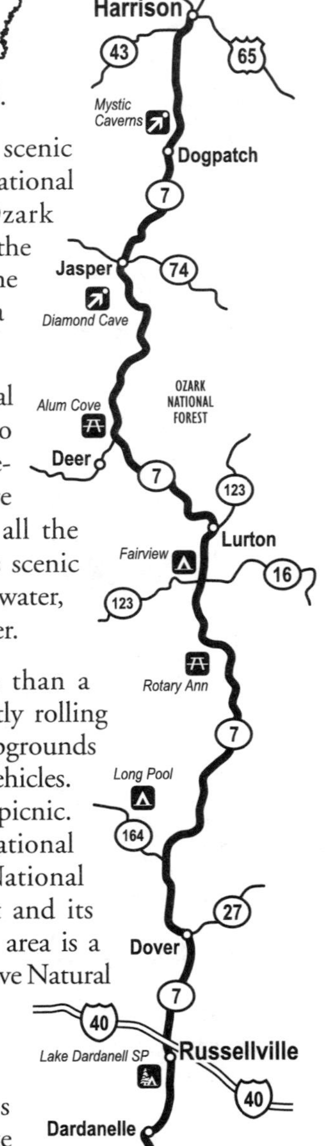

From Harrison, the Arkansas Highway 7 scenic byway travels south through the Ozark National Forest, winding its way through the Ozark Mountains. The byway then descends into the Arkansas River Valley before climbing into the Ouachita Mountains of the Ouachita National Forest.

The byway cuts through the Buffalo National River just south of Dogpatch. The Buffalo National River offers nearly 150 miles of free-flowing river for canoeing or rafting. There are outfitters that will provide you with all the necessary items to enjoy a float down this scenic river of white water, long stretches of calm water, and rock bluffs reaching high above the river.

The Ozark National Forest covers more than a million acres of hardwood forests and gently rolling mountains. There are numerous public campgrounds that offer campsites for tents or recreational vehicles. You'll also find many areas for enjoying a picnic. Hiking trails are plentiful through the national forest. The 160-mile Ozark Highlands National Recreation Trail passes through the forest and its wilderness areas. In the Alum Cove picnic area is a short one-mile trail that leads to the Alum Cove Natural Bridge. This 130-foot natural bridge was carved out of the solid rock by a small stream.

The southern portion of the route passes through the Ouachita National Forest. Like the Ozark National Forest, there are numerous camping and picnicking areas throughout. Hundreds of miles of trails lie within the forest, including the 192-mile Ouachita National Recreation Trail. Two camping areas along Arkansas Highway 7 offer a wooded setting next to a meandering stream. Iron Springs has 13 campsites and South Fourche has 7 campsites. Both areas also have picnic facilities, drinking water, and sanitary facilities.

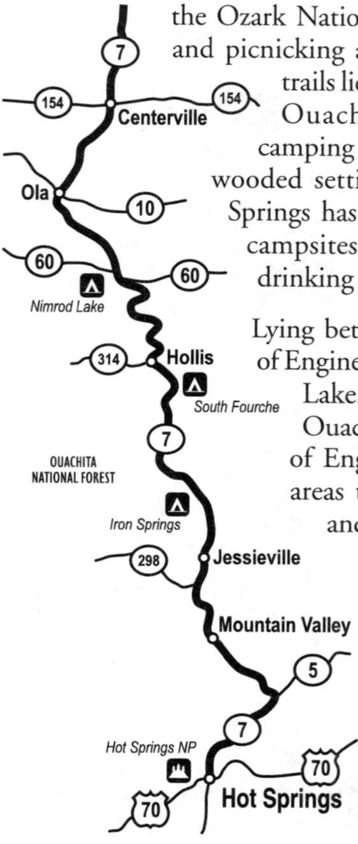

Lying between the national forests are two Corps of Engineers projects, Lake Dardanelle and Nimrod Lake. On the byway's southern end is Lake Ouachita, another Corps project. The Corps of Engineers has developed several public use areas that provide camping facilities for tents and recreational vehicles as well as numerous picnic areas. The lakes also offer opportunities for swimming, fishing, and boating. In addition to the public use areas, Arkansas has developed state parks around each lake.

Information: Ozark-St. Francis National Forest, 605 W Main St, Russelville AR 72801 / 501-968-2354. Lake Dardanelle State Park, 2428 Marina Rd, Russellville AR 72801 / 501-967-5516. Hot Springs National Park, P.O. Box 1860, Hot Springs AR 71902 / 501-624-3383.

Crowley's Ridge Parkway

Crowley's Ridge Parkway is in eastern Arkansas, traveling between Saint Francis and Helena. The byway is nearly 200 miles long and follows a series of US and Arkansas Highways, all of which are two-lane paved roads. The byway is usually open year-round.

The scenic byway begins in Saint Francis and travels south along Crowley's Ridge, a series of rolling hills that stretch from north to south. It is geographically unique; the only other similar land form is found in Siberia. In addition to the scenic qualities of the byway, travelers will pass Civil War sites, museums, historic homes, and a home of Ernest Hemingway. The byway also travels by several state parks and through Saint Francis

National Forest.

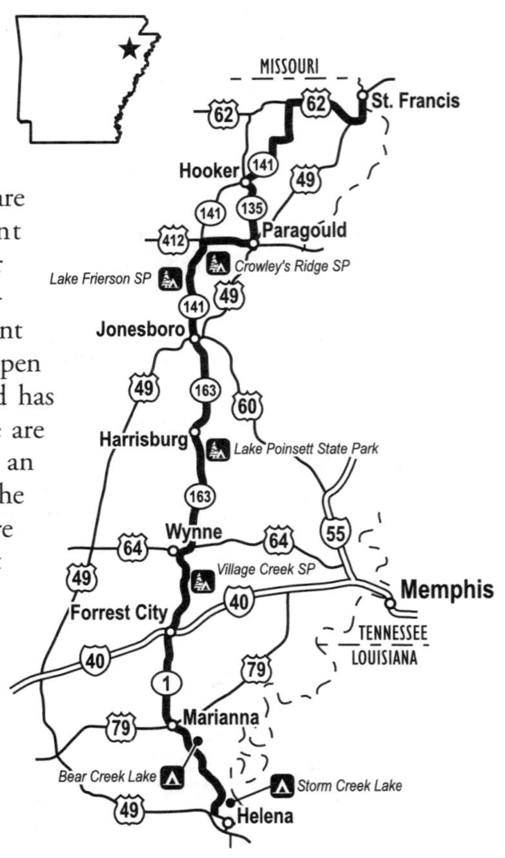

Camping is available in two national forest campgrounds and four state parks. Bear Creek Lake and Storm Creek Lake are campgrounds within Saint Francis National Forest. Bear Creek Lake is open year-round and has 41 RV and tent sites. Storm Creek Lake is open April to mid-September and has 12 RV and tent sites. There are no hookups and both have an RV length limit of 22 feet. The state parks offer a total of more than 150 campsites; most have electric hookups.

Information: Arkansas Department of Parks and Tourism, 1 Capitol Mall, Little Rock AR 72201 / 501-682-1088 or 800-NATURAL.

Mount Magazine

US FS Mount Magazine scenic byway is located in west-central Arkansas about 40 miles east of Fort Smith. The northern access is just south of Paris off AR 109. It travels southeast to Havana and ends at the junction with AR 10. The byway is 30 miles of two-lane paved road suitable for all vehicles. It follows AR 309 and FSR 1606 and is open all year.

This scenic byway travels across the Ozark National Forest through areas of small farms and forests of shortleaf pine, red oak, white oak, and hickory. The byway winds its way through the forest to the top of Mount Magazine, the highest point in Arkansas at 2,753 feet above sea level. The overlook from the top of the mountain offers sweeping vistas of the timber-covered mountains, rugged rock bluffs, and sparkling mountain lakes. Mount Magazine is not only the highest point in Arkansas, but is considered the highest mountain between the Rocky Mountains and the Appalachian Mountains.

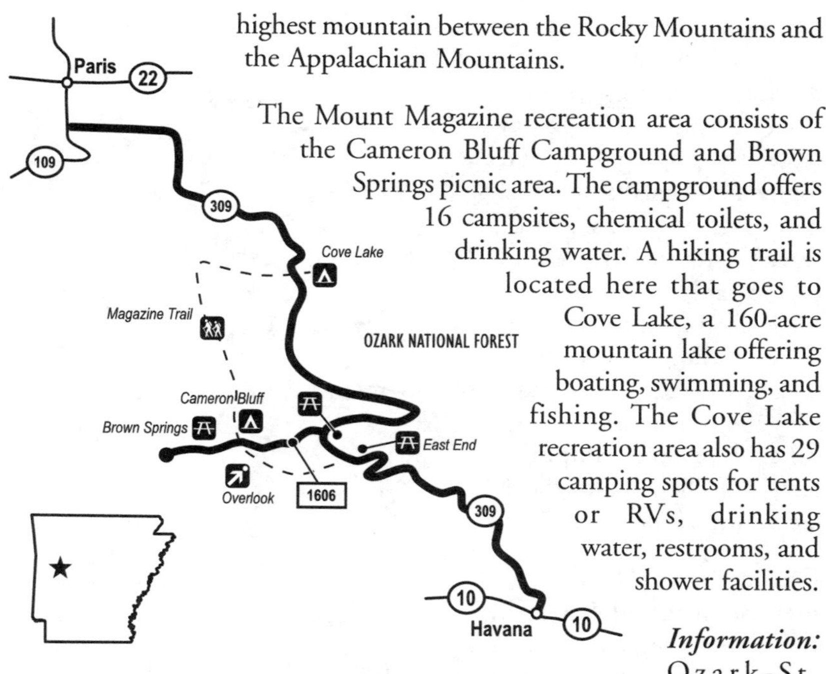

The Mount Magazine recreation area consists of the Cameron Bluff Campground and Brown Springs picnic area. The campground offers 16 campsites, chemical toilets, and drinking water. A hiking trail is located here that goes to Cove Lake, a 160-acre mountain lake offering boating, swimming, and fishing. The Cove Lake recreation area also has 29 camping spots for tents or RVs, drinking water, restrooms, and shower facilities.

Information: Ozark-St. Francis NF, 605 W Main St, Russelville AR 72801 / 501-968-2354.

Ozark Highlands

US FS Ozark Highlands is in northwest Arkansas about 60 miles east of Fort Smith. Southern access is east of Clarksville off US 64. The byway heads north for 45 miles and officially ends at the Ozark National Forest boundary, north of Mossville. Ozark Highlands follows AR 21, a two-lane paved road safe for travel by all types of vehicles. The highway usually remains open year-round.

The Ozark Highlands scenic drive cuts across the Boston Mountains as it winds through Ozark National Forest. Blanketing the byway are large stands of hardwood forest, primarily oak and hickory, with scattered areas of native shortleaf pine. Scenic vistas along the route provide outstanding views of the tree-covered mountains.

Lying near the byway's northern end is the 10,500-acre Upper Buffalo Wilderness with the headwaters of the Buffalo River running through the heart of the area. This wilderness area provides solitude and excellent back country hiking and camping opportunities.

For those interested in a more "civilized" setting, the national forest has developed several campgrounds within the forest. Ozone recreation area is located just off the byway and has eight camping units suitable for tents or recreational vehicles. The park also has drinking water, chemical toilets, and picnic tables. This area was originally the site of a Civilian Conservation Corps camp during the late 1930s and early 1940s. There are several other developed camping areas throughout the forest that are shown on the map.

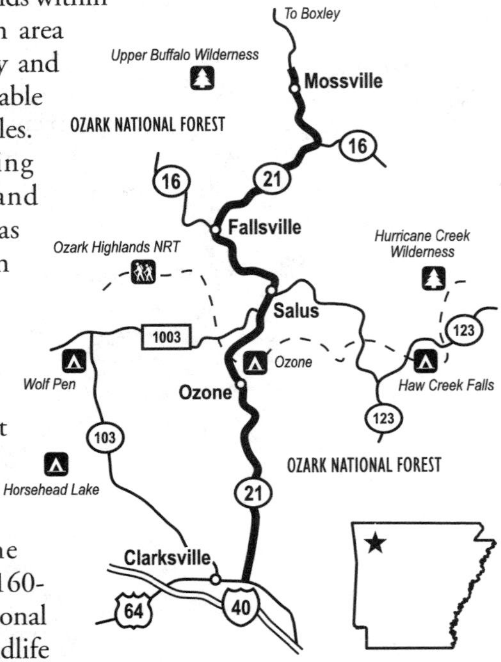

Ozark Highlands Trail may be accessed from the Ozark recreation area. This 160-mile trail cuts across the national forest from west to east. Wildlife is abundant in this area. Keep your eyes on the lookout for mule deer and wild turkey. Black bear also inhabit the region. Occasionally bald eagles and golden eagles are also seen.

Information: Ozark-St. Francis National Forest, 605 W Main St, Russelville AR 72801 / 501-968-2354.

Pig Trail

Pig Trail is in northwest Arkansas about 30 miles east of Fort Smith. The 28-mile byway follows AR 23 between Ozark and Saint Paul. Arkansas Highway 23 is a two-lane paved road suitable for all types of vehicles. It usually remains open year-round.

The Pig Trail crosses the Boston Mountains of the Ozark National Forest showcasing rural America along with spectacular views of timber-covered mountains, clear mountain streams and rivers, isolated farms and ranches, and seasonal waterfalls. Fall brings beautiful colors of red, orange, and gold to these ancient mountains.

The closest campground found along the byway is Redding recreation site, located 3 miles east of the route. This camping area offers 27 units suitable for tents or RVs, restrooms, drinking water, shower facilities, and picnic tables. There are other campgrounds located within the forest if you're willing to venture off the byway. These other camping areas are shown on the map.

There are four wilderness areas within the boundaries of the national forest, lying to the east of this route (see Ozark Highlands and Arkansas Highway 7 scenic byways). These wilderness areas provide excellent opportunities for back county hiking and enjoying the sounds associated with secluded areas. The Ozark Highlands Trail, a National Recreation Trail, crosses this route toward the byway's northern end.

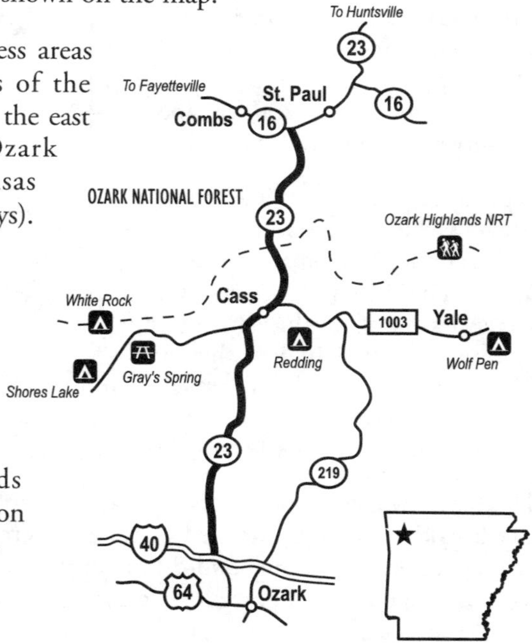

Redding recreation area is adjacent to the Mulberry River, a meandering mountain stream. The river is popular with fishermen as well as canoe enthusiasts. Canoe rentals are available from several outfitters in the area.

Information: Ozark-St. Francis National Forest, 605 W Main St, Russellville AR 72801 / 501-968-2354.

Saint Francis

Saint Francis scenic byway is in east-central Arkansas nearly 60 miles southwest of Memphis, Tennessee. It begins in Marianna and travels south to the intersection with AR 242, north of Helena. The byway is 23 miles long and follows AR 44 and FSR 1900. It travels over a combination of paved and gravel roads that are suitable for all vehicles. The route is generally passable year-round; heavy rain can cause the gravel portion to become slippery.

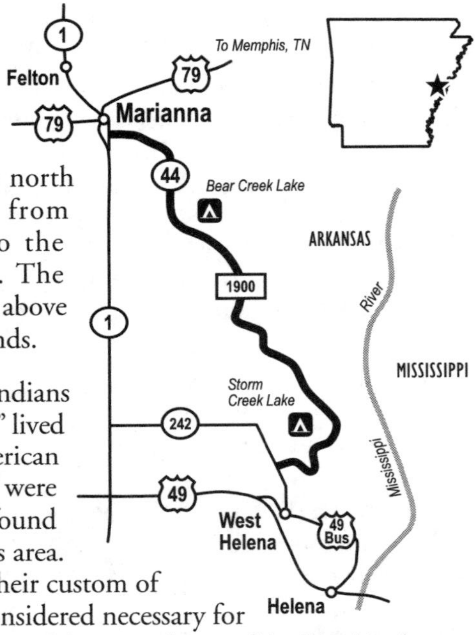

Saint Francis scenic byway rides atop Crowley's Ridge through the hardwood forests of oak and hickory of the Saint Francis National Forest. Crowley's Ridge runs north and south for 200 miles from southern Missouri down to the Mississippi River at Helena. The ridge rises more than 200 feet above the surrounding delta farm lands.

Legend has it that a tribe of Indians known as the "Mound Builders" lived in this area long before the American Indian. The "Mound Builders" were the ancestors of the Indians found by white men moving into this area. The tribal name comes from their custom of burying the dead with tools considered necessary for existence in another world. Some of the mounds can still be found in the area.

There are two developed recreation areas found along the byway. Bear Creek Lake is located near the byway's northern end. This 625-acre lake offers boating, swimming, and fishing opportunities. The lake is stocked with bass, crappie, and bluegill. Two campgrounds are located on the lake offering a total of 41 campsites that can accommodate tents or recreational vehicles, however no hookups are provided. The developed picnic area, Beaver Point, offers 17 picnic tables.

The other developed camping area is located near the southern end of the byway. The 420-acre Storm Creek Lake offers boating and fishing for bass, crappie, or bluegill. A swimming beach is also found here with shower facilities. The campground here has 12 sites for tents and recreational vehicles; no hookups are provided.

Information: Ozark-St. Francis National Forest, 605 W Main St, Russelville AR 72801 / 501-968-2354.

Sylamore

US FS Sylamore scenic drive is 25 miles southeast of Mountain Home in north-central Arkansas. The byway begins in Calico Rock and travels south to Allison and then west to Blanchard Springs Caverns. It follows AR 5, AR 14, and FSR 1110 for a total of 26 miles. All the roads are two-lane paved roads suitable for all types of vehicles and are usually open year-round.

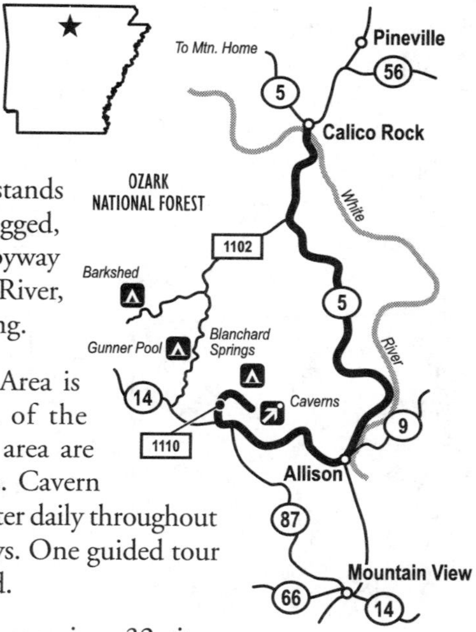

Sylamore scenic byway travels through a beautifully scenic portion of the Ozark National Forest, through a forest of oak and hickory with stands of shortleaf pine, and across rugged, rocky outcrops. Portions of the byway follow the banks of the White River, popular for canoeing and fishing.

Blanchard Springs Recreation Area is perhaps the main attraction of the byway. Within this recreation area are the Blanchard Springs Caverns. Cavern tours depart from the visitor center daily throughout the year except on some holidays. One guided tour is accessible to the handicapped.

Also found in the recreation area is a 32-site campground on the bank of North Sylamore Creek. Picnic tables, drinking water, restrooms, and a sanitary dump station are provided. The day use area has 32 picnic tables, restrooms, and a swimming area with bathhouses and showers. The North Sylamore Trail can be accessed in this area. During the summer months, evening programs about the many facets of the national forest are presented at the Shelter Cave Amphitheater.

Wildlife observers should be on the lookout for white-tailed deer and wild turkey. Birdwatchers can look for more than 150 species of birds, including bluejays, robins, cardinals, warblers, and finches. During the winter months, bald eagles can occasionally be seen soaring overhead.

The Leatherwood Wilderness lies to the west of the byway. This area offers seclusion in a hardwood forest setting. The area also provides opportunities for back country camping and hiking.

Information: Ozark-St. Francis National Forest, 605 W Main St, Russelville AR 72801 / 501-968-2354. Blanchard Springs Caverns, USDA Forest Service, P.O. Box 1279, Mountain View AR 72560 / 501-757-2211. Reservations are recommended during the summer.

California

Ancient Bristlecone

US FS Ancient Bristlecone is south of Bishop in east-central California, near the Nevada state line. The byway begins in Big Pine off US 395 and travels northeast to the road's end at Patriarch Grove on the Inyo National Forest.

Ancient Bristlecone is 36 miles long and follows CA 168 and FSR 4S01, also known as White Mountain Road. The route is usually open year-round but sections may close in winter. The byway follows a paved road to Schulman Grove and then graded dirt to Patriarch Grove. Because of the grade and tight curves, motorhomes and vehicles pulling trailers are not recommended beyond the paved section. Travelers will need to retrace the route back to CA 168.

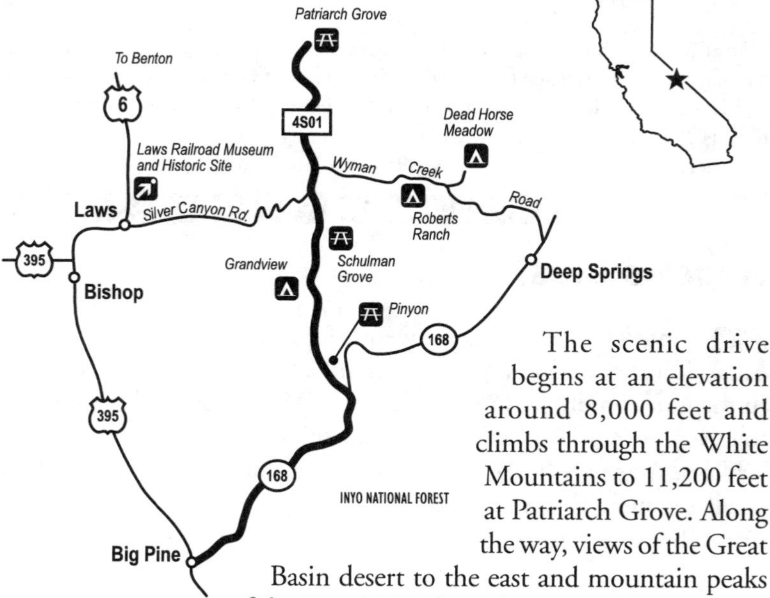

The scenic drive begins at an elevation around 8,000 feet and climbs through the White Mountains to 11,200 feet at Patriarch Grove. Along the way, views of the Great Basin desert to the east and mountain peaks of the Sierra Nevada in the west can be seen. The Ancient Bristlecone Pine Forest, the highlight of the byway, contains the oldest-known living trees on earth. The trees were discovered by Doctor Edmund Schulman, a scientist from Arizona, while searching for old trees that would provide a record of climatic conditions.

Two self-guided nature trails at Schulman Grove give visitors an up-close look at these ancient trees. The oldest living tree, 4,700 year-old Methuselah, is seen along the Methuselah Trail. A trek on the Discovery

Walk takes you to the first tree dated over 4,000 years by Doctor Schulman, the Pine Alpha. The area has a visitor center and picnic facilities.

Farther up the scenic byway is Patriarch Grove, which has picnic facilities and a nature trail. The self-guide trail takes you to Patriarch Tree, the largest Bristlecone Pine in the world.

Information: Inyo National Forest, 873 N Main St, Bishop CA 93514 / 760-873-2400. Laws Railroad Museum & Historical Site, PO Box 363, Bishop CA 93514 / 760-873-5950.

Lodging Invitation

Super 8 Motel - High Sierra Lodge
1005 N. Main St.
Bishop, CA 93514

Phone: 760-873-8426
Fax: 760-873-8060

One of Bishop's finest motels. Clean and comfortable rooms equipped with in-room coffee machines, free extended cable with HBO, and refrigerators. Seasonal outdoor pool and year round indoor jacuzzi. Fish cleaning & freezing facilities and BBQ area. Fantastic fishing! Walking distance to outlet mall and dining. AMEX, MC, Visa, and Discover cards accepted. Located on US Hwy. 395 at the north end of town. We appreciate your business.

Angeles Crest

Angeles Crest is in southwest California, northeast of Los Angeles. The byway's western access is in La Canada off I-210. It travels east to the junction of CA 138, northeast of Wrightwood. The 70-mile route follows CA 2, a two-lane paved road suitable for all vehicles. Angeles Crest is open year-round except a small segment that is closed from late December to early April.

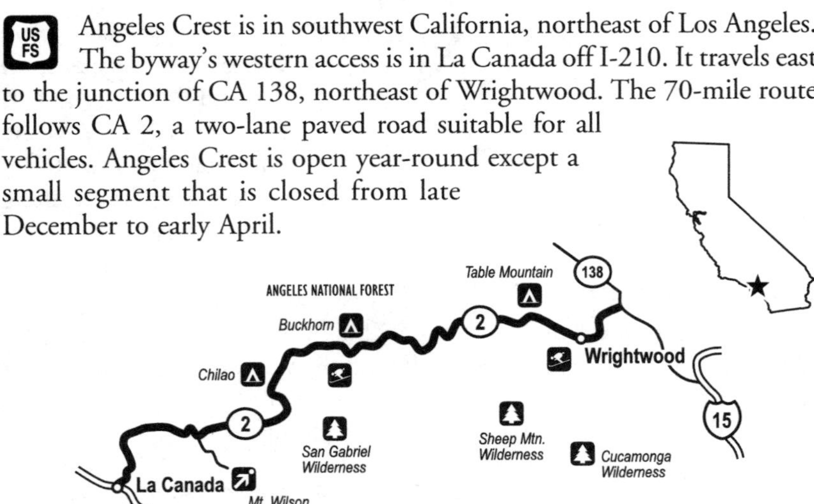

Angeles Crest crosses the San Gabriel Mountains within Angeles National Forest. The byway offers city dwellers an escape from the hustle and bustle of Los Angeles. Panoramic views of Los Angeles, San Fernando Valley, San Gabriel Valley, and Catalina Island, on clear days, reward the byway traveler.

Several campgrounds are along or near the byway. Chilao has over 100 campsites and is open year-round. RVs up to 40 feet can be accommodated. Buckhorn is a smaller campground and has 38 sites. It is open May to November and has an RV length limit of 20 feet. Table Mountain Campground is near the eastern end of the byway. It is operated by a concessionaire and is open May to November. There are 115 campsites; RVs up to 32 feet can be accommodated. Side roads lead to other national forest campgrounds and picnic areas.

San Gabriel and Sheep Mountain wilderness areas surround the byway, providing excellent opportunities for back country hiking. The Pacific Crest National Scenic Trail is also accessed from the byway.

A side trip on Mount Wilson Forest Road leads to the famous, 100-inch telescope at Mount Wilson Observatory. The observatory is open to the public on weekends.

Information: Angeles National Forest, 701 N Santa Anita Ave, Arcadia CA 91006 / 626-574-5200.

Barrel Springs

BLM 2 Barrel Springs Back Country Byway is in northeast California, approximately 50 miles northeast of Alturas. The byway begins in Fort Bidwell and travels east into Nevada, ending at the intersection with Fort Bidwell Road. The 25-mile route follows Barrel Springs Road, which is a single-lane gravel road that can safely be driven in a two-wheel drive, high-clearance vehicle. Keep in mind that Barrel Springs crosses some remote country. Other vehicles may not pass through for one or two days; be prepared for any road emergencies. The byway is generally passable from May through mid-November. Snow closes the byway in winter; it may also become impassable after heavy rain.

Barrel Springs Back Country Byway winds through a maze of rocky rims and rolling hills covered with sagebrush and juniper. The byway offers wide open vistas of the Great Basin Plateau in the shadow of Warner Mountains to the west.

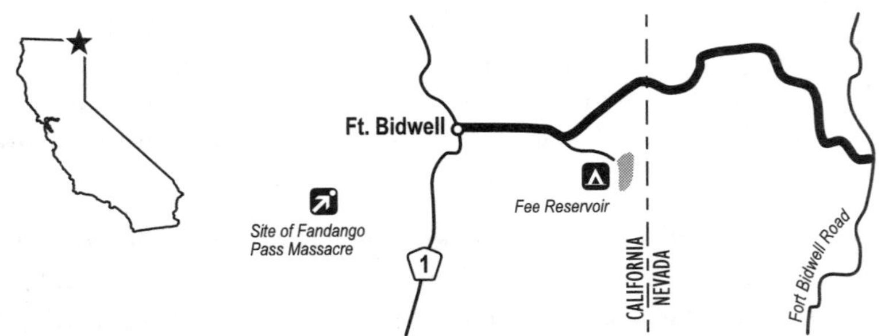

Wildlife watchers will want to be on the lookout for species common to the Great Basin. Mule deer and pronghorn antelope are usually encountered by the byway traveler. Golden eagles, red-tailed hawks, and prairie falcons are commonly seen birds of prey. Coyotes may be seen occasionally, but are more commonly heard in the evening serenading the moon.

A short side trip from the byway is Fee Reservoir. This small desert lake is stocked with trout in the spring and early summer months. A small primitive campground is also located here. Other campgrounds can be found in Modoc National Forest to the west of the byway.

Information: BLM-Susanville Field Station, 2950 Riverside Dr, Susanville CA 96130 / 530-257-0464.

Bradshaw Trail

BLM 3 Bradshaw Trail Back Country Byway is located in southeast California, west of Blythe, near the Arizona state line. The byway's eastern terminus is at the intersection with CA 78, south of Blythe. It travels west to CA 111, ending just south of North Shore. The 70-mile route follows Bradshaw Trail Road, a county-maintained graded dirt road. A four-wheel drive vehicle, dirt bike, all-terrain vehicle, or a similar type is required to travel the byway. The byway is usually passable all year, but temporary closure is possible after heavy rain.

The original Bradshaw Trail was constructed in 1862 by William Bradshaw as an overland stage route from San Bernardino to La Paz, Arizona. It followed Indian trails connecting springs across the desert. The trail was used extensively from 1862 to 1877, but saw fewer users after the completion of the Southern Pacific Railroad to Yuma.

Today the byway is a scenic jeep trail traveling across the Colorado Desert with views of Chuckwalla Mountains in the north and Chocolate

Mountains in the south. The traveler may also see the distant mountains in Arizona. Wildlife observers want to be on the lookout for desert burro, mule deer, and bighorn sheep. Other wildlife in the area includes coyotes, kit fox, and many other small mammals and birds.

Salton Sea, near the byway's western end, is one of the largest saline lakes on earth. It offers excellent boating and fishing. The Salton Sea State Recreation Area has camping and picnicking facilities. Camping is also available in nearby Joshua Tree National Park.

Information: BLM-Palm Springs South Coast Field Office, 690 W Garnet Ave, North Palm Springs CA 92258 / 760-251-4800. Salton Sea SRA, 100-225 State Park Rd., North Shore CA 92254 / 760-393-3059. Joshua Tree National Park, 74485 National Park Dr., Twentynine Palms CA 92277 / 760-367-5529.

Buckhorn

BLM 2 The Buckhorn scenic drive is in northeast California about 50 miles northeast of Susanville. It begins east of Ravendale on Lassen County Road 526. The byway follows Buckhorn Road for 31 miles and ends in Nevada at the junction with NV 447, northeast of Gerlach. Buckhorn Road is a single-lane gravel road that can safely be driven in a two-wheel drive, high-clearance vehicle. The byway travels across some fairly remote country. Other vehicles may not pass through for one or two days; be prepared for any road emergencies. The byway is usually passable from mid-May through mid-November. Snow closes the road in winter; heavy rain can also cause the byway to become impassable.

Buckhorn Back Country Byway travels across the primitive expanses of the Great Basin Plateau through sagebrush-covered hills and stands of aspen, mountain mahogany, and juniper. Small herds of wild horses can

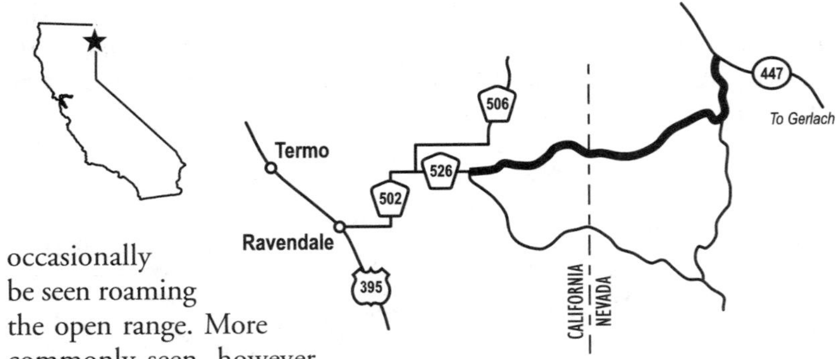

occasionally be seen roaming the open range. More commonly seen, however, are pronghorn antelope and mule deer. Coyotes also inhabit the area, but are usually heard rather than seen. Two intermittent dry lakes provide habitat for ducks, geese and other waterfowl during spring.

There are no developed campgrounds along the byway, however, the BLM permits overnight camping nearly anywhere on BLM-administered lands. To the north of the byway is Modoc National Forest where camping facilities may be found.

Information: BLM-Susanville Field Station, 2950 Riverside Dr, Susanville CA 96130 / 530-257-0464.

Carson Pass Highway

US FS Carson Pass Highway is in east-central California, approximately 60 miles east of Sacramento. The byway travels between the Dew Drop Ranger Station, near Pioneer, and Woodfords. Carson Pass Highway follows CA 88, a two-lane paved road suitable for all types of vehicles, for 58 miles. The highway is usually open all year. Occasional closure is possible in the winter for snow and ice removal.

Carson Pass Highway winds through Eldorado and Toiyabe National Forests. From the Dew Drop Ranger Station, the byway climbs the western slope of the Sierra Nevada, crosses 8,573-foot Carson Pass, and descends the eastern slope into Woodfords. The road follows one of the first trans-Sierra routes into California. The area was first explored in 1844 by John Fremont and mountain main Christopher "Kit" Carson.

The byway presents a variety of recreational opportunities. Many beautiful mountain lakes invite boaters and anglers. Several national forest campgrounds and picnic areas are along the byway. Winter brings recreation in the form of cross-country and downhill skiing, snowmobiling, and sledding. The Mokelumne Wilderness attracts hikers and backpackers as does the Pacific Crest National Scenic Trail.

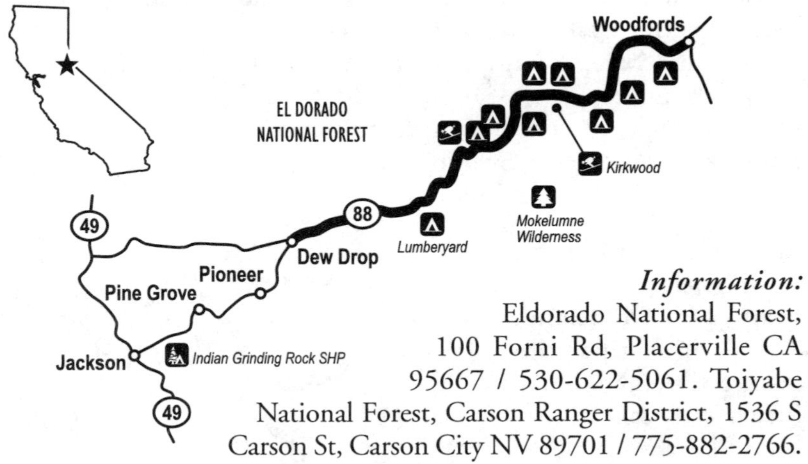

Information: Eldorado National Forest, 100 Forni Rd, Placerville CA 95667 / 530-622-5061. Toiyabe National Forest, Carson Ranger District, 1536 S Carson St, Carson City NV 89701 / 775-882-2766.

Lodging Invitation

Druid House Bed & Breakfast
13887 Druid Lane
Pine Grove, CA 95665

Phone: 209-296-4156
800-267-5781

This three story contemporary mountain retreat in the Sierra foothills offers a sweeping view of the Sacramento Valley and Mt. Diablo. Mixing old and new, the furnishings make the house warm and inviting. The main suite includes a private entrance, deck, patio, bath, hot tub, pellet stove, king 4 poster, wet bar with frig & microwave, and a small bedroom. The main floor suite includes an antique 150 year old sleigh bed, master bath with jacuzzi tub, and a sun room. Both suites offer: cable TV & VCR, phones, bathrobes, central air and heat, wine, beverages and snacks. Full breakfast on weekends and expanded continental on weekdays. Close to skiing • fishing • golf • hiking • rafting • swimming • fine restaurants & cozy cafes • historical sites • shopping • and wineries. Located one mile west of Pine Grove off upper Ridge Road on Druid Lane.

Chimney Peak

The Chimney Peak Back Country Byway is situated in the southern Sierra Nevada Mountains of south-central California. The byway begins approximately 60 miles northwest of Bakersfield, off CA 178. This is the best point to begin the scenic drive.

Chimney Peak is a 39 mile, Type II Back Country Byway. Beginning from CA 178, the byway follows Canebrake Road north to Kennedy Meadows Road and then circles Chimney Peak on Long Valley Loop Road back to its junction with Canebrake Road. The roads are narrow, secondary roads that are washboard-like at times. Some sections may become impassable in winter and early spring. A high-clearance vehicle is recommended; normal passenger cars can usually complete the trip by using extra care.

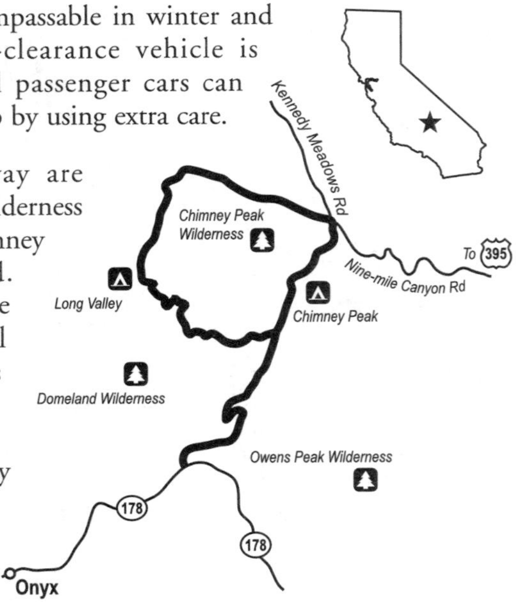

Travelers of the byway are surrounded by three wilderness areas: Owens Peak, Chimney Peak, and Domeland. Trails, including the Pacific Crest National Scenic Trail, take hikers and backpackers into the wilderness areas. The remoteness of the byway lends a feeling of the rugged old west.

Two campgrounds are available to byway travelers: Chimney Creek and Long Valley. Chimney Creek has 36 sites with picnic tables and fire rings. No water or trash receptacles are provided. Long Valley has 13 campsites with picnic tables and fire rings. A trail here will take you to the scenic South Fork Kern River. Pit toilets are available at both campgrounds. Bears do inhabit the area, so take necessary precautions with food and pack out all trash.

Information: BLM-Bakersfield Field Office, 3801 Pegasus Dr, Bakersfield CA 93308 / 661-391-6000.

Death Valley Scenic Byway - Route 190

NSB Death Valley Scenic Byway is in east-central California. The byway follows CA 190 through Death Valley National Park. California Highway 190 is a two-lane paved road suitable for all types of vehicles. The byway is about 55 miles long and remains open year-round.

Death Valley National Park is home to more than 3 million acres of spectacular desert scenery. It contains mountain peaks above 7,000 feet and the lowest point in the western hemisphere. The area near Badwater is 282 feet below sea level. Numerous side roads invite exploration of this vast desert region. More than 350 miles of unpaved and four-wheel drive roads provide access to wilderness camping, hiking, scenery, and historical sites. Ranger guided hikes, talks, and evening programs are presented November through April. A schedule is available at the visitor center in Furnace Creek.

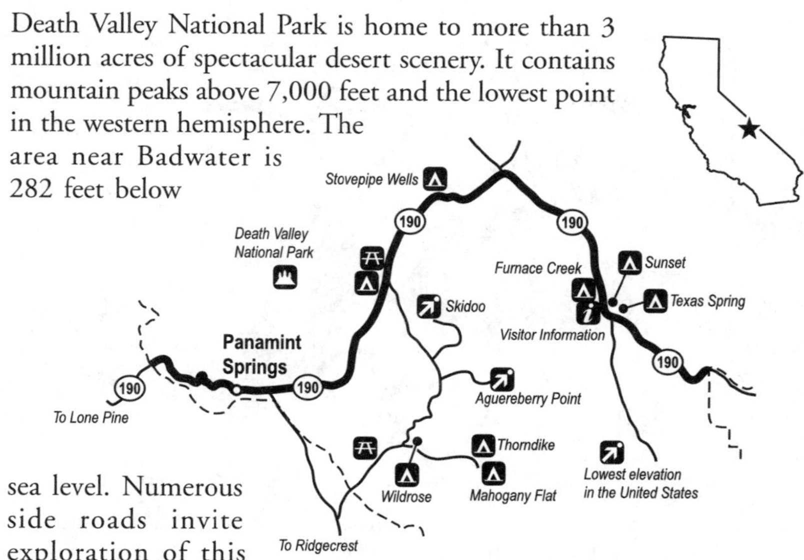

Most visitors come to the park February through mid-April. November is also busy with tourists. A $10 vehicle entrance fee is charged and is valid for seven days. The entrance fee is waived to holders of either the Golden Age or Golden Access Passports.

Those interested in camping must make reservations if staying at the Furnace Creek Campground during the peak season. Other national park campgrounds are along the byway that are first come, first served. A limited number of RV sites are in Texas Spring; it is primarily used for tent camping.

Information: Death Valley National Park, PO Box 579, Death Valley CA 92328 / 760-786-2331.

East Mojave National Scenic Area

1 Black Canyon Road
2 Cedar Canyon Road
3 Cima Road
4 Essex Road
5 Kelbaker Road
6 Kelso-Cima Road
7 Lanfair-Ivenpah Road
8 Wild Horse Canyon

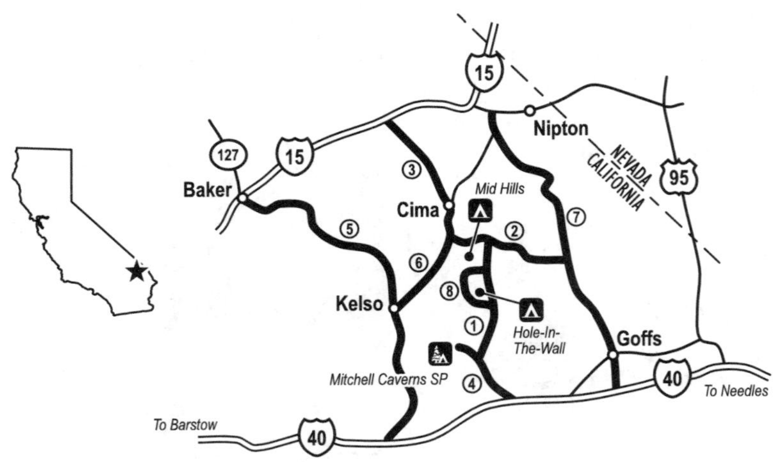

These eight scenic drives are in southeast California, east of Barstow between Interstates 15 and 40. The roads travel through the East Mojave National Scenic Area and are interconnected. All are usually open year-round. Severe thunderstorms can cause the roads to become impassable.

East Mojave National Scenic Area is a unique 1.5 million acre desert region full of scenic, historic, and natural wonders. Table Mountain is a flat-topped mesa visible from many of the routes as are the Providence Mountains. The scenic drives travel through pinyon-juniper woodlands, sage-covered hills, cactus gardens, and colorful volcanic cinder cones and lava beds.

Old mining roads in the New York, Castle, Clark, and Providence Mountains provide opportunities for hiking and mountain biking. Several developed trails are also in the area. Two off-road vehicle trails cross the region: Mojave Road and East Mojave Heritage Trail. Mojave Road is a 130-mile historic Native American trade route that was later developed into a wagon trail. Mojave Road travels east-west through the heart of the National Scenic Area. The East Mojave Heritage Trail, a 700-mile loop beginning and ending in Needles, runs through much of the East Mojave region.

The BLM manages two campgrounds in the National Scenic Area. Hole-in-the-Wall Campground features 37 campsites; some are pull-through. A dump station is also available. Mid Hills Campground has 26 sites. RVs larger than 26 feet may have difficulty maneuvering in the campground. Both campgrounds provide water, restrooms, and picnic tables.

1 • Black Canyon Road

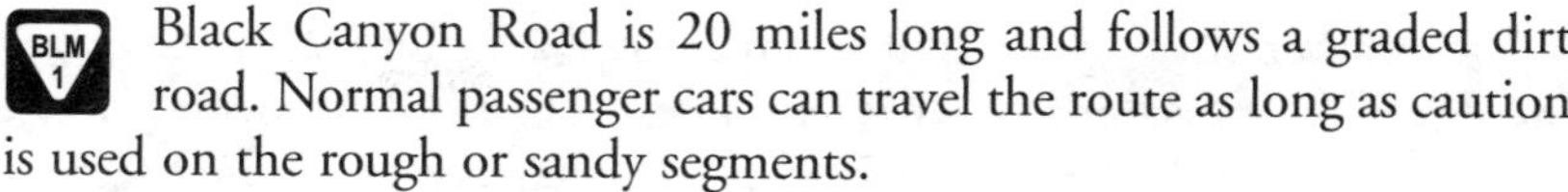

Black Canyon Road is 20 miles long and follows a graded dirt road. Normal passenger cars can travel the route as long as caution is used on the rough or sandy segments.

2 • Cedar Canyon Road

Cedar Canyon Road is 25 miles long and follows a graded dirt road. Passenger vehicles can safely travel the route as long as caution is used on the rough or sandy segments.

3 • Cima Road

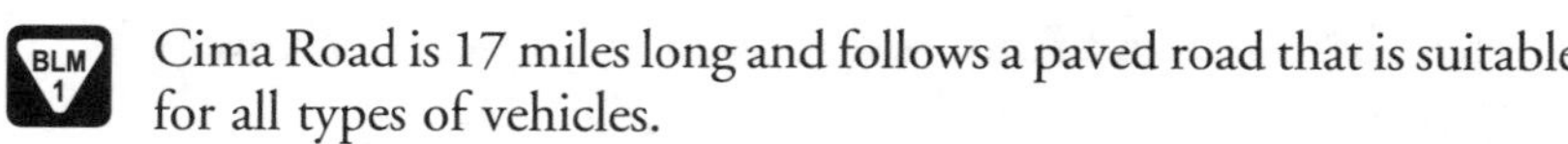

Cima Road is 17 miles long and follows a paved road that is suitable for all types of vehicles.

4 • Essex Road

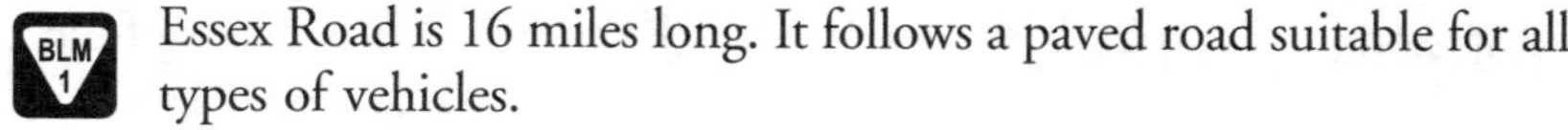

Essex Road is 16 miles long. It follows a paved road suitable for all types of vehicles.

5 • Kelbaker Road

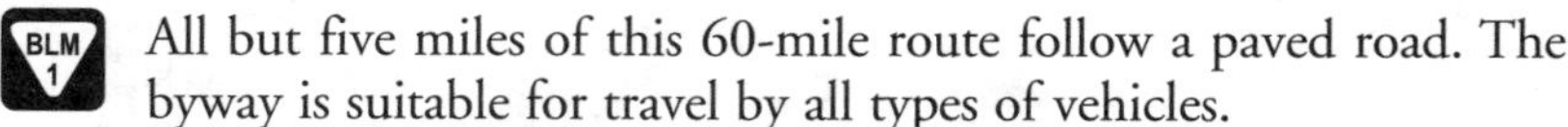

All but five miles of this 60-mile route follow a paved road. The byway is suitable for travel by all types of vehicles.

6 • Kelso-Cima Road

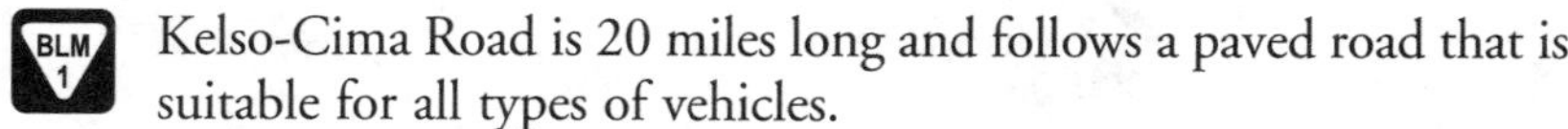

Kelso-Cima Road is 20 miles long and follows a paved road that is suitable for all types of vehicles.

7 • Lanfair-Ivenpah Road

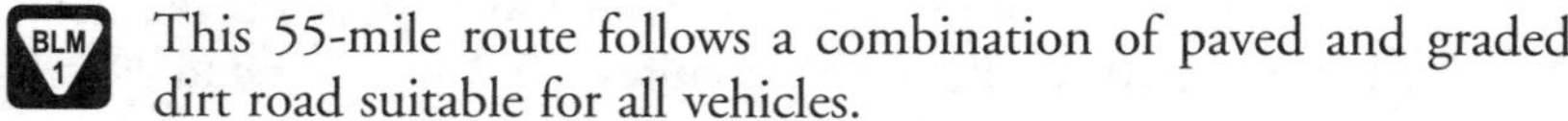

This 55-mile route follows a combination of paved and graded dirt road suitable for all vehicles.

8 • Wild Horse Canyon

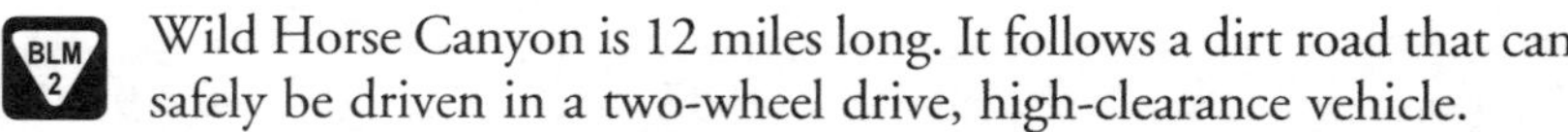

Wild Horse Canyon is 12 miles long. It follows a dirt road that can safely be driven in a two-wheel drive, high-clearance vehicle.

Information: BLM-Needles Field Office, 101 W Spikes Rd, Needles CA 92363 / 760-326-7000.

Feather River

Feather River is located in northeast California, about 65 miles north of Sacramento. Western access is north of Oroville on CA 70. The byway travels north to Belden and then east to the intersection with US 395, near the Nevada border. Feather River is a 130-mile route that follows CA 70, a two-lane paved road suitable for all types of vehicles. Winter driving conditions can be hazardous but otherwise the byway is open year-round.

Feather River follows a route that divides the Sierra Nevada and Cascade Mountain Ranges. The byway provides the lowest pass route through the Sierras. It crosses Plumas National Forest through steep canyon walls covered with moss and ferns, past rock outcrops, and scenic waterfalls.

Bucks Lake Wilderness Area lay south of the byway and attracts back country hikers, horseback riders, and back packers. The Pacific Crest National Scenic Trail is also accessed from the byway in Belden. Several campgrounds and picnic areas are along the route. Others can be found by taking the many side roads into the national forest. The State of California manages two recreation areas: Lake Oroville and Plumas-Eureka. Lake Oroville has over 200 RV and tent campsites; 70 with water and electric hookups. The 15,500-acre lake offers boating, skiing, swimming, and fishing. Plumas-Eureka State Park has 67 RV and tent campsites (24 foot RV length limit), nature and hiking trails, and other amenities.

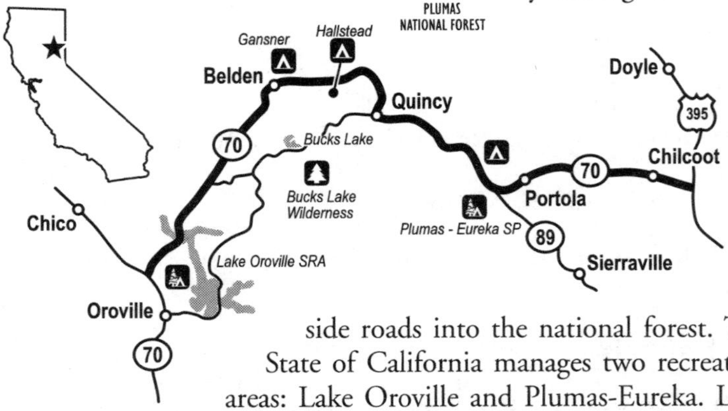

Information: Plumas National Forest, 159 Lawrence St, Quincy CA 95971 / 530-283-2050. Sierra Plumas Eureka State Park, 310 Johnsville Rd, Blairsden CA 96130 / 530-836-2380. Lake Oroville SRA, 400 Glen Dr, Oroville CA 95966 / 530-538-2200.

Lodging Invitation

Bucks Lakeshore Resort
1100 Bucks Lake Road
Bucks Lake, CA 95956

Phone: 916-283-6900
Fax: 916-283-6909

Bucks Lakeshore Resort, an alpine lodge with restaurant, offers 11 cabins (7 lakefront), RV Park & campground, and a 60-berth marina. Guests enjoy summer water sports rentals, lakeview patio dining as well as lounge with 180 degree lakeview and fireplace. Winter sports include x-country skiing, snowmobiling and snow bus to lodge. Over 100 miles of groomed snow roads start at your cabin door; northern California snow park nearby. Food, supplies, gas & on/off sale liquor are available in the Lakeshore Country Store. Wonderful low-season packages available October - December and April - May.

The Feather Bed
542 Jackson St.
P.O. Box 3200
Quincy, CA 95971

Phone: 530-283-0102
800-696-8624

The Feather Bed allows you to step back to a gracious and simpler time. Far from the crowds and urban noise —close to nature. You may choose a guest room upstairs in the main house or a private guest house, all with private baths and separate entrances. Your stay includes an abundant country breakfast in the Victorian dining room. A short walk takes you to a theatre, the County Museum, shops and restaurants. Guests can enjoy fishing, water sports, golfing, horseback riding, snowmobiling, cross country skiing, bird watching, hiking, biking, fall colors, picnicking, or just relaxing on the front porch. Located on the corner of Jackson Street and Court Street, just behind the Court House.

A/C H

Jacinto Reyes

US FS Jacinto Reyes is in southwest California, approximately 15 miles north of Ventura. The byway's southern terminus is just west of Ojai on CA 150. The northern end of the byway is east of Cuyama on CA 166. Jacinto Reyes follows CA 33, a two-lane pave road suitable for all vehicles, for 56 miles. Thirty-seven miles are officially designated a National Forest Scenic Byway. The byway is usually open all year.

Traveling across Los Padres National Forest, the byway begins nearly at sea level, winds through the coastal mountains to an elevation of 5,020 feet, and makes a dramatic descent into Cuyama Valley. Views of the Pacific Ocean and distant Channel Islands are possible at times.

A portion of the byway is accompanied by Sespe Creek, of which 32 miles are preserved as a Wild and Scenic River. The creek runs through beautiful

Sespe Gorge, a popular spot with rock climbers. Four wilderness areas surround the scenic byway: Sespe, Dick Smith, Matilija, and Chumash. A preserved wilderness setting where no motor vehicles are permitted, the areas attract hikers, back packers, and equestrians. An interesting spot worth visiting is Bellyache Springs. Contrary to its name, the spring produces water of exceptional quality. Visitors are also treated to a cascading waterfall.

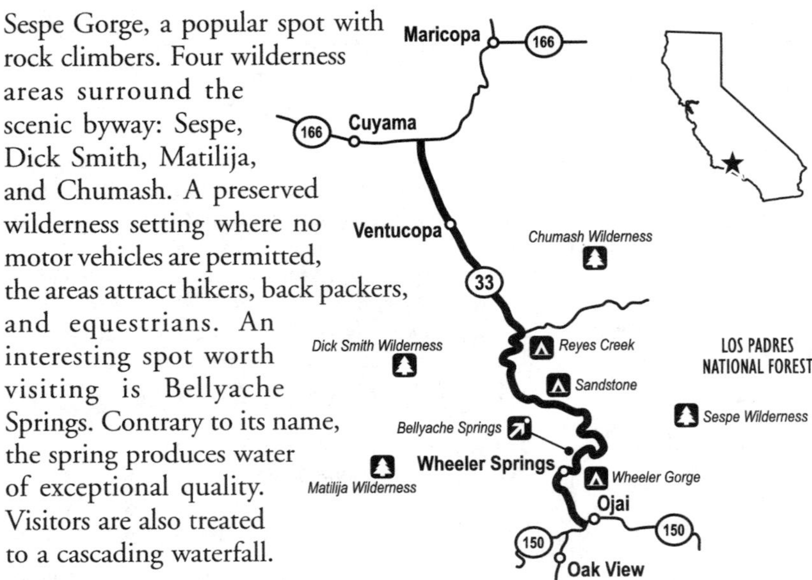

Information: Los Padres National Forest, 6144 Calle Real, Goleta CA 93117 / 805-683-6711.

Lodging Invitation

Capri Motel	Phone:	805-646-4305
1180 E. Ojai Ave.	Fax:	805-646-4144
Ojai, CA 93023		

Located just across from Soule Golf Course, the Capri Motel is adjacent to tennis and golf. Each air-conditioned room has a private balcony with sliding glass doors so you can enjoy the view. Cable TV, courtesy coffee and all the amenities for the traveler. Rooms are always fresh and airy. Relax in the large adult pool while your children are playing in their pool, try the jacuzzi or simply enjoy the lawn area. AMEX, Discover, MC, and Visa cards accepted.

A/C H

Judy Andreen Sierra Heritage

US FS This scenic byway is in east-central California, northeast of Fresno. The byway begins in Clovis and travels northeast to Kaiser Meadow, near Mono Hot Springs. Sierra Heritage is 70 miles long and follows CA 168 to Huntington Lake and then FSR 80 to Kaiser Meadow. Both roads are two-lane paved roads suitable for all vehicles. The last mile of FSR 80 to Kaiser Meadow is basically one lane and is suitable only for passenger vehicles. From Clovis to Huntington Lake, the byway is open all year. The portion from Huntington Lake to Kaiser Meadow is closed in winter.

Beginning at an elevation of about 500 feet, the byway winds through the Sierra Nevada to about 9,500 feet. The route crosses the Sierra National Forest through oak, ponderosa pine, and mixed conifer forests. A beautiful display of wildflowers add color to the foothills in spring and the mountains in summer.

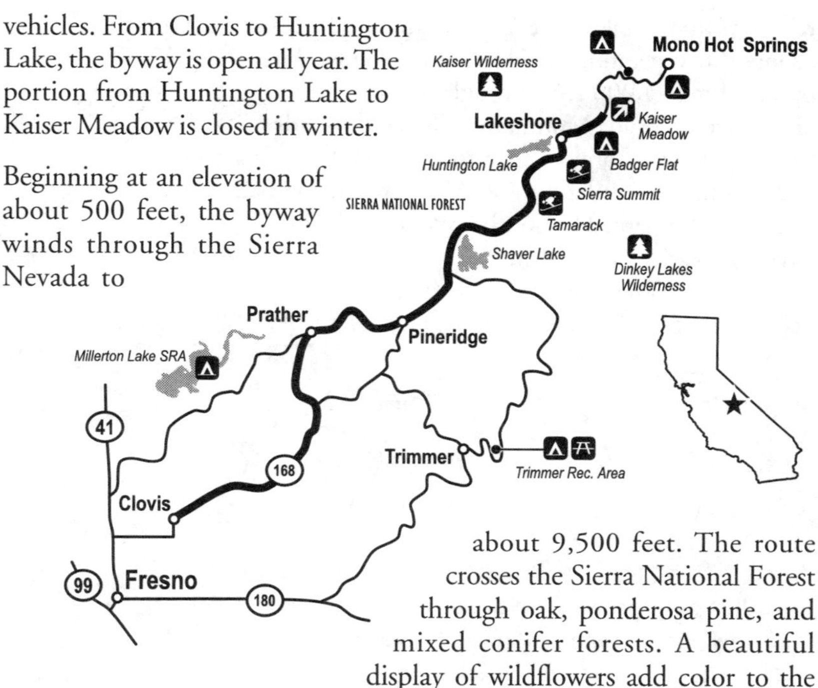

Shaver Lake offers developed camping facilities and excellent trout fishing. Farther up the byway is Huntington Lake. It's rated one of the top sailing lakes in California; sailboat races are held throughout the summer. Huntington Lake also has camping facilities. Hiking trails provide access to two wilderness areas. White Bark Vista near Kaiser Meadow has a gentle half-mile nature trail with sweeping views of the Sierra Nevada Mountains.

Information: Sierra National Forest, 1600 Tollhouse Rd, Clovis CA 93612 / 209-297-0706. Millerton Lake SRA, 5290 Millerton, Friant CA 93626 / 209-822-2332.

Kings Canyon

US FS Kings Canyon is in central California, approximately 35 miles east of Fresno. The byway officially begins at the Sequoia National Forest boundary and travels east into Kings Canyon National Park. The 50-mile route follows CA 180, a two-lane paved road suitable for all vehicles. It is generally open mid-April to early November. The byway ends in the national park; travelers will need to retrace the route back to Wilsonia.

Kings Canyon takes the traveler through dramatic changes in vegetation, wildlife, and geology. First the byway climbs 4,000 feet through the western foothills of the Sierra Nevada Mountains. Then it descends 3,700 feet into Kings Canyon only to climb 2,000 feet again and end in beautiful Zumwalt Meadow. Nearly half of the route is accompanied by South Fork of the Kings River, a National Wild and Scenic River. The byway also bisects the rugged Monarch Wilderness.

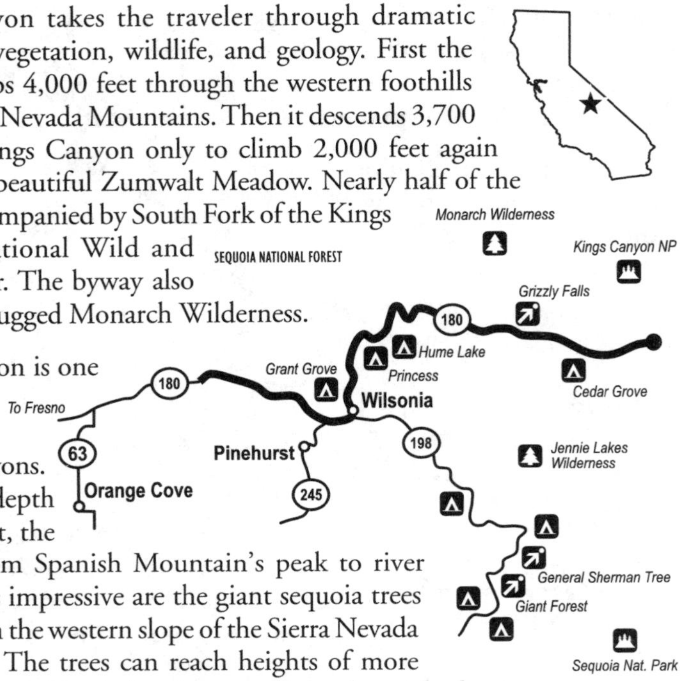

Kings Canyon is one of North America's deepest canyons. It reaches a depth of 8,200 feet, the distance from Spanish Mountain's peak to river level. Just as impressive are the giant sequoia trees that grow on the western slope of the Sierra Nevada Mountains. The trees can reach heights of more than 300 feet, with 40-foot bases and branches eight feet in diameter. A nature trail in Grant Grove will take you among these magnificent trees and the huge General Grant Tree.

Information: Sequoia National Forest, 900 W Grand Ave, Porterville CA 93257 / 559-784-1500. Kings Canyon and Sequoia National Parks, 47050 Generals Hwy, Three Rivers CA 93271 / 559-565-3341.

Lassen

US FS The Lassen scenic byway is in northeast California, about 40 miles east of Redding. It forms a loop of 172 miles and follows California State Highways 36, 44, 89, and 147, which are two-lane paved roads suitable for all vehicles. Portions may temporarily close in winter, otherwise the roads are open year-round.

Lassen passes through a region known as the Crossroads. It is here that peaks of the Sierra Nevada and Cascade mountains merge with the sagebrush of the Great Basin. The byway travels through Lassen Volcanic National Park for 30 miles. Lassen Peak erupted in May 1914, beginning a seven year cycle of sporadic outburst. The national park gives interesting insight into the workings of active volcanoes. The rest of the byway travels through Lassen National Forest.

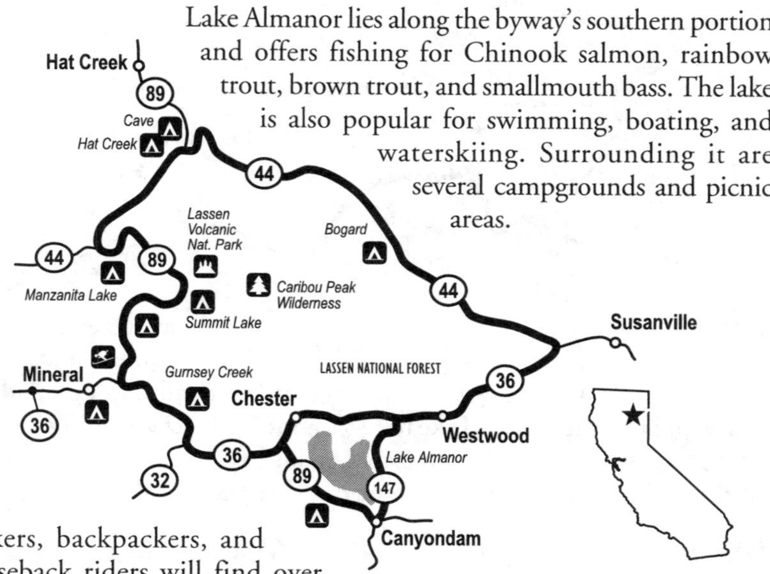

Lake Almanor lies along the byway's southern portion and offers fishing for Chinook salmon, rainbow trout, brown trout, and smallmouth bass. The lake is also popular for swimming, boating, and waterskiing. Surrounding it are several campgrounds and picnic areas.

Hikers, backpackers, and horseback riders will find over 460 miles of trails within Lassen National Forest. They range from wide, easy-walking trails to rugged, steep trails requiring more endurance. The Pacific Crest National Scenic Trail is also accessed from the byway.

Information: Lassen National Forest, 55 S Sacramento St, Susanville CA 96130 / 530-257-2151. Lassen Volcanic National Park, PO Box 100, Mineral CA 96063 / 530-595-4444.

Lee Vining Canyon

US FS Lee Vining Canyon is in east-central California between Mono Lake and Yosemite National Park. The byway begins just south of Lee Vining and travels west through Inyo National Forest to the Tioga Pass entrance of Yosemite National Park. The byway follows CA 120, a two-lane paved road safe for travel by all vehicles. Lee Vining Canyon is 12 miles long and is normally open Memorial Day to early November.

The byway is the highest vehicle crossing in the Sierra Nevada Mountains. It climbs 3,200 feet to an elevation of 9,945 feet at Tioga Pass. Byway travelers are treated to mountain meadows and rugged peaks. Lee Vining Creek flows alongside the byway. In autumn, large stands of aspen paint the canyon with colors of gold. Wildlife observers should be on the lookout for bighorn sheep.

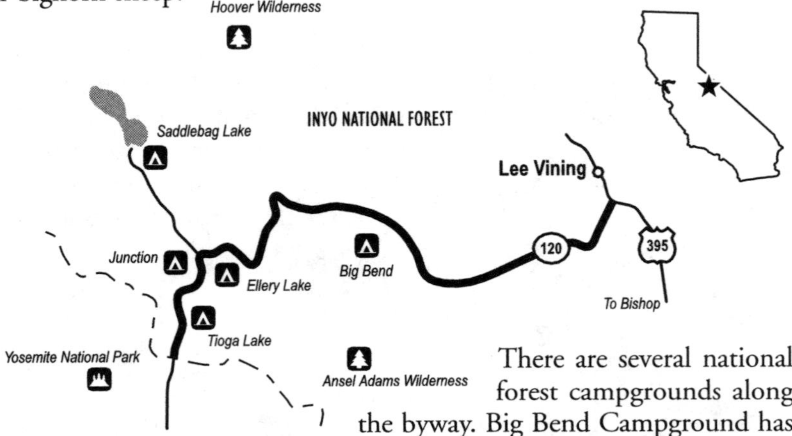

There are several national forest campgrounds along the byway. Big Bend Campground has 17 RV and tent sites. Ellery Lake has 15 campsites. Junction and Tioga Lake campgrounds each have 13 campsites. Saddlebag Lake is a short side trip off the byway and has 20 sites. None of the campgrounds have hookups.

Information: Inyo National Forest, 873 N Main St, Bishop CA 93514 / 760-873-2400. Yosemite National Park, PO Box 577, Administration Bldg, Yosemite CA 95389 / 209-372-0200.

Owens Valley to Death Valley

BLM 2 This scenic byway is in east-central California south of Bishop, near the Nevada state line. Western access is east of Big Pine off CA 168. The byway travels southeast to the northern entrance of Death Valley National Park. The 63-mile byway follows Death Valley Road, which is a county maintained road. The first 32 miles are paved; the remaining is graded dirt. You can safely drive this route in a two-wheel drive, high-clearance vehicle. Owens Valley to Death Valley is usually passable all year but may close temporarily after heavy rain.

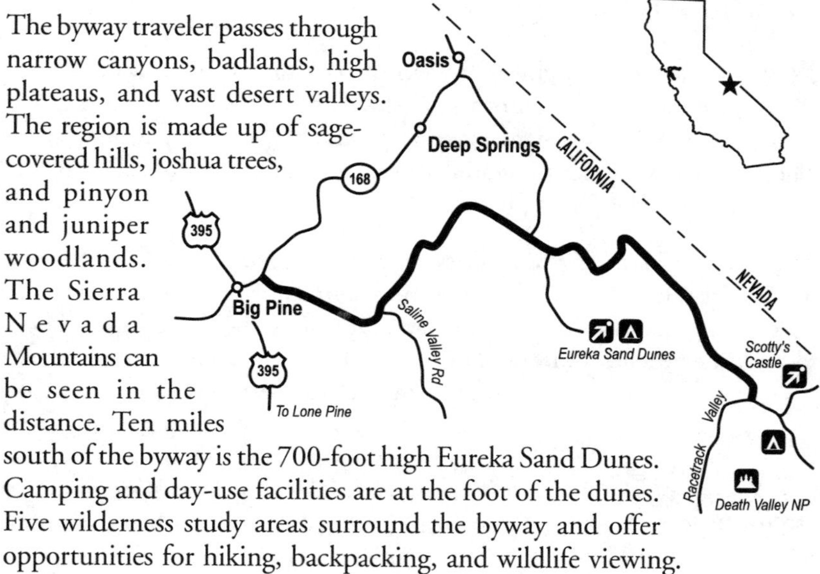

The byway traveler passes through narrow canyons, badlands, high plateaus, and vast desert valleys. The region is made up of sage-covered hills, joshua trees, and pinyon and juniper woodlands. The Sierra Nevada Mountains can be seen in the distance. Ten miles south of the byway is the 700-foot high Eureka Sand Dunes. Camping and day-use facilities are at the foot of the dunes. Five wilderness study areas surround the byway and offer opportunities for hiking, backpacking, and wildlife viewing.

Death Valley National Park contains the lowest point in the western hemisphere. The valley received its name from gold seekers that died crossing the region, believing it to be a shortcut to California's gold fields. Attractions found in the northern unit are Scotty's Castle and Ubehebe Crater. Guided tours of Scotty's Castle are offered throughout the year. Nearby is a national park campground with 30 RV and tent sites.

Information: BLM-Ridgecrest Field Office, 300 S Richmond Rd, Ridgecrest CA 93555 / 760-384-5400. Death Valley National Park, PO Box 579, Death Valley CA 92328 / 760-786-2331.

Lodging Invitation

Super 8 Motel - High Sierra Lodge   Phone: 760-873-8426
1005 N. Main St.   Fax: 760-873-8060
Bishop, CA 93514

One of Bishops finest motels. Clean and comfortable rooms equipped with in-room coffee machines, free extended cable with HBO, and refrigerators. Seasonal outdoor pool and year round indoor jacuzzi. Fish cleaning & freezing facilities and BBQ area. Fantastic fishing! Walking distance to outlet mall and dining. AMEX, MC, Visa, and Discover cards accepted. Located on US Hwy. 395 at the north end of town. We appreciate your business.

Pacific Coast Highway

Pacific Coast Highway follows the coastline of the Pacific Ocean in west-central California. It travels between Monterey and San Simeon on CA 1, a two-lane paved road suitable for all types of vehicles. The byway is 95 miles long and is usually open year-round. Fog in the summer can make driving hazardous.

The Pacific Coast Highway rides atop the rugged cliffs of California's scenic coastline, offering the sights and sounds of ocean waves crashing upon rocky shores. Miles of state park land along the shore allow visitors to walk the beaches and watch playful sea otters or migrating gray whales in winter. On the northern end is Point Lobos State Reserve, which contains one of the few remaining native Monterey cypress tree groves. The area has walking trails and observation platforms. Other state park areas along the byway offer camping and picnicking.

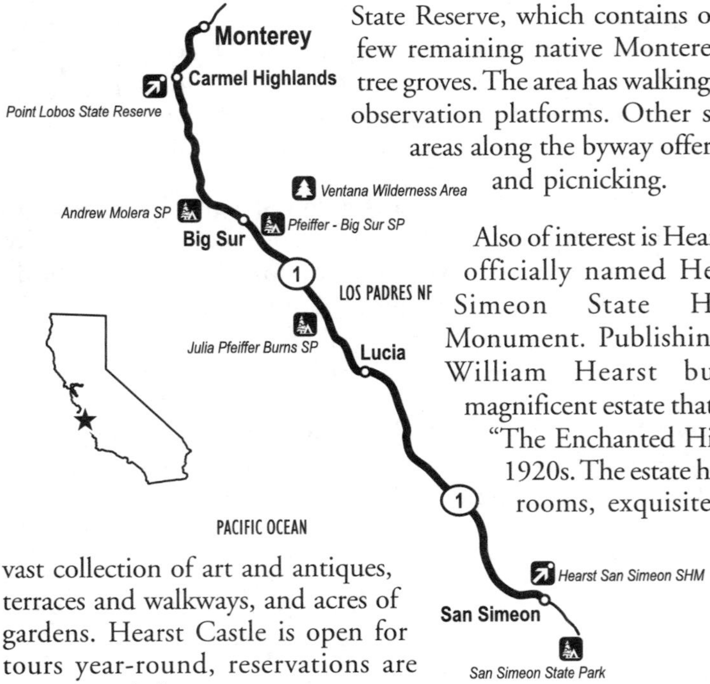

Also of interest is Hearst Castle, officially named Hearst San Simeon State Historical Monument. Publishing tycoon William Hearst built this magnificent estate that he called "The Enchanted Hill" in the 1920s. The estate houses 165 rooms, exquisite pools, a vast collection of art and antiques, terraces and walkways, and acres of gardens. Hearst Castle is open for tours year-round, reservations are recommended.

Information: Los Padres National Forest, 6144 Calle Real, Goleta CA 93117 / 805-683-6711. Pfeiffer-Big Sur State Park and Julia Pfeiffer Burns

State Park, MAF Big Sur Station 1, Big Sur CA 93920 / 831-667-2315. Andrew Molera State Park, phone 831-667-2315.

Lodging Invitation

The Martine Inn	Phone:	831-373-3388
255 Oceanview Blvd.		800-852-5588
Pacific Grove, CA 93950	Fax:	831-373-3896

This gracious mansion, built in 1899, sits high atop the cliffs of Pacific Grove overlooking the rocky coastline of Monterey Bay. The 19 bedrooms, many with wood-burning fireplaces, include a private bath, authentic antiques, and private telephone. Your stay includes a full breakfast — elegance in presentation is a part of the dining experience. Guests are invited to play pool in the game room, relax in the six-person hot tub, read in the library, sunbathe in the landscaped-enclosed courtyard or watch whales, sea otters and sailboat races from the parlor or sitting rooms. Area activities include picnics on the beach • golf • scuba diving • bicycling • tennis • historical tours • boating • and much more.

Palms to Pines

Palms to Pines scenic byway is in southern California near Palm Springs. The byway follows CA 74 and CA 243 for 67 miles between Banning and Palm Desert. Both state highways are two-lane paved roads suitable for all types of vehicles. Both are generally open year-round.

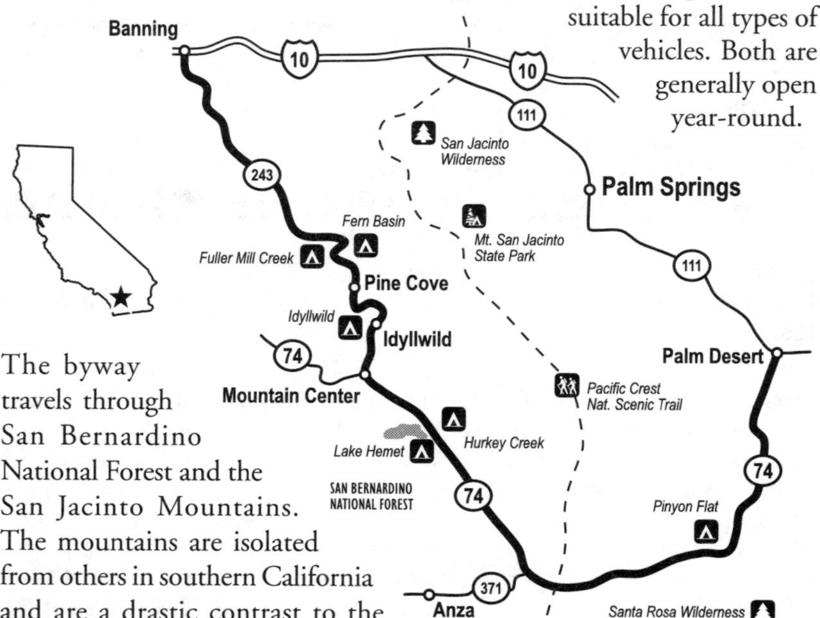

The byway travels through San Bernardino National Forest and the San Jacinto Mountains. The mountains are isolated from others in southern California and are a drastic contrast to the surrounding desert. Byway travelers are taken from a desert oasis to snow-capped mountains. Among the wildlife inhabiting the area are bald eagles, usually seen around Lake Hemet in the winter, and bighorn sheep.

Two wilderness areas can be accessed from the byway: San Jacinto and Santa Rosa. Trailheads into San Jacinto are located near Idyllwild. The Pacific Crest National Scenic Trail is also accessed from the byway. In all, over 150 miles of trails run throughout the national forest.

Those interested in camping have several campgrounds to choose from. Fern Basin is a national forest campground with 24 RV and tent sites. It is open May through October and limits the size of RVs to 18 feet. Hurkey Creek is a county-operated campground with over 100 sites. Mount San Jacinto State Park has several developed camping areas.

Information: San Bernardino National Forest, 1824 S Commercenter Cir, San Bernardino CA 92408 / 909-383-5588. Mt. San Jacinto State Park, 25905 Hwy 243, Idyllwild CA 92549 / 909-659-2607.

Lodging Invitation

Casa Cody B & B Country Inn	Phone:	760-320-9346
175 S. Cahuilla Rd.		800-231-2639
Palm Springs, CA 92262	Fax:	760-325-8610

A romantic, historic hideaway nestled against the spectacular San Jacinto Mountains in the heart of Palm Springs Village. The Casa Cody — hacienda adobe style architecture Santa Fe decor — offers guests 23 single story rooms, studios, and one & two bedroom units with private patios. Kitchens and fireplaces in some units. Facilities include two pools and secluded spa. Rates: $79 - $199, summer less, all credit cards accepted. From Palm Canyon Drive (State Route 111) turn west on Tahquitz Canyon to Cahuilla Road, turn left.

A/C H

Edelweiss Lodge	Phone:	909-659-2787
Pine Cove, CA 92549	E-mail:	edelweis@pe.net
MAIL - P.O. Box 1747		
Idyllwild, CA 92549		

If you're truly looking to get away from it all, come & enjoy the Edelweiss experience. A romantic, rustic retreat located in Pine Cove, only 3 miles above Idyllwild and 1000 feet higher, the property is filled with tall Pines, Cedars, and Oak trees. The 11 individual cabins, accommodating 1 to 6 people, are fully outfitted with equipped kitchens, woodburning fireplaces, and color TV with video player. Guests enjoy the shops, restaurants and various festivities in Idyllwild and for more active pursuits—hiking, fishing, mountain biking, and rock climbing. The many activities throughout the year keep things interesting.

International Lodge Phone: 760-346-6161
74-380 El Camino 800-874-9338 reservations
Palm Desert, CA 92260 Fax: 760-568-0563

"Best Kept Secret In The Desert" — The International Lodge offers 52 spacious, luxurious, and individually decorated condo's. Amenities include: color TV • direct dial phones • air conditioning • kitchen • private patio • two heated pools • jacuzzi hot pool • laundry room • convenient parking in front of condo • 16 person conference room and wet bar. Adults only. No pets. Open all year, 3 star rated.

A/C H

Palm Springs Marquis Resort Phone: 760-322-2121
150 S. Indian Canyon Dr. 800-223-1050
Palm Springs, CA 92262 Fax: 760-322-2380

In the heart of Palm Springs, overlooking the beautiful San Jacinto Mountains you will find this intimate and luxurious hotel. The resort's 265 elegant rooms and suites are decorated in contemporary California style decor. Lush garden settings make dining a special experience at the resort. Guests will enjoy two outdoor heated swimming pools with whirlpools and two championship tennis courts. Walking distance to a host of fine restaurants, shopping, art galleries, museum, and casino. Amenities include: full bath facilities • hair dryers • A/C • coffee maker • telephone • cable TV • refrigerator • radio • and private balcony or patio. If you are bringing the kids be sure to ask about the Kamp Wannakombak children's program — It's a great time for the kids while you spend some time alone.

A/C H

Shilo Inn-Palm Springs Desert Resort Phone: 760-320-7676
1875 N. Palm Canyon Drive 800-222-2244
Palm Springs, CA 92262-9213 Fax: 760-320-9543

Enjoy the spectacular San Jacinto Mountain Range from this beautiful resort hotel located near the aerial tramway. All 124 guestrooms and suites feature a microwave • refrigerator • coffee maker • satellite TV with premium channels • and much more. VCR and movie rentals are available to guests. Facilities include a spectacular courtyard with gazebo, outdoor family and adult pools & spas, steam room, sauna, fitness center and guest laundromat. Amenities include free local calls, USA Today newspaper, continental breakfast and airport shuttle. Meeting space is available for up to 60 people. Restaurants are located nearby.

A/C

Super 8 Lodge Phone: 760-322-3757
1900 N. Palm Canyon Dr. 800-800-8000
Palm Springs, CA 92262 Fax: 760-323-5290

The Super 8 Lodge offers travelers comfort, convenience, and affordability in a resort setting. Amenities include: one 8-minute free long distance call each day of stay • electronic locks • in-room refrigerator • remote control TV with preferred channels • guest laundry • outdoor heated pool / whirlpool. Close to shopping, attractions, entertainment and gambling.

A/C H

Rim of the World

Rim of the World is in southwest California near San Bernardino. The byway begins at Mormon Rocks Fire Station on CA 138, just west of I-15. It travels southeast following CA 138, CA 18, and CA 38 and ends in Redlands. The state highways are usually open all year and are two-lane paved roads suitable for all types of vehicles. Rim of the World is 115 miles long.

Rim Of The World offers some of the most naturally beautiful scenery in southern California. Sweeping views of the San Bernardino Mountains reward the byway traveler as it follows similar routes taken by travelers of the past. Native Americans, Mormon pioneers, and miners all came through this area with different destinations in mind.

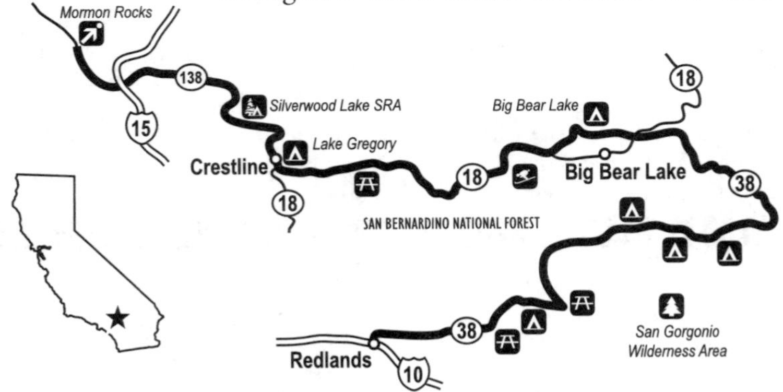

Rim of the World passes through San Bernardino National Forest, which offers a variety of recreational opportunities. San Gorgonio Wilderness is nearly 57,000 acres of granite ridges, subalpine meadows, and placid lakes. It lies southeast of the byway and offers excellent hiking and backpacking opportunities. Numerous campgrounds and picnic areas are all along the byway. Some of the more secluded camping areas can be reached by taking a short drive off the byway.

The State of California manages a recreation area at Silverwood Lake. The 100-acre lake attracts visitors interested in swimming, fishing, and boating. The campground here has 136 RV and tent sites available year-round. Visitors will also find miles of paved trails.

Information: San Bernardino National Forest, 1824 S Commercenter Cir, San Bernardino CA 92408 / 909-383-5588. Silverwood Lake SRA, 14651 Cedar Cir, Hesperia CA 92345 / 760-389-2303.

Lodging Invitation

Shore Acres Lodge & Vacation Rentals Phone: 909-866-8200
P.O. Box 110410 800-524-6600
Big Bear Lake, CA 92315 Fax: 909-866-1580

Year-round mountain recreation in a pristine alpine setting tucked away from traffic and big city noises. Established in 1907 as a "Gentlemen's" hunting and fishing lodge, Shore Acres Lodge & Vacation Rentals offers one of the most picturesque spots on Big Bear Lake. Accommodations include eleven classic mountain style cabins, located on 2 pine shaded, lakefront acres where the fish are really biting — two steps to Big Bear Lake or fly fish off your back porch. Guests will also enjoy the clean fresh air, singing birds and the smell of pine and manzanita. Close to shopping • restaurants • ski resorts • golf • and family fun.

Saline Valley

BLM 2

Saline Valley scenic byway is located in east-central California, near the Nevada border. Southern access is southeast of Keeler off CA 190. The byway travels north to the junction of Owens Valley to Death Valley scenic byway. Saline Valley is 82 miles long and follows Saline Valley Road, which is mostly a county-maintained graded dirt road. Ten miles of the byway are paved. The road is subject to temporary closure after periods of heavy rain, otherwise it is generally open year-round. A two-wheel drive, high-clearance vehicle is required to safely travel the route.

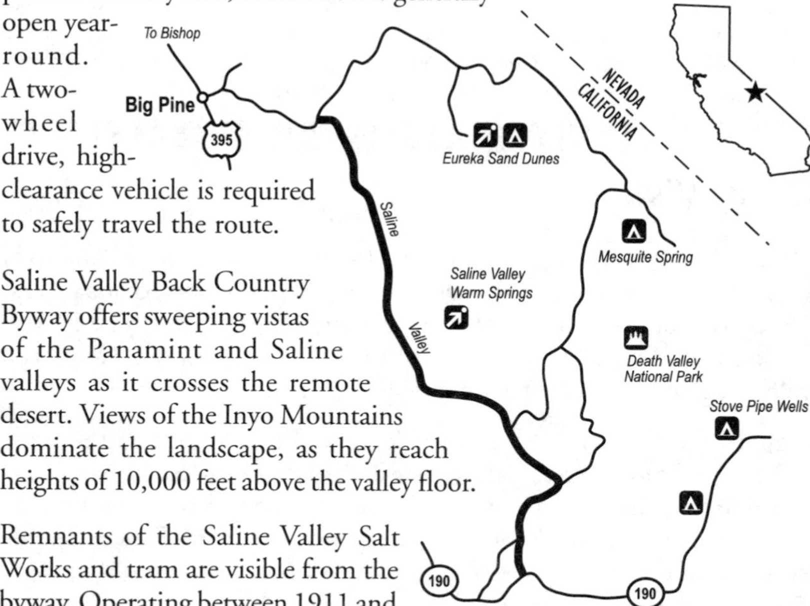

Saline Valley Back Country Byway offers sweeping vistas of the Panamint and Saline valleys as it crosses the remote desert. Views of the Inyo Mountains dominate the landscape, as they reach heights of 10,000 feet above the valley floor.

Remnants of the Saline Valley Salt Works and tram are visible from the byway. Operating between 1911 and

1913, it was once the steepest tramway in the United States. It rises from 1,100 feet to 8,500 feet at Inyo Crest and then drops 3,600 feet at Swansea in Owens Valley. The area is listed on the National Register of Historic Places.

Saline Valley Warm Springs is a BLM special management area that provides warm spring bathing and camping. The area is located six miles east of Saline Valley Road.

Death Valley National Park is east of the byway. Side roads provide access to the park where the lowest point in the western hemisphere resides. The national park also offers camping facilities and interesting sights to visit.

Information: BLM-Ridgecrest Field Office, 300 S Richmond Rd, Ridgecrest CA 93555 / 760-384-5400. Inyo National Forest, 873 N Main St, Bishop CA 93514 / 760-873-2400. Death Valley National Park, PO Box 579, Death Valley CA 92328 / 760-786-2331.

Sierra Vista

US FS The Sierra Vista scenic byway is located in east-central California, between Yosemite National Park and Kings Canyon National Park. The byway forms an open loop between Bass Lake and North Fork, with a side trip ending at the junction with CA 41. The byway is about 100 miles long and is usually passable mid-May to mid-November.

Beginning in North Fork, the byway follows Minarets Road northeasterly to Beasore Road. It then follows Beasore Road southwest to Bass Lake. The side road that is also a part of the byway follows Sky Ranch Road to CA 41. Minarets Road is a two-lane paved road from North Fork to Beasore Road. From this point, the first eight miles of Beasore Road has a graded dirt surface; expect to travel at slow speeds on this portion. The rest of

Beasore Road to Bass Lake is paved. The entire byway is safe for travel by all types of vehicles.

The Sierra Vista scenic byway begins at an elevation of 3,000 feet and climbs to more than 7,000 feet as it crosses Sierra National Forest. Several scenic overlooks provide sweeping views of the surrounding Sierra Nevada Mountains. Redinger Overlook provides an excellent view of Redinger Lake and the San Joaquin River. Mile High Overlook offers spectacular views of the Minarets, Mount Ritter, and Mammoth Mountain as well as views of Mammoth Pool Reservoir and the San Joaquin River.

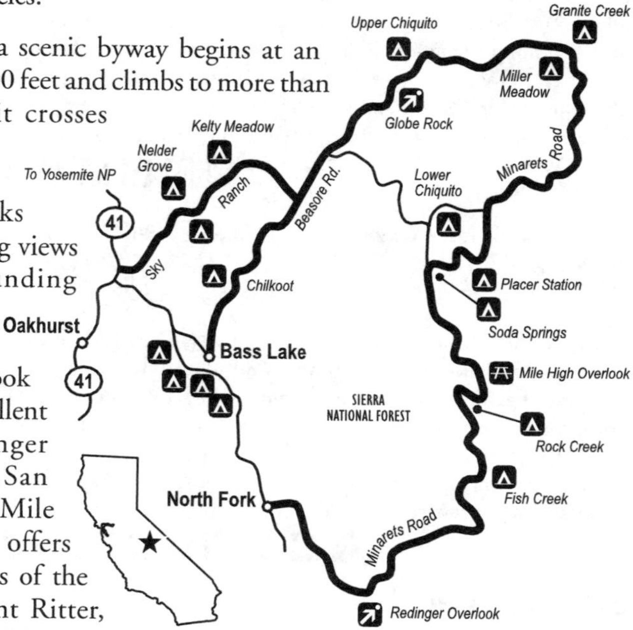

Those interested in camping will find plenty of camp-grounds along the byway. All campgrounds operate on a first-come, first-served basis; no reservations are accepted. Nelder Grove, located along Sky Ranch Road, is a popular camping area. Here there are over 100 giant sequoias intermingled with pine, fir, and incense cedar. Shadow of the Giants National Recreation Trail, located in Nelder Grove, is a one-mile, self-guided trail along the banks of Nelder Creek. Be sure to check out "Granddad and the Grandkids," an isolated, mature sequoia tree that has one large branch outstretched over younger sequoias growing beneath.

Information: Sierra National Forest, 1600 Tollhouse Rd, Clovis CA 93612 / 209-297-0706.

Lodging Invitation

High Sierra RV
40389 Hwy. 41
Oakhurst, CA 93644

Phone: 209-683-7662

Camp along the river in rustic mountain atmosphere with all the amenities of full hook-ups, yet within easy walking distance to shopping, restaurants, and theaters. Only 17 miles to Yosemite National Park. Facilities & Features include: hot showers • phone hook-ups • RV dump • laundry room • bathrooms • pay phone • fishing • swimming • picnic tables • cable TV hook-ups • 30 amp service • city water & sewer. Rates from $15.00 to $25.00 per night. Weekly and monthly rates available. From the junction of Hwy. 41 & 49, travel north 0.4 miles on Hwy. 41 and enter right on Golden Oak Loop at the "High Sierra RV" sign.

Shilo Inn - Oakhurst / Yosemite
40644 Highway 41
Oakhurst, CA 93644-9621

Phone: 209-683-3555
800-222-2244
Fax: 209-683-3386

Located at the Southern Gateway to Yosemite National Park, Bass Lake, and Badger Pass Ski Area, this Shilo Inn offers travelers 80 mini-suites. All rooms are complete with a microwave • refrigerator • wet bar • and satellite TV with premium channels. VCR and movie rentals are also available. Facilities include an outdoor heated pool and spa for use during the warmer seasons as well as a sauna, steam room, fitness center and guest laundromat. Amenities include free local calls, USA Today newspaper and continental breakfast. Meeting space is available. A restaurant is located adjacent to the hotel.

Smith River

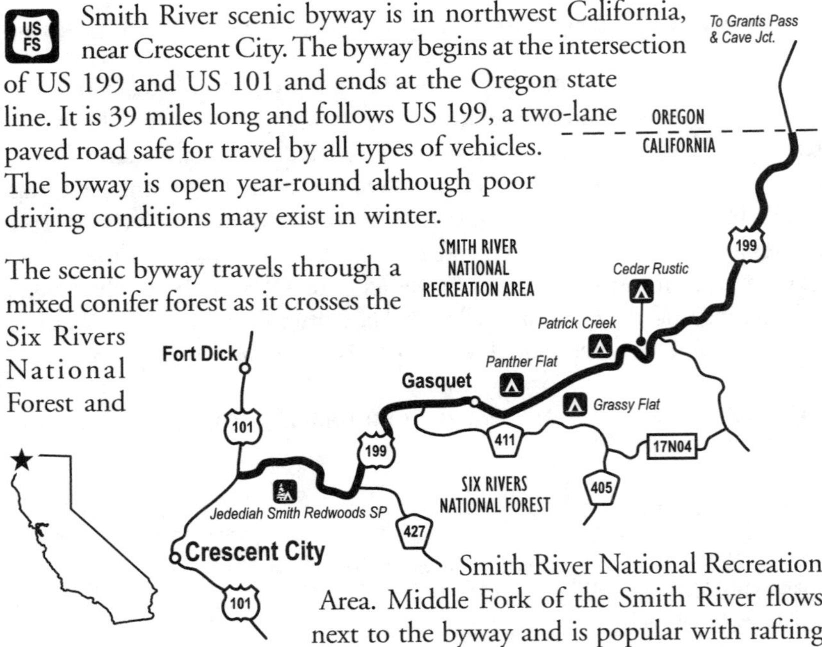

Smith River scenic byway is in northwest California, near Crescent City. The byway begins at the intersection of US 199 and US 101 and ends at the Oregon state line. It is 39 miles long and follows US 199, a two-lane paved road safe for travel by all types of vehicles. The byway is open year-round although poor driving conditions may exist in winter.

The scenic byway travels through a mixed conifer forest as it crosses the Six Rivers National Forest and Smith River National Recreation Area. Middle Fork of the Smith River flows next to the byway and is popular with rafting enthusiasts as well as anglers. Among the fish inhabiting the river are Chinook salmon, steelhead trout, and rainbow trout. Several access points are along the byway. The river is part of the Wild and Scenic River program and is the only undammed watershed in California.

Smith River provides access to a variety of recreational activities. There are several developed campgrounds directly along the byway. Near the western end is Jedediah Smith Redwoods State Park. The campground here has over 100 campsites set among the giant trees. Those interested in hiking, backpacking, or horseback riding will find several trails throughout the area. Trails range from under one mile long to more than 15 miles.

Information: Six Rivers National Forest, 1330 Bayshore Way, Eureka CA 95501 / 707-442-1721. Jedediah Smith Redwoods State Park & Smith River NRA, 1375 Elk Valley Rd, Crescent City CA 95531 / 707-464-6101.

State of Jefferson

This byway is in northwest California near the Oregon border. The byway's southeast access is in Yreka off I-5. It heads northwest, crosses into Oregon, and ends at the junction with US 199. State of Jefferson follows CA 263, CA 96, and Grayback Road. The roads are two-lane paved roads suitable for all vehicles. The byway is 108 miles long and is generally open year-round but temporary closure is possible during winter.

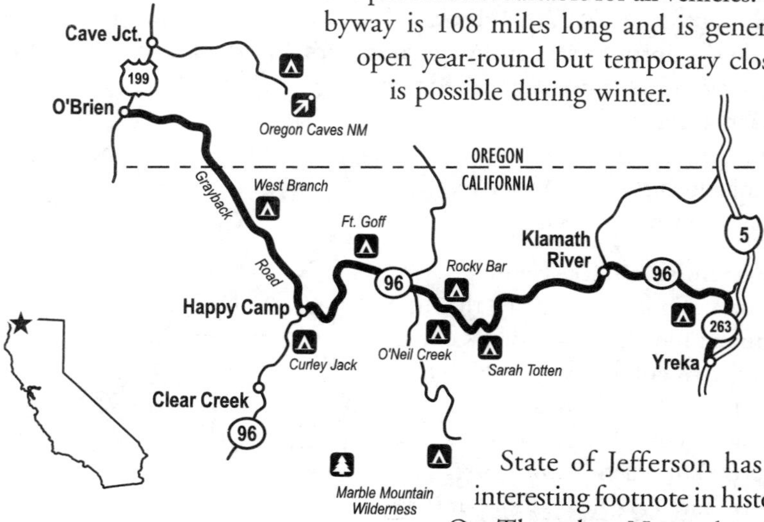

State of Jefferson has an interesting footnote in history. On Thursday, November 27, 1941, the State of Jefferson "seceded" from California and Oregon to form the 49th state of the Union. Several counties in northern California and southern Oregon proclaimed their independence to protest the lack of good roads and other basic services. Armed miners displaying the State of Jefferson seal stopped traffic at the "border" on US 99 (now CA 263) to distribute the "Proclamation of Independence." The proclamation declared an intent to "secede each Thursday until further notice." Movement for secession, however, was stopped abruptly by the attack on Pearl Harbor. Nowadays the byway traveler is free to cross this beautiful territory known as Klamath National Forest.

Much of the byway follows the meandering Klamath River, a National Wild and Scenic River. Anglers may wish to spend some time attempting to catch salmon or trout. The river is also enjoyed by rafting, canoeing, kayaking, and tubing enthusiasts. Several campgrounds are situated along the banks of the river. Among the wildlife inhabiting the area are deer, otters, geese, ducks, and bears. Bald eagles have occasionally been seen riding the wind currents.

Information: Klamath National Forest, 1312 Fairlane Rd, Yreka CA 96097 / 530-842-6131.

Sunrise

US FS The Sunrise scenic byway is about 45 miles east of San Diego in southwest California. It begins one mile east of Pine Valley off I-8 and travels north to end at the junction with CA 79. The byway follows County Road S1, a two-lane paved road safe for all types of vehicles, and is 24 miles long. Temporary closure is possible during winter, otherwise the byway is open year-round.

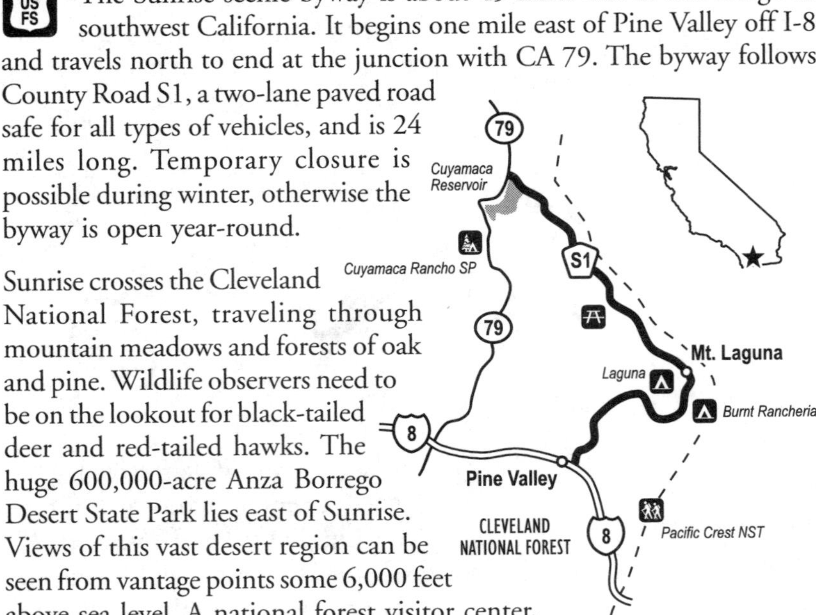

Sunrise crosses the Cleveland National Forest, traveling through mountain meadows and forests of oak and pine. Wildlife observers need to be on the lookout for black-tailed deer and red-tailed hawks. The huge 600,000-acre Anza Borrego Desert State Park lies east of Sunrise. Views of this vast desert region can be seen from vantage points some 6,000 feet above sea level. A national forest visitor center, open weekends through summer, is in Mount Laguna. Information about the byway and national forest are found here.

Those interested in staying overnight will find two national forest campgrounds: Burnt Rancheria and Laguna. Both campgrounds are in the Laguna Recreation Area. Burnt Rancheria has a total of 108 campsites; 11 are tent-only. The campground is set among pine and oak trees and is open mid-May through October. Laguna is open year-round and has 103 campsites, of which 23 are for tent campers only. There are no RV hookups at either campground. Additional camping facilities are available in Cuyamaca Rancho State Park, near the north end of the byway.

In addition to camping, Laguna Recreation Area attracts hikers, mountain bikers, and horseback riders. There are several trails ranging from under one mile long to more than ten miles. The Pacific Crest National Scenic Trail crosses the recreation area. Trails can also be found in the state park.

Information: Cleveland National Forest, 10845 Rancho Bernardo Rd - Suite 200, San Diego CA 92127 / 619-673-6180. Cuyamaca Rancho State Park, 12551 Hwy 79, Descanso CA 90216 / 760-765-0755.

Tioga Road / Big Oak Flat Road

NSB Located in east-central California, the byway begins in the community of Big Oak Flat. The byway travels east and ends at the Tioga Pass entrance to Yosemite National Park. Lee Vining Canyon scenic byway picks up where this one ends and continues east. The byway follows CA 120 (Big Oak Flat Road and Tioga Pass Road in the national park), a two-lane paved road suitable for all vehicles. It is approximately 80 miles long; 64 miles are officially designated a National Scenic Byway. Tioga Pass Road in the national park is closed during winter. The rest of the byway usually remains open year-round.

Yosemite National Park is one of the crown jewels of the National Park System. It was established in 1890 to preserve a portion of the Sierra Nevada Mountains that stretch along California's eastern flank. The byway offers spectacular views of the mountains and meadows and valleys covered with wildflowers. Much of the surrounding land is undisturbed by man. In fact, nearly 95 percent of the park is preserved wilderness and many miles of its rivers are National Wild and Scenic Rivers.

Recreational opportunities are abundant within Yosemite National Park. Birdwatchers will delight in the more than 200 species of birds inhabiting the area. Other wildlife found here include black bear, mule deer, and mountain lion. Numerous campgrounds provide a total of over 800 campsites for RVers and tent campers. Anglers will be tempted by the many rivers teaming with cutthroat, steelhead, and golden trout. Miles of trails invite the hiker to explore the unspoiled wilderness.

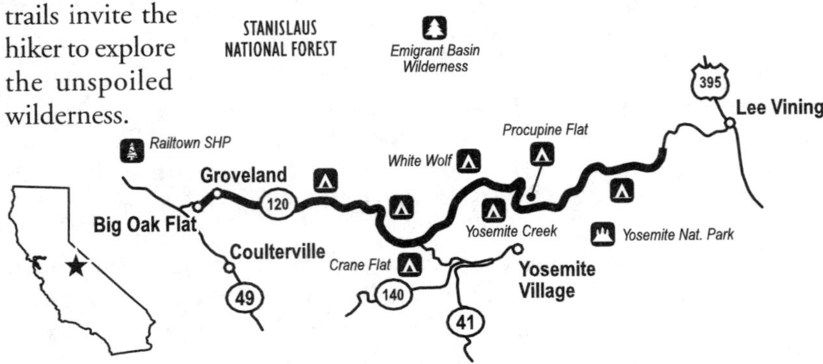

Information: Stanislaus National Forest, 19777 Greenley Rd, Sonora CA 95370 / 209-532-3671. Sierra National Forest, 1600 Tollhouse Rd, Clovis CA 93612 / 209-297-0706. Yosemite National Park, PO Box 577, Administration Bldg, Yosemite CA 95389 / 209-372-0200.

Lodging Invitation

Marble Quarry RV Park
11551 Yankee Hill Rd.
P.O. Box 850
Columbia, CA 95310

Phone: 209-532-9539
Fax: 209-532-8631

A clean, family oriented, haven for an enjoyable camping experience — shade trees galore. A *Park* - not just a place to park! Short walking distance to historic Columbia or old quarry. Central location for caves • museums • movies • railroad • fishing • boating • antique shopping • restaurants • and much more.

The Groveland Hotel
18767 Main St.
P.O. Box 289
Groveland, CA 95321

Phone: 209-962-4000
Fax: 209-962-6674
E-mail: peggy@groveland.com
Internet: www.groveland.com

The Groveland Hotel provides you with a magnificent setting — from the most delightful lodging and sumptuous dining to enjoying your favorite outdoor activities and revisiting California's historic past. A gracious restoration with antiques, down comforters and private baths, complete with foothills hospitality. In addition to all the comforts of Grandma's House, nearby amenities include golf • tennis • swimming • world class white-water rafting • horseback riding • fishing • and hiking. The town of Groveland offers great little shops for browsing and antiquing. The walking tour of town will guide you through some of the Gold Rush era's most historic areas. Only 23 miles from Yosemite.

Trinity Heritage

US FS Trinity Heritage is located in northwestern California, about 45 miles northwest of Redding. The byway begins in Weaverville and travels northeast, ending at the junction with I-5 north of Weed. It follows CA 3 and FSR 17, which are two-lane paved roads safe for travel by all vehicles. The byway is about 120 miles long. California Highway 3 is usually open year round. Forest Service Road 17 is closed late November through May.

Trinity Heritage climbs more than 4,000 feet as it crosses the Shasta-Trinity National Forests. Several scenic vistas offer beautiful views of the surrounding mountains, including Mount Shasta. Much of the byway follows the shores of 16,000-acre Clair Engle Lake, which has a rugged and densely forested shoreline and hundreds of hidden coves. Most development on the lake is limited to the western shore. The lake is in the Trinity Unit of the Whiskeytown-Shasta-Trinity National Recreation Area. Several developed campgrounds are available to those interested in staying overnight.

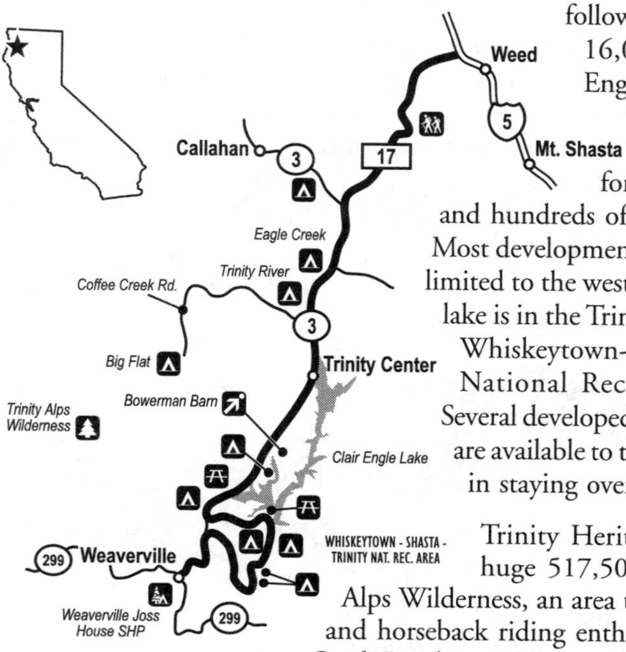

Trinity Heritage skirts the huge 517,500-acre Trinity Alps Wilderness, an area used by hiking and horseback riding enthusiasts. Coffee Creek Road provides access to the heart of this preserved wilderness. At road's end is a small, five-site campground. In the spring, large herds of deer may be seen in the meadows. Thousands of miners lived along Coffee Creek and its tributaries during the Gold Rush. Evidence of their activity is visible from the road.

Bowerman Barn is a short distance off the byway and is worth seeing. It has a foundation of hand-laid stone, mortise and tenon framework, and whipsawn pine boards attached with hand-forged square nails. It's one of the last of its kind.

Information: Shasta-Trinity National Forests, 2400 Washington Ave, Redding CA 96001 / 530-244-2978. Weaverville Joss House SHP, PO Box 1217, Weaverville CA 96093 / 530-623-5284. Whiskeytown-Shasta-Trinity NRA, PO Box 188, Whiskeytown CA 96095 / 530-246-1225.

Trinity River

US FS Trinity River is in northwest California, traveling between I-5 and US 101. Eastern access is near Redding and its western near Arcata. The byway is approximately 140 miles long and follows CA 299. The road is a two-lane paved road suitable for all types of vehicles. It is usually passable year-round but winter driving conditions can be hazardous.

The Trinity River scenic byway crosses Shasta-Trinity National Forests with a small portion running through Six Rivers National Forest. Trinity River meanders alongside much of the byway and attracts anglers in search of salmon or trout. Anglers are also attracted to the Trinity Alps Wilderness, which boasts more than 60 alpine lakes. It is California's largest wilderness area and is also used by hikers, equestrians, and backpackers.

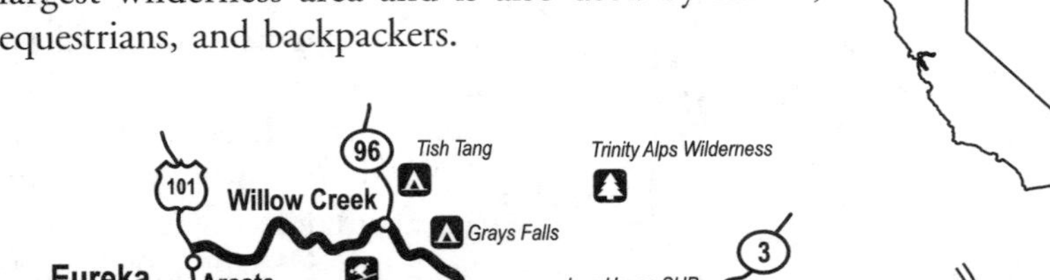

Whiskeytown Lake is next to the byway near the eastern terminus. It is part of the Whiskeytown-Shasta-Trinity National Recreation Area, which is managed by the National Park Service. Lake fishing is good either from the shore or from a boat. Rainbow and brown trout, kokanee salmon, largemouth bass, smallmouth bass, and spotted bass inhabit the lake. The recreation area also has developed camping facilities for RVers and tent campers. Several national forest campgrounds are also along or near the byway.

Information: Shasta-Trinity National Forests, 2400 Washington Ave, Redding CA 96001 / 530-244-2978. Weaverville Joss House SHP, PO Box 1217, Weaverville CA 96093 / 530-623-5284. Whiskeytown-Shasta-Trinity NRA, PO Box 188, Whiskeytown CA 96095 / 530-246-1225.

Yuba Donner

US FS Yuba Donner is in northeast California, about 80 miles northeast of Sacramento. The byway forms a loop drive through Tahoe National Forest. It follows CA 20, CA 49, CA 89, and I-80. All roads followed are suitable for all types of vehicles. Yuba Donner is 170 miles long and usually open year-round.

Yuba Donner travels through the foothills and mountains of the northern Sierra Nevada Mountains. It winds through miles of forests and valleys with meandering rivers and streams. The area is rich with gold mining

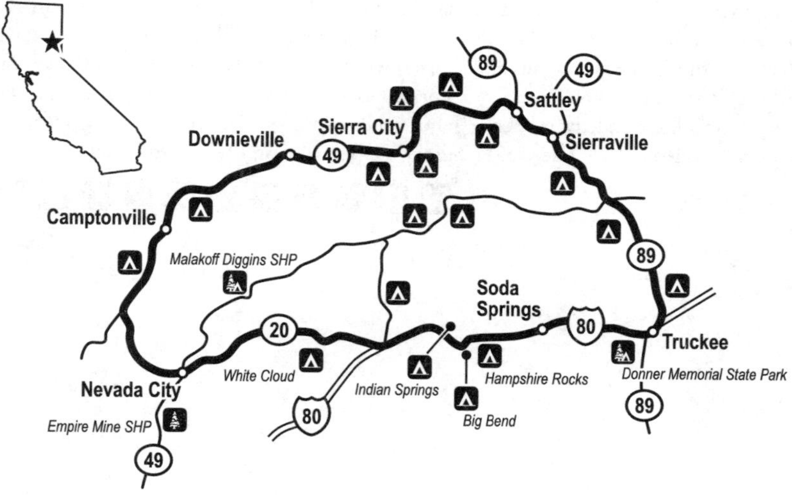

history and immigrant and transportation history, including Native American trade routes and campsites of the ill-fated Donner Party.

The Donner Party was actually composed of two families, the Donners and the Reeds, who left Illinois in 1846 and headed for California under the leadership of George Donner. After having difficulty crossing the Great

Salt Lake in Utah, they were trapped in the Sierra Nevada Mountains by heavy November snow. They were forced to camp for the winter at a small lake, now named Donner Lake. They suffered tremendous hardships; members of the group resorted to cannibalism in order to survive. Forty-seven of the original 87-member party were eventually brought into California by rescue parties over what is now known as Donner Pass.

Information: Tahoe National Forest, 631 Coyote St, Nevada City CA 95959 / 530-265-4531. Donner Memorial State Park, 12593 Donner Pass Rd, Truckee CA 96161 / 530-582-7892. Malakoff Diggins SHP, 23579 N Bloomfield Rd, Nevada City CA 95959 / 530-265-2740. Empire Mine SHP, 10791 E Empire St, Grass Valley CA 95975 / 530-273-8522.

Lodging Invitation

Coachland RV Park
10500 Highway 89 North
Truckee, CA 96161

Phone: 530-587-3071
Fax: 916-587-6976

Coachland RV Park offers a quiet and relaxing environment on 55 acres of pines in the clean crisp air of the High Sierras. Facilities include 131 full hook-up pull through RV spaces with cable TV. On-site laundry, restrooms, and picnic tables. Historical downtown Truckee with it's fine restaurants and shops is within walking distance. Nearby attractions and activities include: golf courses • major ski resorts • Nevada casinos • excellent fishing in numerous lakes and rivers • Lake Tahoe • hiking • mountain biking • river rafting • mines and museums of "The Gold Country". Open all year. Only ¼ mile from I-80.

Colorado

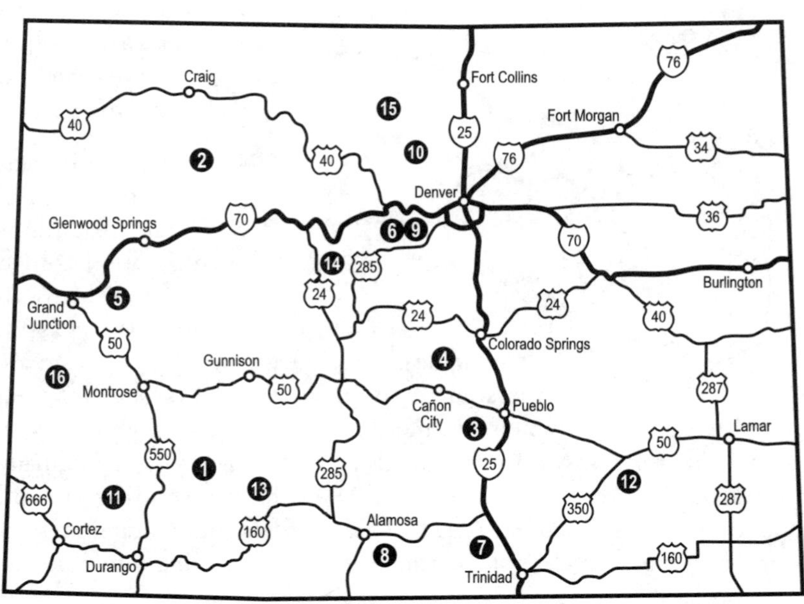
Craig
Fort Collins
Fort Morgan
Denver
Glenwood Springs
Grand Junction
Burlington
Colorado Springs
Gunnison
Montrose
Cañon City
Pueblo
Lamar
Cortez
Durango
Alamosa
Trinidad
40
25
76
34
36
70
285
24
50
287
550
666
160
350
1
2
3
4
5
6
7
8
9
10
11
12
13
14
15
16

Alpine Loop

Alpine Loop Back Country Byway is in southwest Colorado about 100 miles southeast of Grand Junction. The byway forms a loop drive between Lake City and the towns of Ouray and Silverton. Alpine Loop is 65 miles long and is generally open late June through October.

Near Ouray, the byway follows Mineral Creek Road to Engineer Pass. From Silverton, the byway follows Animas River Road to Cinnamon Pass. The northern segment from Lake City follows Henson Creek Road to Engineer Pass. The southern portion from Lake City follows Lake Fork of the Gunnison River Road to Cinnamon Pass. The roads are marked with "Alpine Loop" signs. Two-thirds of the byway is paved and is suitable for all types of vehicles. The rest is a dirt surface and requires a four-wheel drive vehicle to complete.

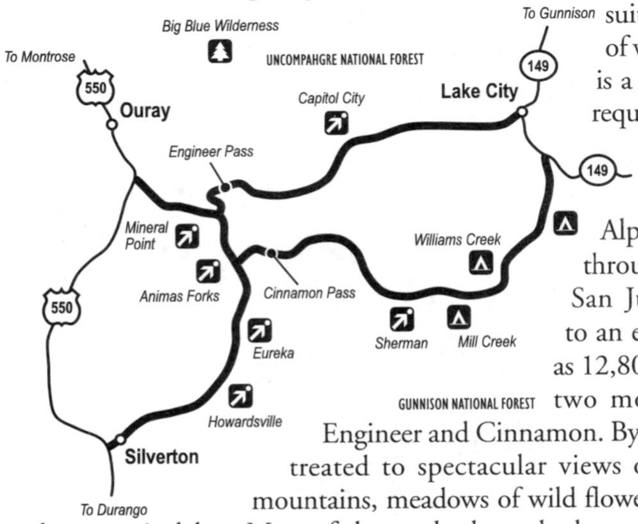

Big Blue Wilderness
To Montrose
550
Ouray
UNCOMPAHGRE NATIONAL FOREST
Capitol City
Lake City
To Gunnison
149
Engineer Pass
149
Mineral Point
Animas Forks
Cinnamon Pass
Williams Creek
550
Eureka
Sherman
Mill Creek
Howardsville
GUNNISON NATIONAL FOREST
Silverton
To Durango

Alpine Loop winds through the beautiful San Juan Mountains to an elevation as high as 12,800 feet. It crosses two mountain passes: Engineer and Cinnamon. Byway travelers are treated to spectacular views of snow-capped mountains, meadows of wild flowers, ghost towns, and mountain lakes. Most of the roads along the byway were originally constructed by prospectors in the late 1800s for transporting ore and supplies. Today, the roads are used by four-wheelers and mountain bikers. Four-wheel drive vehicles may be rented in the surrounding communities.

Several hiking trails are accessed from the byway, including five that lead to peaks over 14,000 feet. Those not interested in hiking may wish to photograph or explore the byway's many ghost towns. Anglers will find lakes, rivers, and streams teaming with rainbow, brook, and cutthroat trout. Three campgrounds are along the byway for those interested in staying overnight.

Information: BLM-Gunnison Field Office, 216 N Colorado Ave, Gunnison CO 81230 / 970-641-0471. Uncompahgre National Forest, Ouray Ranger District, 2505 S Townsend, Montrose CO 81401 / 970-240-5400. Gunnison National Forest, Gunnison Ranger District, 216 N Colorado St, Gunnison CO 81230 / 970-641-0471.

Flat Tops Trail

US FS Flat Tops Trail is in northwest Colorado about 100 miles northeast of Grand Junction. It crosses the White River and Routt National Forests between Meeker and Yampa. The byway follows CR 8 and FSR 16 over a combination of paved and gravel-surfaced roads. Most vehicles are able to complete the entire 82-mile route. Flat Tops Trail receives two to ten feet of snow in winter and is not maintained for automobile use. It is open for snowmobile and cross-country ski use.

The Flat Tops Trail crosses sage-covered hills, meadows, and working ranches as it winds through two national forests. Byway travelers are also treated to forests of lodgepole pine, spruce, fir, and aspen. The byway climbs across 10,343-foot Ripple Creek Pass before leaving White River National Forest. Vaughn Lake is nearby and offers fishing for rainbow and brown trout.

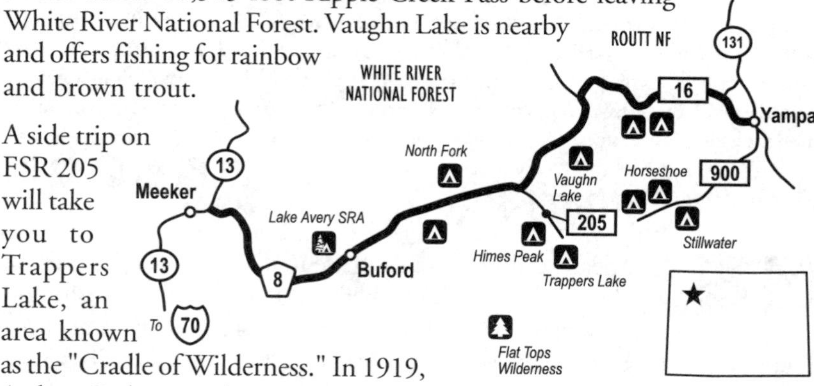

A side trip on FSR 205 will take you to Trappers Lake, an area known as the "Cradle of Wilderness." In 1919, Arthur Carhart made recommendations to cease further development of roads and homes around the lake. His efforts to protect the natural beauty of the area led to a wilderness protection movement, which ultimately led to the Wilderness Act of 1964. Visitors will find four camping areas with a total of nearly 60 RV and tent sites. An RV length limit of 22 feet exists for each camping area.

Information: Routt National Forest, Yampa RD, PO Box 7, Yampa CO 80483 / 970-638-4516. White River National Forest, PO Box 948, Glenwood Springs CO 81602 / 970-945-2521. Lake Avery SRA, Colorado State Parks, 1313 Sherman St #618, Denver CO 80203 / 303-866-3437.

Lodging Invitation

Buford Hunting & Fishing Lodge Phone: 970-878-4745
20474 RBC #8
Meeker, CO 81641

The Buford Lodge is located adjacent to the beautiful White River in the center of the White River National Forest offering excellent fishing and hunting. The rustic and modern housekeeping cabins, some with fireplaces or wood stoves and televisions, date back to 1908. RV sites are also available. Located on the property in an 85 year-old log building is the new Buford White River Historical Museum. The on-site grocery store, which is on the National Registry of Historic Places, is stocked with sporting goods, gifts, gas and propane. Dining is available at the nearby restaurant. The Buford Lodge will help arrange hunt/drop camps and provide guides to those interested in a real wilderness experience. Located 22 miles east of Meeker on Trappers Lake Road (County Road 8) at Buford, near milepost 20.

JML Outfitters Phone: 970-878-4749
300 County Road 75
Meeker, CO 81641

JML Outfitters is located 2 miles off the Flat Tops Trail Scenic Byway on Papoose Creek, 30 miles east of Meeker. Scenic and serene rustic setting in the White River National Forest. Guest rooms or private cabin available. Open year-round. Summer guests enjoy fishing, horseback riding, camping, mountain biking, photography, stargazing and watching wildlife. Fall features aspen gold and hunting. This winter wonderland includes snowshoeing, cross country skiing and snowmobiling. License #288.

Frontier Pathways

Frontier Pathways is in south-central Colorado near Pueblo. The byway follows CO 96 between Pueblo and Westcliffe and CO 165 between Colorado City and Rockvale. Both state highways are two-lane paved roads suitable for all types of vehicles. Portions of the 103-mile byway may close in winter, otherwise it usually remains open year-round.

From Pueblo, Frontier Pathways crosses the grassy plains of eastern Colorado before climbing 2,000 feet to Hardscrabble Pass and McKenzie Junction. The beautiful Sangre de Cristo Mountains dominate the western sky. Travelers can continue traveling west of McKenzie Junction and descend into Wet Mountain Valley between lush green slopes of the Wet Mountains. Or travelers can head south on CO 165, travel through San Isabel National Forest and Greenhorn Valley to Colorado City.

Camping is available in Lake Pueblo State Park and San Isabel National Forest. Ophir Creek Campground is in the national forest and has 31 campsites. There are three campgrounds in the Lake Isabel Recreation Area with a total of 52 campsites. La Vista Campground in the recreation area has 19 sites with electric hookups. Lake Pueblo State Park offers hundreds of campsites, most with electric hookups. It remains open year-round; the national forest campgrounds are open spring to fall.

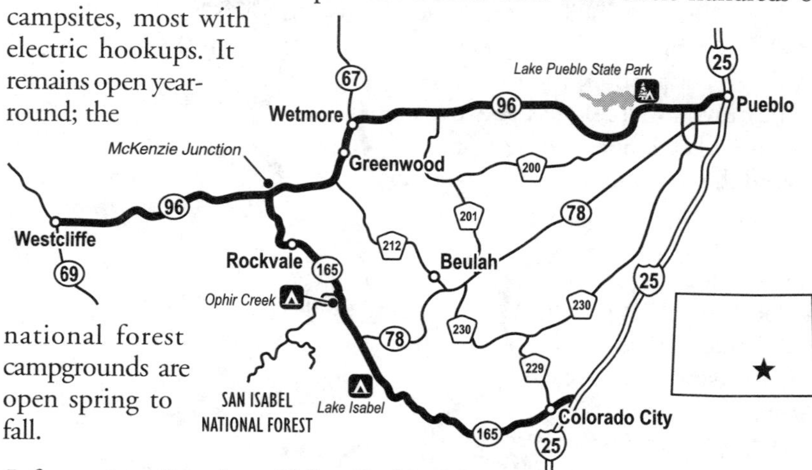

Information: Greenhorn Valley C of C, PO Box 125, Colorado City CO 81019 / 719-676-3000. Pike and San Isabel National Forest, 1920 Valley Dr, Pueblo CO 81008 / 719-545-8737. Lake Pueblo State Park, 640 Pueblo Reservoir Rd, Pueblo CO 81005 / 719-561-9320.

Gold Belt Tour

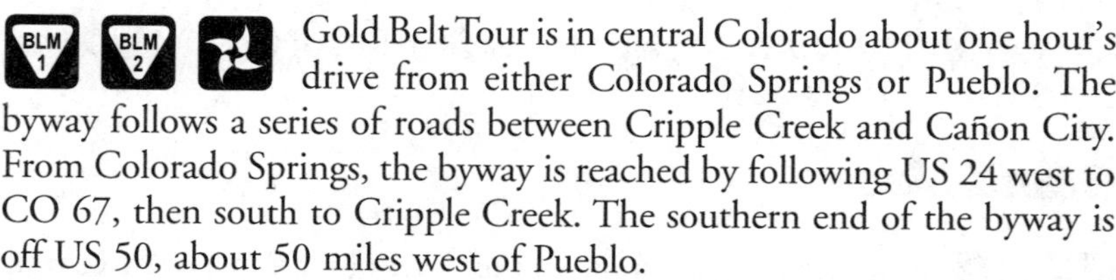

Gold Belt Tour is in central Colorado about one hour's drive from either Colorado Springs or Pueblo. The byway follows a series of roads between Cripple Creek and Cañon City. From Colorado Springs, the byway is reached by following US 24 west to CO 67, then south to Cripple Creek. The southern end of the byway is off US 50, about 50 miles west of Pueblo.

Much of the 122-mile route follows two-lane paved roads suitable for all vehicles. Phantom Canyon road is a rough, gravel-surfaced road. Vehicles over 25 feet should not attempt this segment of the byway. The upper portion of Shelf Road is also a gravel-surfaced road; it requires the use of a four-wheel drive vehicle. All the roads are usually passable year-round; heavy snow can close portions of the route. Phantom Canyon Road and the upper portion of Shelf Road should be avoided in wet weather.

In the 1890s, mining towns of the region enjoyed the greatest gold boom Colorado has ever known. The back country byway is named for the historic Florence and Cripple Creek Railroad, the "Gold Belt Line," which linked the gold camps with Florence and Cañon City. Phantom Canyon Road follows the old railroad grade.

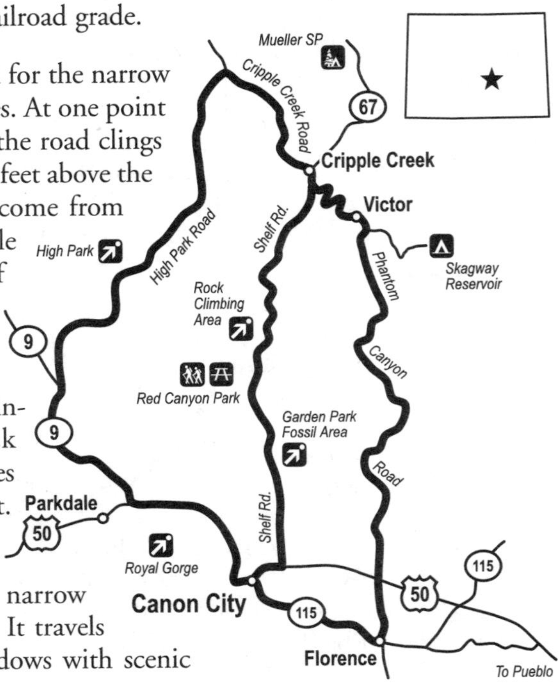

Shelf Road is so named for the narrow "shelf" on which it rides. At one point on the upper portion, the road clings to the canyon wall 200 feet above the stream bed. Climbers come from around the world to scale the limestone walls of Shelf Road. South of the rock climbing area is Red Canyon Park, a 500-acre park containing unusual red rock formations. Some spires reach heights of 100 feet.

High Park Road is an alternate route to the narrow confines of the others. It travels across wide open meadows with scenic mountain vistas.

Information: BLM-Royal Gorge Field Office, 3170 E Main St, Canon City CO 81212 / 719-269-8500. Mueller State Park, PO Box 49, Divide CO 80814 / 719-687-2366.

Grand Mesa

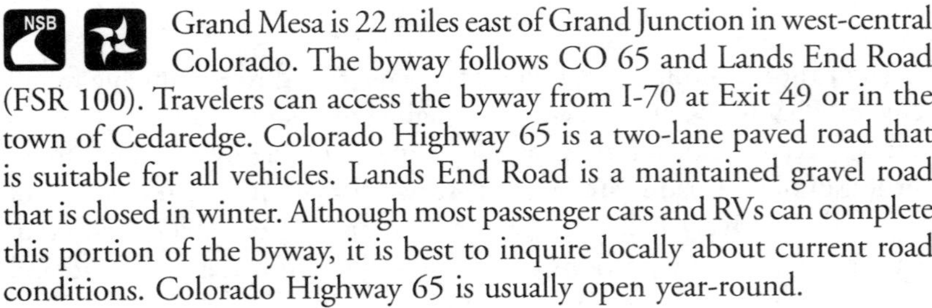

Grand Mesa is 22 miles east of Grand Junction in west-central Colorado. The byway follows CO 65 and Lands End Road (FSR 100). Travelers can access the byway from I-70 at Exit 49 or in the town of Cedaredge. Colorado Highway 65 is a two-lane paved road that is suitable for all vehicles. Lands End Road is a maintained gravel road that is closed in winter. Although most passenger cars and RVs can complete this portion of the byway, it is best to inquire locally about current road conditions. Colorado Highway 65 is usually open year-round.

From the exit off I-70, you begin in the canyon of Plateau Creek with sandstone walls rising 400 to 1,000 feet above the highway. The road continues climbing from the town of Mesa to an elevation of around

11,000 feet. It is here that you've reached the top of Grand Mesa, the world's largest flat-top mountain. The panoramic view from the top is simply astounding. In a short drive you've traveled from the pinyon-juniper desert canyon to a cool, evergreen forest.

Over 300 stream-fed lakes teaming with rainbow, brook, and cutthroat trout are scattered across the Mesa. Several national forest campgrounds offer the perfect spot for pitching a tent or settling in your RV. Among the facilities are picnic tables, drinking water, fire rings, and pit toilets. There are no hookups or dump stations. During winter, the area becomes a haven for cross-country and downhill skiing as well as snowmobiling. Hiking, backpacking, mountain biking, and horseback riding are enjoyed in warmer months.

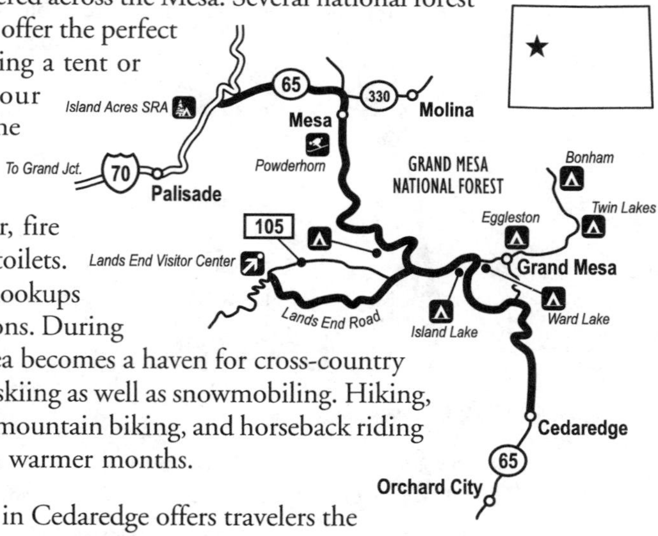

Pioneer Town in Cedaredge offers travelers the chance to turn back the clock. Authentic stores and the Cedaredge Town Jail, along with period clothes and memorabilia from the past 100 years, create a realistic old-west atmosphere.

Information: Grand Mesa-Uncompahgre & Gunnison National Forests, 2250 Hwy 50, Delta CO 81416 / 970-874-6600. Island Acres SRA, Colorado State Parks, 1313 Sherman St #618, Denver CO 80203 / 303-866-3437.

Guanella Pass

US FS

Guanella Pass is in central Colorado, 45 miles west of Denver. The byway's northern access is in Georgetown and its southern in Grant. It is 22 miles long and follows Guanella Pass Road. The first ten miles from Georgetown is paved; the remaining is gravel. Large RVs or vehicles pulling trailers are not recommended on the byway. Guanella Pass is usually maintained year-round except for days following heavy snow. Caution should be exercised if traveling the byway in winter.

From an elevation of 8,500 feet in Grant, Guanella Pass climbs through Geneva Creek Canyon, passes Scott Gomer Creek Falls, and enters the large mountain meadow of Geneva Park. The park is surrounded by mountains exceeding 13,000 feet. Just beyond the park is a side trip worth taking. A rough road (recommended only for high-clearance vehicles) leads to the townsite of Geneva City. The remains lie in a basin near the headwaters of Geneva Creek where cabins and mills dot the landscape. The townsite is on private property; take only pictures. Also, the road to the townsite is popular with mountain bikers; please use caution!

Perhaps the highlight of the byway is the summit of Guanella Pass where travelers are rewarded with panoramic views of the surrounding mountains. Hiking enthusiasts gather here to begin their exploration of nearby Mount Evans Wilderness. It also attracts cross-country skiers in winter. Once beyond the summit, the byway descends into Georgetown with South Clear Creek flowing alongside.

Gold mining lured prospectors to Georgetown in 1859, but silver became the town's claim to fame. Georgetown was known as the "Silver Queen" and once boasted of more than 5,000 residents. Over 200 Victorian structures were built during the silver mining boom. The Georgetown Silver Plume Mining District is a National Historic Landmark.

Information: Arapahoe and Roosevelt National Forests, 240 W Prospect Rd, Fort Collins CO 80526 / 970-498-2770.

Highway of Legends

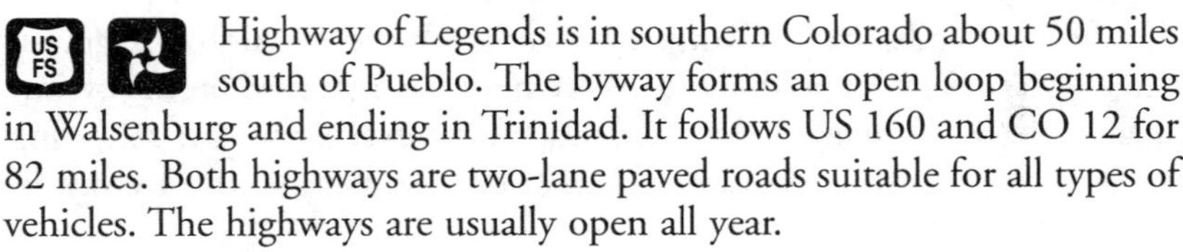

Highway of Legends is in southern Colorado about 50 miles south of Pueblo. The byway forms an open loop beginning in Walsenburg and ending in Trinidad. It follows US 160 and CO 12 for 82 miles. Both highways are two-lane paved roads suitable for all types of vehicles. The highways are usually open all year.

Highway Of Legends crosses San Isabel National Forest through the Sangre de Cristo ("Blood of Christ") Mountains. The Spanish Peaks and a variety of unique geological formations are seen from the byway. Some of the more interesting formations are: Stonewall, Dakota Wall, Devil's Stairsteps, and the Profile Rock.

Sitting quietly among the pine trees near the byway's midpoint is Monument Lake, one of many high altitude lakes along the drive. In the center of the lake is a rock formation jutting 15 feet above the water's surface. This is the "monument" for which the lake is named. It's a natural rock formation said to represent two Indian chiefs. Camping and picnicking facilities may be found around the lake.

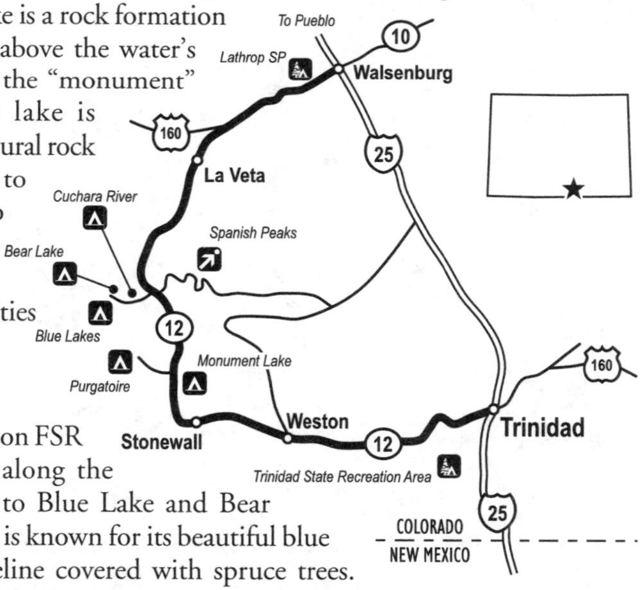

A short side trip on FSR 413 takes you along the Cuchara River to Blue Lake and Bear Lake. Blue Lake is known for its beautiful blue color and shoreline covered with spruce trees. Beyond Blue Lake lies pristine Bear Lake. San Isabel National Forest manages campgrounds around each lake. A total of 30 RV and tent sites are available. There are also several nature and hiking trails in the area. Camping is also available in Lathrop State Park and Trinidad State Park.

Information: Pike and San Isabel National Forests, 1920 Valley Dr, Pueblo CO 81008 / 719-545-8737. Trinidad State Park, 32610 CO 12, Trinidad CO 81082 / 719-846-6951. Lathrop State Park, 70 CR 502, Walsenburg CO 81089 / 719-738-2376.

Los Caminos Antiguos

Los Caminos Antiguos is in south-central Colorado about 120 miles southwest of Pueblo. The byway begins in Alamosa, travels by the Great Sand Dunes National Monument, and then heads south to end at the New Mexico state line. It follows CO 17, CO 142,

CO 150, CO 159, US 160, and US 285. A short segment also follows Six Mile Lane between CO 17 and CO 150. All the roads are two-lane paved roads suitable for all types of vehicles. The byway is 152 miles long and is usually open year-round.

Los Caminos Antiguos explores the rich heritage of Colorado's San Luis Valley and its blend of distinctive cultures. The byway passes through Fort Garland, site of an 1858 fort that is now a state museum. It travels through Colorado's oldest community, San Luis. Travelers can also visit Colorado's oldest church, Our Lady of Guadalupe, located in Conejos near Antonito. In Antonito, you can take a ride on a narrow-gauge steam train through the Rio Grande National Forest.

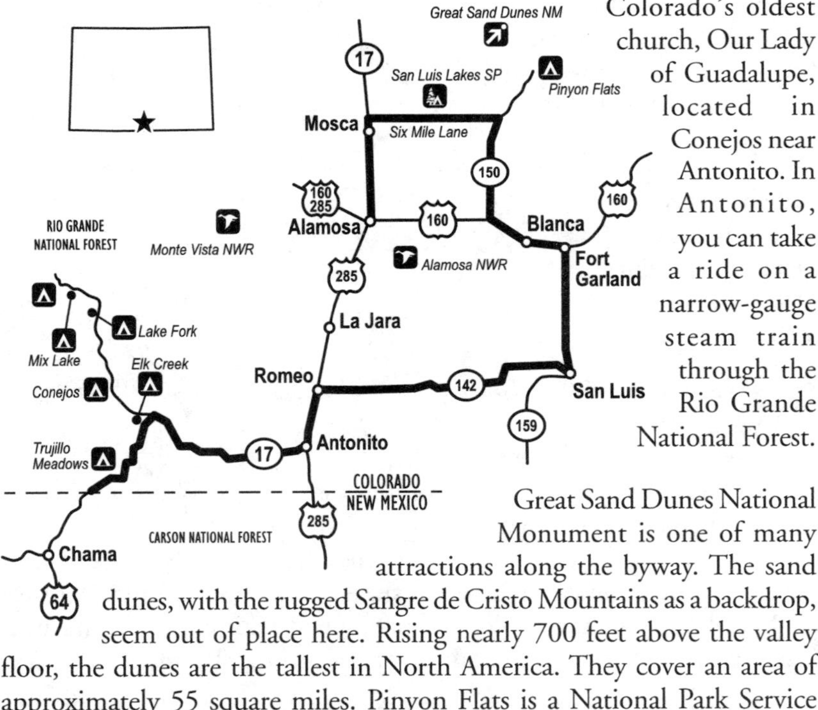

Great Sand Dunes National Monument is one of many attractions along the byway. The sand dunes, with the rugged Sangre de Cristo Mountains as a backdrop, seem out of place here. Rising nearly 700 feet above the valley floor, the dunes are the tallest in North America. They cover an area of approximately 55 square miles. Pinyon Flats is a National Park Service campground near the foot of the dunes and has 88 RV and tent campsites.

Information: BLM-San Luis Resource Area, 1921 State St, Alamosa CO 81101 / 719-589-4975. Rio Grande National Forest, 1803 W Hwy 160, Monte Vista CO 81144 / 719-852-5941. Carson National Forest, 208 Cruz Alta Rd, Taos NM 87571 / 505-758-6200. Great Sand Dunes National Monument, 11500 Hwy 150, Mosca CO 81146 / 719-378-2312. San Luis Lakes State Park, PO Box 175, Mosca CO 81146 / 719-378-2020. Cumbres & Toltec Scenic Railroad, PO Box 668, Antonito CO 81120 / 719-376-5483.

Mount Evans

Mount Evans is approximately 30 miles west of Denver in central Colorado. It begins near Idaho Springs and travels south through Arapaho National Forest to the summit of Mount Evans. The byway follows CO 103 and CO 5, which are two-lane paved roads. Colorado Highway 103 is suitable for most vehicles including those pulling trailers 25 feet long or less. Colorado Highway 5 is not recommended for large RVs or vehicles pulling trailers. The byway is 28 miles long. Highway 5 is usually open Memorial Day through Labor Day.

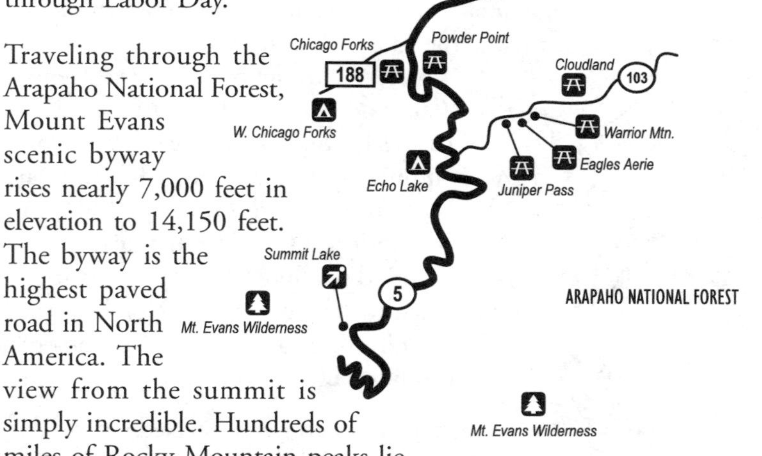

Traveling through the Arapaho National Forest, Mount Evans scenic byway rises nearly 7,000 feet in elevation to 14,150 feet. The byway is the highest paved road in North America. The view from the summit is simply incredible. Hundreds of miles of Rocky Mountain peaks lie north, south, and west; the plains can be seen in the east. Surrounding the summit is preserved wilderness, known as the Mount Evans Wilderness. Trailheads along the byway provide access to this large wilderness area.

As you climb the byway you'll pass two scenic alpine lakes, both containing trout. Echo Lake and Summit Lake have park areas managed by the city of Denver. A campground is located at Echo Lake and has a total of 16 campsites. Another campground with 11 sites is but a short drive off the byway on FSR 188.

A visitor center is located at the start of the byway in Idaho Springs, just off I-70. The center offers educational and interpretive exhibits, nature and historical literature, guidebooks and reference books, and a self-guided tape tour of the Mount Evans scenic drive.

Information: Arapahoe and Roosevelt National Forests, 240 W Prospect Rd, Fort Collins CO 80526 / 970-498-2770.

Peak to Peak

Peak to Peak is in north-central Colorado about 30 miles west of Denver. The byway's northern terminus is in Estes Park. It travels south through Roosevelt National Forest and ends at the junction with US 6. The byway follows CO 7, CO 72, and CO 119; all are two-lane paved roads suitable for all types of vehicles. Peak to Peak is 60 miles long and usually remains open year-round. Delays are possible during winter for snow removal.

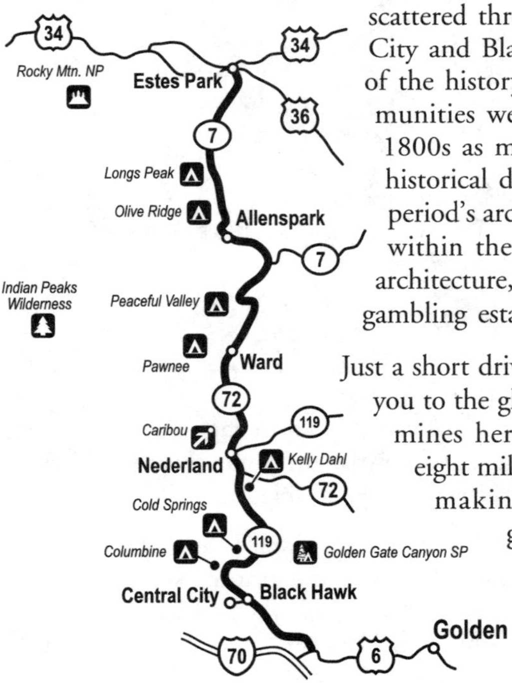

Views of the snow-capped Continental Divide and high mountain valleys are offered to travelers along this route. Relics from the late 1800s mining boom days are scattered throughout the area. Central City and Blackhawk are two examples of the history of the area. These communities were established in the late 1800s as mining towns and are now historical districts with much of that period's architecture preserved. Today, within these structures of historical architecture, one will find casino-style gambling establishments.

Just a short drive west of Nederland takes you to the ghost town of Caribou. The mines here produced an estimated eight million dollars worth of silver, making it one of Colorado's greatest silver mines. Silver bricks from Caribou were laid in a side-walk in Central City for a visit by Ulysses S. Grant in 1872. When the bottom fell out of the silver market in 1893, Caribou was left to become a ghost town.

In the charming mountain village of Estes Park you'll find the historic Stanley Hotel, built in 1909 by F.O. Stanley. Mr. Stanley would transport guests from the Lyons rail station in Stanley Steamers along the very roads now known as the Peak To Peak scenic byway.

Information: Arapahoe and Roosevelt National Forests, 240 W Prospect Rd, Fort Collins CO 80526 / 970-498-2770. Rocky Mountain National Park, 1000 W US Hwy 36, Estes Park CO 80517 / 970-586-1206. Golden Gate Canyon State Park, 3873 Hwy 46, Golden CO 80403 / 303-582-3707.

Lodging Invitation

Gold Lake Mountain Resort & Spa
3371 Gold Lake Road
Ward, CO 80481

Phone: 800-450-3544
Fax: 303-459-9080
Internet: www.goldlake.com

At the Gold Lake Mountain Resort & Spa you'll enjoy the ambiance of our artistically restored cabins and the endless recreational opportunities provided by the Rocky Mountain wilderness. Relax in a lake side hot pool overlooking the Continental Divide or pamper yourself with a restorative treatment at the full service spa — then indulge in healthy gourmet cuisine at Alices restaurant.

Romantic RiverSong Inn
1765 Lower Broadview Rd.
Estes Park, CO 80517
MAIL: P.O. Box 1910

Phone: 970-586-4666
Fax: 970-577-1961
E-mail: riversng@frii.com
Internet: http://www.romanticriversong.com

RiverSong, a romantic nine-room country Inn, is nestled at the end of a winding country lane on 30 wooded acres. There are trout streams and ponds, hiking trails and tree swings. Many of the rooms have breathtaking views of the snowcapped peaks and nearby Rocky Mountain National Park. After a candlelight dinner prepared by their own chef, guests can enjoy a whirlpool tub for two in front of a crackling fire. At RiverSong, you'll be lulled to sleep by the melody of the mountain stream. Small elopement weddings performed by Innkeeper at the Inn or mountain top.

The Baldpate Inn, Ltd.
4900 S. Hwy. 7
P.O. Box 4445
Estes Park, CO 80517

Phone: 970-586-KEYS
970-586-6151

For a classic mountain getaway, The Baldpate Inn offers a unique bed and breakfast experience during the summer and fall. Nestled in the pine forest on the side of Twin Sisters Mountain, near the Lily Lake Visitors Center of Rocky Mountain National Park. First opening in 1917, the lodge is built from native hand-hewed timber and includes five massive stone fireplaces. The Inn's spacious front porch and many of the twelve guest rooms and three cabins command a most spectacular view of the area. All rates include a delightful gourmet breakfast each morning and complimentary snacks in the evening. In January 1996 The Baldpate Inn was listed on the National Register of Historic Places.

Located seven miles south of Estes Park on Colorado route 7.

Woodlands on Fall River
1888 Fall River Road
Estes Park, CO 80517

Phone: 800-721-2279 / 970-586-0404
Fax: 970-586-3297
Internet: www.estes-park.com/woodlands

The Woodlands on Fall River offers all riverfront suites in a dramatic mountain setting. Amenities include: separate living rooms and bedrooms • kitchens • in-room phones • cable TV with HBO • VCRs and free video library. Large private decks and patios with individual gas grills facing river. In-room 2 person spa tub; many suites with jetted bathtubs. Outdoor hot tub on beautifully landscaped grounds. Close to Rocky Mountain National Park. Sorry, no pets. Handicapped accessible.

San Juan Skyway

Beautiful San Juan Skyway is in southwest Colorado. It forms a 236-mile loop that follows US 160, US 550, CO 62, and CO 145. The highways are two-lane paved roads suitable for all types of vehicles. Winter driving conditions can be hazardous and require extra caution. Portions may temporarily close for snow removal.

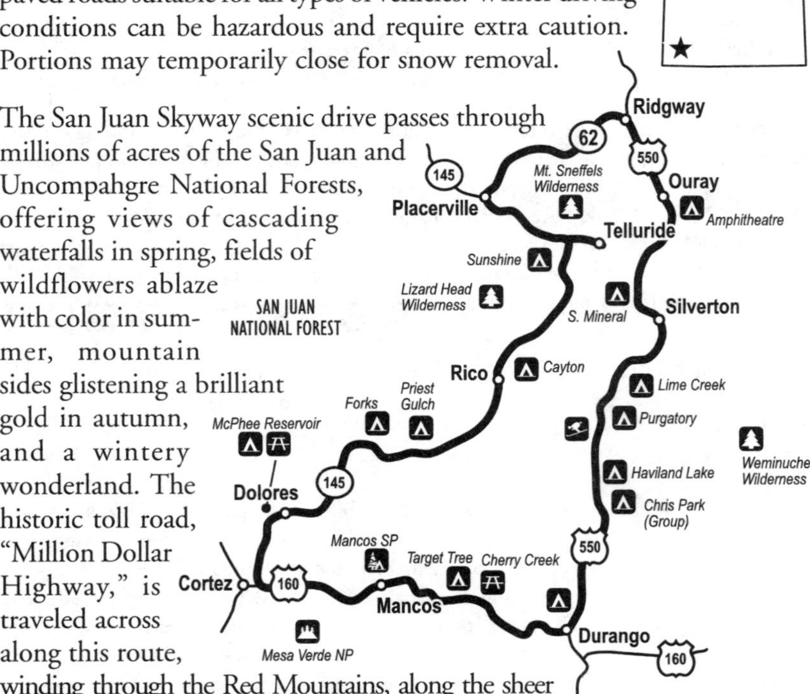

The San Juan Skyway scenic drive passes through millions of acres of the San Juan and Uncompahgre National Forests, offering views of cascading waterfalls in spring, fields of wildflowers ablaze with color in summer, mountain sides glistening a brilliant gold in autumn, and a wintery wonderland. The historic toll road, "Million Dollar Highway," is traveled across along this route, winding through the Red Mountains, along the sheer sides of the Uncompahgre Gorge, and through tunnels above scenic waterfalls.

There are three wilderness areas accessed along the byway. These areas provide excellent opportunities for hiking, backpacking, or horseback riding in the wild San Juan Mountains. Numerous other trails found all along the byway range from short, gentle walking trails to more rigorous hiking trails leading deep into the national forests.

Campgrounds are in no short supply along this byway. Whether you're searching for a highly developed campsite with the amenities of home or a small, secluded spot to pitch a tent, you're sure to find what you're looking for. Many camping areas are situated along streams or lakeshores offering excellent opportunities for trout fishing.

The town of Cortez is located south of Dolores and is known as the "Archeological Center of the United States." To the east of Cortez is the Mesa Verde National Park, showcasing the cliff dwellings once inhabited by the Anasazi Indians. Guided tours, a museum, camping, and lodging are available here. To the southwest is the famous Four Corners Monument where you can stand in four states at once.

Durango was founded in 1880 and served the once booming mining industry. Many restored historic landmarks line the streets of downtown. Also found here is the historic Durango and Silverton Narrow-Gauge Railroad. Visitors can ride the train, from May through October, for a unique sight-seeing trip through the rugged mountains. The station is located downtown at the south end of Main.

The town of Telluride is a Victorian mining town founded in the late 1800s and is now an international ski resort. Butch Cassidy's first bank robbery took place here. Located in the area are four-wheel drive roads that lead to other historic mining towns within the forest.

Information: San Juan National Forest, 15 Burnett Ct, Durango CO 81301 / 970-247-4874. Grand Mesa-Uncompahgre & Gunnison National Forests, 2250 Hwy 50, Delta CO 81416 / 970-874-6600. Mancos State Park, c/o Navajo State Park, Box 1697, Arboles CO 81121 / 970-883-2208. Durango & Silverton Narrow-Gauge RR, 479 Main Ave, Durango CO 81301 / 970-247-2733.

Lodging Invitation

A Bed & Breakfast on Maple Street	Phone:	800-665-3906 / 970-565-3906
102 S. Maple Street	Fax:	970-565-2090
P.O. Box 327	E-mail:	maple@fone.net
Cortez, CO 81321	Internet:	http://subee.com/maple/home.html

A unique Rocky Mountain log and rock house and new in downtown Cortez. Inside you'll find a warm western Colorado welcome and a generous helping of hospitality. All rooms offer private baths, queen beds, and air conditioning — Antiques abound. Relax in the gazebo-enclosed hot tub or enjoy the beautiful flower garden. Walking distance to restaurants, shopping or Native Indian Dancing. BIG Appetite? BIG Breakfast! Smoke-free. Rates: $69.00 and up. Winter rates available. New duplex cabin.

Anasazi Motor Inn	Phone:	970-565-3773
640 S. Broadway		800-972-6232
Cortez, CO 81321	Fax:	970-565-1027

The Anasazi Motor Inn, with 87 units, is fully equipped to make your stay in this beautiful area an enjoyable one. Amenities include: restaurant • lounge • heated pool • spa • and conference facilities with a capacity of 300 people. AAA and AARP discounts available. Visa, MC, Discover, AMEX, and Diners Club cards welcomed.

Kelly Place	Phone:	970-565-3125
14663 Road G		800-745-4885
Cortez, CO 81321	Fax:	970-565-3540

Kelly Place is an outdoor ed center and unique "Bed & Breakfast" near the "Trail of the Ancients", a Colorado Scenic and Historic Byway. The adobe-style lodge and cabins with kitchenettes and fireplaces are located on 100 acres, 10 miles west of Highway 160/666 in red-rock McElmo Canyon.

Purgatory Village Hotel	Phone:	800-693-0175 / 970-247-3397
5 Skier Place	Fax:	970-382-2248
Durango, CO 81301	E-mail:	gmpvh@frontier.net
	Internet:	http://www.creativelinks.com/pvh

A deluxe lodging property located at the base of Purgatory Ski Resort. Accommodations include hotel rooms, studios with kitchenettes, and condominiums with your choice of one, two, and three bedroom units. Among the many amenities is 24 hour front desk service and daily housekeeping. You'll also enjoy a wide variety of outdoor activities. Rated by Condé Nast Traveler magazine as one of the top 40 ski lodging properties in the U.S.!

River House B & B	Phone:	970-247-4775
495 Animas View Dr.		800-254-4775
Durango, CO 81301	Fax:	970-259-1465

The River House is a large, sprawling, southwestern home facing the Animas River. Guests dine in a large atrium filled with plants, a fountain, and eight skylights. Antiques, art, and artifacts from around the world decorate the seven bedrooms, snooker and music rooms. Enjoy a soak in the hot tub before a relaxing massage or retiring to the living room to watch a favorite video on the large screen TV, and enjoy the warmth of the fire in the beautiful stone and brass fireplace. Comfort, casualness, and fun are the themes at River House.

Riversbend Bed & Breakfast
42505 Hwy. 160
Mancos, CO 81328

Phone: 970-533-7353
800-699-8994
Internet: www.riversbend.com

Riversbend serves as a hub for the many area activities and is your haven for rest and relaxation when the day is over. In this 2-story log inn located on the Mancos River, you are welcomed by the charm of yesteryear as you are engulfed by the soft glow of the overhead hurricane lamps, the hominess and warmth of the log walls and antiques, the crisp white priscillas. Guests drift off to sleep between cool white sheets that smell of Colorado sunshine and awaken to the tantalizing scent of a scrumptious gourmet breakfast. Take your morning glass of juice to the hot tub and enjoy an invigorating warm massage as you listen to the sound of the gently rushing river. Count the stars in their splendid array of brilliance under the canopy of night sky after a day of horse back riding, exploring Mesa Verde National Park (7 miles), riding the narrow gauge train (25 miles). Come, refresh yourself, and experience the exhilarating, yet peaceful, Colorado lifestyle. Gaye and Jack look forward to meeting you!

Tomahawk Lodge
728 South Broadway
Cortez, CO 81321

Phone: 970-565-8521
800-643-7705
Fax: 970-564-9793

The Tomahawk Lodge welcomes travelers with 39 clean, cozy rooms. Economy rates • coffee around the clock • swimming pool • cinemax • and free local calls. Near restaurants, stores, and all major attractions.

A/C

Santa Fe Trail

NSB

Santa Fe Trail is in southeast Colorado. It follows US 350 from Trinidad to La Junta and US 50 east to the Kansas state line. Both highways are two-lane paved roads that are suitable for all types of vehicles. The byway is nearly 190 miles long and usually remains open year-round.

Santa Fe Trail retraces the route once trekked by pioneers heading west in the 1800s. The Mountain Branch of the trail traveled through what is today Trinidad and crossed Raton Pass, a mountain gap used by Native Americans for centuries. Near the byway's midpoint is Bent's Old Fort, once a trading post and cultural melting pot, now a National Historic Site. Santa Fe Trail crosses southeast Colorado's prairie with the mountains in the distance. A portion of the byway passes through Comanche National Grassland.

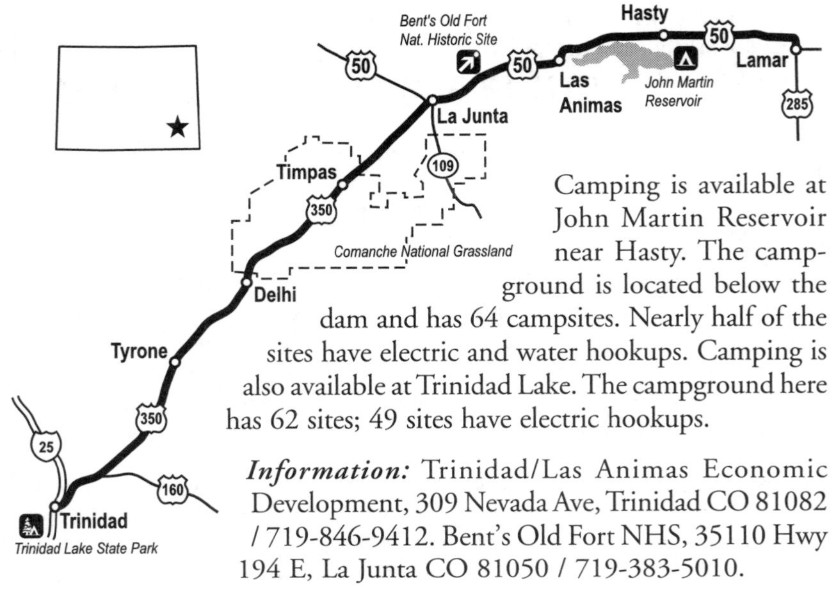

Camping is available at John Martin Reservoir near Hasty. The campground is located below the dam and has 64 campsites. Nearly half of the sites have electric and water hookups. Camping is also available at Trinidad Lake. The campground here has 62 sites; 49 sites have electric hookups.

Information: Trinidad/Las Animas Economic Development, 309 Nevada Ave, Trinidad CO 81082 / 719-846-9412. Bent's Old Fort NHS, 35110 Hwy 194 E, La Junta CO 81050 / 719-383-5010.

Silver Thread Highway

US FS

The Silver Thread scenic byway is approximately 50 miles northwest of Alamosa in southwest Colorado. Its southern terminus is in South Fork on US 160. The byway follows CO 149 northwest through Creede to Lake City. Colorado Highway 149 is a two-lane paved road that is suitable for all vehicles. Silver Thread Highway is 75 miles long and is generally passable year-round.

The Silver Thread Highway has been a passageway from Creede to Lake City since the 1870s. It was once a toll road and stage route for the miners. Traveling through the Gunnison and Rio Grande National Forests, this scenic route offers spectacular views of the San Juan Mountains, cascading waterfalls, and historic mining towns. Flowing alongside much of the byway are the waters of the Rio Grande River.

Wildlife observers will delight in seeing Rocky Mountain Sheep grazing along the highway. In fall, winter, and early spring, elk are commonly seen as they descend to the lower elevations for winter range. Other wildlife found in the area includes mule deer, coyotes, porcupines, and bears.

Those interested in extending their stay will find several national forest campgrounds. Campground facilities vary from primitive to more developed. Many of the camping areas are situated on the banks of the

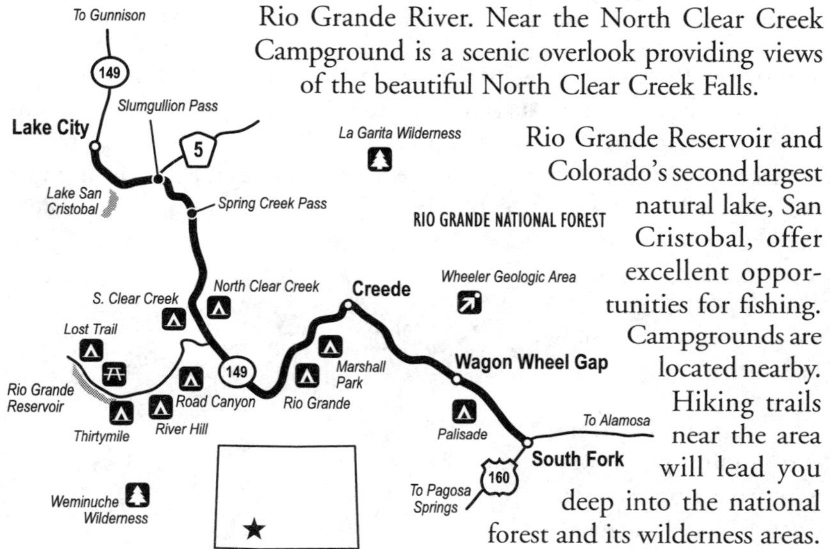

Rio Grande River. Near the North Clear Creek Campground is a scenic overlook providing views of the beautiful North Clear Creek Falls.

Rio Grande Reservoir and Colorado's second largest natural lake, San Cristobal, offer excellent opportunities for fishing. Campgrounds are located nearby. Hiking trails near the area will lead you deep into the national forest and its wilderness areas.

Information: Rio Grande National Forest, Creede Ranger District, PO Box 270, Creede CO 81130 /719-658-2556. San Juan National Forest, 15 Burnett Ct, Durango CO 81301 / 970-247-4874.

Lodging Invitation

Foothills Lodge	Phone:	719-873-5969
0035 Silver Thread Lane		800-510-3897 reservations
P.O. Box 264	Fax:	719-873-5969
South Fork, CO 81154-0264	E-mail:	fhlodge@amigo.net

A relaxing—great escape! Choose from modern log cabins with aspen paneling, kitchens and woodburning fireplaces or uniquely decorated lodge apartments. Rooms with one to two bedrooms and anywhere from one queen size bed to four double beds — accommodating up to eight people. You'll enjoy hot showers, fresh towels daily, cable TV, phones, and indoor hot tub. Outdoor recreation includes hunting • skiing • snowmobiling • sightseeing • and Gold Medal fishing in the Rio Grande. Adjacent to the lodge you can enjoy a good meal at the Hungry Logger Restaurant or Croaker's Saloon. Located on Hwy. 160 (milepost 160), at the south end of town.

Top of the Rockies

NSB

Top of the Rockies is about 75 miles west of Denver in central Colorado. It's 82 miles long and follows US 24 and CO 91. A seven-mile segment to Twin Lakes follows CO 82. All the roads are two-lane paved roads suitable for all types of vehicles. The byway is usually passable year-round but extra caution should be used in winter.

Top of the Rockies crosses the Continental Divide twice and traces the Arkansas River nearly to its source in the area of Fremont Pass. Mount Elbert and Mount Massive rise over 14,000 feet and dominate the landscape between Granite and Leadville. Leadville is the highest incorporated community in the United States. Just north of Leadville, the byway splits. The western route follows US 24 through the White River National Forest. The eastern route follows CO 91 and crosses Fremont Pass near Climax.

The national forests surrounding the byway offer extensive opportunities for outdoor recreation. Several campgrounds are situated around the Twin Lakes area with a total of 213 RV and tent sites. The campgrounds are usually open spring to fall. There are no hookups available. Off US 24 near Redcliff is the Hornsilver Campground, managed by the national forest. It offers 12 campsites and has an RV length limit of 16 feet.

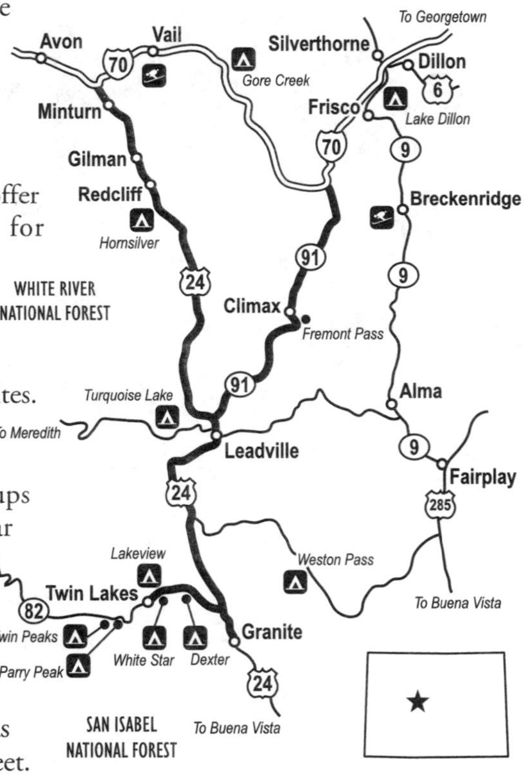

Information: Greater Leadville Area Chamber of Commerce, PO Box 861, Leadville CO 80461 / 719-486-3900. White River National Forest, PO Box 948, Glenwood Springs CO 81602 / 970-945-2521. San Isabel National Forest, 1920 Valley Dr, Pueblo CO 81008 / 719-545-8737.

Trail Ridge Road / Beaver Meadow Road

This scenic byway is in north-central Colorado about 30 miles west of Loveland. It begins in Estes Park and heads southwest to

Grand Lake through Rocky Mountain National Park. The byway follows US 36 and US 34 for a total of 53 miles. Both US Highways are two-lane paved roads suitable for all types of vehicles. Trail Ridge Road through the national park is usually open Memorial Day to mid-October.

Trail Ridge and Beaver Meadow Roads take the visitor to the "top of the world" as it reaches 12,183 feet above sea level, higher than any other continuous paved highway in the United States. In fact, Trail Ridge Road stays above treeline, the alpine tundra, for eleven beautiful miles. Views to the north, south, east, and west extend into Wyoming and three national forests adjacent to Rocky Mountain National Park. The Alpine Visitor Center, located at Fall River Pass, provides exhibits explaining the life of the alpine tundra. This is also a good place to stop for a snack before continuing on.

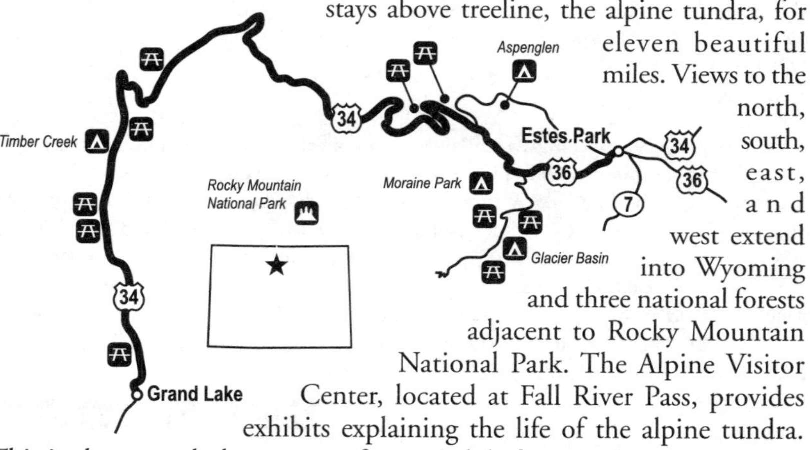

Rocky Mountain National Park was born in 1915, several years after Enos Mills, a naturalist, writer, and conservationist, began campaigning in 1909 for preservation of this pristine area. In addition to the rugged and majestic mountain scenery, the park offers plenty of opportunities for horseback riding, camping, fishing, hiking, skiing, and snowmobiling. A side trip worth taking is the 10-mile road to Bear Lake. This little alpine lake offers a half-mile, wheelchair accessible trail that surrounds the lake. The area is heavily used and is often congested; you can expect parking lots to be full between 10:00 a.m. and 3:00 p.m. on summer days.

Information: Arapahoe & Roosevelt National Forest, 240 W Prospect Rd, Fort Collins CO 80526 / 970-498-2770. Rocky Mountain National Park, 1000 W US Hwy 36, Estes Park CO 80517 / 970-586-1206.

Lodging Invitation

Romantic RiverSong Inn	Phone:	970-586-4666
1765 Lower Broadview Rd.	Fax:	970-577-1961
Estes Park, CO 80517	E-mail:	riversng@frii.com
MAIL: P.O. Box 1910	Internet:	http://www.romanticriversong.com

RiverSong, a romantic nine-room country Inn, is nestled at the end of a winding country lane on 30 wooded acres. There are trout streams and ponds, hiking trails and tree swings. Many of the rooms have breathtaking views of the snowcapped peaks and nearby Rocky Mountain National Park. After a candlelight dinner prepared by their own chef, guests can enjoy a whirlpool tub for two in front of a crackling fire. At RiverSong, you'll be lulled to sleep by the melody of the mountain stream. Small elopement weddings performed by Innkeeper at the Inn or mountain top.

The Baldpate Inn, Ltd.
4900 S. Hwy. 7
P.O. Box 4445
Estes Park, CO 80517

Phone: 970-586-KEYS
970-586-6151

For a classic mountain getaway, The Baldpate Inn offers a unique bed and breakfast experience during the summer and fall. Nestled in the pine forest on the side of Twin Sisters Mountain, near the Lily Lake Visitors Center of Rocky Mountain National Park. First opening in 1917, the lodge is built from native hand-hewed timber and includes five massive stone fireplaces. The Inn's spacious front porch and many of the twelve guest rooms and three cabins command a most spectacular view of the area. All rates include a delightful gourmet breakfast each morning and complimentary snacks in the evening. In January 1996 The Baldpate Inn was listed on the National Register of Historic Places. Located seven miles south of Estes Park on Colorado route 7.

Victoria Cottages
P.O. Box 14
Grand Lake, CO 80447

Phone: 970-627-8027
Fax: 970-627-8027
E-mail: VictoriaCottages@juno.com

Victoria Cottages offers this romantic getaway bordering the Rocky Mountain National Park. Nestled in the pines with a view of Grand Lake, this two room story-book cabin with stone fireplace offers all the comforts of home. Walk to town for shopping, fine dining, horseback riding, hiking, golf and activities for the kids — all in breathtaking surroundings.

Woodlands on Fall River
1888 Fall River Road
Estes Park, CO 80517

Phone: 800-721-2279 / 970-586-0404
Fax: 970-586-3297
Internet: www.estes-park.com/woodlands

The Woodlands on Fall River offers all riverfront suites in a dramatic mountain setting. Amenities include: separate living rooms and bedrooms • kitchens • in-room phones • cable TV with HBO • VCRs and free video library. Large private decks and patios with individual gas grills facing river. In-room 2 person spa tub; many suites with jetted bathtubs. Outdoor hot tub on beautifully landscaped grounds. Close to Rocky Mountain National Park. Sorry, no pets. Handicapped accessible.

Unaweep / Tabeguache

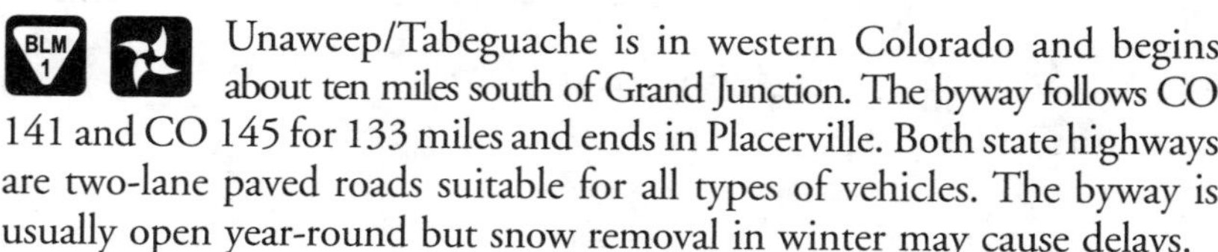

Unaweep/Tabeguache is in western Colorado and begins about ten miles south of Grand Junction. The byway follows CO 141 and CO 145 for 133 miles and ends in Placerville. Both state highways are two-lane paved roads suitable for all types of vehicles. The byway is usually open year-round but snow removal in winter may cause delays.

The byway circles the Uncompahgre National Forest, traveling through 1,200-foot granite walls rising above lush green fields. This area was once the home of Ute Indians and a hideout for Butch Cassidy. Structures built by Native American hunters and gatherers, petroglyphs, geological formations, and waterfalls are some of the highlights of the byway.

A variety of wildlife inhabits this region of Colorado including black bear, mountain lion, bobcat, coyotes, and various rodents and reptiles. The large meadows and south-facing canyon slopes provide winter habitat for mule deer and elk. Wild turkeys and pheasants may also be spotted in the meadows. During the winter months, the watchful eye may catch glimpses of bald eagles perched in the cottonwood trees along West Creek or the Dolores and San Miguel rivers.

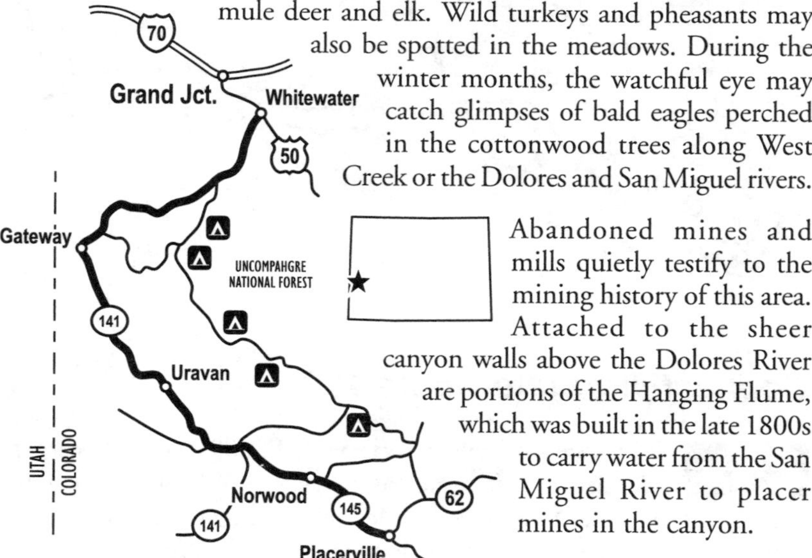

Abandoned mines and mills quietly testify to the mining history of this area. Attached to the sheer canyon walls above the Dolores River are portions of the Hanging Flume, which was built in the late 1800s to carry water from the San Miguel River to placer mines in the canyon.

The many side roads found along the byway lead into the Uncompahgre National Forest and offer challenges to four-wheel drive and mountain bike enthusiasts. The national forest also has several developed camping areas available.

Information: Uncompahgre National Forest, 2250 Hwy 50, Delta CO 81416 / 970-874-6600. BLM-Uncompahgre Field Office, 2505 S Townsend Ave, Montrose CO 81401 / 970-240-5300.

Connecticut

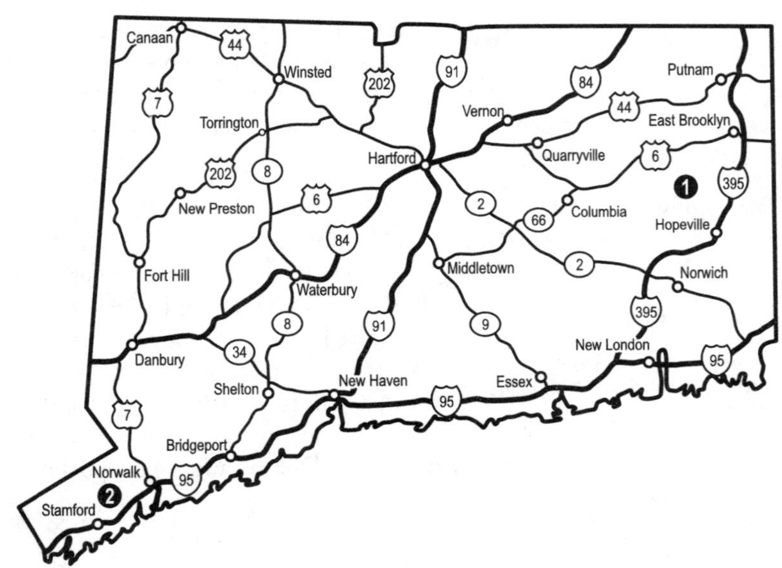

Connecticut State Route 169

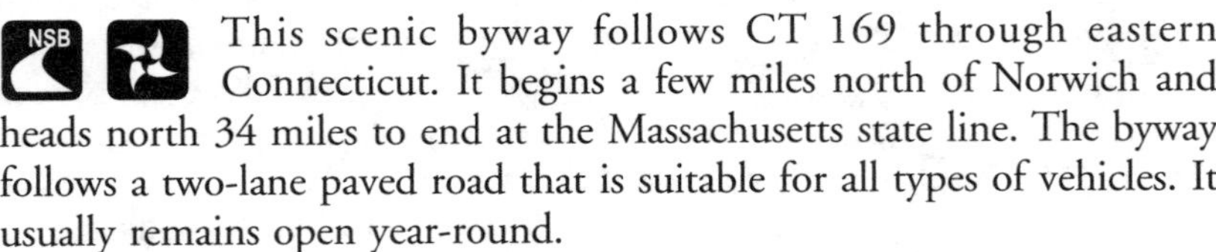

This scenic byway follows CT 169 through eastern Connecticut. It begins a few miles north of Norwich and heads north 34 miles to end at the Massachusetts state line. The byway follows a two-lane paved road that is suitable for all types of vehicles. It usually remains open year-round.

Connecticut State Route 169 takes the traveler through gently rolling New England hills covered with corn stalks and apple orchards. Small farms dot the countryside; their livestock pastures enclosed with stone fences and grain elevators standing proudly. Fall strikes this area ablaze with brilliant colors of orange, red, and gold. Each town you pass through seems to proudly display its various architectural styles, teaming with history.

In Canterbury, you'll discover the Prudence Crandall House, New England's first school for black women. The museum, listed as a National Historic Landmark, features changing exhibits, period furnishings, a research library, and gift shop. In Woodstock is the Roseland Cottage, circa 1846. This was built by publisher Henry Bowen for use as a summer home. Listed as a National Historic Landmark, the landscape has the original 1850 boxwood parterre garden.

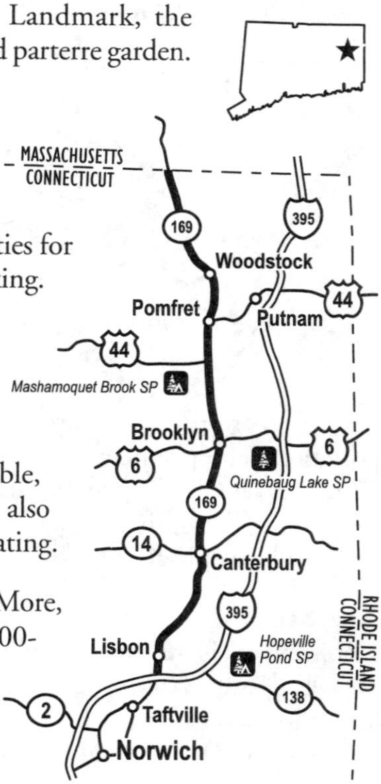

For those interested in extending their stay in the area , the 916-acre Mashamoquet Brook State Park offers 55 campsites for tents and recreational vehicles. The park also offers opportunities for fishing, swimming, hiking, and picnicking.

Hopeville Pond State Park is located to the east of the byway's southern terminus. This 554-acre park also offers camping and picnicking facilities. There are 82 campsites available, many with electrical hookups. You can also enjoy hiking, swimming, fishing, and boating.

Information: Connecticut's Mystic & More, PO Box 89, New London CT 06320 / 800-To-Enjoy. Northeast Connecticut Visitors District, PO Box 598, Putnam CT 06260 / 860-928-1228. Mashamoquet Brook SP, Route 44, Pomfret CT 06259 / 860-928-6121. Quienebaug Lake & Hopeville Pond State Parks, State Parks Division, Bureau of Outdoor Recreation, Dept. of Environmental Protection, 79 Elm St, Hartford CT 06106 / 860-424-3200.

Merritt Parkway

Merritt Parkway is in southwest Connecticut and travels from the New York state line east to the Housatonic River. Merritt Parkway is also known as CT 15, which is a four-lane divided highway suitable for most types of vehicles. Connecticut regulations restrict the use of Merritt Parkway to "non-commercial motor vehicles that do not exceed 7,500 pounds, 24 feet in length, eight feet in height, and seven feet six inches in width." The byway runs for 38 miles and is usually open all year.

The Merritt Parkway is a unique driving experience in that it is listed on the National Register of Historic Places for its bridges. The 38-mile parkway was built in the 1930s as Connecticut's first divided-lane, limited access highway. The tree-lined corridor is a unique achievement in highway landscape, bridge design and engineering. Originally there were 72 bridges constructed, of which 69 remain, and no two were alike in design.

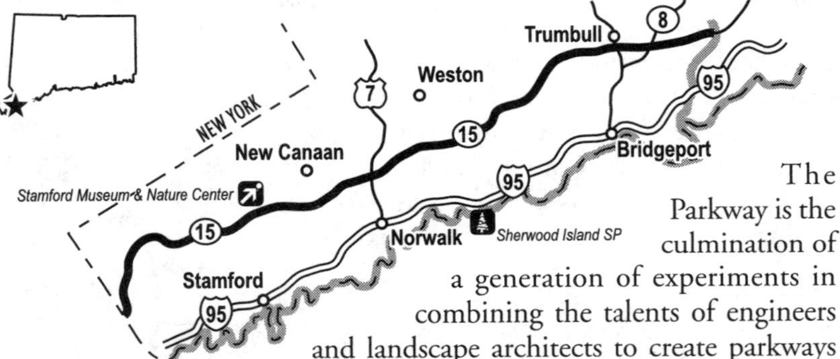

The Parkway is the culmination of a generation of experiments in combining the talents of engineers and landscape architects to create parkways that served recreational purposes, were scenic, and provided safe transportation. The planners of the parkway's landscape, A. Earl Wood and Weld Thayer Chase, gave priority to fitting the road into the natural surroundings. The spring brings brilliant displays from the flowering trees and shrubs, while autumn brings its own display of magnificent colors.

The Barlett Arboretum is a facility operated by the University of Connecticut. Here you can enjoy a wide variety of plants indigenous to New England. Walking trails invite inspection of swamps, woodlands, and cultivated gardens. The Sherwood Island State Park offers wide sandy beaches on the Long Island Sound, waterside picnic areas, and fishing jetties.

Information: Connecticut's Office of Tourism, 505 Hudson St, Hartford CT 06067 / 860-270-8075.

Lodging Invitation

Roger Sherman Inn
195 Oenoke Ridge
New Canaan, CT 06840

Phone: 203-966-4541
Fax: 203-966-0503

Dating back to the mid-1700's, the beautifully refurbished Roger Shermann Inn provides guests with charming and up-to-date accommodations. The indoor and outdoor award-winning dining makes the Inn the perfect retreat in an atmosphere of light-hearted elegance. Located only two miles north of the Merritt Parkway, at exit 37.

FLORIDA

1 Apalachee Savannahs, *102*

Apalachee Savannahs

US FS Apalachee Savannahs is in northwest Florida about 45 miles west of Tallahassee. The byway begins in Bristol and travels south to the junction with US 98, east of Apalachicola. Apalachee Savannahs is 60 miles long and follows CR 12, FL 379, and FL 65. The roads are two-lane paved roads suitable for all vehicles and generally remain open all year. Thirty-two miles are officially designated a National Forest Scenic Byway.

The Apalachee Savannahs scenic byway traverses the Apalachicola National Forest through the landscape of gentle slopes, longleaf pine flats, savannahs, cypress bogs, and numerous sloughs and creeks. Over one hundred species of wildflowers grow among the grasses and sedges of the savannahs, offering a beautiful display of seasonal color. Flowing alongside much of the byway is the meandering Apalachicola River.

Recreational opportunities are abundant along this byway. The Florida National Scenic Trail crosses the national forest and can be accessed from the byway. The trail passes through the 23,432-acre Bradwell Bay Wilderness, mainly a large fresh water swamp with several hundred acres of pine, mixed hardwoods, and titi.

Several developed recreation areas are located along the byway. Camel Lake offers 10 campsites situated next to a small natural lake. Access to the Florida National Scenic Trail is provided. Cotton Landing is a smaller recreation area with only four campsites available. Wright Lake has a 21-unit campground set in a wooded area along the shores of the lake. The Hickory Landing Recreation Area provides 10 camping units and access to the Apalachicola River for boating and fishing.

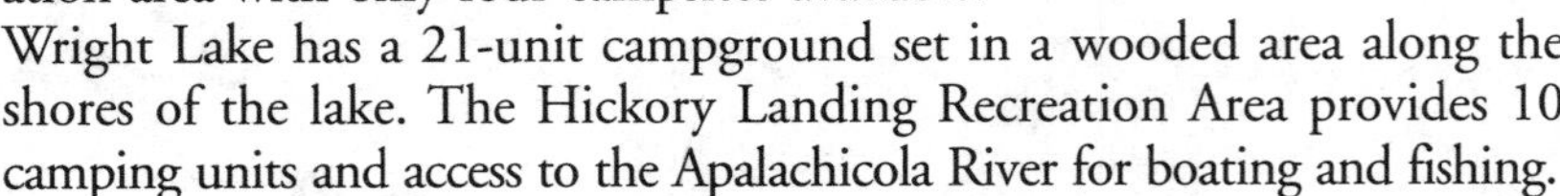

Fishing, hiking, and picnicking are among the attractions of Fort Gadsden State Historic Site. This site also offers interpretive exhibits depicting the history of the fort and its role in Florida's history.

Information: National Forests In Florida, 325 John Knox Rd Suite F100, Tallahassee FL 32303 / 850-942-9300. Fort Gadsden State Historical Site, PO Box 157, Sumatra FL 32335 / 904-670-8988.

GEORGIA

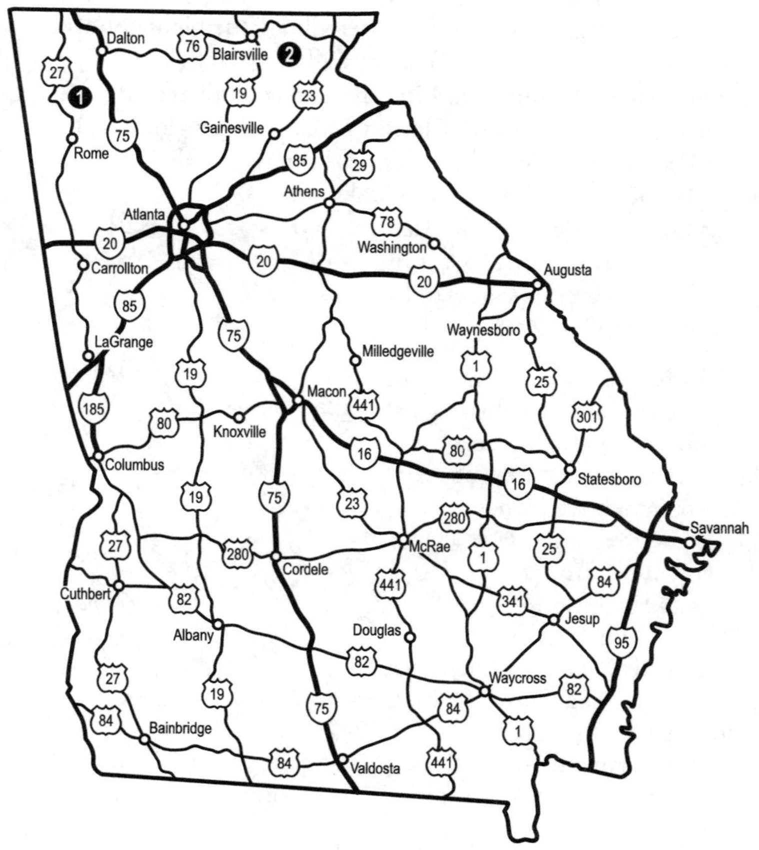

Dalton
76
Blairsville
2
27
1
19
23
Gainesville
75
Rome
85
29
Athens
Atlanta
78
Washington
20
20
20
Carrollton
Augusta
85
Waynesboro
75
LaGrange
Milledgeville
1
19
25
Macon
185
441
301
80
Knoxville
16
80
Columbus
16
Statesboro
19
75
23
280
Savannah
27
280
McRae
1
25
Cordele
84
Cuthbert
441
82
341
Jesup
Albany
Douglas
95
82
27
Waycross
82
19
84
75
84
Bainbridge
1
84
Valdosta
441

Ridge and Valley

Ridge and Valley is in northwest Georgia about 75 miles northwest of Atlanta. It forms a loop drive between Villanow and Armuchee. The byway is 47 miles long and follows a series of roads: US 27, GA 136, GA 156, Armuchee, Thomas Ballenger, Floyd Springs, Johns Creek, Pocket, and Furnace Creek roads. The roads are two-lane paved roads suitable for all vehicles. They usually remain open year-round.

The Ridge and Valley scenic byway crosses the Chattahoochee National Forest offering excellent scenery of long parallel ridges with broad valleys situated in between. Two beautiful waterfalls are the highlight of the 218-acre Keown Falls Scenic Area. A short walking trail leads to the scenic waterfalls. Picnic facilities have been constructed for your enjoyment. Nearby is John's Mountain Overlook, the site of an old fire tower that has since been removed. The spectacular view from the platform looks west as far as Lookout Mountain in Alabama and Tennessee. A three-mile walking trail departs from the overlook, goes to Keown Falls, and returns to the overlook.

Wildlife observers will delight in the many species found in this region of Georgia. White-tailed deer and wild turkey are among some of the wildlife commonly seen. Those interested in extending their stay will find camping and picnicking facilities at the Pocket Recreation Area. This area was once the site of a Civilian Conservation Corps encampment utilized from 1938 to 1942. A three-mile loop trail here will take you deep into the wooded countryside. The campground offers 27 campsites, restrooms, and drinking water.

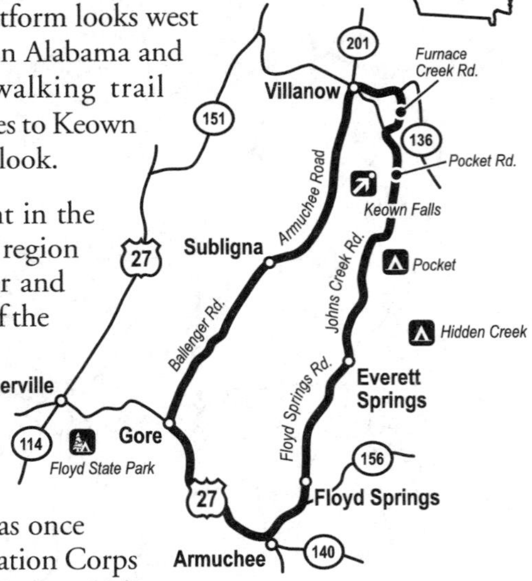

There are two privately-owned lakes along the byway that are open to the public, Lake Marvin and Lake Arrowhead. The lakes offer good warm water fishing in a beautiful woodland setting.

Information: Chattahoochee and Oconee National Forests, 1755 Cleveland Hwy, Gainesville GA 30501 / 770-536-0541.

Russell - Brasstown

Russell - Brasstown is in northeast Georgia about 90 miles north of Atlanta. The byway forms a loop beginning and ending near Helen. It follows GA 75, GA 180, and GA 348 for a total of 38 miles. The state highways are two-lane paved roads suitable for all vehicles. The roads are usually open year-round; extra caution should be exercised in winter.

The Russell - Brasstown scenic byway crosses the Chattahoochee National Forest winding through forested hills, mountains, and valleys. The headwaters of the Chattahoochee River are completely encircled by the byway.

Brasstown Bald is Georgia's highest mountain and is adjacent to the byway. The view from the 4,784-foot high mountain is spectacular. The visitor center here offers slide programs and interpretive exhibits. Picnicking facilities along with restrooms and drinking water are available. A short quarter-mile walking trail from the parking lot leads to the summit.

Of interest to hikers and backpackers is the Appalachian National Scenic Trail which crosses the byway. Several wilderness areas also provide opportunities for hiking and backpacking in a secluded, primitive setting.

A short side trip off the byway worth taking is GA 356 to the Anna Ruby Falls Scenic Area. In this 1,600-acre area, twin waterfalls merge to form Smith Creek. It is necessary to walk a half-mile trail to reach the falls. Five scenic waterfalls can be seen within the 170-acre High Shoals Scenic Area. A one-mile hiking trail will take you to the waterfalls.

Andrews Cove is the only developed national forest campground along the byway. The campground is situated on Andrews Creek and has 11 units available to campers. Restrooms and drinking water are also provided.

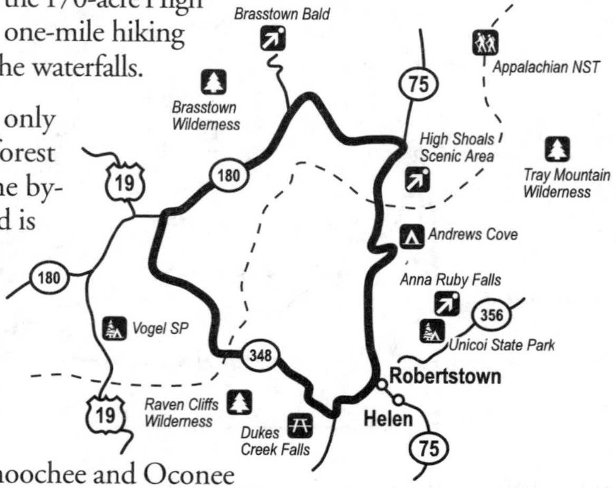

Information: Chattahoochee and Oconee NF, 1755 Cleveland Hwy, Gainesville GA 30501 / 770-536-0541. Unicoi State Park, PO Box 997, Helen GA 30545 / 706-878-3982. Vogel State Park, 7485 Vogel State Park Rd, Blairsville GA 30512 / 706-745-2628.

Idaho

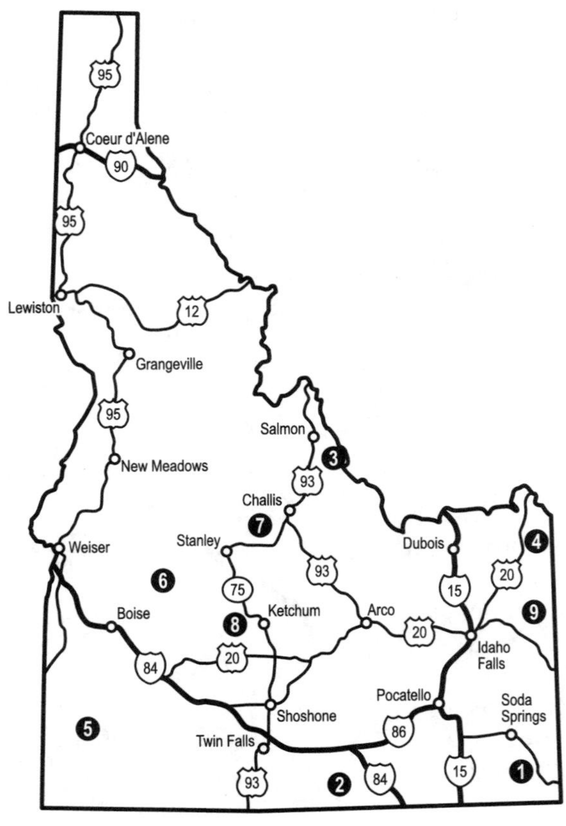
95
Coeur d'Alene
90
95
Lewiston
12
Grangeville
95
Salmon
3
New Meadows
93
Challis
7
Stanley
Weiser
6
Dubois
4
93
20
75
15
Ketchum
Arco
9
Boise
8
20
Idaho Falls
20
84
Pocatello
Soda Springs
Shoshone
5
86
Twin Falls
1
15
84
2
93

Bear Lake - Caribou

This scenic byway is located in southeast Idaho about 55 miles east of Pocatello. It begins in Freedom and travels southwest to the Utah state line. The byway is 115 miles long and follows ID 34, US 30, and US 89, all of which are two-lane paved roads suitable for all vehicles. Heavy snowfall may temporarily close portions of the byway, otherwise it remains open all year.

The Bear Lake - Caribou scenic byway travels along the shores of Bear Lake, across rolling farm lands, open livestock ranges, and through forested canyons. The northern portion runs through the Caribou National Forest with scenic vistas of the Caribou Mountains to the north.

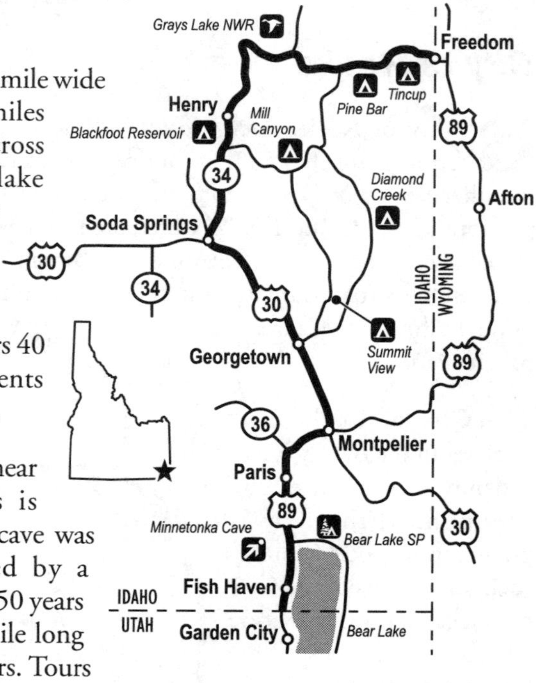

Bear Lake is a large, eight-mile wide lake that stretches 20 miles from north to south across Idaho and Utah. The lake offers excellent rainbow and cutthroat trout fishing in addition to swimming and sailing. Bear Lake State Park offers 40 campsites suitable for tents and recreational vehicles.

To the west of the byway near its southern terminus is Minnetonka Cave. The cave was accidentally discovered by a grouse hunter more than 50 years ago. The cave is a half-mile long cavern with nine chambers. Tours operate from mid-June through Labor Day. The national forest has developed three campgrounds near the cave.

The northern portion of the byway crosses the Caribou National Forest, alongside Blackfoot Reservoir and Grays Lake National Wildlife Refuge. Blackfoot Reservoir is popular for fishing and boating. Grays Lake National Wildlife Refuge is an excellent place to see the largest concentration of sandhill crains in the United States during summer.

Information: Caribou National Forest, Federal Building Suite 172, 250 S 4th Ave, Pocatello ID 83201 / 208-236-7500. Bear Lake State Park, Box 297, Paris ID 83261 / 208-945-2790.

Lodging Invitation

Three Sisters Motel
112 South 6th Street
Montpelier, ID 83254

Phone: 208-847-2324

Attractive motel centrally located. Very clean rooms with reasonable rates. Fridges and microwaves in most rooms. Direct dial phones in all rooms with free local calls. Guaranteed reservations available. AAA & AARP discounts. Visa, MC, Discover, and AMEX cards accepted. Located on the corner of Highway 89 and 6th Street. Family owned and operated.

City of Rocks

BLM 1

City of Rocks Back Country Byway is in south-central Idaho approximately 75 miles southwest of Pocatello. Travelers can begin in either Burley or Declo; both are just south of I-84. The byway follows portions of ID 27 and ID 77, which are two-lane paved roads suitable for all vehicles. From Oakley to Almo, the byway follows a graded dirt road and is subject to closure in winter. From Almo to ID 77, the byway follows a two-lane paved road.

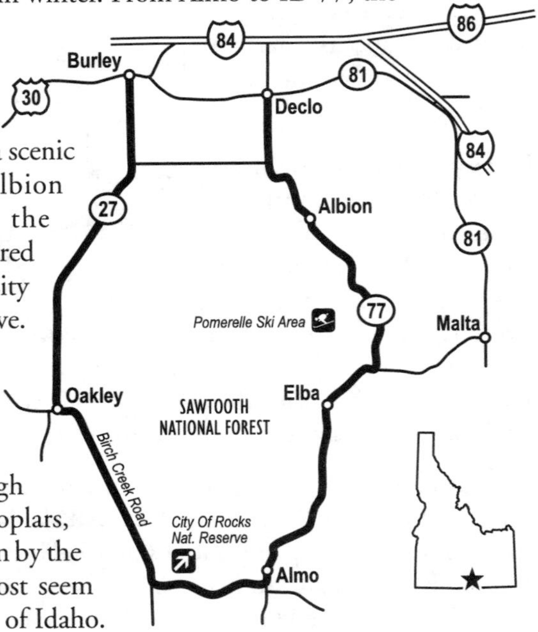

The City of Rocks Back Country Byway is a scenic journey around the Albion Mountains, through the granite spires and sculptured rock formations of the City of Rocks National Reserve. The byway also travels across southern Idaho's sage-covered valleys and wide open spaces. You'll also pass through patches of Lombardy poplars, first brought to this region by the pioneers. The trees almost seem out of place for this part of Idaho.

The City of Rocks National Reserve is administered cooperatively by the National Park Service and Idaho Department of Parks and Recreation. This area is rich in history. The Shoshone and Bannock Indians once traveled, hunted, and gathered pinyon nuts here. Emigrants following the California Trail or Salt Lake Alternate Trail passed through this area, often signing their names on the rocks with axle grease. Recreational opportunities for camping and rock climbing are among the attractions available here.

Information: BLM-Snake River Resource Area, 15 E 200 S, Burley ID 83318 / 208-677-6686. Sawtooth National Forest, Burley Ranger District, 3650 S Overland Ave, Burley ID 83318 / 208-678-0430. City of Rocks National Reserve, PO Box 169, Almo ID 83312 / 208-824-5519.

Lodging Invitation

Lewis and Clark

BLM 1

Lewis and Clark forms a loop beginning and ending in Tendoy, which is located in east-central Idaho. The byway is nearly 40 miles long and follows Old Highway 28, FSR 185, Warm Springs Road, and Lewis and Clark Highway. The roads are primarily single-lane, gravel-surfaced roads suitable for passenger vehicles. In some areas, grades exceed five percent. Lewis and Clark is normally closed to vehicles November through early June but remains open for snowmobiles.

The Lewis and Clark Back Country Byway passes through stands of fir and pine trees, across mountain meadows, and rolling hills as it climbs the Bitterroot Range to the Continental Divide and Lemhi Pass. The byway offers magnificent views of the Bitterroot and Beaverhead Mountains and the Salmon and Lemhi Valleys.

President Thomas Jefferson commissioned the expedition to explore and map the vast new territory west of the Mississippi River acquired by the United States in the Louisiana Purchase of 1803. The Lewis and Clark expedition began in May of 1804 and crossed Lemhi Pass late in the summer of 1805. Here the expedition unfurled the flag of the United States for the first time west of the Rocky Mountains, laying claim to the Pacific Northwest. At the top of Lemhi Pass is a memorial to the one woman of the expedition who served as a guide and interpreter.

The byway passes the site of Fort Lemhi, built in 1855 by Mormon missionaries. The remote outpost once had over 100 inhabitants before being abandoned in 1858. The remains of the fort are on private property, obtain permission from the landowner before inspecting!

Agency Creek Campground is a small campground maintained by the BLM. There are four campsites, all with picnic tables and fire rings. Pit toilets are also provided. There is no drinking water or trash receptacles.

Information: BLM-Salmon Field Office, Rt 2 Box 610, Salmon ID 83467 / 208-756-5400.

Mesa Falls

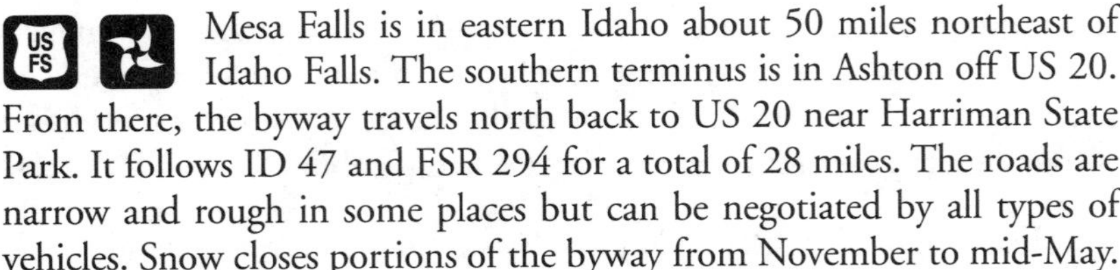

Mesa Falls is in eastern Idaho about 50 miles northeast of Idaho Falls. The southern terminus is in Ashton off US 20. From there, the byway travels north back to US 20 near Harriman State Park. It follows ID 47 and FSR 294 for a total of 28 miles. The roads are narrow and rough in some places but can be negotiated by all types of vehicles. Snow closes portions of the byway from November to mid-May.

The Mesa Falls scenic drive travels across the Targhee National Forest, winding through scenic farmland before entering Three Rivers Canyon and climbing to a mixed forest of lodgepole pine, Douglas-fir, and aspen.

Views of the west slopes of the Tetons, the Mesa Falls, and the Henry's Fork of the Snake River are but a few of the highlights found along the byway.

The Mesa Falls are the last undisturbed major waterfalls of the Columbia River system, with the Upper Mesa Falls plummeting 100 feet and the lower falls dropping 70 feet. The Lower Mesa Falls were chosen as the site for a Civilian Conservation Corps project. CCC crews constructed a stone overlook that provides a panoramic view of both falls.

The Three Rivers area is a popular spot for camping, fishing, inner tubing, and hiking. The rails of the Yellowstone Railway, which once operated as a passenger railroad through Idaho to Yellowstone National Park, have been removed and it is now used for hiking, bicycling, cross-country skiing, and snowmobiling.

The national forest offers several developed campgrounds along the byway as well as throughout the national forest. The Warm River Campground is a popular spot that offers 12 units, drinking water, and restrooms. Henry's Lake State Park is located north of the byway and has 50 campsites. Other facilities found in the state park include drinking water, showers, and recreational vehicle hookups.

Information: Targhee National Forest, Ashton Ranger District, Box 858 Ashton ID 83420 / 208-652-7442. Harriman State Park, HC 66 Box 500, Island Park ID 83429 / 208-558-7368.

Owyhee Uplands

Owyhee Uplands Back Country Byway is in southwest Idaho, 75 miles south of Boise. The byway begins near Grand View and travels west for 101 miles. It ends south of Jordan Valley, Oregon off US 95. Owyhee Uplands follows Deep Creek-Mud Flat Road, which is a narrow, gravel road. There are short grades of 12 percent at plateau breaks. The byway is generally open June through September.

The Owyhee Uplands scenic drive travels across a remote area in Idaho with a small portion crossing into Oregon. This route travels through juniper and mountain mahogany woodlands, sheer-walled river canyons, mountain valleys, and sagebrush covered hills. To the south and west, the vast desert expanse is framed by the Santa Rosa and Steens Mountains. In the spring, wildflowers growing in the open fields add a splash of color to the desert landscape.

There is only one campground located directly along the byway, the primitive BLM-operated North Fork Campground. The BLM also maintains Cove Campground, just a few miles south of the byway's eastern end. This campground offers 26 units for tents and recreational vehicles and also has drinking water, shower facilities, and restrooms. The BLM does permit dispersed camping nearly anywhere on BLM land.

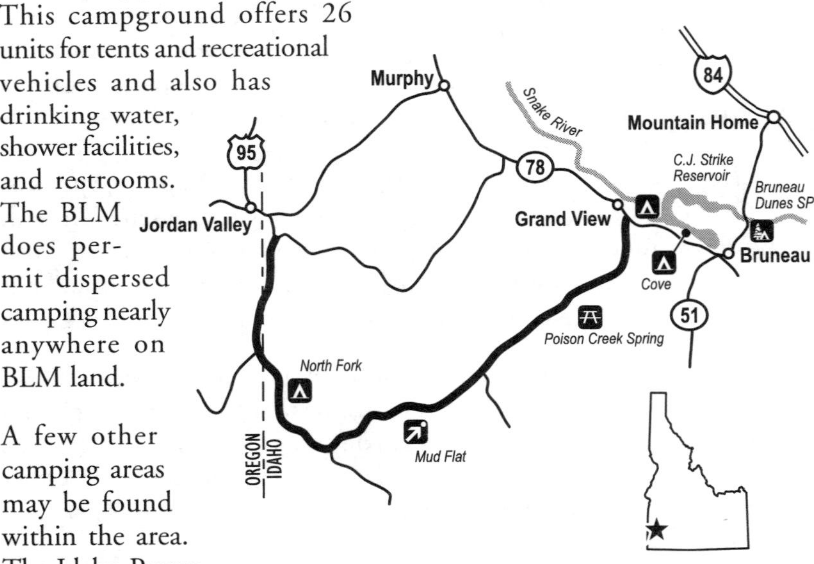

A few other camping areas may be found within the area. The Idaho Power Company maintains three parks near the C.J. Strike Reservoir's dam with a total of 50 campsites available, some being pull-through sites. The reservoir offers abundant fishing and boating opportunities.

Farther east of the byway is Bruneau Dunes State Park. This 4,800-acre park encompasses sand dunes reaching heights of several hundred feet. There are also several lakes within the park that offer good fishing. The campground here has 48 sites, some with hookups, drinking water, shower facilities, flush toilets, and a dump station.

Information: BLM-Boise Field Office, 3948 Development Ave, Boise ID 83705 / 208-384-3300. Bruneau Dunes State Park, HC 85 Box 41, Mountain Home ID 83647 / 208-366-7919.

Ponderosa Pine

The Ponderosa Pine scenic byway is located in west-central Idaho near Boise. It can be accessed from the south at Exit 57 on I-84. It then heads north across the Boise National Forest to end in Stanley. Ponderosa Pine is 130 miles long and follows ID 21, a two-lane paved road suitable for all vehicles. The highway is narrow with some steep grades but has passing lanes. Avalanche conditions exist during winter in the Banner Summit Area; road closure can be frequent.

The Ponderosa Pine scenic byway winds through the Boise National Forest with a small portion through the Challis National Forest and Sawtooth National Recreation Area. The byway passes through dense forests of pine, across high mountain valleys, and along portions of the Boise River, Lucky Peak Lake, and the South Fork of the Payette River. Visitors to the byway are treated to spectacular views of the rugged Sawtooth Mountains. Much of the Sawtooth Mountains are protected from development by the 217,000-acre Sawtooth Wilderness. This wilderness area provides excellent opportunities for hiking, backpacking, and horseback riding.

Boise National Forest is rich with wildlife. In the higher elevations are mountain lions and black bears. Mule deer and elk may be seen grazing early in the morning or evening. Birdwatchers will want to be on the lookout for hummingbirds, larks, swallows, and many more species. Bald eagles, hawks, and falcons can also be seen flying overhead.

If you're interested in staying awhile, the national forest offers several camping areas directly along the byway. You can venture into the forest from the many side roads to find more camping and picnicking opportunities.

Information: Sawtooth National Forest, 2647 Kimberly Rd E, Twin Falls ID 83301 / 208-737-3200. Boise National Forest, 1249 S Vinnell Way, Boise ID 83709 / 208-373-4100. Salmon-Challis National Forest, RR 2 Box 600, Salmon ID 83467 / 208-756-5100.

Lodging Invitation

Shilo Inn - Boise Airport
4111 Broadway Avenue
Boise, ID 83705-5302

Phone: 208-343-7662
800-222-2244
Fax: 208-344-0318

Located only 1 mile from Boise International Airport, this Shilo Inn offers travelers 125 guestrooms & suites. All rooms feature a microwave • refrigerator • coffee maker • satellite TV with premium channels • VCP and more. Movie rentals are also available. Facilities include an outdoor pool to enjoy during the warmer seasons as well as an indoor spa, sauna, steam room, fitness center and guest laundromat. Amenities include free local calls, USA Today newspaper, continental breakfast and airport shuttle. Meeting space is available for up to 50 people. A restaurant is located adjacent to the hotel.

Shilo Inn - Boise Riverside
3031 Main Street
Boise, ID 83702-2048

Phone: 208-344-3521
800-222-2244
Fax: 208-384-1217

This newly renovated Shilo Inn is located on the banks of the picturesque Boise River which harbors the Greenbelt's 25 miles of hiking and biking trails. All 112 guestrooms are complete with microwave • refrigerator • satellite TV with premium channels • and VCP. Movie rentals are available at front desk. Facilities include an indoor pool, spa, sauna, steam room, fitness center and guest laundromat. Amenities include free local calls, USA Today newspaper, continental breakfast and airport shuttle. Meeting space for up to 75 people is available. A restaurant & lounge is located adjacent to the hotel.

Torrey's Burnt Creek Inn
HC 67, Box 725
Stanley, ID 83278

Phone: 888-838-2313

For an enjoyable and relaxing outdoor experience, Torrey's Burnt Creek Inn offers private riverside modern log cabins with kitchenettes and RV hook-ups. On-site amenities include: laundromat • showers • restaurant • convenience store • and gift shop. Guests enjoy great fishing on the Famed River of No Return—Salmon River.

Salmon River

Salmon River scenic byway travels from Stanley to Lost Trail Pass on the Idaho-Montana border. The byway is in central

Idaho, approximately 130 miles northwest of Boise. It follows ID 75 and US 93 for 161 miles. Both highways are two-lane paved roads safe for travel by all types of vehicles. There are no passing lanes and some tight curves that require slow speeds. Salmon River scenic byway is generally open year-round but extra caution is needed in winter.

The Salmon River scenic drive passes through the Challis and Salmon National Forests and a portion of the Sawtooth National Recreation Area. Flowing alongside the byway for almost its entire length is the cool blue water of the Salmon River. As the byway travels through forested canyons and valleys, spectacular vistas of the Bitterroot, Salmon River, Lemhi, and Lost River Mountains come into view.

The Challis and Salmon National Forests provide access to the 2.3 million acre Frank Church River of No Return Wilderness. There are more acres of roadless wilderness in this region than anywhere else in the lower 48 states. This vast wilderness area offers excellent fishing, hunting, hiking, backpacking, and horseback riding.

Those less interested in the primitive back country experience of the wilderness will find plenty of opportunities for pitching a tent or parking their RV in a developed campground. Numerous public campgrounds are located directly along or a short distance off the byway.

If you're driving this byway in a high-clearance or four-wheel-drive vehicle, you might consider taking a side trip known as the Custer Motorway Adventure Road. This side trip explores the historic Yankee Fork Mining District and will take you past ghost towns and abandoned mining sites of the late 1800s.

Information: Sawtooth National Forest, 2647 Kimberly Rd E, Twin Falls ID 83301 / 208-737-3200. Salmon-Challis National Forest, RR 2 Box 600, Salmon ID 83467 / 208-756-5100.

Lodging Invitation

Torrey's Burnt Creek Inn
HC 67, Box 725
Stanley, ID 83278
Phone: 888-838-2313

For an enjoyable and relaxing outdoor experience, Torrey's Burnt Creek Inn offers private riverside modern log cabins with kitchenettes and RV hook-ups. On-site amenities include: laundromat • showers • restaurant • convenience store • and gift shop. Guests enjoy great fishing on the Famed River of No Return—Salmon River.

Sawtooth

Sawtooth begins in Shoshone, which is 25 miles north of Twin Falls in central Idaho. It heads north through national forest land and the Sawtooth National Recreation Area and ends in Stanley. The 116-mile route follows ID 75, a two-lane paved road safe for travel by all types of vehicles. Five to six percent grades are encountered from Galena Summit to Stanley. The byway remains open year-round but extra caution should be used during winter. Sixty-one miles are officially designated a National Forest Scenic Byway.

Beginning in Idaho's high desert region, the byway climbs north along the scenic Wood River, passes through the forested landscape of Sawtooth National Forest, crosses Galena Summit at 8,701 feet, and then descends to Stanley. The overlook near Galena Summit provides panoramic views into the Sawtooth Mountains and wilderness area.

The Shoshone Ice Caves are natural lava tubes in which air currents have formed striking ice sculptures. The caves are located 90 feet below the earth's surface and maintain a year-round temperature below freezing. Guided tours of the ice caves are offered during the summer.

The visitor center for the 756,000-acre Sawtooth National Recreation Area is located north of Ketchum and is open year-round. Visitors will find information and exhibits here. This vast recreation area offers nearly unlimited opportunities for camping, picnicking, hiking, backpacking, fishing, and bicycling.

The Sawtooth National Forest also offers opportunities for camping, picnicking, and hiking. Several public campgrounds have been developed along the byway as well as within the national forest.

Information: Sawtooth National Forest, 2647 Kimberly Rd E, Twin Falls ID 83301 / 208-737-3200. Salmon-Challis National Forest, RR 2 Box 600, Salmon ID 83467 / 208-756-5100.

Lodging Invitation

Torrey's Burnt Creek Inn
HC 67, Box 725
Stanley, ID 83278

Phone: 888-838-2313

For an enjoyable and relaxing outdoor experience, Torrey's Burnt Creek Inn offers private riverside modern log cabins with kitchenettes and RV hook-ups. On-site amenities include: laundromat • showers • restaurant • convenience store • and gift shop. Guests enjoy great fishing on the Famed River of No Return—Salmon River.

Teton

US FS

This scenic drive is in eastern Idaho about 50 miles east of Idaho Falls. It follows ID 31, ID 32, and ID 33 between Ashton and Swan Valley. The state highways are two-lane paved roads suitable for all types of vehicles. Six percent grades and sharp curves are encountered at Pine Creek Pass. The byway usually remains open year-round. Twenty miles are designated a National Forest Scenic Byway; the rest is a state scenic byway.

The Teton scenic byway begins in Swan Valley with views of the Snake River and Caribou Mountains to the south. The byway then begins climbing through the Targhee National Forest along Pine Creek to the 6,764-foot Pine Creek Pass. Spectacular views of the Teton Mountains in Wyoming can be seen from here.

Several national forest campgrounds can be found along or near this portion of the byway. Near the byway's southern terminus is Falls Campground with 24 sites, drinking water, and pit toilets. Just beyond Pine Creek Pass is a small national forest campground. Pine Creek Campground has 11

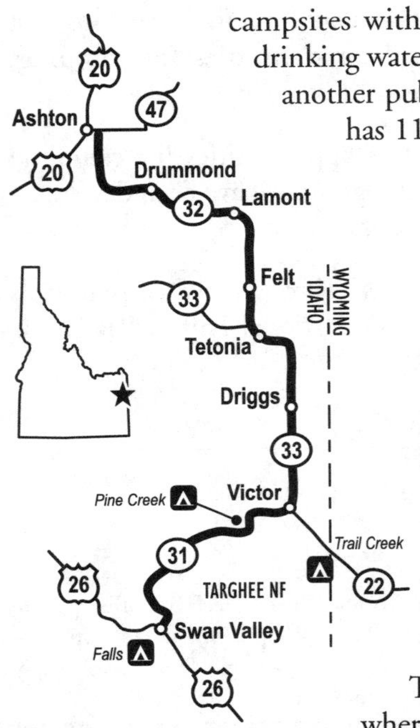

campsites with picnic tables, fire rings, toilets, and drinking water. About six miles southeast of Victor is another public campground named Trail Creek; it has 11 campsites.

A variety of wildlife inhabits the mountains and valleys of the national forest. Elk and mule deer may be seen grazing in the fields; the best time to view them is early in the morning or evening. Other wildlife includes black bear, coyotes, and moose. Hawks can often be seen gliding on the wind currents.

After traveling through the national forest, the byway continues north across rolling agricultural land through the communities of Victor, Driggs, and Tetonia. The byway ends near Ashton where the Mesa Falls scenic byway begins.

Information: Targhee National Forest, Palisades Ranger District, 3659 E Ririe Hwy, Idaho Falls ID 83401 / 208-523-1412.

Illinois

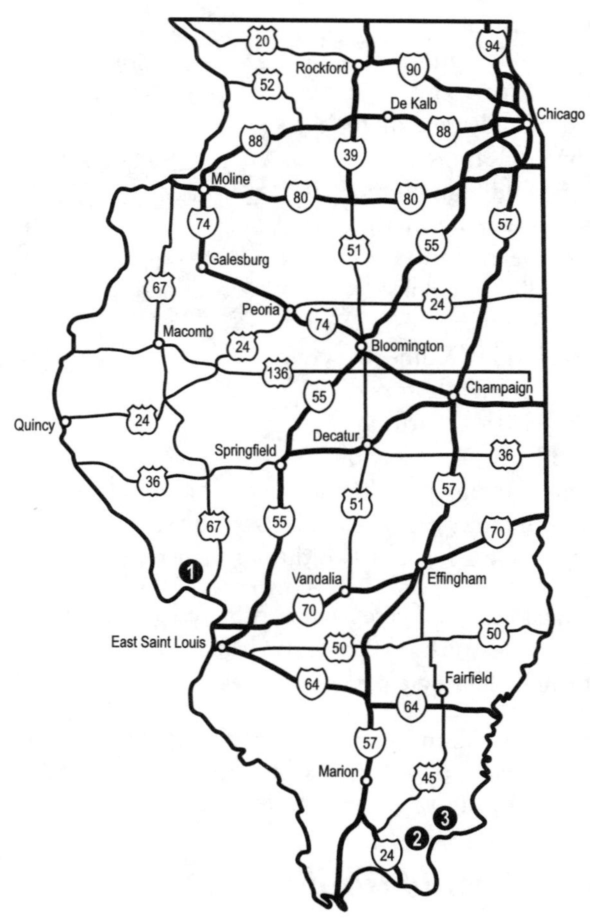
20
94
Rockford
90
52
De Kalb
Chicago
88
88
39
Moline
80
80
74
57
51
55
Galesburg
67
24
Peoria
74
Macomb
Bloomington
24
136
Champaign
55
Quincy
24
Decatur
Springfield
36
36
57
51
67
55
70
1
Vandalia
Effingham
70
50
East Saint Louis
50
Fairfield
64
64
57
Marion
45
3
2
24

Meeting of the Great Rivers

NSB Meeting of the Great Rivers is in southwest Illinois about 20 miles north of Saint Louis, Missouri. The byway begins in Alton at the Melvin Price Lock and Dam and travels north to Kampsville. It follows IL 100, Eldred Road, and IL 108 for a total of 50 miles. The byway reaches Kampsville via a ferry across the Illinois River. The roads followed are two-lane paved roads suitable for all vehicles.

Meeting of the Great Rivers follows the Mississippi River between Alton and Pere Marquette State Park and the Illinois River to Kampsville. Dense woodland and high bluffs add to the scenic beauty of the byway. In fall, the region is decorated with vibrant color. The byway traveler passes through several small communities with Victorian homes and rural areas with charming farmhouses and barns. A variety of wildlife inhabits the region including deer, otter, and beaver. In January and February, bald eagles can be seen. In November and March thousands of white pelicans stay a week or two during their migration.

Camping is available in the Pere Marquett State Park. It has 117 RV and tent sites; 82 have electric hookups. It also features nature trails, horseback riding, and fishing. The state park is open all year.

Information: Greater Alton/Twin Rivers Convention and Visitors Bureau, 200 Piasa St, Alton IL 62002 / 618-465-6676 or 800-258-6645. Pere Marquette State Park, PO Box 158, Grafton IL 62037 / 618-786-3323.

Ohio River Scenic Route

NSB Ohio River Scenic Route begins near Fort Defiance State Park in southern Illinois and travels northeast to the Indiana state line. It follows a series of US, state, and county highways that are suitable for all vehicles. The byway is nearly 190 miles long. A portion runs through Shawnee National Forest and is also known as the Shawnee Hills on the Ohio Scenic Byway.

The Ohio River Scenic Route crosses an area rich in history and natural beauty. In Shawneetown and Golconda there are several historic buildings dating back to the early 1800s. Fort Massac State Park in Metropolis, Illinois' first state park, features a reconstructed fort from the French and Indian War of the late 1700s. Re-creations of pioneer life and other activities take place in the park throughout the

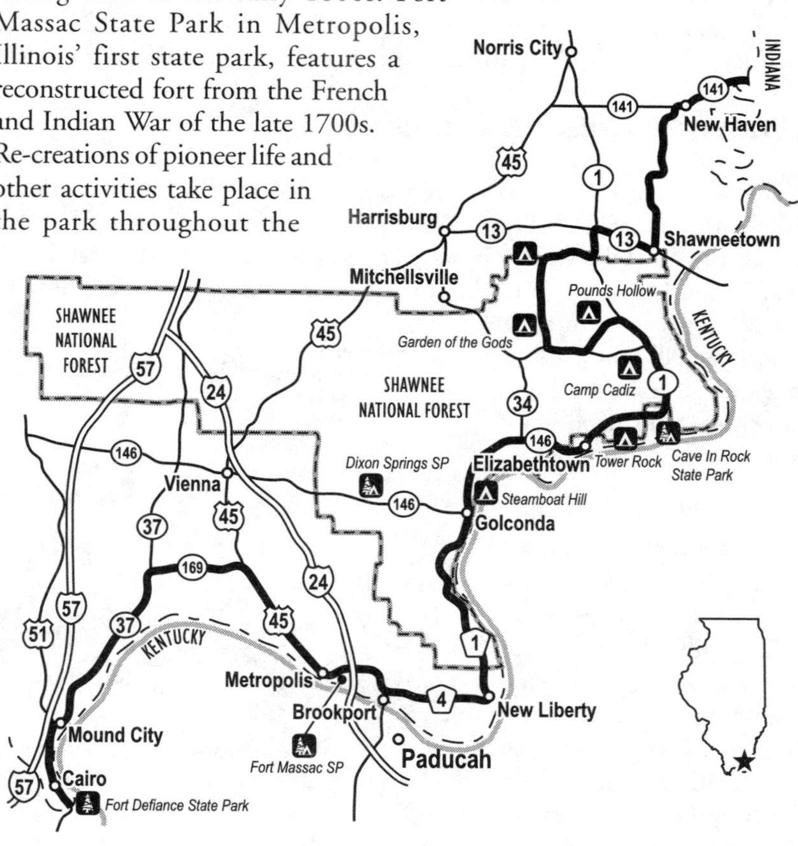

year. A campground with 48 RV and tent sites is located in the park. Cave-In-Rock State Park features a small cave once used by outlaws that preyed on travelers of the Ohio River. Visitors to the park can enjoy lunch or dinner at the restaurant overlooking the river.

A portion of the byway travels across Shawnee National Forest where visitors will find hundreds of miles of trails, several campgrounds, and preserved wilderness areas. Garden of the Gods features eight miles of trails winding through unique rock formations. A small, 12-site campground is located here.

Information: Southernmost Illinois Tourism Bureau, PO Box 278, Ullin IL 62992 / 618-845-3777 or 800-248-4373. Shawnee National Forest, 50 Hwy 145 S, Harrisburg IL 62946 / 618-253-7114. Cave-In-Rock State Park, PO Box 338, Cave-In-Rock IL 62919 / 618-289-4545. Fort Massac State Park, 1308 E 5th St, Metropolis IL 62960 / 618-524-4712. Dixon Springs State Park, RR 2, Golconda IL 62938 / 618-949-3394.

Shawnee Hills on the Ohio

US FS Shawnee Hills on the Ohio is in southern Illinois. It begins in Mitchellsville and travels south along the banks of the Ohio River to end in New Liberty. The byway follows OH 34, Karbers Ridge Road, OH 1, OH 146, and CR 1. All the roads are two-lane paved roads suitable for all types of vehicles. Shawnee Hills on the Ohio is about 70 miles long and usually remains open year-round.

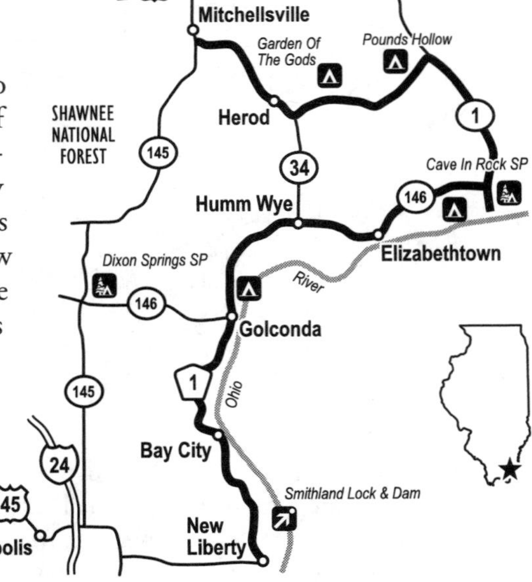

Shawnee Hills on the Ohio travels through the heart of the Shawnee National Forest, winding through gently rolling hills and ridgetops before descending to follow the Ohio River. Shawnee National Forest preserves over 250,000 acres of hardwood forest, meandering streams, and placid lakes.

White-tailed deer can be found throughout the national forest and are most commonly seen along the forested creek bottoms. Alert wildlife observers may occasionally catch a glimpse of a wild turkey or two. Fishermen will find largemouth bass, bluegill, catfish, and crappie in the many creeks and lakes throughout the national forest.

A short distance off the byway is the Garden of the Gods Recreation Area and Wilderness. There are eight miles of trails that wind above and below the bluffs and sandstone rock formations. The campground located here has 12 RV and tent sites, a picnic area, and drinking water.

Cave-In-Rock State Park has a campground with 48 sites for tents and recreational vehicles. Hookups are also available at many of the sites. A short hiking trail here leads to a cave that was once a pirate's den in the 1790s. The cave was also used as the headquarters for outlaws and gangs.

Near the end of the byway is Smithland Lock and Dam, a facility operated by the Corps of Engineers. There is a picnic area for enjoying a lunch while watching the locks in operation.

Information: Shawnee National Forest, 50 Hwy 145 S, Harrisburg IL 62946 / 618-253-7114. Cave In Rock State Park, PO Box 338, Cave-In-Rock IL 62919 / 618-289-4545. Dixon Springs State Park, RR 2, Golconda IL 62938 / 618-949-3394.

INDIANA

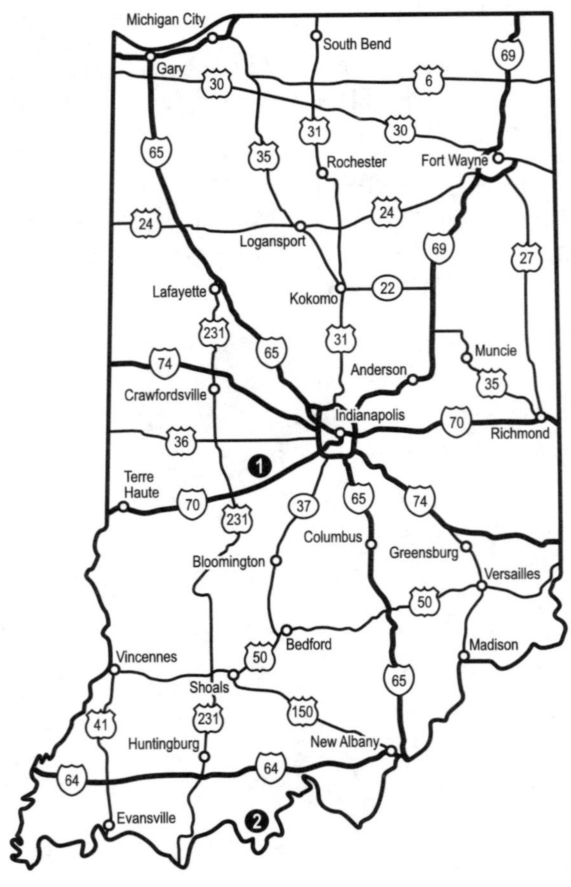

Michigan City
South Bend
Gary
30
6
69
31
30
65
35
Rochester
Fort Wayne
24
24
Logansport
69
27
Lafayette
Kokomo
22
231
31
65
74
Muncie
Anderson
Crawfordsville
35
Indianapolis
70
36
Richmond
1
Terre Haute
70
231
37
65
74
Columbus
Greensburg
Bloomington
Versailles
50
Bedford
Madison
Vincennes
50
Shoals
65
231
150
41
Huntingburg
New Albany
64
64
Evansville
2

Indiana National Road

Indiana National Road follows US 40 across mid-Indiana from the Illinois state line to the Ohio state line. The byway is 180 miles long and remains open year-round. US Highway 40 is a two-lane paved road suitable for all vehicles.

The National Road was the first federally funded highway in the United States. It ran from Cumberland, Maryland to Vandalia, Illinois. The portion running through Indiana was built between 1828 and 1834. Travelers of the byway today will find 32 historic places listed on the National Register of Historic Sites including: the James Whitcomb Riley Birthplace, the Indiana State Capitol, and Highland Lawn Cemetery in Terre Haute.

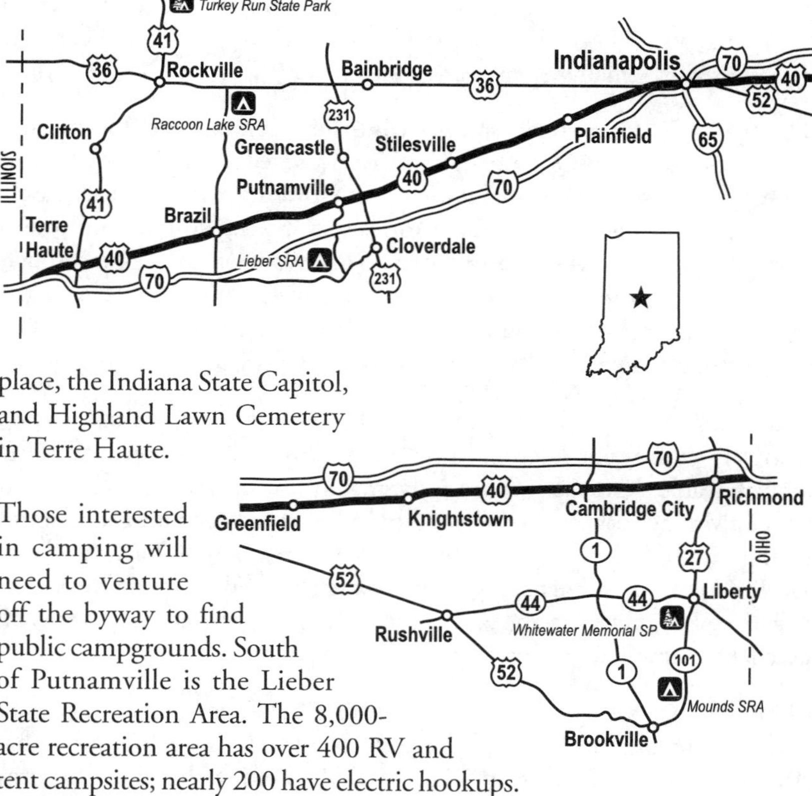

Those interested in camping will need to venture off the byway to find public campgrounds. South of Putnamville is the Lieber State Recreation Area. The 8,000-acre recreation area has over 400 RV and tent campsites; nearly 200 have electric hookups. Facilities are limited in winter, but the area remains open year-round. Near the byway's eastern end is Whitewater Memorial State Park, located south of Richmond. It has over 300 campsites and some cabins available for rent.

Information: Historic Landmarks Foundation of Indiana, Box 284, Cambridge City IN 47327 / 765-478-3172. Old National Road Welcome Center / 800-828-8414. Lieber SRA, 1317 W Lieber Rd Ste 1, Cloverdale IN 46120 / 765-795-4576. Raccoon Lake SRA, 160 S Raccoon Pkwy, Rockville IN 47872 / 765-344-1412. Turkey Run State Park, Rt 1 Box 164, Marshall IN 47859 / 765-597-2635. Mounds SRA, Brookville Lake, PO Box 100, Brookville IN 47012 / 765-647-2657. Whitewater Memorial State Park, 1418 S State Rd 101, Liberty IN 47353 / 765-458-5565.

Ohio River Scenic Route

NSB Ohio River Scenic Route crosses southern Indiana from the Illinois state line to the Ohio state line. The byway is 302 miles long and primarily follows two-lane paved roads. The main routes followed are: IN 56, IN 62, and IN 66. For detailed directions, please see the side bar. The byway usually remains open year-round.

The byway winds through southern Indiana's rolling hills, forests, and farmlands, and at times it clings to the river's edge. As you travel this route, you'll pass through quaint towns with towering church spires, stately mansions, and historic buildings. You'll pass cypress swamps and travel atop rock outcrops peering over the Ohio River, and leisurely pass through dense hardwood forests. At times you'll be given sweeping views of the river, while other times you hardly know it's there. Below is just a small sample of the many attractions and scenery you will discover along this route.

Something you wouldn't expect to find in Indiana is a cypress swamp, complete with water lilies and rare birds. This makes for an interesting and enjoyable short side trip from the main route of the scenic drive. Just west of Mount Vernon in southwestern Indiana, you can take IN 69 south to the Hovey Lake State Fish and Wildlife Area, a 4,300-acre wetland. Here, you can do some fishing or enjoy a relaxing boat ride on the waters of Hovey Lake. Next to the lake is the Twin Swamps Nature Preserve, an excellent example of a cypress swamp, in Indiana!

North of Rockport on IN 162, just east of US 231, is Lincoln State Park and the Lincoln Boyhood National Memorial. It is on this farm that Abraham Lincoln lived from 1816 to 1830. During this time, he grew from a seven-year-old boy to a 21-year-old man. Log farm buildings are staffed by costumed interpreters during the summer months. Visitors are invited to participate in the daily chores that Abe and his family would have performed including breaking flax, splitting wood, or making butter.

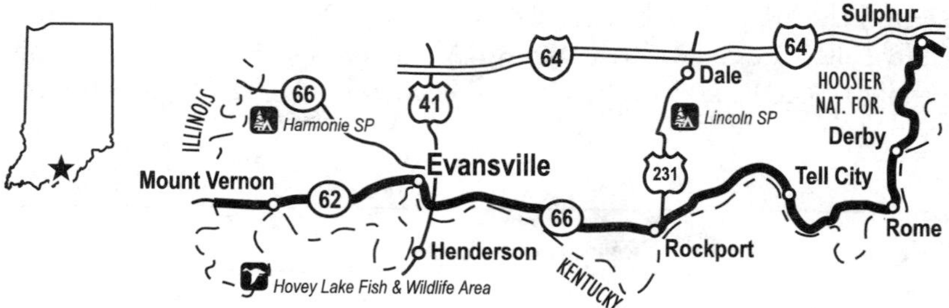

The Ohio River Scenic Route passes through portions of the 80,000-acre Hoosier National Forest. The byway travels along the Ohio River in the forest's southern portion before turning north, passing through stands of hardwoods, pine and cedar, springs, caves, and sinkholes. Several recreation areas are available throughout the national forest that provide camping (no hookups) and picnicking facilities.

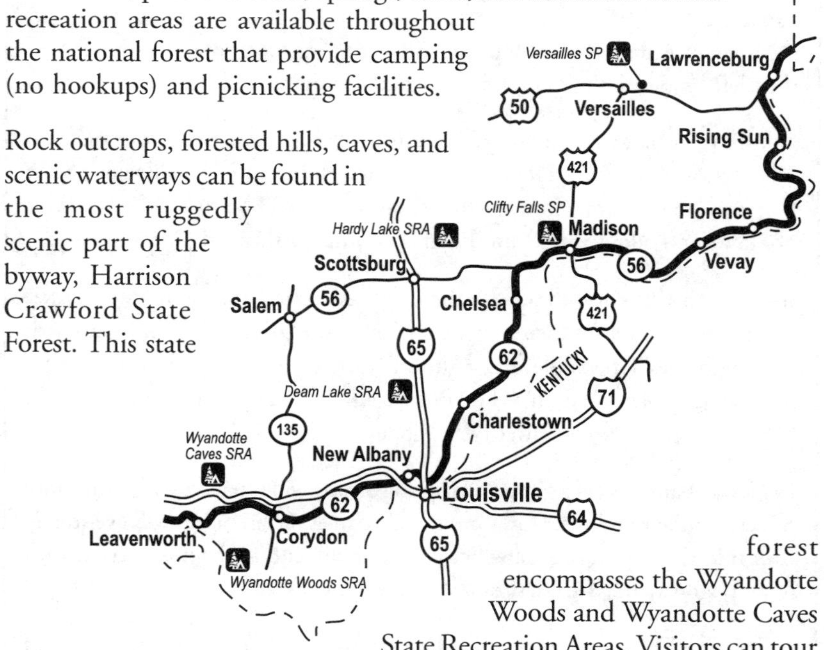

Rock outcrops, forested hills, caves, and scenic waterways can be found in the most ruggedly scenic part of the byway, Harrison Crawford State Forest. This state forest encompasses the Wyandotte Woods and Wyandotte Caves State Recreation Areas. Visitors can tour the caves that were once used by prehistoric people for mining operations.

Information: Hoosier National Forest, 811 Constitution Ave, Bedford IN 47421 / 812-275-5987. Harmonie State Park, Rt 1 Box 5A, New Harmony IN 47631 / 812-682-4821. Lincoln State Park, Box 216, Lincoln City IN 47552 / 812-937-4710. Harrison Crawford State Forest, 7240 Old Forest Rd SW, Corydon IN 47112 / 812-738-8232. Wyandotte Caves SRA, 7315 S Wyandotte Cave Rd, Leavenworth IN 47137 / 812-738-2782.

Deam Lake SRA, 1217 Deam Lake Rd, Borden IN 47106 / 812-246-5421.
Clifty Falls State Park, 1501 Green Rd, Madison IN 47250 / 812-273-8885.
Versailles State Park, Box 205 US 50, Versailles IN 47042 / 812-689-6424.

Following the Ohio River Scenic Route

The following description is traveling the route from east to west.

Begin at the Indiana-Ohio border and follow U.S. 50 west to Oberting Road. Follow Oberting Road to the town of Greendale. In Greendale, turn left onto Ridge Avenue (State Highway 1), which will become Main Street in Lawrenceburg. In Lawrencburg, turn right (west) on U.S. 50 and follow to the town of Aurora. In Aurora, you will want to turn left onto George Street, then left on Second Street, and then south on State Highway 56.

Continue traveling south on SH 56, through Rising Sun, until you reach the intersection with State Highway 156. State Highway 156 will rejoin State Highway 56 in Vevay. Continue traveling west on SH 56 to SH 62, just west of Hanover. Follow SH 62 until you reach the outskirts of Jeffersonville.

In Jeffersonville, you will want to turn left on Allison Lane, right onto Market Street, left on Walnut Street, right on Riverside Drive, right on Sherwood, left on South Clark Boulevard, right on Harrison Avenue, left on Randolph Avenue, then westward on SH 62 once again. State Highway 62 will become Spring Street when you enter New Albany.

In New Albany, State Highway 62 (Spring Street) will intersect with Vincennes Street; turn left and then right onto Main Street. Main Street will eventually turn into the Corydon Pike which, in turn, will end at the intersection with State Highway 62. Turn left onto State Highway 62.

Follow State Highway 62 westward until you reach the town of Sulpher and the intersection with State Highway 66. Turn left onto State Highway 66 and follow it until you reach State Highway 662 near Newburgh. Follow SH 662 west to Interstate 164. Follow I-164 west to Evansville. I-164 will become Veterans Memorial Drive and then Riverside Drive in Evansville. Follow this route until you reach the intersection with State Highway 62 (Lloyd Expressway) From here on out, you'll want to follow State Highway 62 west through Mt. Vernon to the Indiana-Illinois state line.

Kentucky

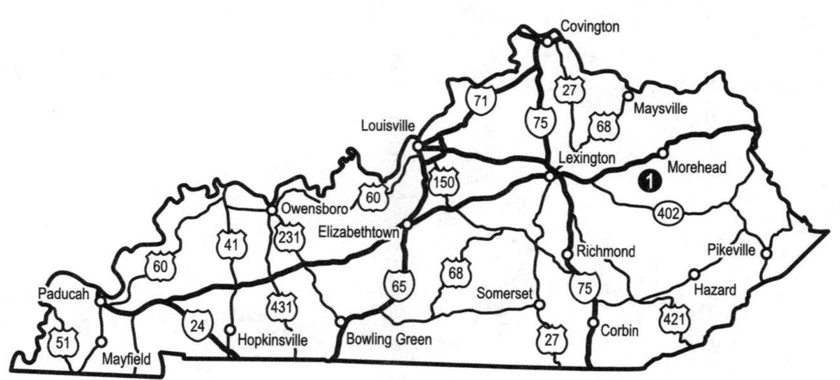

Zilpo Road

Zilpo Road is in the forested hills of eastern Kentucky approximately 60 miles east of Lexington. The short, nine-mile byway ends on the western shore of Cave Run Lake at the Zilpo Recreation Area. It follows FSR 918, which is a wide two-lane paved road suitable for all vehicles. The byway is open year-round.

Zilpo Road is a ridgetop route running through the hardwood forests of Daniel Boone National Forest. The road is a wide, gently curving road among trees that offer beautiful colors of orange, red, and gold during autumn. Wildlife observers will want to stay alert and be looking for white-tailed deer foraging among the woods. The patient observer may also see an occasional wild turkey. Woodpeckers, owls, and whippoorwills make their presence known within the forest. Hawks, osprey, and the bald eagle can also be seen soaring on the wind currents.

Cave Run Lake is perhaps the main attraction of this byway. It is a 7,390-acre lake constructed on the Licking River by the Corps of Engineers. The lake provides excellent fishing and boating opportunities. The Zilpo Recreation Area is a 355-acre park offering 172 wooded campsites, some with hookups. Facilities include restrooms with showers, a boat ramp, swimming beach, drinking water, walking trails, and two dump stations. On the other side of the lake is the 700-acre Twin Knobs Recreation Area. Each of the 277 campsites found here will accommodate large recreational vehicles or tents. Restrooms with showers, a swimming beach, and walking trails are among the facilities offered. Weekly programs are offered at the amphitheater.

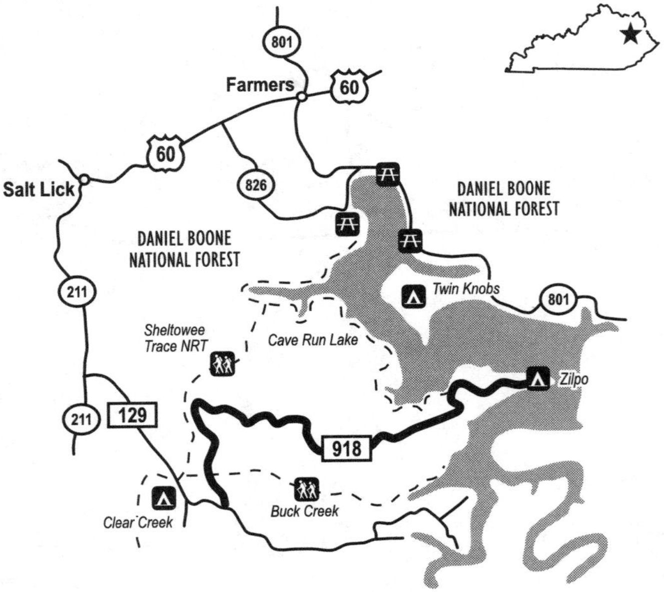

A smaller, more primitive camping area is found near the beginning of the byway, the Clear Creek Campground. This campground has 21 units with picnic tables and chemical toilets.

The Zilpo Road scenic byway runs through the heart of the Pioneer Weapons Wildlife Management Area. This 7,480-acre area provides hunters the opportunity to experience hunting the way Daniel Boone did years ago. Hunting is limited to pioneer weapons such as the bow and arrow, cross bow, and black powder firearms.

Information: Daniel Boone National Forest, 1700 Bypass Rd, Winchester KY 40391 / 606-745-3100.

Louisiana

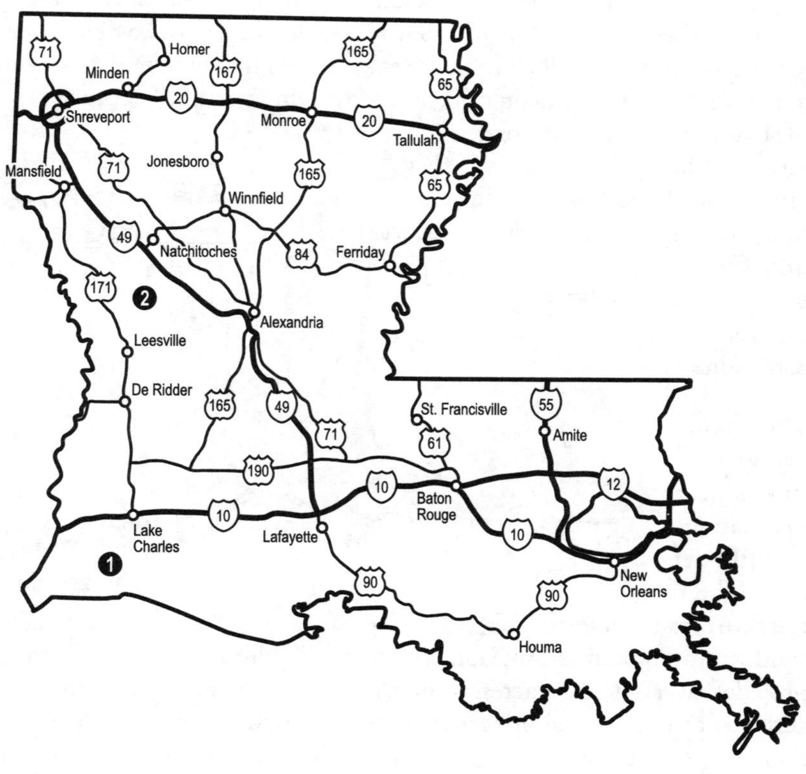

71
Homer
Minden
167
165
65
20
Shreveport
Monroe
20
Tallulah
71
Jonesboro
165
Mansfield
65
Winnfield
49
Natchitoches
84
Ferriday
171
2
Alexandria
Leesville
De Ridder
165
49
71
St. Francisville
55
Amite
61
190
10
12
Baton
Rouge
10
Lake
Charles
Lafayette
10
1
90
New
Orleans
90
Houma

Creole Nature Trail

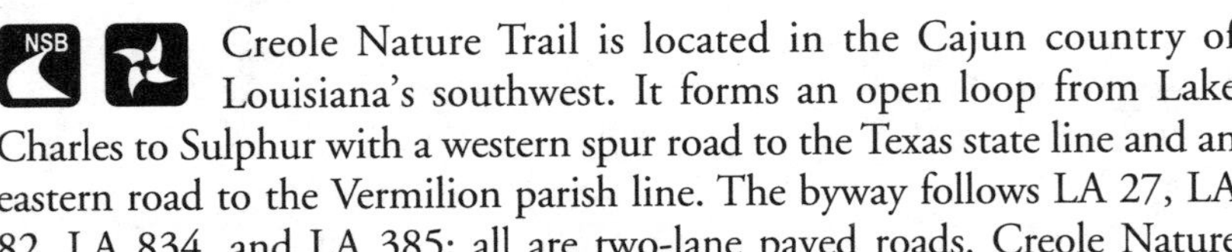

Creole Nature Trail is located in the Cajun country of Louisiana's southwest. It forms an open loop from Lake Charles to Sulphur with a western spur road to the Texas state line and an eastern road to the Vermilion parish line. The byway follows LA 27, LA 82, LA 834, and LA 385; all are two-lane paved roads. Creole Nature Trail is open year-round and is 180 miles long.

Visitors to the Creole Nature Trail can begin their journey in Sulphur, just north of Interstate 10. From here, the byway travels south through the marshlands of southern Calcasieu and Cameron Parishes to Holly Beach on the Gulf of Mexico. From Holly Beach, the byway continues east along the coast of the Gulf of Mexico through the town of Cameron to Creole. From Creole, you can continue driving north to the byway's end in Lake Charles. You also have the option of driving west from Holly Beach to the Texas state line or east from Creole to the byway's end at the Vermilion parish line.

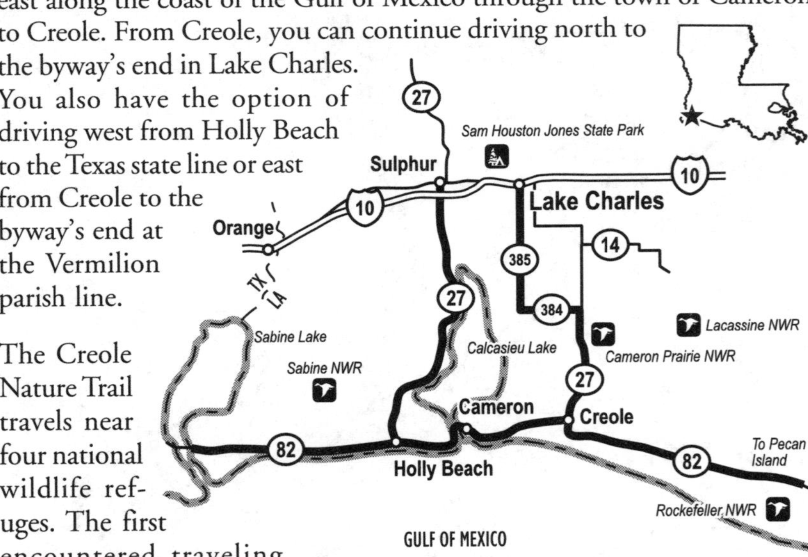

The Creole Nature Trail travels near four national wildlife refuges. The first encountered traveling south from Sulphur is the Sabine National Wildlife Refuge. This refuge provides over 124,000 acres of marshland for migrating waterfowl in addition to recreational opportunities for the byway traveler. A 1½-mile trail here provides excellent opportunities for viewing the wildlife, including alligators. Over 150 miles of canals, bayous, and waterways are open to the public for boating and fishing.

The Cameron Prairie National Wildlife Refuge plays host to ducks, geese, herons, egrets, and the endangered peregrine falcon. A boardwalk here overlooks the marsh. The Rockefeller and Lacassine NWR offer a total of nearly 117,000 acres of marshland. The Rockefeller NWR is open to the public from March 1 through December 1 for the purpose of sight-seeing and sport fishing. Lacassine NWR is primarily a freshwater marshland with a variety of wildlife including alligator, coyote, mink, muskrat, and white-tailed deer.

Camping and picnicking facilities may be found in the Sam Houston Jones State Park in Lake Charles. The park offers 73 RV and tent campsites, some with electrical hookups. The park also has 12 cabins available for rent.

Information: Southwest Louisiana/Lake Charles C&VB, 1211 N Lakeshore Dr, Lake Charles LA 70601 / 318-436-9588 or 800-456-SWLA. Sam Houston Jones State Park, 107 Sutherland Rd, Lake Charles LA 70611 / 318-855-2665 or 888-677-7264.

Longleaf Trail

Longleaf Trail is in west-central Louisiana about 35 miles northwest of Alexandria. It begins about five miles south of Derry off LA 119 and travels west across the Kisatchie National Forest. It ends at the intersection with LA 117, south of Bellwood. Longleaf Trail follows FSR 59, a two-lane paved road suitable for all vehicles. It remains open year-round and is 17 miles long.

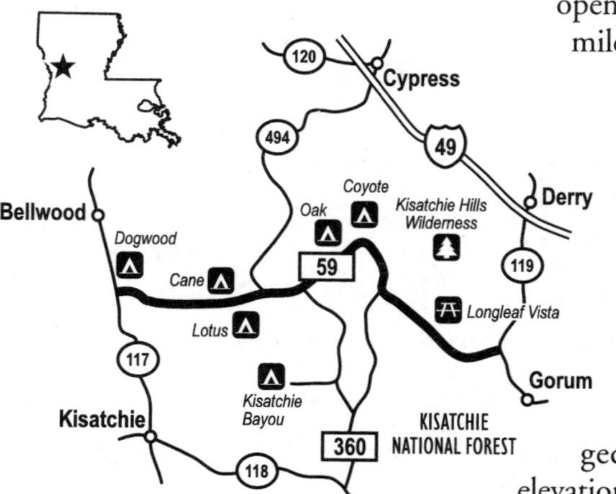

The Longleaf Trail National Forest Scenic Byway travels across the Kisatchie National Forest through some of the most unique scenery in the state. The terrain along the byway is unusually rugged for Louisiana, with elevations ranging from 120 to 400 feet above sea level. The byway offers many scenic vistas of mesas, buttes, and sandstone outcrops set against the backdrop of longleaf pines. The trail was originally constructed as a single-lane road by the Civilian Conservation Corps around 1935.

The Kisatchie Hills Wilderness lies next to the byway and is known locally as the "Little Grand Canyon" because of its steep slopes, rock outcrops, and mesas. Hiking and horseback riding trails lead you into this wilderness area. The Longleaf Vista Picnic Area is surrounded on three sides by this 8,700-acre wilderness area. A 1½-mile nature trail is located here as is a small visitor center. Restrooms and drinking water are also provided.

Wildlife observers will find white-tailed deer, foxes, opossums, squirrels, raccoons, and coyotes inhabiting the area. An occasional roadrunner can also be seen. Birdwatchers will delight in the numerous songbirds.

Most of the camping areas along the byway are primitive but do have drinking water or restroom facilities. Dogwood Campground is the most developed and has 20 RV and tent sites, drinking water, and flush toilets. Kisatchie Bayou has 17 walk-in sites and only one drive-in unit. Drinking water and vault toilets are provided. There is no water at Coyote, Cane, and Oak Campgrounds.

Information: Kisatchie National Forest, PO Box 5500, Pineville LA 71361 / 318-473-7160.

MARYLAND

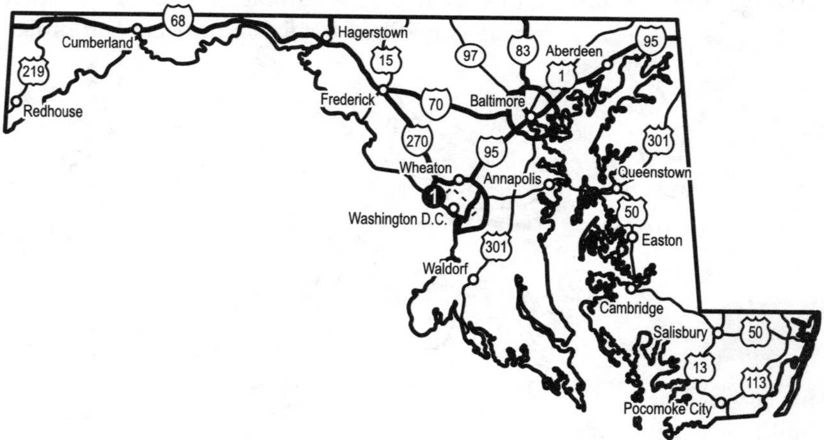

George Washington Memorial Parkway

Virginia section see page 306

George Washington Memorial Parkway is in northeast Virginia and south-central Maryland. Portions of the scenic drive pass through Washington, D.C. The segment described here is north of the District of Columbia; see Virginia for the other segment. The byway follows a four-lane divided highway named Clara Barton Parkway. Its short—six miles long—and remains open year-round.

The George Washington Memorial Parkway preserves the natural scenery along the Potomac River, connecting historic sites from Mount Vernon, past the Nation's Capital, to the Great Falls of the Potomac. The many historic sites are complemented by the scenic countryside. The banks of the Potomac River are covered with willows, elders, and birches. Autumn brings vibrant colors to the parkway as the red maples, oaks, sumacs, and hickories proudly display their autumn attire. It is not unusual to see white-tailed deer, raccoon, wild turkey, and opossum in the area.

The Clara Barton National Historic Site was the home of American Red Cross founder, Clara Barton, from 1897 to 1904. The 38-room house was designed by Clara and was first used as a Red Cross warehouse. Over 30 large closets in the building were used for storage of relief supplies. It was later modified for living quarters and offices in 1897. The building is furnished with original and period artifacts that provide interesting insights into the character of Clara Barton and the American Red Cross. Guided tours are given daily from 10:00 a.m. to 5:00 p.m.

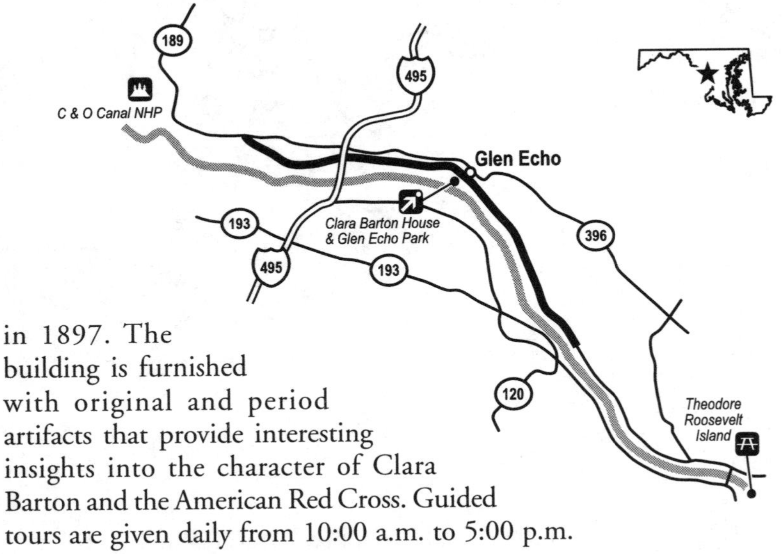

Glen Echo Park is located adjacent to the Clara Barton National Historic Site. Glen Echo is now an arts and cultural center where classes are taught year-round by well-known artists and professionals. It was once an amusement park that served the Washington area until 1967. An antique, hand-carved and hand-painted Dentzel Carousel operates on summer weekends. The gallery offers monthly exhibitions of Glen Echo's artists.

Information: George Washington Memorial Pkwy, Turkey Run Park, McLean VA 22101 / 703-289-2500. C & O Canal NHP Headquarters, Box 4, Sharpsburg MD 21782 / 301-739-4200. Clara Barton House NHS, 5801 Oxford Rd, Glen Echo MD 20812 / 301-492-6245. Glen Echo Park, 7300 MacArthur Blvd, Glen Echo MD 20812 / 301-492-6229 main office or 301-492-6282 events hotline.

Michigan

1 Black River, *138*
2 River Road, *139*
3 Whitefish Bay, *140*

Black River

Black River scenic byway is in the western corner of Michigan's Upper Peninsula, near the Wisconsin state line. The byway begins in Bessemer and travels north to the road's end on the shores of Lake Superior. Black River is 15 miles long and follows North Moore Street, Saint Johns Road, and Black River Road (CR 513). All are two-lane paved roads suitable for all types of vehicles. The byway is open year-round.

The Black River scenic byway crosses the Ottawa National Forest alongside the meandering Black River through areas of old growth hemlock and hardwoods of the Black River Valley. The byway offers scenic views of the distant Porcupine Mountains. In autumn, the byway is bathed in colors of red, orange, and gold.

Near the byway's northern end are five cascading waterfalls. Short hiking trails provide access to each of the falls. Difficulty levels range from easy to strenuous as there may be a series of steps and steep grades. None of the trails are accessible to the handicapped.

The byway ends at the Black River Recreation Area, a popular spot throughout the year. A day use area provides picnic tables, restrooms, and drinking water. The campground here has 40 RV and tent sites, drinking water, flush toilets, and a dump station. A boat ramp on the Black River provides access to Lake Superior.

Those interested in hiking or backpacking will find access to the North Country National Scenic Trail. Much of the trail parallels the Black River. This hiking trail begins in New York, cuts through seven states, and ends in North Dakota where it links up with the Lewis and Clark National Historic Trail.

Information: Ottawa National Forest, Bessemer Ranger District, 500 N Moore St, Bessemer MI 49911 / 906-667-0261.

River Road

This byway is in northeast Michigan about 90 miles north of Saginaw. It travels alongside the AuSable River between Oscoda and Hale. From Oscoda the byway follows River Road to MI 65, which it follows into Hale. The byway is 30 miles long and is open year-round. The roads followed are two-lane paved roads safe for all types of vehicles.

The River Road scenic byway travels across the AuSable River Valley, following a portion of an early Indian trail along the AuSable River. The trail connected a Chippewa village at the mouth of the Riviere aux Sables (River of Sand) with the main north-south trails of interior Michigan. There are several platforms on the high banks above the river that provide panoramic views of the river and the surrounding forest.

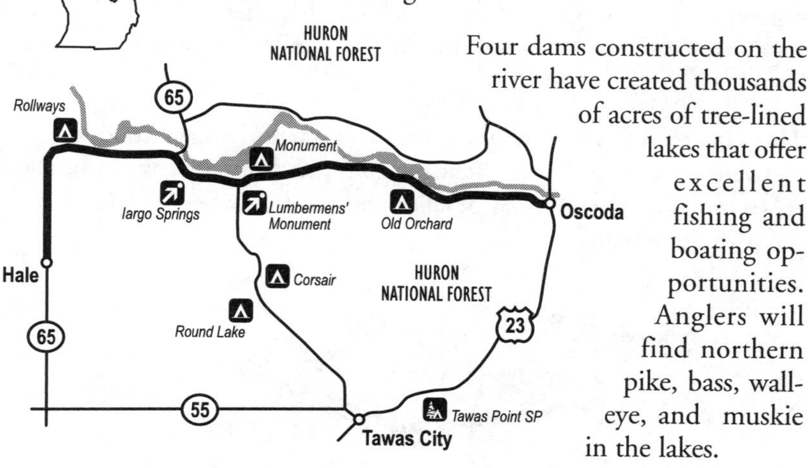

Four dams constructed on the river have created thousands of acres of tree-lined lakes that offer excellent fishing and boating opportunities. Anglers will find northern pike, bass, walleye, and muskie in the lakes.

Those interested in prolonging their stay will find several campgrounds. Old Orchard Park is a highly developed park on the banks of the AuSable River with 500 campsites. Hookups are available at 200 of the campsites. The park also has restrooms, showers, picnic areas, swimming beach, and drinking water. Rollways and Monument Campgrounds provide a total of 40 campsites with picnic tables, fire rings, drinking water, and restrooms. Two other national forest campgrounds are located a short distance off the byway that provide an additional 45 campsites to choose from.

Midway along the byway is Lumbermens' Monument. This nine-foot bronze statue was erected in 1932 as a memorial to Michigan's logging era. A visitor center has information on the monument and the surrounding area. Guided walks of the grounds are given.

Farther west on the byway is the Iargo Springs Interpretive Site. The Chippewa once used this site for pow-wows with as many as 500 gathering at one time. They believed the springs held mystical or curative powers. An overlook provides views of the AuSable River Valley.

Information: Huron-Manistee National Forest, 1755 S Mitchell St, Cadillac MI 49601 / 517-739-0728.

Whitefish Bay

US FS Whitefish Bay is on Michigan's Upper Peninsula about 15 miles west of Sault Sainte Marie. It begins in Bay Mills and heads west across Hiawatha National Forest to the junction with MI 123. The byway follows FSR 3150 and FSR 42, which are two-lane paved roads suitable for all types of vehicles. Whitefish Bay is 27 miles long and remains open year-round.

The Whitefish Bay scenic byway travels through the hardwood forests of Hiawatha National Forest, often hugging the shores of Lake Superior. It passes miles of undisturbed beaches and sand dunes with several access roads to the beaches.

Panoramic views of Lake Superior and Canada at Spectacle Lake Overlook are impressive and should not be missed. You may also wish to visit Point Iroquois Lighthouse, which is listed on the National Register of Historic Places. Visitors are welcome to climb to the top of the 65-foot lighthouse for a panoramic view of Lake Superior. A museum tells the stories of lightkeepers and their families through family album photographs, antiques, and artifacts.

There are two national forest campgrounds located along the byway, Monocle Lake and Bay View. Monocle Lake Campground has 39 campsites set among northern hardwood, aspen, red maple, and white birch. Fire rings and picnic tables are provided at each site. A boat ramp provides access to the lake. Bay View Campground is situated on the shores of Lake Superior and has 24 campsites. Fire rings and picnic tables are also provided at each site. Other public campgrounds are scattered throughout the national forest.

Brimley State Park is to the east of the byway and is more developed than the national forest campgrounds. The park has 270 sites for tents and recreational vehicles, many with electrical hookups. It also has laundry facilities, restrooms with showers, and a swimming beach.

Information: Hiawatha National Forest, 2727 N Lincoln Rd, Escanaba MI 49829 / 906-786-4062. Tahquamenon Falls State Park, 41382 W MI 23, Paradise MI 49768 / 906-492-3415. Brimley State Park, 9200 W 6 Mile Rd, Brimley MI 49715 / 906-248-3422.

MINNESOTA

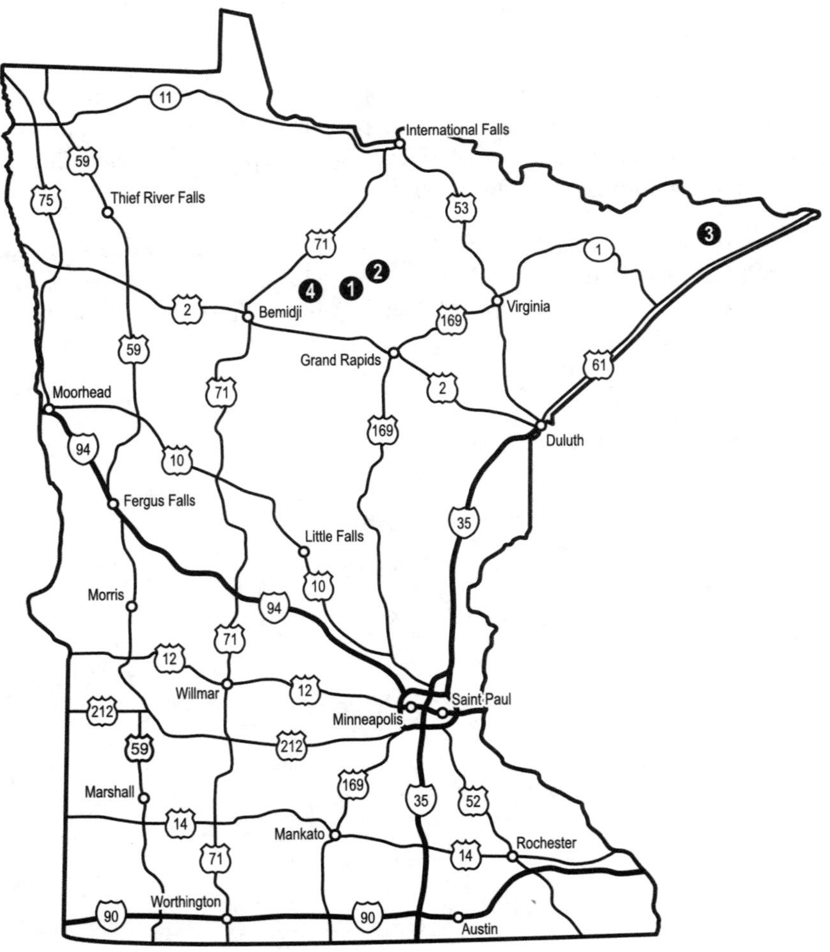

International Falls
Thief River Falls
Bemidji
Virginia
Grand Rapids
Moorhead
Duluth
Fergus Falls
Little Falls
Morris
Willmar
Saint Paul
Minneapolis
Marshall
Mankato
Rochester
Worthington
Austin
11
59
75
53
71
1
2
169
61
10
94
35
12
212
52
14
90
1
2
3
4

Avenue of Pines

Avenue of Pines is 15 miles northwest of Grand Rapids in north-central Minnesota. The byway begins near Deer River and follows MN 46 northwest to the junction with US 71 in Northome. Minnesota Highway 46 is a two-lane paved road suitable for all vehicles and usually remains open year-round. Avenue of Pines is 46 miles long.

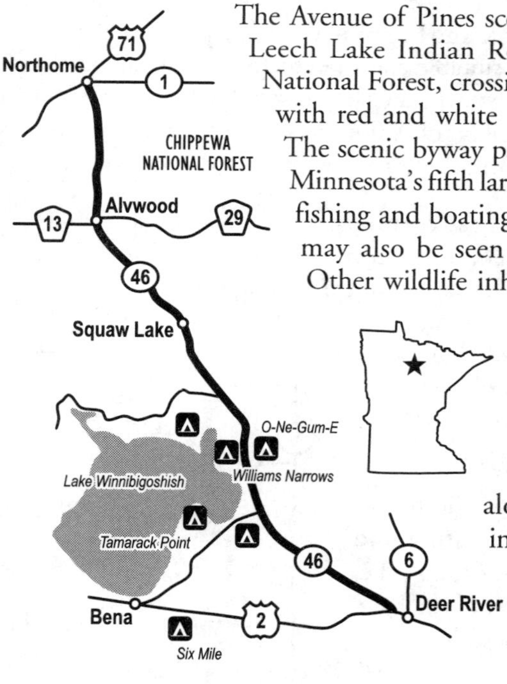

The Avenue of Pines scenic byway travels through Leech Lake Indian Reservation and Chippewa National Forest, crossing low rolling hills covered with red and white pines and numerous lakes. The scenic byway passes Lake Winnibigoshish, Minnesota's fifth largest lake that offers excellent fishing and boating opportunities. Bald eagles may also be seen circling around the lake. Other wildlife inhabiting the region include osprey, white-tailed deer, black bear, gray wolf, and numerous waterfowl.

Cut Foot Sioux Visitor Center is located midway along the byway and offers information and displays on the natural resources of the area. Films and presentations are given throughout the summer months. The Cut Foot Sioux National Recreation Trail is located near here. This trail follows the approximate location of the early fur trade routes and overland portages used by Indians. Also near the visitor center is the Cut Foot Sioux Ranger Station, which was constructed in 1904. The original log cabin is listed as a National Historic Site.

Chippewa National Forest was the first national forest established east of the Mississippi. It offers over 600,000 acres of land for a variety of recreational uses. Several national forest campgrounds have been developed along the byway, with more available throughout the forest. A large number of lakes and rivers provide excellent canoeing opportunities. Fishermen will find excellent fishing for muskie, walleye, northern pike, bass, and sunfish. Numerous trails cross the national forest providing opportunities for hiking, horseback riding, and bicycling.

Information: Chippewa National Forest, Rt 3 Box 244, Cass Lake MN 56633 / 218-335-8600.

Edge of the Wilderness

Edge of the Wilderness byway is in north-central Minnesota and begins in Grand Rapids. It follows MN 38, a two-lane paved road suitable for all vehicles, north for nearly 50 miles to Effie. The 22-mile segment traveling through Chippewa National Forest is designated a National Forest Scenic Byway. Edge of the Wilderness usually remains open year-round; delays are possible during winter.

The Edge Of The Wilderness scenic byway winds through forests of oak, birch, and aspen, skirting the shores of numerous lakes. The variety of trees along the byway create a beautiful show of fall color. Wildlife observers will want to be on the lookout for beaver, white-tailed deer, osprey, and eagles. Coyotes and the gray wolf also inhabit this region of Minnesota.

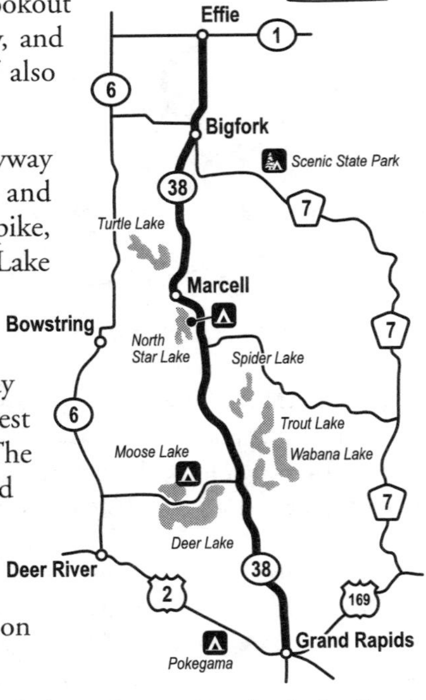

The many lakes adjacent to the byway provide opportunities for boating and fishing. Anglers will find northern pike, muskie, walleye, bass, and sunfish. Lake trout can also be found in some of the lakes.

Those wishing to lengthen their stay will find a developed national forest campground at North Star Lake. The campground has 42 sites for tents and recreational vehicles, drinking water, restrooms, picnic tables, and fire rings. Additionally, there are primitive national forest campsites on Spider, Trout, and Wabana Lakes.

Approximately seven miles east of Bigfork on County Road 7 is the Scenic State Park. This park offers 117 campsites, some with electrical hookups.

Facilities include restrooms, showers, drinking water, and a dump station. Picnicking, swimming, fishing, and boating are among the activities offered. Boat rentals are available for those that didn't bring their own. The park also offers miles of hiking, cross-country skiing, and snowmobiling trails.

Information: Chippewa National Forest, Rt 3 Box 244, Cass Lake MN 56633 / 218-335-8600. Scenic State Park, HC 2 Box 17, Bigfork MN 56628 / 218-743-3362.

North Shore Drive / Gunflint Trail

US FS North Shore Drive / Gunflint Trail is in northeastern Minnesota about 80 miles northeast of Duluth. The North Shore Drive portion begins in Schroeder and travels northeast to the national forest boundary, east of Red Cliff. The Gunflint Trail section starts in Grand Marais and travels northwest to the road's end near the Canadian border. The scenic drive follows US 61 and Gunflint Trail, which is also known as CR 12. Both roads are two-lane paved roads suitable for all types of vehicles and remain open year-round. North Shore Drive is officially designated a National Forest Scenic Byway.

Travelers to this scenic drive are treated to spectacular views of Lake Superior to the south and a vast expanse of hardwood forests to the north.

US Highway 61 follows the lake's shoreline as it crosses Superior National Forest. The forest offers numerous opportunities for camping, picnicking, hiking, and fishing. During winter, this area becomes a haven for snowmobile and cross-country ski enthusiasts. Opportunities also exist for watching deer and moose make their way through the woods or gazing at eagles soaring gracefully in the sky.

Many side roads tempt the traveler to turn off the main route and explore the wilderness. If you do find yourself tempted, you'll be rewarded with beautiful scenery. These side roads also provide access to miles of hiking trails and crystal-clear lakes for paddling a canoe.

The Gunflint Trail will take you through the Boundary Waters Canoe Area Wilderness and deeper into the national forest. It offers anglers the opportunity for trying their luck at catching brook and rainbow trout, walleye, bass, and northern pike. Those interested in hiking will find access to the Superior Hiking Trail, Border Route Trail, and Kekekabic Trail. In winter, there are miles of well groomed trails for cross-country skiing, snowmobiling and snowshoeing. For additional detailed information on the recreational possibilities refer to The Gunflint Trail Association listed below.

Information: Superior National Forest, 8901 Grand Ave Pl, Duluth MN 55808 / 218-626-4300. The Gunflint Trail Association, PO Box 205, Grand Marais MN 55604 / 800-338-6932. Temperance River State Park, Box 33, Schroeder MN 55613 / 218-663-7476. Cascade River State Park, 3481 W Hwy 61, Lutsen MN 55612 / 218-387-3053. Judge C.R. Magney State Park, 4051 E Hwy 61, Grand Marais MN 55604 / 218-387-3039.

Lodging Invitation

Cascade Lodge	Phone:	218-387-1112 / 800-322-9543
HC 3, Box 445	Fax:	218-387-1113
Lutsen, MN 55612	Internet:	http://www.cascadelodgemn.com

Located in the midst of Cascade River State Park and overlooking Lake Superior offering spectacular views. Accommodation options include rooms in the historic main lodge, log cabins with fireplaces and a house. Some units include kitchens and whirlpools. Distinctive family restaurant and gift shop. Nearby fishing, tennis, golf, and alpine skiing. Outstanding hiking, cross country skiing, and mountain bike trails begin at the lodge. The hiking trails connect to the Superior Hiking trail and the ski trails with the North Shore ski trail system. Open all year. AAA rated. Located on Hwy. 61 midway between Lutsen and Grand Marais, 100 miles NE of Duluth.

The Gunflint Trail Association	Phone:	800-338-6932
P.O. Box 205		218-387-2870
Grand Marais, MN 55604		

Each season on The Gunflint Trail offers a variety of activities everyone can enjoy. The

Gunflint Trail lodges, cabins, campsites, and outfitters are unique, privately owned resorts operated by families and individuals in the pioneer tradition. They have a knowledge and love of this wilderness area and an eagerness to share its beauty and recreational opportunities with you. The resorts and businesses listed below are members of The Gunflint Trail Association. These establishments along the Trail have joined together to help make your vacation here a memorable experience. You may contact the association at the address listed above for general information on the area and/or the members listed below for detailed information on their location.

Association Members:

Association Members	Cabin	Campground	Bed & Breakfast	Canoe Outfitters
Bearskin Lodge, 800-338-4170	•			
Borderland Lodge Resort, 800-451-1667	•			
Boundary Country Trekking, 800-322-8327	•			
Boundary Waters Adventures, 800-894-0128	•			
Clearwater Canoe Outfitters & Lodge, 800-527-0554	•			•
Golden Eagle Lodge, 800-346-2203	•			
Gunflint Lodge, 800-328-3325	•			
Gunflint Northwoods Outfitters, 800-362-5251	•			
Gunflint Pines Resort & Campground, 800-533-5814	•	•		
Heston's Country Store & Cabins, 800-338-7230	•			
Hungry Jack Lodge, 800-338-1566	•	•		
Hungry Jack Outfitters, 800-648-2922				•
Loon Lake Lodge, 800-552-6351	•			
Nor'Wester Lodge & Canoe Outfitters, 800-992-4FUN	•	•		•
Old Northwoods Lodge, 800-682-8264	•			
Pincushion Mountain Bed & Breakfast, 800-542-1226			•	
Rockwood Lodge & Outfitters, 800-942-2922	•			•
Sea Island Lodge Resort & Dining Room, 800-346-8906	•			
Seagull Creek Fishing Camp, 800-531-5510	•			
Seagull Outfitters, 800-346-2205				•
Spirit of the Land Island Hostel, 800-454-2922	•			
Superior Properties, 800-950-4360	•			
Superior-North Canoe Outfitters, 800-852-2008				•
Top of the Trail Outfitters, 800-869-0883				•
Trail Center, 800-972-3066	•			
Trout Lake Resort, 800-258-7688	•			
Tuscarora Lodge & Outfitters, 800-544-3843	•			•
Voyageur Canoe Outfitters, 800-777-7215				•
Way of the Wilderness Canoe Outfitters, 800-346-6625				•
Windigo Lodge, 800-535-4320	•	•		

Scenic Highway

Scenic Highway is in north-central Minnesota about 20 miles east of Bemidji. The byway's northern terminus is near Blackduck on

US 71. It travels south across the Chippewa National Forest and Leech Lake Indian Reservation to the junction with US 2. Scenic Highway is 12 miles long and follows Beltrami County Road 39 and Cass County Road 10. Both are two-lane paved roads safe for travel by all types of vehicles. Delays are possible during winter, otherwise the byway remains open all year.

Scenic Highway crosses the Chippewa National Forest through mixed stands of hardwood trees, evergreens, and wetlands. The southern portion of the byway travels adjacent to the shores of Cass Lake. Beautiful fall colors decorate the byway with colors of orange, red, and gold. White-tailed deer can sometimes be seen from the byway foraging among the open wetlands. These areas are also good locations for spotting a great blue heron or two.

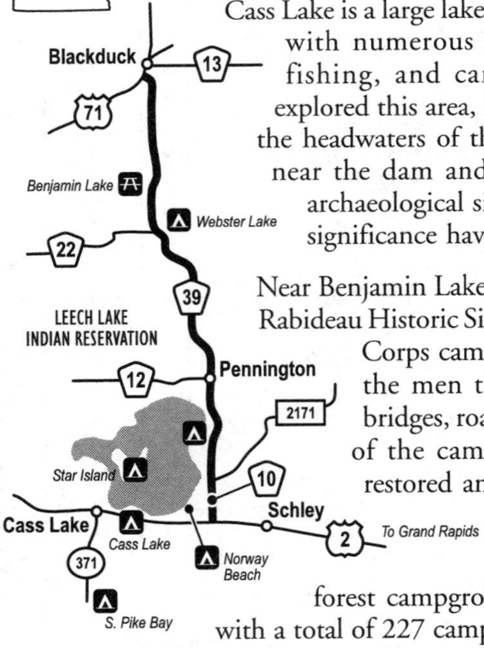

Cass Lake is a large lake on the west side of the byway with numerous opportunities for boating, fishing, and camping. When Lewis Cass explored this area, he thought he had discovered the headwaters of the Mississippi River. Located near the dam and along the river are several archaeological sites where artifacts of historic significance have been discovered.

Near Benjamin Lake Recreation Area is the Camp Rabideau Historic Site. This Civilian Conservation Corps camp was built in 1935 to house the men that constructed fire towers, bridges, roads, and trails in the area. Four of the camp's 15 buildings have been restored and are open to the public for touring during the summer.

There are several national forest campgrounds surrounding Cass Lake with a total of 227 campsites. Facilities vary but most provide drinking water, picnic tables, and fire rings. Near the byway's northern end is the Webster Lake Campground with 24 campsites. To the west of the byway, north of Bemidji is Lake Bemidji State Park. There are 98 campsites available with many having RV hookups. The park also offers miles of hiking, snowmobiling, and cross-country skiing trails.

Information: Chippewa National Forest, Rt 3 Box 244, Cass Lake MN 56633 / 218-335-8600. Lake Bemidji State Park, 3401 State Park Rd NE, Bemidji MN 56601 / 218-755-3843.

Mississippi

1 Natchez Trace Parkway, *150*

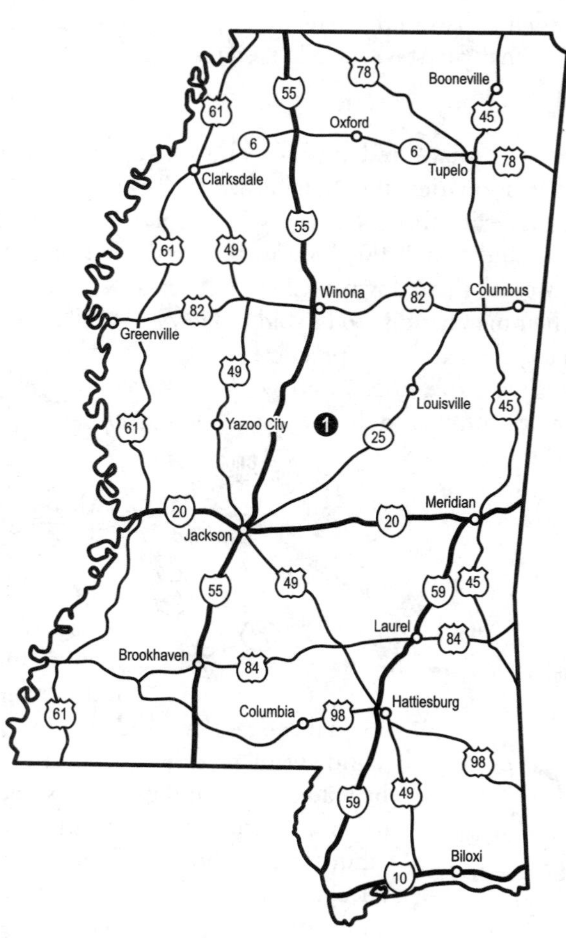

Natchez Trace Parkway

Alabama section see page 9 / Tennessee portion see page 272

This historic route generally follows the old Indian trace, or trail, between Nashville, Tennessee and Natchez, Mississippi. This is the longest portion of the parkway as it crosses Mississippi from Natchez to the Alabama state line, a distance of 310 miles. The parkway is a two-lane paved road suitable for all types of vehicles and remains open year-round. A small 17-mile portion running through Tombigbee National Forest is officially designated a National Forest Scenic Byway.

Once trekked by Indians and trampled into a rough road by traders, trappers, and missionaries, the Natchez Trace Parkway is now a scenic 445-mile route traveling from Natchez, Mississippi to Nashville, Tennessee. In the late 1700s and early 1800s, "Kaintucks," as the river merchants were called, would float downriver on flatboats loaded with their merchandise to be sold in New Orleans. Since there wasn't any practical way to return by river, the boats were dismantled and the lumber sold. The Natchez Trace would be the only pathway home.

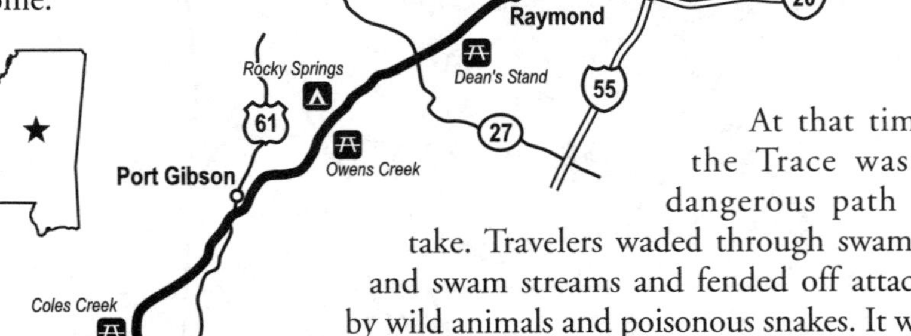

At that time, the Trace was a dangerous path to take. Travelers waded through swamps and swam streams and fended off attacks by wild animals and poisonous snakes. It was also necessary to keep an eye open for murderous bandits and Indian attacks. The terrain of the trace was rough, too. A broken leg of a lone traveler would often mean certain death. The dangers of the route earned the Trace the nickname "Devil's Backbone." Modern-day travelers don't have these dangers to face as they travel this historic route.

You can begin your drive on the parkway in the historic town of Natchez. Natchez boasts an incredible 500 antebellum structures, including homes, churches, and public buildings. Prior to the Civil War, more than half of the millionaires in the United States lived in Natchez. Several of the beautiful mansions are open year-round for guided tours.

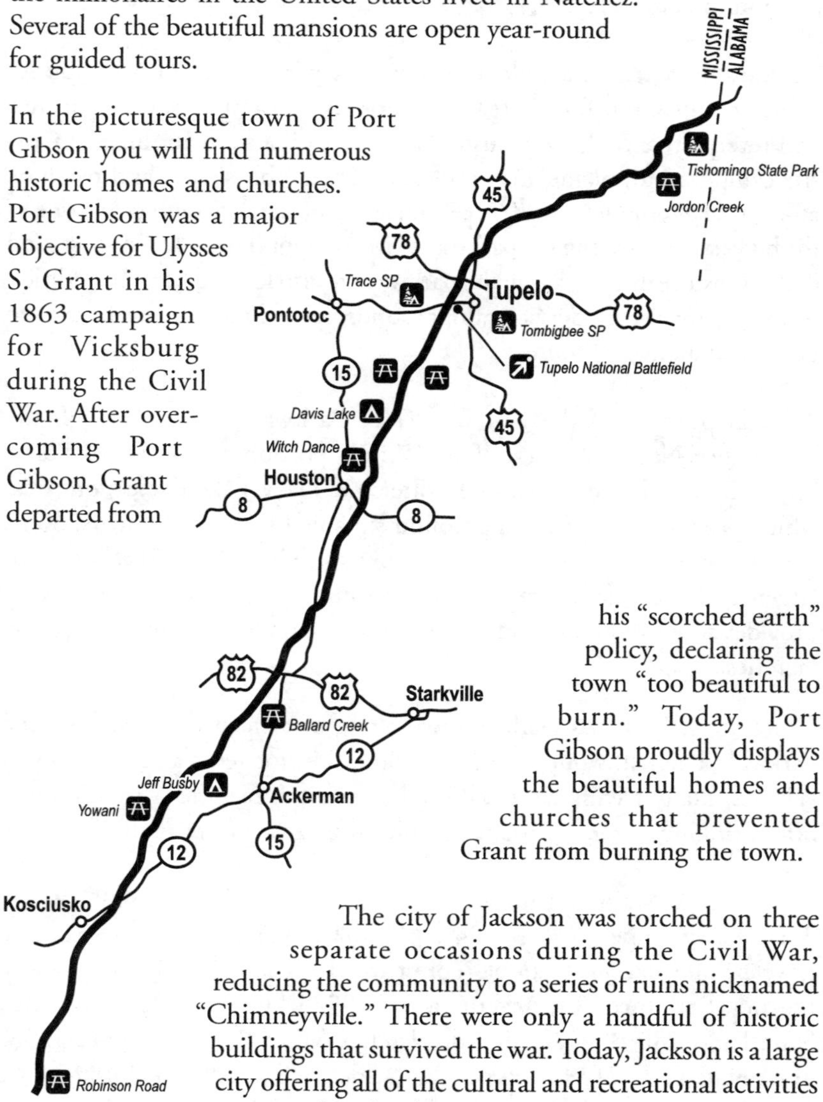

In the picturesque town of Port Gibson you will find numerous historic homes and churches. Port Gibson was a major objective for Ulysses S. Grant in his 1863 campaign for Vicksburg during the Civil War. After overcoming Port Gibson, Grant departed from his "scorched earth" policy, declaring the town "too beautiful to burn." Today, Port Gibson proudly displays the beautiful homes and churches that prevented Grant from burning the town.

The city of Jackson was torched on three separate occasions during the Civil War, reducing the community to a series of ruins nicknamed "Chimneyville." There were only a handful of historic buildings that survived the war. Today, Jackson is a large city offering all of the cultural and recreational activities associated with a large city.

On the parkway's northern end is the city of Tupelo. It is here that the parkway headquarters and visitor center are located. A museum within the visitor center houses artifacts and displays chronicling the history and development of the old Natchez Trace and the modern parkway. Audiovisual programs tell the story of the historic trail. A nature trail is also found here.

Recreational activities are plentiful along the parkway. The Rocky Springs recreation area, north of Port Gibson, offers 22 campsites, a picnic area, and interpretive trails. Jeff Busby Park, west of Ackerman, offers an 18-site campground, picnic area, trails, and an exhibit shelter and overlook atop Little Mountain. At 603 feet in elevation, Little Mountain is one of the highest points along the parkway in Mississippi. The only service station and campstore directly along the parkway are also located here. In addition to the National Park Service campgrounds, several picnic areas have been developed along the route.

A small portion of the Natchez Trace Parkway travels through the Tombigbee National Forest. This 17-mile portion is a National Forest Scenic Byway. The national forest offers the Davis Lake Recreation Area, which provides a 24-site campground suitable for tents or trailers. Some of the campsites have electrical hookups. The lake is stocked with largemouth bass, catfish, crappie, and bream. The Witchdance picnic area provides access to hiking and horseback riding trails, in addition to picnic facilities.

There are several state parks located along or a short distance from the parkway. The parks offer numerous campsites for tents and recreational vehicles, many having electrical hookups. Other facilities vary but most offer drinking water, restrooms, picnic areas, and nature trails.

Information: National Park Service, Natchez Trace Pkwy, 2680 Natchez Trace Pkwy, Tupelo MS 38804 / 662-680-4025 or 800-305-7417 for traveler information. National Forest In Mississippi, Tombigbee Ranger District, Rt 1 Box 98A, Ackerman MS 39735 / 601-285-3264. Natchez State Park, 280-B Wickcliff Rd, Natchez MS 39120 / 601-442-2658. Trace State Park, 2139 Faulkner Rd, Belden MS 38826 / 662-489-2958. Tombigbee State Park, 264 Cabin Dr, Tupelo MS 38801 / 662-842-7669. Tishomingo State Park, PO Box 880, Tishomingo MS 38873 / 662-438-6914. Casey Jones Railroad Museum State Park, 10501 Vaughan Rd #1, Vaughan MS 39179 / 601-673-9864.

Lodging Invitation

Cabot Lodge - Jackson North
120 Dyess Road
Ridgeland, MS 39157

Phone: 601-957-0757
800-342-2268
Fax: 601-957-0757

Designed around a most hospitable concept, Cabot Lodge offers you such a relaxing atmosphere, you'll get the feeling you never left home. Right away you'll notice the beautiful atrium with its central fireplace, antler chandeliers, unique wooden end tables and comfortable furniture. The walls of windows lead you out into the courtyards where the gardens are meticulously maintained. All 208 attractive guest rooms offer such amenities as satellite TV, movie channels and direct dial phones. The front desk stocks a complimentary supply of travel necessities available on request. Your stay includes a generous complimentary deluxe continental breakfast and a two hour cocktail reception in the evening. Located in northeast Jackson off I-55 north, just minutes from the Natchez Trace exit.

Fairview Inn
734 Fairview Street
Jackson, MS 39202

Phone: 888-948-1908 / 601-948-3429
Fax: 601-948-1203
E-mail: fairview@fairviewinn.com

Colonial Revival mansion on National Register of Historic Places. Eight elegant rooms and suites all with private baths, cable TV, phones, and data ports. Full breakfast. AAA 4-Diamond. Named a "Top Inn of 1994" by Country Inns Magazine. In 1996 presented an Award of Excellence in the field of Hospitality and Fine Cuisine by Country Inns and The James Beard Foundation. AMEX, Discover, MC, and Visa cards accepted.

MISSOURI

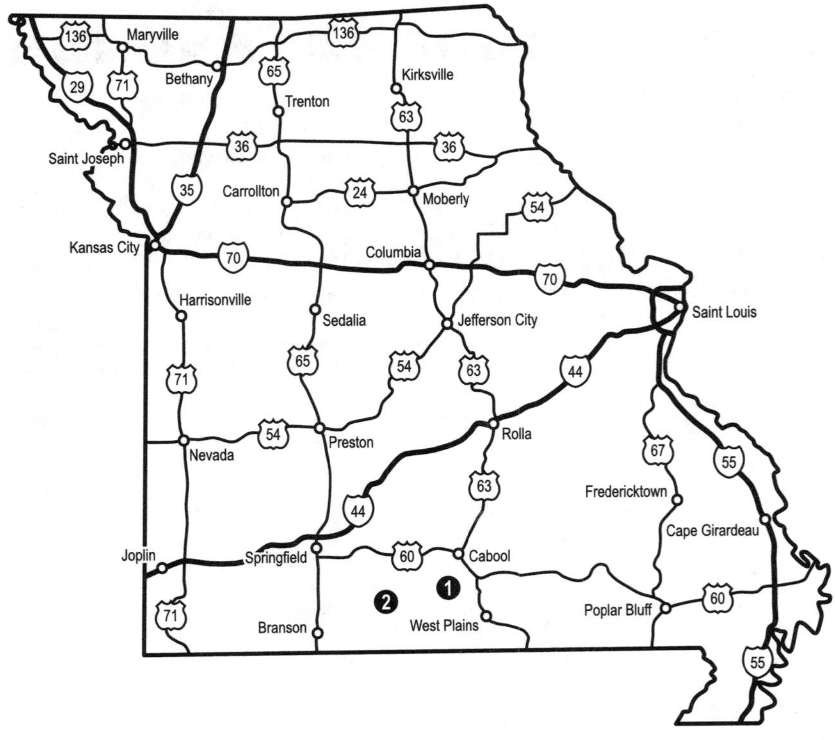
136
Maryville
Bethany
29
71
65
136
Kirksville
Trenton
63
36
36
Saint Joseph
35
Carrollton
24
Moberly
54
Kansas City
70
Columbia
70
Saint Louis
Harrisonville
Sedalia
Jefferson City
65
54
63
44
71
54
Preston
Rolla
Nevada
67
55
63
Fredericktown
44
Cape Girardeau
Joplin
Springfield
60
Cabool
1
2
Poplar Bluff
60
71
Branson
West Plains
55

Blue Buck Knob

US FS Blue Buck Knob is in south-central Missouri about 75 miles east of Springfield. It begins in Cabool and travels south through the Mark Twain National Forest to the intersection with MO 14. The byway is nearly 30 miles long and follows Missouri Highways 76, 181, and "AP." The state highways are two-lane paved roads suitable for all vehicles. Blue Buck Knob generally remains open year-round.

The Blue Buck Knob scenic byway travels through Missouri's Ozark hill country within the Mark Twain National Forest. It twists and turns through farmland, open pastures, and densely wooded hillsides. Many tree-lined spur roads tempt the byway traveler to take a side trip and further explore the national forest.

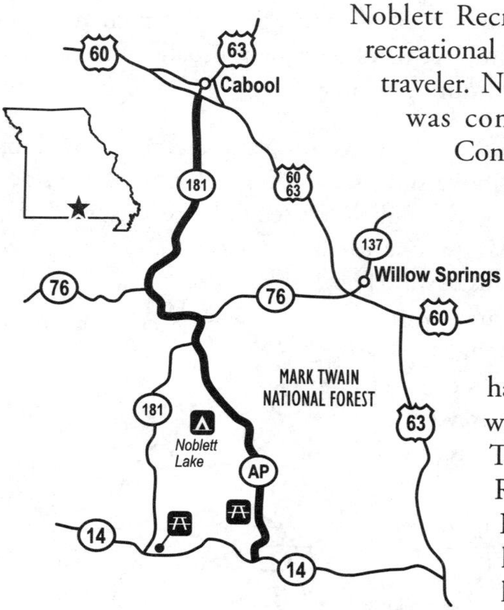

60
63
Cabool
181
60
63
137
Willow Springs
76
76
60
MARK TWAIN NATIONAL FOREST
181
63
Noblett Lake
AP
14
14

Noblett Recreation Area offers diverse recreational opportunities for the byway traveler. Noblett is a 27-acre lake that was constructed by the Civilian Conservation Corps during the 1930s. The remains of the CCC camp are accessible just a few miles away by gravel road. A boat ramp provides access to this scenic lake set among the hardwood trees. A nine-mile walking trail circles the lake. The northern trailhead of the Ridge Runner National Recreation Trail is also located here. This hiking trail heads south through the forest to the North Fork Recreation Area. A campground is in Noblett Recreation Area and has 25 tree-shaded sites with picnic tables and fire rings. No hookups are provided. Fishermen may wish to spend some time trying to pull bass, bluegill, crappie, or catfish from the lake.

Other recreational activities are available throughout the national forest. Wildlife observers will want to be on the lookout for white-tailed deer or wild turkey that were reintroduced to Missouri in the 1930s. The North Fork of the White River offers canoeing enthusiasts a pleasurable float among rugged rock outcrops and densely wooded forests. Horseback riding, hunting, and hiking are also popular recreational opportunities on the Mark Twain National Forest.

Information: Mark Twain National Forest, 401 Fairgrounds Rd, Rolla MO 65401 / 573-364-4621.

Glade Top Trail

US FS Glade Top Trail is in southwest Missouri about 55 miles southeast of Springfield. To reach the northern terminus from Ava, follow MO 5 south to MO "A." Follow MO "A" to CR 409 and take CR 409 to the national forest entrance, where the byway officially begins. Glade Top Trail is 23 miles long and follows FSR 147 and FSR 149, which are two-lane gravel roads suitable for most vehicles. The roads usually remain open year-round; caution is needed during winter.

The Glade Top Trail cuts across the Mark Twain National Forest traveling through narrow ridge tops above the surrounding rolling countryside. Numerous scenic vistas of the Springfield Plateau to the west and the Saint Francis and Boston Mountains to the south reward the traveler of this byway. The changing seasons paint the area with brilliant colors of red and orange in autumn. Dogwood, serviceberry, redbud, and wild fruit trees make their presence known in the spring.

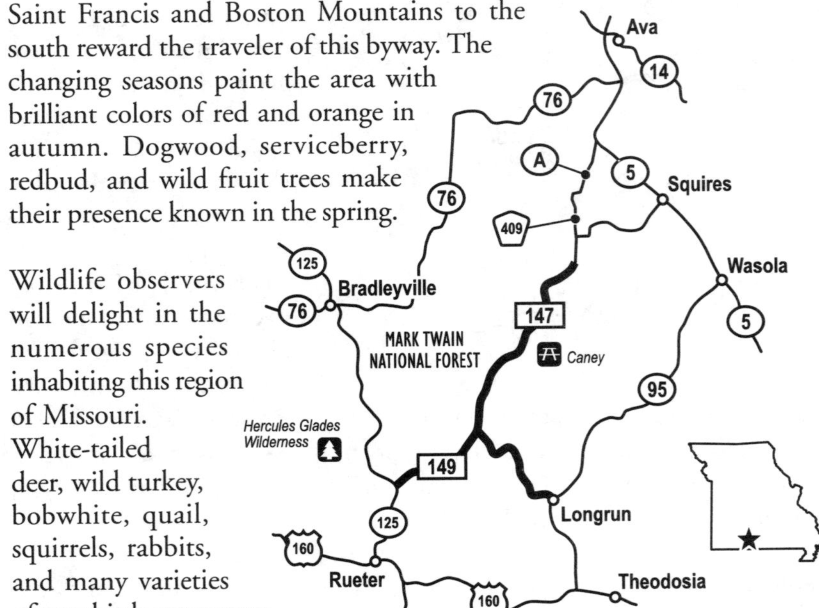

Wildlife observers will delight in the numerous species inhabiting this region of Missouri. White-tailed deer, wild turkey, bobwhite, quail, squirrels, rabbits, and many varieties of songbirds are among the wildlife seen along the byway. The glades also provide a home for wildlife not often encountered in the Ozarks, such as the roadrunner.

Developed recreational facilities are limited. There are no public campgrounds along the byway, however, the Caney Picnic Area provides a nice spot for taking a break and enjoying lunch. A short hiking trail here leads to a small but interesting cave. The nearest national forest camping facilities are 30 miles northwest on MO 125.

The Mark Twain National Forest provides other recreational pursuits in addition to picnicking. Numerous side roads make for a pleasurable drive, taking you farther into the national forest. They also offer a challenge to those interested in bicycling. The Hercules Glades Wilderness to the west of the byway has several trails for hiking or horseback riding. Many rivers and streams running through the forest provide anglers with the opportunity to catch bass, bluegill, catfish, or crappie.

Branson lies approximately 30 miles west of the byway and offers music shows, a scenic train ride, and opportunities for outdoor recreation.

Information: Mark Twain National Forest, 401 Fairgrounds Rd, Rolla MO 65401 / 573-364-4621.

MONTANA

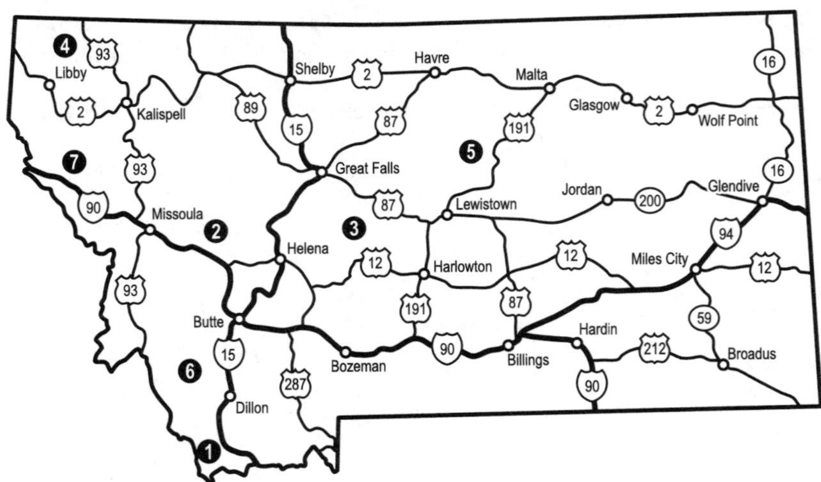

Libby
Kalispell
Shelby
Havre
Malta
Glasgow
Wolf Point
Great Falls
Lewistown
Jordan
Glendive
Missoula
Helena
Harlowton
Miles City
Butte
Hardin
Bozeman
Billings
Broadus
Dillon
93
2
89
15
87
191
16
90
200
12
94
59
212
287

Big Sheep Creek

BLM 1

Big Sheep Creek is in southwest Montana about 25 miles south of Dillon. It begins in Dell on I-15 and ends at the junction with MT 324, east of Grant. The 50-mile route follows Big Sheep Creek and Medicine Lodge Roads. The roads are primarily two-lane gravel roads; a short stretch is a narrow, dirt road. Two-wheel drive vehicles can safely drive the byway. Motorhomes and vehicles pulling trailers should not attempt to complete the byway. Big Sheep Creek Back Country Byway is usually open May through early October.

From Dell, the Big Sheep Creek Back Country Byway makes its way through steep canyon walls with Big Sheep Creek flowing alongside. This spring-fed creek attracts bighorn sheep and deer, which are commonly seen in the evening. Numerous side roads tempt the byway traveler to further explore the canyon on foot, by bicycle, or in the comfort of your vehicle.

Once through the canyon, the byway heads north through the open spaces of Medicine Lodge Valley, surrounded by the Tendoy Mountains to the east and the Bitterroot Range to the west. Through this portion of the byway, Medicine Lodge Creek meanders nearby. Side roads from here will take you into the Beaverhead National Forest for hiking and backpacking opportunities.

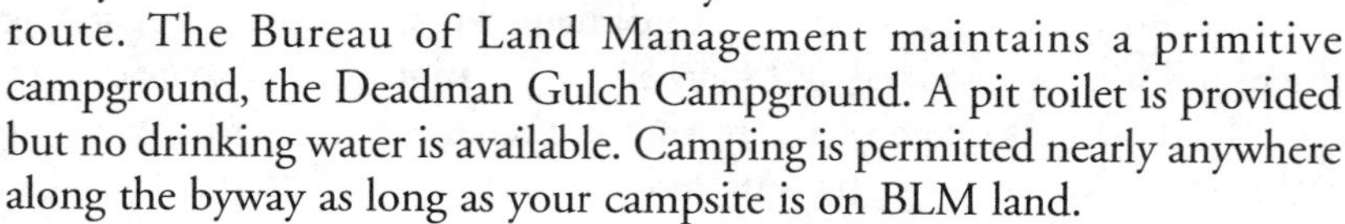

Developed recreational facilities are nearly nonexistent on this back country route. The Bureau of Land Management maintains a primitive campground, the Deadman Gulch Campground. A pit toilet is provided but no drinking water is available. Camping is permitted nearly anywhere along the byway as long as your campsite is on BLM land.

More developed camping facilities may be found in the Clark Canyon Reservoir area and Bannack State Park. The state park, north of Grant, is the site of Montana's first major gold discovery and a well-preserved ghost town. The town once boasted of a population over 3,000 and became the state's first territorial capital in 1864. There are 30 campsites available for tents and recreational vehicles; there are no hookups.

Information: BLM-Dillon Field Office, 1005 Selway Dr, Dillon MT 59725 / 406-683-2337. Beaverhead National Forest, 420 Barrett St, Dillon MT 59725 / 406-683-3900. Bannack State Park, 4200 Bannack Rd, Dillon MT 59725 / 406-834-3413.

Garnet Range

Garnet Range is approximately 30 miles east of Missoula in western Montana. It begins south of Greenough on MT 200 and travels east to the area of Reynolds City ghost town. The byway is 12 miles long and follows Garnet Range Road, which is accessible by car in good weather from May through October. From January through April, the route is marked and groomed as a National Winter Recreation Trail for snowmobile use and cross-country skiing.

From MT 200, the Garnet Range scenic byway climbs 2,000 feet into the evergreen forest of the Garnet Mountains and offers spectacular views of the Mission, Rattlesnake, Swan, and Sapphire mountain ranges. The byway provides access to one of the best-preserved ghost towns remaining in Montana, the gold mining town of Garnet.

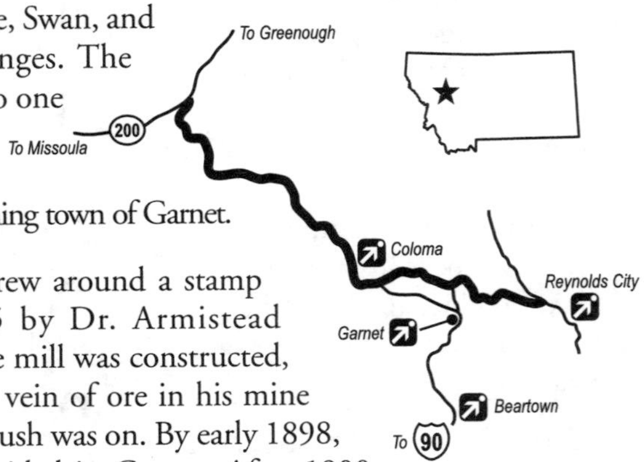

The town of Garnet grew around a stamp mill erected in 1895 by Dr. Armistead Mitchell. Soon after the mill was constructed, Sam Ritchey hit a rich vein of ore in his mine just west of town. The rush was on. By early 1898, nearly 1,000 people resided in Garnet. After 1900 the gold, however, became scarce and difficult to mine. By 1905 many of the mines were abandoned and Garnet's population shrunk to 150. Fire in 1912 destroyed much of the town and the advent of World War I in 1914 drew most of the remaining residents away to defense-related jobs. By the 1920s, Garnet had become a ghost town.

The Garnet Range byway is part of a 55-mile system of snowmobile and cross-country ski trails. A visitor center is located in Garnet and offers more detailed information on the town and the recreational opportunities found in the area. During winter, there are two cabins in Garnet that are available for rent.

Information: BLM-Missoula Field Office, 3255 Fort Missoula Rd, Missoula MT 59804 / 406-329-3914.

Kings Hill

Kings Hill is in central Montana about 25 miles southeast of Great Falls. It follows US 89 for 70 miles between Armington and White Sulphur Springs. US 89 is a two-lane paved road suitable for all types of vehicles and generally remains open year-round. Driving the byway in winter requires extra caution.

The Kings Hill National Forest Scenic Byway travels through dense forests, limestone canyons, and grassy meadows as it crosses the Little Belt Mountains. The byway crosses Kings Hill Pass at an elevation of 7,393 feet. An observation tower near the pass provides panoramic views of the surrounding mountains. The meandering Belt Creek follows alongside most of the byway from Kings Hill Pass northward.

A variety of wildlife is found within the national forest and this part of Montana. Mule deer and elk may be seen grazing along streams or in meadows. Golden eagles or red-tailed hawks can be seen gracefully soaring above. Another form of wildlife inhabiting this area that you may not necessarily wish to see is the black bear.

The byway traveler is provided with numerous opportunities for outdoor recreation. Winter brings cross-country skiers and snowmobilers to the area for its many miles of groomed trails. Downhill skiing is also a popular wintertime activity. Warmer months bring anglers to the area's many lakes and streams. Species of fish include rainbow, cutthroat, and brook trout, among others.

Several camping areas are located directly along the byway and within the national forest. Facilities will vary but most provide campsites with picnic tables and fire rings, restrooms, and drinking water. A couple of miles north of the Many Pines Campground is a short hiking trail that leads to the scenic Memorial Falls.

Information: Lewis And Clark National Forest, 1101 15th St N, Great Falls MT 59401 / 406-791-7700.

Lake Koocanusa

US FS Lake Koocanusa scenic byway is located in northwestern Montana, northeast of Libby. The byway forms a loop drive around Lake Koocanusa between Libby and Eureka. It is 88 miles long and follows MT 37 and FSR 228, which are two-lane paved roads suitable for all vehicles. Temporary closure is possible during winter, otherwise the byway remains open year-round.

The Lake Koocanusa scenic byway travels across Kootenai National Forest through ponderosa pine, lodgepole pine, and Douglas fir. The lake for which the byway is named is a 90-mile long reservoir reaching into Canada. It was created by the construction of Libby Dam. Many scenic turnouts provide excellent views of the lake and surrounding mountains. A visitor center at the dam provides information and guided tours of the 370-foot high structure.

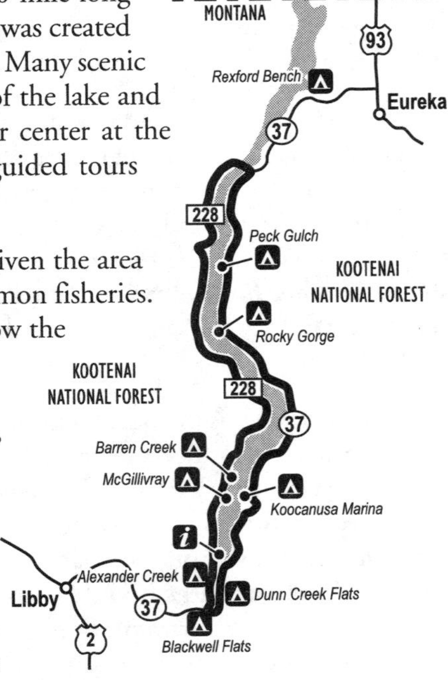

Excellent fishing in the lake has given the area a reputation as one of the best salmon fisheries. The lake and Kootenai River below the dam provide excellent opportunities for catching rainbow, westslope, cutthroat, bull trout, kokanee salmon, and brook trout.

Several recreation areas are located along the byway. Rocky Gorge has 120 campsites suitable for tents and recreational vehicles. A boat ramp gives access to the lake. Peck Gulch has restrooms, a boat ramp, and plenty of sites for picnicking or camping. The Barron Creek Recreation Site has a boat ramp and dispersed camping areas. McGillivray Recreation Site is a campground and day use area with group picnic shelters. Overnight camping, ball fields, a swimming beach, and a boat ramp are available. A short boat ride from this recreation area will take you to Yarnell Islands, which have camping and picnicking facilities.

Numerous side roads invite further exploration of Kootenai National Forest. The forest offers a total of 35 camping areas with over 600 campsites. Dispersed camping is also permitted nearly anywhere on public lands. Five national recreation trails are within the national forest for those interested in hiking or backpacking. Little North Fork Trail is near the byway and guides you to a scenic waterfall.

Information: Kootenai National Forest, 506 US Hwy 2 W, Libby MT 59923 / 406-293-6211. Lake Koocanusa, U.S. Army Corps of Engineers, 17115 MT 37, Libby MT 59923 / 406-293-7751 or 406-293-5577 visitor center.

Missouri Breaks

BLM 2 Located in north-central Montana, Missouri Breaks lies about 40 miles north of Lewiston. Eastern access is in the Charles M. Russell National Wildlife Refuge at US 191. It forms a loop drive back to US 191 with four side trips to scenic overlooks along the Missouri River. The 73-

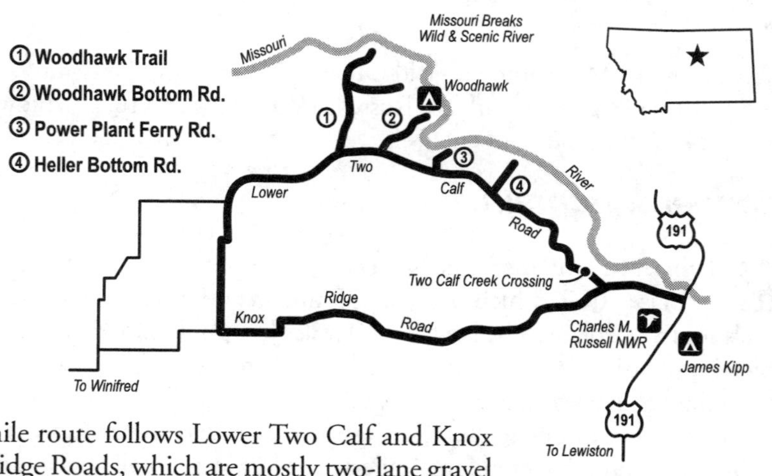

mile route follows Lower Two Calf and Knox Ridge Roads, which are mostly two-lane gravel and dirt roads that can be negotiated by passenger cars in dry weather.

Large RVs and vehicles pulling trailers should not attempt the Two Calf Creek Crossing nor the side roads off Lower Two Calf Road. Missouri Breaks is generally passable May through October.

The Missouri Breaks Back Country Byway crosses a ruggedly beautiful landscape alongside portions of the Upper Missouri National Wild and Scenic River. A 149-mile segment was designated in 1976 as a wild and scenic river to preserve the river and its natural surroundings. Much of the river is the same today as Lewis and Clark saw it in May of 1805 on their journey to the Pacific Northwest.

Several side trips off the main route lead to scenic overlooks on the Missouri River. Woodhawk Trail takes you to Sunshine and Deweese Ridges where the river flows almost directly beneath you. Woodhawk Bottom Road will take you down to the banks of the river. A BLM campground here has five sites with picnic tables for those interested in staying overnight.

A variety of wildlife inhabits the area. Some 60 species of mammals, 233 species of birds, and 20 species of amphibians and reptiles may be found here. Wildlife observers will want to be on the lookout for antelope, white-tailed deer and mule deer, elk, and bighorn sheep. Prairie dogs, beaver, pheasant, sage grouse, and a large variety of song birds may also be seen.

Camping is available at the Woodhawk Campground and at James Kipp Recreation Area in the Charles M. Russell National Wildlife Refuge. The James Kipp Recreation Area has 28 sites with picnic tables and fire rings. A boat ramp provides access to the river. Pit toilets and drinking water are also available.

Information: BLM-Lewistown Field Office, PO Box 1160, Lewiston MT 59457 / 406-538-7461. Charles M Russell NWR, PO Box 110, Lewistown MT 59457 / 406-538-8706.

Pioneer Mountains

US FS Pioneer Mountains scenic byway is in southwest Montana. It begins in Wise River, which is about 35 miles southwest of Butte, and travels south to Polaris. The byway is 40 miles long and follows FSR 484, which is primarily a two-lane paved road suitable for all vehicles. A portion of FSR 484 is a narrow, gravel road that requires slow speeds. This segment of road is near Elkhorn Hot Springs and is not recommended for motorhomes and vehicles pulling trailers. The byway is usually open mid-May to mid-November.

The scenic byway crosses Beaverhead National Forest through lodgepole pine forests and across numerous parks and meadows. Outstanding views of the Pioneer Mountain Range are provided as the byway ascends the divide separating the Wise River and Grasshopper Creek drainages. Both Wise River and Grasshopper Creek flow alongside the byway.

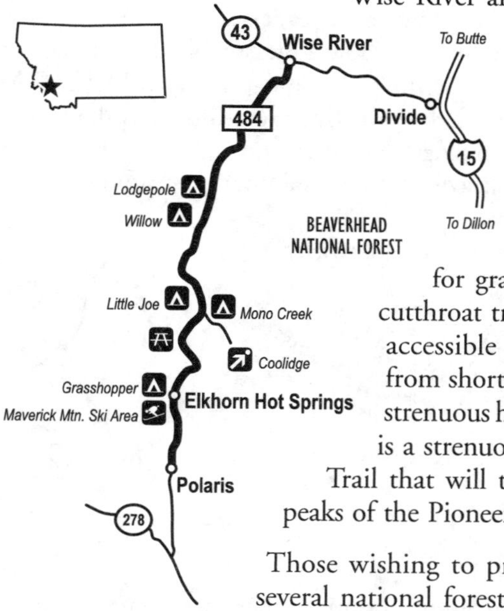

The national forest offers nearly unlimited opportunities for outdoor recreation. The forest's many rivers and creeks provide excellent fishing for grayling, rainbow, brook, and cutthroat trout. Many hiking trails are accessible from the route and range from short, easy walks to longer, more strenuous hikes. The Pioneer Loop Trail is a strenuous 35-mile National Scenic Trail that will take you along the western peaks of the Pioneer Mountains.

Those wishing to prolong their stay will find several national forest campgrounds from which to choose. Lodgepole and Willow Campgrounds provide a total of 12 campsites set among pine trees along the Wise River. Little Joe offers four sites on the river, while Mono Creek Campground has five sites set back about one mile from the byway. Grasshopper is the largest of the campgrounds; it has 24 campsites. All of the campgrounds except Little Joe can accommodate recreational vehicles up to 16 feet long.

A short side trip off the byway will take you to the ghost town of Coolidge. This historic town was built in the 1920s to provide a home base for miners who worked in the Elkhorn silver mine. Remnants of the Elkhorn Mill remain for inspection by visitors.

Information: Beaverhead National Forest, 420 Barrett St, Dillon MT 59725 / 406-683-3900.

Saint Regis to Paradise

The Saint Regis to Paradise scenic byway is located in western Montana about 70 miles northwest of Missoula. It is 22 miles long and follows MT 135 from Saint Regis to the junction with MT 200. The state highway is a two-lane paved road safe for travel by all types of vehicles. It usually remains open year-round but winter driving requires extra caution.

Originally a meandering trail used by homesteaders in the late 1800s, the Saint Regis to Paradise scenic byway is now a pleasurable drive along the scenic Clark Fork River. It travels through the flat, forested Dolan Flats into the canyon walls of the Clark Fork River, which divides the Coeur d'Alene and Cabinet Mountain ranges. Elk, deer, and bighorn sheep inhabit the canyon region and the heavily forested mountains surrounding the route. Bald eagles are occasionally seen, especially during fall and winter months.

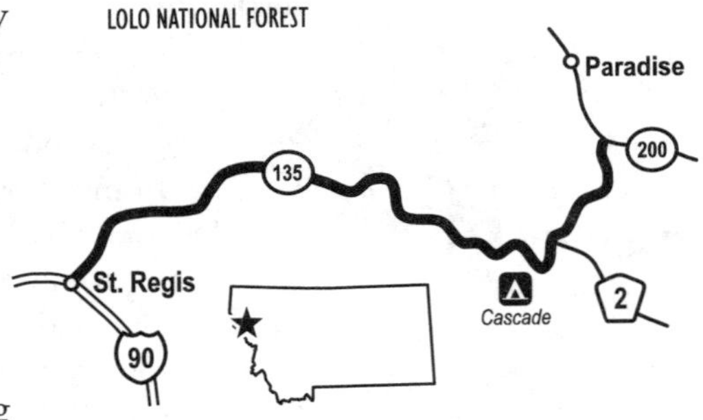

Clark Fork River provides excellent opportunities for those interested in fishing or rafting. The river rapids are of varying levels of difficulty, offering a challenging float trip for all skill levels. If you're not interested in rafting, there are numerous spots where you can enjoy a lunch while watching others float on the river.

Those interested in camping will find only one national forest campground along the byway. Cascade Campground has ten sites that can accommodate recreational vehicles up to 22 feet long. The campground is open from mid-May to the end of October. Other facilities available include drinking water, restrooms, a boat ramp, and hiking trail.

About 25 miles east of the northern end of the byway is the 19,000-acre National Bison Range. This natural grassland area was established in 1908 to protect one of the most important remaining herds of American bison. About 400 of these shaggy animals roam the land. Self-guided auto tours are available year-round. A visitor center provides more information on the bison and the area. Other wildlife in the area includes white-tailed deer, mule deer, bighorn sheep, and pronghorn.

Information: Lolo National Forest, Plains Ranger District, PO Box 429 Plains MT 59859 / 406-826-3821.

Nevada

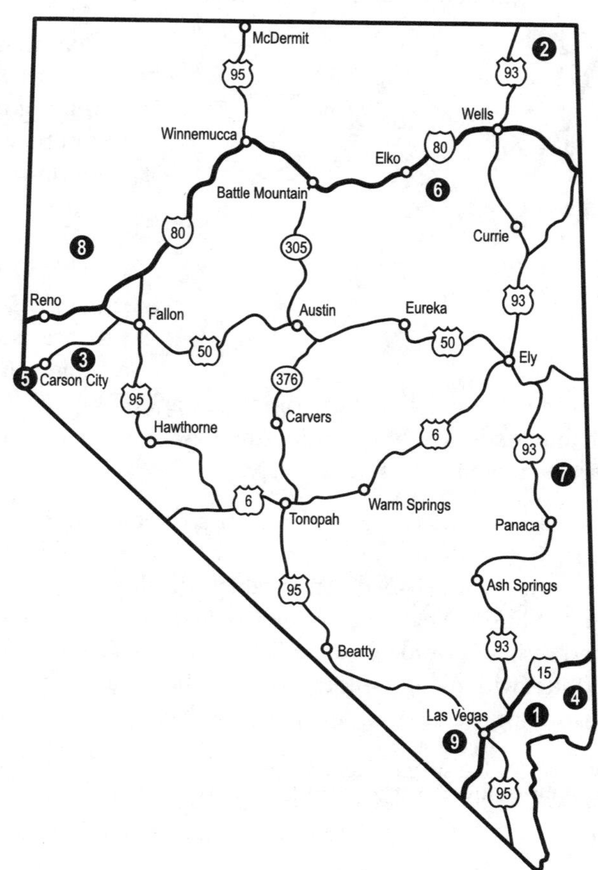

McDermit
2
95
93
Wells
Winnemucca
Elko
80
Battle Mountain
6
80
305
Currie
8
93
Reno
Fallon
Austin
Eureka
50
50
Ely
3
5
Carson City
376
95
Carvers
6
Hawthorne
93
7
6
Warm Springs
Tonopah
Panaca
Ash Springs
95
Beatty
93
15
4
1
Las Vegas
9
95

Bitter Springs Trail

BLM 2 Bitter Springs Trail is about 45 miles northeast of Las Vegas in southeast Nevada. It can be accessed from I-15 by taking Exit 75 and then traveling east. The byway is 28 miles long and follows Bitter Springs Road, which is a single-lane dirt road that requires a two-wheel drive, high-clearance vehicle. The byway usually remains open year-round.

Bitter Springs Trail travels through the foothills of the Muddy Mountains, past abandoned mining operations, and brightly colored sandstone hills. One of the more interesting sites encountered along the route is the Bitter Ridge, a sweeping arc that cuts for eight miles across a rolling valley. Side roads invite the byway traveler to explore the many canyons, but unless you're in a four-wheel drive vehicle, it is not recommended that you attempt to take these side roads.

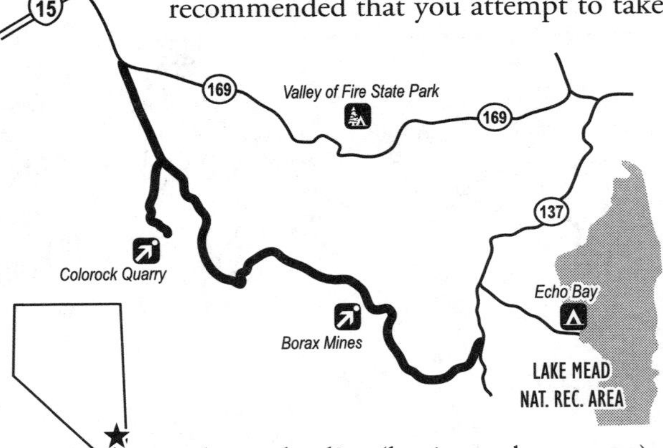

Remnants of the American Borax mining operation can be seen along the byway. Several mine buildings still stand, along with 30-foot deep cisterns that were once used to hold water, mine tunnels, and adits (horizontal passages). Evidence of early human inhabitants is also found along the byway; on many of the canyon walls are pictographs and petroglyphs.

There are no developed recreational facilities directly along the byway, however, camping areas are not too far away. Valley of Fire State Park offers 50 campsites with shaded picnic tables, drinking water, restrooms, and shower facilities. Near the byway's eastern terminus is Echo Bay Campground in Lake Mead National Recreation Area. The campground has over 150 sites with picnic tables and grills. There is also a dump station, restrooms, drinking water, a marina, and a lodge.

Information: BLM-Las Vegas Field Office, 4765 Vegas Dr, Las Vegas NV 89107 / 702-647-5000. Valley of Fire State Park, PO Box 515, Overton NV 89040 / 702-397-2088. Lake Mead NRA, 601 Nevada Hwy, Boulder City NV 89005 / 702-293-8990.

California Trail

The California Trail scenic byway is in northeast Nevada about 75 miles northeast of Elko. It can be accessed in either Thousand Springs or Jackpot on US 93. California Trail is 76 miles long and follows Elko County Roads C765, C763, C761, and C762. All the roads are gravel and are suitable for passenger cars except under adverse weather conditions. The byway is generally open May through October.

California Trail Back Country Byway follows the footsteps and wagon trains of settlers who used this route as the path to a better life in California. Trailmarkers along the byway identify the California Trail. Wagon wheel ruts made by the pioneers can still be seen at many places along the byway. The Mammoth Ruts site is located on private property, please respect the landowners' rights and obtain permission before exploring this site.

As you travel this scenic byway, you'll also be retracing part of the path of the old Magic City Freight Line. This route was once used by horse-drawn wagons to haul goods between Toana, Nevada and Magic City, Idaho (now known as Twin Falls).

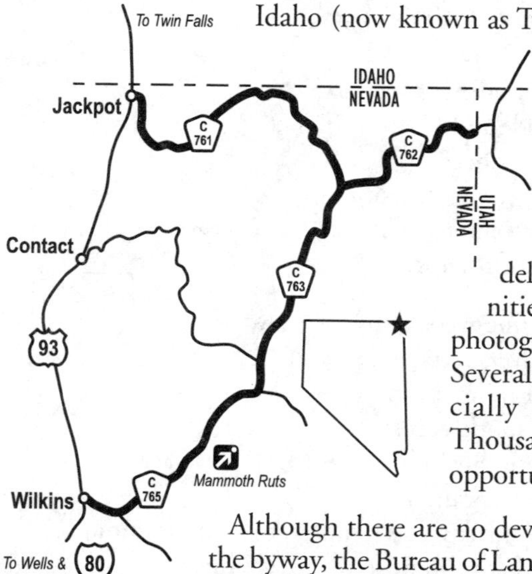

Though this byway travels through isolated countryside, opportunities for outdoor recreation are plentiful. Photographers and wildlife observers will delight in the many opportunities for spotting mule deer or photographing nature's work of art. Several streams and creeks, especially Rock Spring Creek and Thousand Springs Creek provide opportunities for the angler.

Although there are no developed campgrounds along the byway, the Bureau of Land Management does permit dispersed camping nearly anywhere on BLM land. It is best to obtain maps from the BLM that will delineate public lands from private property before setting up camp. Developed camping areas can be found in the Toiyabe National Forest, which lies to the west of the byway.

Information: BLM-Elko Field Office, 3900 E Idaho St, Elko NV 89801 / 775-753-0200.

Fort Churchill to Wellington

Fort Churchill to Wellington is in west-central Nevada ten miles east of Carson City. The eastern terminus is near Fort Churchill State Historic Park off US 95A. The byway heads west to Dayton and then south to end at the junction with NV 208 near Wellington. It follows NV 2B, Como, Sunrise Pass, and Upper Colony Roads for a total of 67 miles. The roads vary from relatively smooth gravel to rough dirt roads. The graveled sections are mostly two lanes while the rougher segments are single lane with steep grades. A four-wheel drive vehicle is necessary to complete the byway; a two-wheel drive, high-clearance vehicle can travel most of the route. Most of the byway is passable year-round. The portion through the Pine Nut Mountains is usually closed in winter.

Fort Churchill SHP is the site of a military establishment that was erected in 1860 to defend settlers and riders of the Pony Express Trail. The stone buildings were used for less than a decade and abandoned in 1869. The fort once had more than 60 buildings; the remains invite exploration. A visitor center has more information on the history of the fort.

Leaving the fort, you continue west along the banks of the Carson River, retracing the Pony Express Trail for 21 miles. From Dayton, the byway heads south across the rugged Pine Nut Mountains. This region is home to wild horses, mountain lions, mule deer, bobcats, and coyotes. Once across the mountains, the route smooths out a bit and continues south to Wellington.

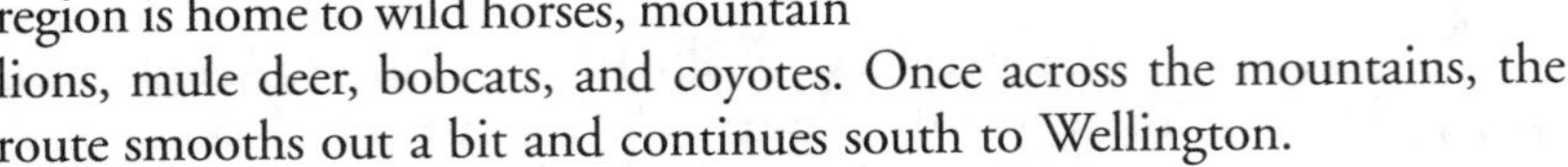

Camping facilities can be found in Fort Churchill SHP and Dayton State Park. The ten-site campground and picnic area in Dayton SP were built on the site of Rock Point Quartz Mill, which dates to 1861.

Information: BLM-Carson City Field Office, 5665 Morgan Mill Rd, Carson City NV 89701 / 775-885-6000. Dayton State Park, PO Box

412, Dayton NV 89403 / 775-687-5678. Ft. Churchill SHP, Old Fort Churchill Rd, Silver Springs NV 89429 / 775-577-2345.

Gold Butte

BLM 2 Gold Butte is in southeast Nevada about 80 miles northeast of Las Vegas. It begins south of Mesquite off NV 170 and travels south to the ghost town of Gold Butte. The byway is 62 miles long and follows Gold Butte Road, splitting at Devil's Throat. The first 24 miles follow a narrow paved road suitable for passenger vehicles. Traveling east of Devil's Throat, the road is a relatively smooth gravel road that is also suitable for passenger cars. The segment heading west from Devil's Throat is a lightly maintained dirt road that requires a high-clearance, two-wheel or four-wheel drive vehicle. Gold Butte Back Country Byway remains open year-round.

Gold Butte Back Country Byway travels across a desert landscape among the foothills of the Virgin Mountains and red rock formations. The Virgin River is seen peacefully flowing alongside the first several miles of the byway. To the east you'll see Virgin Peak towering 8,000 feet above the desert floor. Side roads can take you to the top of this mountain peak.

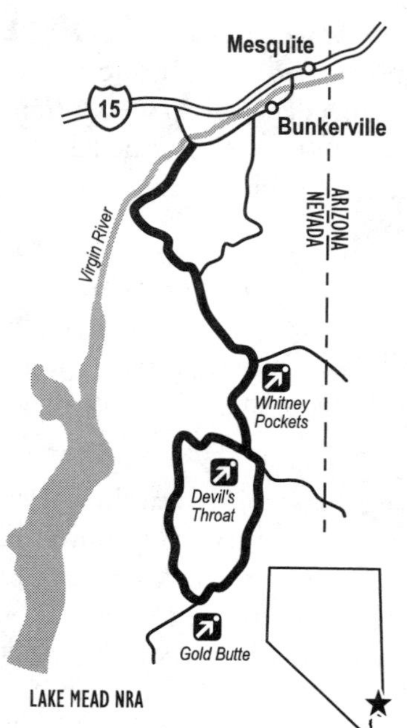

This area is rich in history. Three separate Native American cultures are known to have settled here. Their petroglyph carvings can be seen etched into the rocks. Early non-Indian explorers were followed by the Mormon colonizers who settled in the Mesquite and Bunkerville area in 1877.

Desert wildlife thrives along the byway. Wildlife observers will want to remain alert for the occasional bighorn sheep or mule deer. Mountain lions and the desert tortoise also make their home in this area. Patient observers may occasionally catch a glimpse of wild horses or herds of burro.

The byway passes colorful sandstone rock formations in the area of Whitney Pockets. This area was partially named for a local family and the pockets that have been etched into the cliffs by erosion. The remnants of a Civilian Conservation Corps projects can also be seen in this area.

The byway continues to a split in the road at Devil's Throat, a 100-foot wide by 100-foot deep sinkhole that continues to expand. Whether you turn left or right at this point, you'll end up at the historic mining town of Gold Butte. This town was established in 1908 to service the many mining operations in the area. The town once boasted of a store, hotel, stable, and post office.

Information: BLM-Las Vegas Field Office, 4765 W Vegas Dr, Las Vegas NV 89107 / 702-647-5000. Lake Mead NRA, 601 Nevada Hwy, Boulder City NV 89005 / 702-293-8990.

Lake Tahoe East Shore Drive

Lake Tahoe East Shore Drive is in west-central Nevada about 15 miles west of Carson City. It follows the eastern shore of Lake Tahoe between the cities of King's Beach and South Lake Tahoe. The byway is 30 miles long and follows NV 28 and US 50. Both highways are two-lane paved roads suitable for all types of vehicles. They usually remain open all year.

Lake Tahoe is the largest alpine lake in North America. It stretches for 22 miles north to south and is 12 miles wide. It is said that a white dinner plate can be seen in these crystal-clear waters to a depth of 75 feet. A tram near the lake's south shore takes visitors up 2,000 feet above the lake for spectacular panoramic views of the lake and Lake Tahoe Basin.

Near the byway's northern end is Incline Village. Located here is the Ponderosa Ranch, which was the filming site for the television show "Bonanza." It is now a theme park featuring a petting farm, saloon and a museum. Visitors can stroll through the original Cartwright ranch house and a recreated Western town. The museum displays automobiles, carriages and an antique gun collection.

Recreational opportunities are plentiful along this scenic byway. In winter, the area provides excellent opportunities for cross-country skiing, downhill skiing, snowmobiling, and sledding. Lake Tahoe attracts sailboats and water-skiers during the warmer months. Miles of alpine beaches can be found within Lake Tahoe Nevada State Park and around the lake that provide the perfect spot for a family outing. Numerous side roads and trails provide hiking and mountain biking opportunities. The 63,475-acre

Desolation Wilderness on the California side offers hiking, backpacking, and horseback riding. The Pacific Crest National Scenic Trail also passes through here.

Numerous camping areas are along the byway and within the surrounding national forest land. Washoe Lake State Park is located north of Carson City off US 395. The campground has 50 sites for tents and recreational vehicles with some sites having hookups. It also has drinking water, picnic areas, restrooms, a dump station, and a boat ramp. In South Lake Tahoe is a county park with 170 campsites. Hookups are available at many of the sites. Other facilities include restrooms, picnic areas, shower facilities, and a boat ramp. On the California side is 593-acre Emerald Bay State Park. There are 100 campsites suitable for tents and recreational vehicles. Just north of this state park is the D.L. Bliss State Park which, has 167 campsites. This 1,237-acre park also offers miles of hiking trails.

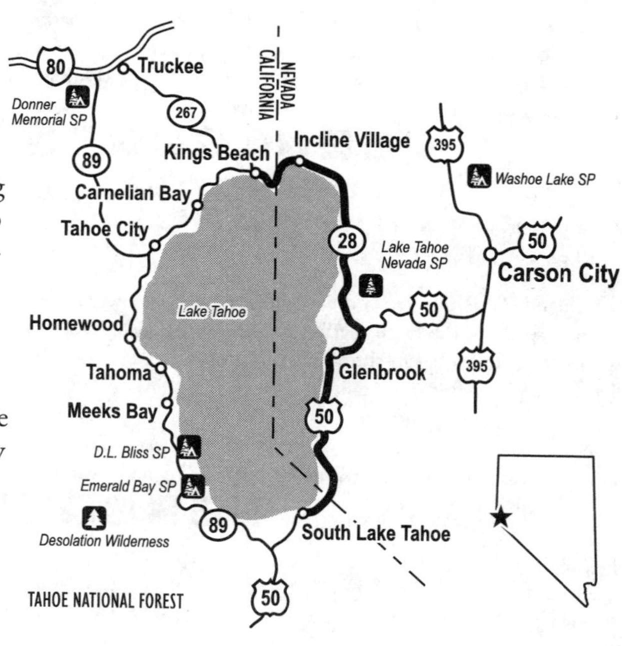

Information: Tahoe National Forest, 631 Coyote St, Nevada City CA 95959 / 530-265-4531. Lake Tahoe Nevada State Park, PO Box 8867, Incline Village NV 89452 / 775-831-0494. Mormon Station SHP, 2295 Main St, Genoa NV 89411 / 775-782-2590. Washoe Lake SRA, 4855 E Lake Blvd, Carson City NV 89704 / 775-687-4319. Emerald Bay State Park, SR 89, Tahoe City CA 96142 / 530-541-3030. D.L. Bliss State Park, PO Box 266, Tahoma CA 96142 / 530-525-7277. Donner Memorial State Park, 12593 Donner Pass Rd, Truckee CA 96161 / 530-582-7892.

Lodging Invitation

Carson Station Hotel / Casino
900 S. Carson Street
Carson City, NV 89701

Phone: 702-883-0900
800-501-2929
Fax: 702-882-7569

The Carson Station Hotel & Casino offers travelers 92 spacious, newly remodeled hotel rooms. The full service casino with cabaret lounge treats guests to live entertainment • sports book • sports bar • restaurant • snack bar • and valet parking. Located near historical district, museums, shopping, state capitol complex, and Governor's Mansion. Only 25 minutes to Lake Tahoe and Reno. Special low-season drive-up packages. We cater to traveling golf groups. Friendly, professional staff.

A/C H

Coachland RV Park
10500 Highway 89 North
Truckee, CA 96161

Phone: 530-587-3071
Fax: 916-587-6976

Coachland RV Park offers a quiet and relaxing environment on 55 acres of pines in the clean crisp air of the High Sierras. Facilities include 131 full hook-up pull through RV spaces with cable TV. On-site laundry, restrooms, and picnic tables. Historical downtown Truckee with it's fine restaurants and shops is within walking distance. Nearby attractions and activities include: golf courses • major ski resorts • Nevada casinos • excellent fishing in numerous lakes and rivers • Lake Tahoe • hiking • mountain biking • river rafting • mines and museums of "The Gold Country". Open all year. Only ¼ mile from I-80.

H

Lampliter Motel
4143 Cedar Avenue
South Lake Tahoe, CA 96150

Phone: 916-544-2936
Fax: 916-544-5249

A quiet location, two blocks off Highway 50, yet in the center of everything. Cozy, spotless, and individually decorated rooms complete with continental breakfast & warm hospitality. You'll want to relax in the elevated spa and enjoy the beautiful views. Guests can dine at the restaurant across the street or walk ¼ block to casino food & entertainment. Only three short blocks away from the marina, golf course and our private beach where you can swim & enjoy all water sports in the crystal waters of Lake Tahoe. Free or low cost shuttles are available to most winter and summer attractions or Reno/Tahoe airport. At Lake Tahoe, the LAMPLITER is THE PLACE to stay! AAA & AARP discounts.

A/C H

Tahoe Colony Inn
3794 Montreal Road
South Lake Tahoe, CA 96150

Phone: 530-544-6481
800-338-5552

At the Tahoe Colony Inn, a 104 unit resort, the Eldorado National Forest is your backyard — with shopping, theaters and restaurants in front. Walking distance to restaurants and casinos, only 3 blocks from Lake Tahoe. Minutes away from golf • skiing • fishing • horseback riding • shopping • and miniature golf. Free continental breakfast and shuttle service to casinos. Year round pool & spa. Discount activity coupons. AAA, AARP & Senior discounts.

Viking Motor Lodge
4083 Cedar Avenue
South Lake Tahoe, CA 96150

Phone: 530-541-5155 / 800-288-4083
Fax: 530-541-5643
E-mail: vikingslt@aol.com

The 76 unit Viking Motor Lodge is conveniently located to the area's many attractions. Only 3 blocks from Lake Tahoe and access to private beach, 1½ blocks to casino's, and 10 minutes to ski slopes. Amenities include: free local calls • cable color TV & HBO • heated pool & spa — open all year • fireplaces in some units • free continental breakfast • free parking • and meeting facilities.

Lamoille Canyon Road

Lamoille Canyon Road scenic byway is located in northeast Nevada approximately 20 miles southeast of Elko. The byway begins near Lamoille off NV 227. It travels south through the Humboldt National Forest to the Roads End Picnic Area. Travelers will need to retrace the route back to NV 227. Lamoille Canyon Road is 12 miles long and follows FSR 660, which is a two-lane paved road suitable for all types of vehicles. It is generally open May through October.

Lamoille Canyon Road travels through the canyon carved by Lamoille Creek, which flows alongside much of the byway. The canyon is a beautifully rugged canyon with three perennial streams, sheer rock cliffs, and scenic ribbon-like waterfalls. Two other canyons can be seen from the byway: Right Fork Lamoille Canyon and Thomas Canyon. These canyons and the rivers which carved them provide excellent fishing opportunities. A small stand of Bristlecone pine exists within Thomas Canyon.

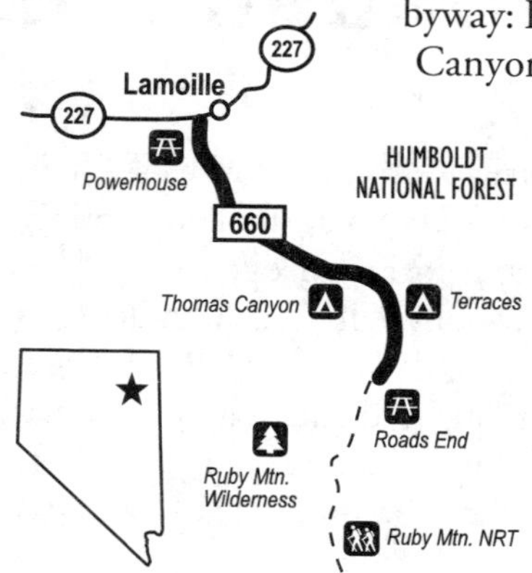

Some of the wildlife seen along the byway includes mule deer, yellow-bellied marmots, red-tailed hawks, cottontail rabbits, and coyotes. Other wildlife inhabiting the region includes snow partridge, mountain goats, and bighorn sheep.

Byway travelers will find two national forest campgrounds in Lamoille Canyon. Thomas Canyon Campground offers 42 campsites with picnic tables and fire rings. Terraces Campground is more primitive and has only nine tent campsites. Two picnic areas provide the perfect spot for enjoying an afternoon lunch. Powerhouse Picnic Area is located near the byway's beginning and Roads End Picnic Area is, where else, at the end of the byway.

The Ruby Mountain National Recreation Trail can be accessed from the Roads End Picnic Area. This trail extends south for 40 miles through some spectacular scenery. There are eight lakes, with excellent opportunities for fishing, that can be reached from the Ruby Mountain Trail. Other hiking trails can be found along the byway for those interested in hiking, backpacking, mountain biking, or horseback riding.

Information: Humboldt National Forest, 2035 Last Chance Rd, Elko NV 89801 / 775-738-5171.

Lodging Invitation

Shilo Inn - Elko	Phone:	702-738-5522
2401 Mountain City Highway		800-222-2244
Elko, NV 89801-4496	Fax:	702-738-6247

The Elko Shilo Inn is conveniently located near golf courses, convention center, gaming and equestrian center. The 70 fully equipped mini-suites provide guests with a microwave • refrigerator • wet bar • and satellite TV with premium channels. VCR and movie rentals are also available. Facilities include a 24-hour indoor pool, spa, sauna, steam room, fitness center and guest laundromat. Amenities include free local calls, USA Today newspaper, continental breakfast and airport shuttle to Harris Field/Elko Airport. Meeting space for up to 80 people is available. Several restaurants are located nearby.

Mount Wilson

Mount Wilson Back Country Byway is 90 miles south of Ely in eastern Nevada. Northern access is off US 93 at the Pony Springs Rest Area. The byway travels southeast and forms an open loop drive back to US 93, near the town of Pioche. Mount Wilson is 62 miles long and follows County Roads 441, 440, 431, and 430, BLM Road 4045, and NV 322. The roads are a combination of paved and gravel roads that can be safely driven in a two-wheel drive, high-clearance vehicle. Mount Wilson is open May through October; it can become impassable after heavy rain.

The Mount Wilson scenic byway begins in the arid, brush-covered desert landscape common to Nevada and takes you to the forested slopes of Mount Wilson. It passes through the thick pinyon-juniper forest, climbing into pockets of ponderosa pine, fir, mountain mahogany, and aspen. Spring offers a colorful display as the wildflowers growing along the byway proudly make their presence known. Not to be outdone, fall displays its own show of colors, with the golden color of aspen set among leaves of yellow, red, and orange. The byway then descends from the mountains and enters the broad valleys of Camp and Meadow Valleys.

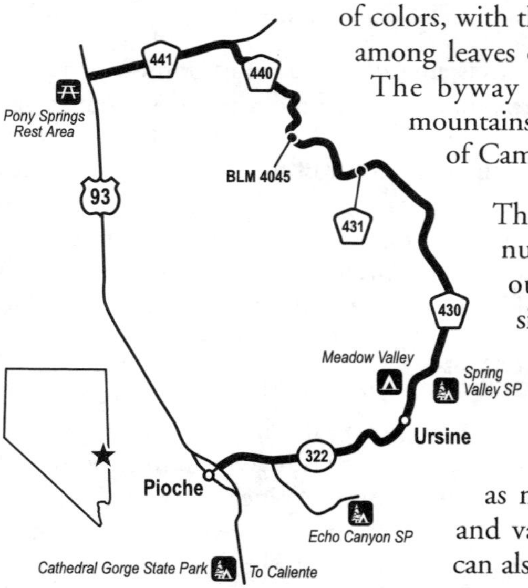

The back country byway offers numerous opportunities for outdoor recreation. Several side roads invite exploration by the hiker and mountain biker. There's never a bad time to watch for wildlife, which includes such species as mule deer, coyotes, hawks, and various lizards. Wild horses can also be seen at times.

Those interested in fishing will find a 65-acre lake stocked with brown trout, rainbow trout, and Alabama striped bass in Spring Valley State Park. The park also offers the opportunity to camp overnight at any one of its 37 sites. Some of the campsites have electrical hookups. Several pioneer ranches, old stone homes, and a cemetery dating to the pioneer days exist within the park.

Situated in a narrow, steep-walled canyon is the BLM operated Meadow Valley Campground. It has six tent-only campsites with picnic tables and fire rings. Pit toilets are provided but there is no drinking water. You can stay here up to 14 days if you want to.

Information: BLM-Ely Field Office, 702 N Industrial Way, HC 33 Box 33500, Ely NV 89301 / 775-289-1800. Spring Valley State Park, Star Rt 89063 Box 201, Pioche NV 89043 / 775-962-5102. Echo Canyon State Park, Star Rt Box 295, Pioche, NV 89043 / 775-962-5103. Cathedral Gorge State Park, PO Box 176, Panaca NV 89042 / 775-728-4460.

Pyramid Lake

Pyramid Lake is 30 miles north of Reno in west-central Nevada. It lies entirely within the Pyramid Lake Indian Reservation and follows NV 445, NV 446, and NV 447. The state highways are two-lane paved roads suitable for all vehicles. Pyramid Lake National Scenic Byway is 40 miles long and remains open year-round.

Pyramid Lake scenic drive travels along the beautiful shores of Pyramid Lake, named for the rock formation that resembles a pyramid. The byway travels in the shadows of the rugged Virginia Mountains, which lie south of the byway. A side trip from the main route of the byway takes you into the mountains where Sugarloaf Peak stands a proud 5,291 feet above sea level. Other mountain peaks reach heights above 8,000 feet. Another mountain range lies north of Pyramid Lake, where Pah-Rah Peak stretches 7,800 feet above sea level.

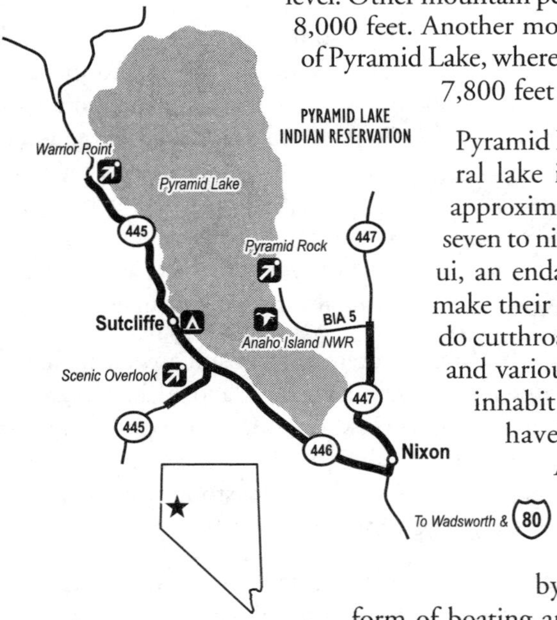

Pyramid Lake is the largest natural lake in Nevada, measuring approximately 30 miles long and seven to nine miles wide. The Cui-ui, an endangered species of fish, make their home in these waters as do cutthroat trout. White pelicans and various other shorebirds also inhabit this region; their safe haven being the 750-acre Anaho Island National Wildlife Refuge.

Recreation along the byway is mostly in the form of boating and fishing. A marina is located in Sutcliffe and provides all the necessary equipment for such activities. Swimming is also a popular activity on the lake. Beaches can be found at Pelican Point and Warrior Point. The mountains that surround the lake offer excellent opportunities for hiking, horseback riding, and backpacking. Please note that Tribal permits are required for fishing and boating and may be obtained in Sutcliffe.

Information: Pyramid Lake Paiute Tribe, PO Box 256, Nixon NV 89424 / 775-574-1000. Pyramid Lake Marina, phone 775-476-1156.

Red Rock Canyon

Red Rock Canyon is in southern Nevada about 20 miles west of Las Vegas. It can be reached from Las Vegas by traveling west on NV 159. The byway is 13 miles long and follows Red Rock Canyon Road, which is a one-way, paved road suitable for all vehicles. Red Rock Canyon remains open year-round.

Red Rock Canyon Back Country Byway traverses the arid desert landscape, passing rock formations that rise 2,000 feet above the valley floor. The sheer cliff walls are cut by deep canyons where hidden desert springs provide water that supports the diversity of wildlife inhabiting this area. Bighorn sheep can be seen by the watchful eye of the wildlife observer. Cougars, kit fox, coyotes, bobcat, and birds of prey also inhabit the area. Wild horses and burros can also be seen.

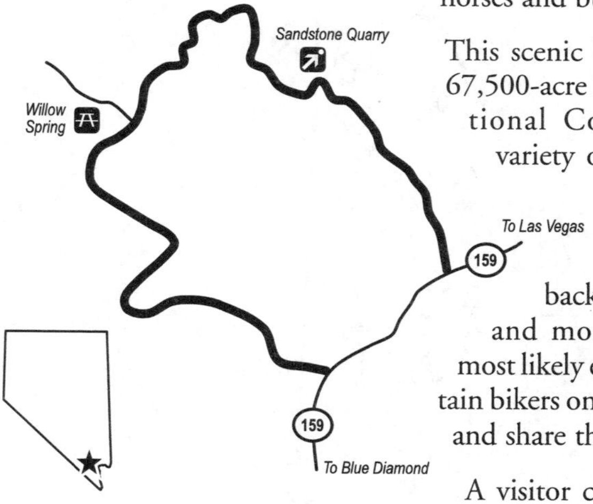

Sandstone Quarry
Willow Spring
To Las Vegas
159
159
To Blue Diamond

This scenic byway travels through 67,500-acre Red Rock Canyon National Conservation Area. A variety of activities can be enjoyed in the area including hiking, backpacking, horseback riding, rock climbing, and mountain biking. You'll most likely encounter many mountain bikers on the byway, be cautious and share the road with them.

A visitor center is located at the entrance of the byway. It has information and exhibits on the area and its recreational opportunities. For example, a brochure is available that lists and briefly describes 15 hiking trails. Other materials provide information on the plant and animal life of this rugged desert area.

One site of interest you'll encounter along the byway is Sandstone Quarry. A short walk takes you to the historic quarry dating from the turn of the century. Trails here will take you farther into the conservation area.

Information: BLM-Las Vegas Field Office, 4765 W Vegas Dr, Las Vegas NV 89108 / 702-647-5000. BLM-Caliente Field Station, PO Box 237, Caliente NV 89008 / 775-726-8100. Spring Mountain Ranch State Park, PO Box 124, Blue Diamond NV 89004 / 702-875-4141.

New Hampshire

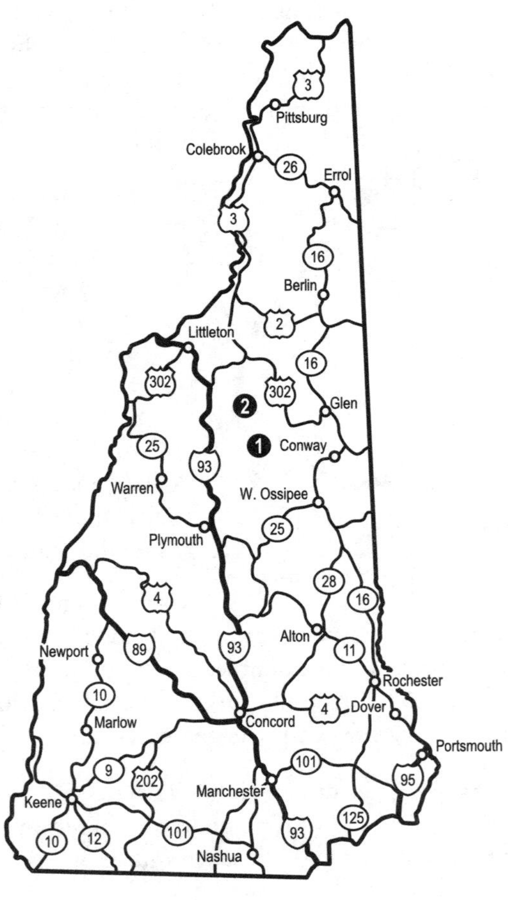

Kancamagus Scenic Byway

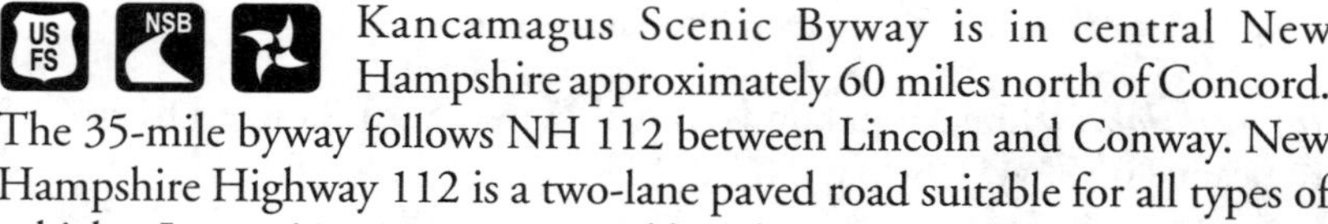

Kancamagus Scenic Byway is in central New Hampshire approximately 60 miles north of Concord. The 35-mile byway follows NH 112 between Lincoln and Conway. New Hampshire Highway 112 is a two-lane paved road suitable for all types of vehicles. It remains open year-round but driving the byway in winter calls for extra caution.

Kancamagus Scenic Byway climbs nearly 3,000 feet as it crosses the beautiful White Mountains. The waters of Swift River flow alongside the byway once you cross Kancamagus Pass. Several scenic vistas along the route provide panoramic views of the surrounding mountains.

There are several hiking trails along the byway. Some trails are short walking trails while others are long and more strenuous. A pleasant walk along the Sabbaday Brook Trail, west of Passaconaway Campground, will lead you to the beautiful Sabbaday Falls. Other trails near here will take you to the top of 4,140-foot Mount Tripyramid. Several wilderness areas surround the byway. These pristine areas offer excellent hiking, back country camping, and horseback riding. The Appalachian National Scenic Trail can be accessed in the Pemigewasset and Presidential Range-Dry River Wilderness Areas.

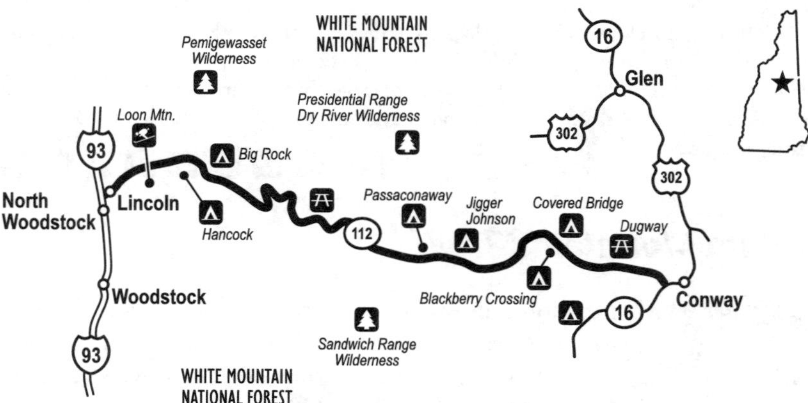

The White Mountain National Forest has developed numerous camping and picnicking areas along this scenic byway. There are six public campgrounds from which to choose for an overnight stay. Jigger Johnson Campground is the largest and has 75 sites. Hancock Campground follows in size with 56 campsites. Forty-nine sites are available at Covered Bridge; Passaconaway has 33 sites; Big Rock offers 28 campsites; Blackberry

Crossing has 20 sites. Facilities found in each campground includes drinking water, picnic tables, and restrooms. None of the campgrounds have electrical hookups for recreational vehicles.

Information: White Mountain National Forest, Saco Ranger District, 33 Kancamagus Hwy, Conway NH 03818 / 603-447-5448.

Lodging Invitation

Kancamagus Motor Lodge
Route 112 (Kancamagus Hwy.)
Lincoln, NH 03251

Phone: 800-346-4205
603-745-3365
Fax: 603-745-6691

Located in the middle of the White Mountain region, at the start of the Kancamagus Highway with great mountain views. Close by to every imaginable activity and attraction, one could easily spend a week in this area. Modern, quiet, and spotless rooms — cable TV • A/C • phone • and in room, private steam bath. The Terrace Restaurant offers excellent and inexpensive dining. Need help? Ask for expert advice on touring the most rugged area in the northeast. AAA & Mobil good value rated. Rates from $38.00 to $64.00, double.

A/C

Three Rivers House
RR 1, Box 72
S. Main St.
N. Woodstock, NH 03262

Phone: 603-745-2711
800-940-2711
Fax: 603-745-2773

The Three Rivers House is centrally located in the heart of the White Mountains National Forest at the western entrance of the Kancamagus Highway. Amenities include: rooms & suites • gas fireplaces • A/C • whirlpools • color cable TV • and private baths. Guests enjoy the nearby attractions, skiing, hiking, golf, and shopping. Visa, MC, Disc., & AMEX cards accepted.

A/C

White Mountains Trail

NSB

White Mountains Trail is in central New Hampshire. It begins in North Woodstock and heads north to Twin Mountain. From Twin Mountain it travels south to Conway. The byway is approximately 70 miles long and follows US 3, I-93, US 302, and NH 16. The roads are two- and four-lane paved roads suitable for all vehicles. White Mountains Trail is usually open year-round.

White Mountains Trail travels across central New Hampshire among the beautiful White Mountains. Travelers are treated to views of mountains, valleys, gorges, waterfalls, and unique rock formations. Several turnouts provide scenic views of the surrounding mountains. In Bretton Woods, visitors can take the historic Mount Washington Cog Railway to the summit of the highest mountain in the Northeast. Rail excursions of varying length are offered from the Conway Scenic Railroad in Conway.

The byway is never far from the White Mountains National Forest where outdoor recreation opportunities abound. Hikers can access the Appalachian National Scenic Trail. Numerous other trails accessed from the byway range from short, easy walks to wilderness adventures. There is only one national forest campground located directly along the byway.

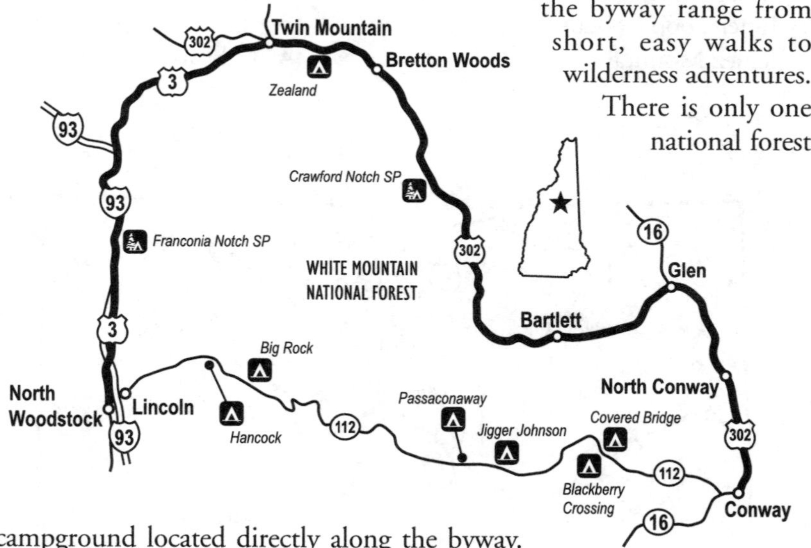

Zealand Campground, between Twin Mountain and Bretton Woods, has a total of 11 campsites. The small campground is open May to October.

White Mountains Trail passes through two state parks: Franconia Notch and Crawford Notch. Franconia Notch State Park is 6,440 acres situated between Franconia and Kinsman mountain ranges. It contains several interesting natural features including "Old Man of the Mountain." The campground here has 97 sites. Crawford Notch State Park is 5,775 acres and contains two beautiful waterfalls, among other natural features. It has a primitive, 30-site campground. Both campgrounds are open May through October.

Information: White Mountain National Forest, Saco Ranger District, 33 Kancamagus Hwy, Conway NH 03818 / 603-447-5448. Franconia Notch State Park, Franconia NH 03580 / 603-823-5563. Crawford Notch State Park, New Hampshire Division of Parks and Recreation, PO Box 1856, Concord NH 03302 / 603-271-3556.

NEW MEXICO

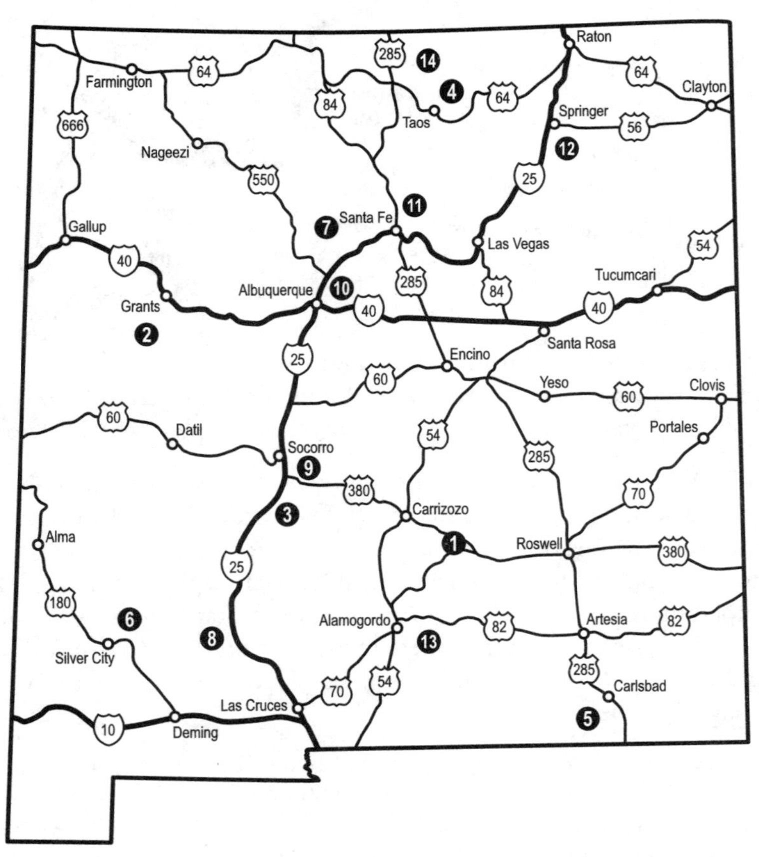

Raton
285
14
Farmington
64
84
4
64
64
Clayton
Taos
Springer
56
666
Nageezi
12
550
25
11
Santa Fe
7
Gallup
Las Vegas
54
40
Tucumcari
Albuquerque
10
285
84
40
40
Grants
2
Santa Rosa
25
Encino
60
Yeso
60
Clovis
60
Datil
Portales
Socorro
54
9
285
380
70
3
Carrizozo
Alma
1
Roswell
380
25
180
6
Alamogordo
Artesia
82
82
8
13
Silver City
285
Carlsbad
70
54
Las Cruces
5
10
Deming

Billy the Kid

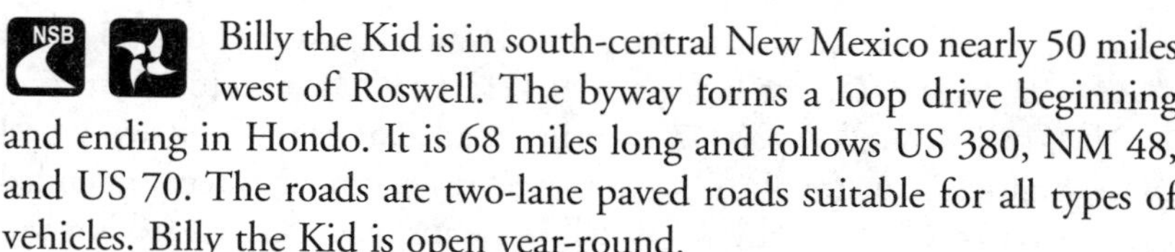

Billy the Kid is in south-central New Mexico nearly 50 miles west of Roswell. The byway forms a loop drive beginning and ending in Hondo. It is 68 miles long and follows US 380, NM 48, and US 70. The roads are two-lane paved roads suitable for all types of vehicles. Billy the Kid is open year-round.

Billy the Kid travels through a region of grassy plains and pine forests, and through towns of historic significance. Lincoln's main street is lined with adobe homes and commercial buildings that date back to the late 1800s. It is here that Billy the Kid was tried, convicted, and sentenced to hang. Before the law carried out its sentence, Billy killed the prison guards and escaped from the Lincoln County Courthouse. Sheriff Pat Garrett eventually tracked him to Fort Sumner, where Billy was killed on July 14, 1881. Travelers of the byway can tour the Old Lincoln County Courthouse Museum.

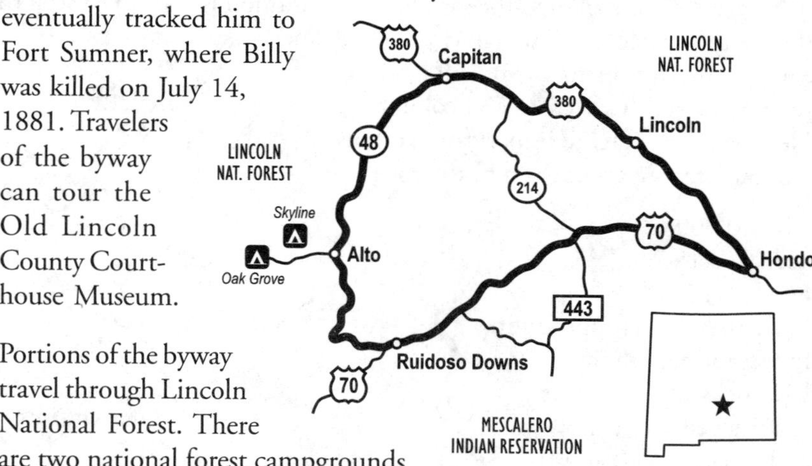

Portions of the byway travel through Lincoln National Forest. There are two national forest campgrounds near the byway, west of Alto: Skyline and Oak Grove. Skyline Campground is one mile west of Alto on NM 532, then four miles northwest on FSR 117. It has 17 RV and tent sites; RVs are limited to 16 feet long. Oak Grove Campground is five miles west of Alto on NM 532. It has 29 RV and tent sites; RVs are limited to 16 feet long. There are no hookups or drinking water at either campground and both are open mid-May to mid-September.

Information: Village of Ruidoso, 313 Cree Meadows Dr. (PO Drawer 69), Ruidoso NM 88345 / 505-258-4014 or 505-258-3017. Lincoln National Forest, Smokey Bear Ranger District, 901 Mechem Dr., Ruidoso NM 88345 / 505-257-4095.

Chain of Craters

BLM 2 Chain Of Craters is in west-central New Mexico about 25 miles southwest of Grants. It follows CR 42 south for 36 miles to the junction of NM 117. County Road 42 is a dirt road that requires a two-wheel drive, high-clearance vehicle. A four-wheel drive vehicle is recommended during wet weather. The byway usually remains open year-round but can become impassable during and after periods of inclement weather.

The Chain Of Craters Back Country Byway travels through portions of the El Malpais National Monument and National Conservation Area. The byway crosses a brush-covered landscape with views of sandstone bluffs rising above the desert floor. This rugged and desolate area was once inhabited by Indians, and crossed by Spanish and American explorers who carved their names in the sandstone. Inscription Rock can be seen to the west in El Morro National Monument. The earliest inscription dates to 1605 by Juan de Onate, a Spanish governor and colonizer of New Mexico. Native American symbols and pictures are also carved in the rock.

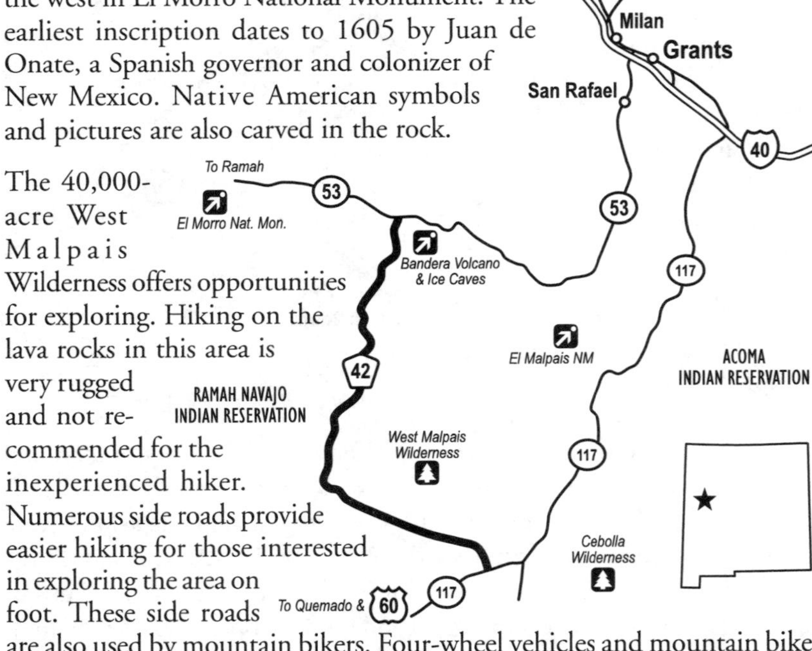

The 40,000-acre West Malpais Wilderness offers opportunities for exploring. Hiking on the lava rocks in this area is very rugged and not recommended for the inexperienced hiker. Numerous side roads provide easier hiking for those interested in exploring the area on foot. These side roads are also used by mountain bikers. Four-wheel vehicles and mountain bikes are prohibited from the wilderness area. The Continental Divide National Scenic Trail follows a portion of the byway along the northern area.

There are no developed public campgrounds along the byway, however, dispersed camping is permitted on BLM land. Be sure to bring your own water as none is available.

Information: BLM-Albuquerque Field Office, 435 Montano Rd NE, Albuquerque NM 87107 / 505-761-8700. El Malpais National Monument, PO Box 939, Grants NM 87020 / 505-285-4641. El Morro National Monument, RR 2 Box 43, Ramah NM 87321 / 505-783-4226. Bandera Volcano & Ice Caves, Ice Caves Trading Co, 12000 Ice Caves Rd, Grants NM 87020 / 888-Ice-Cave.

El Camino Real

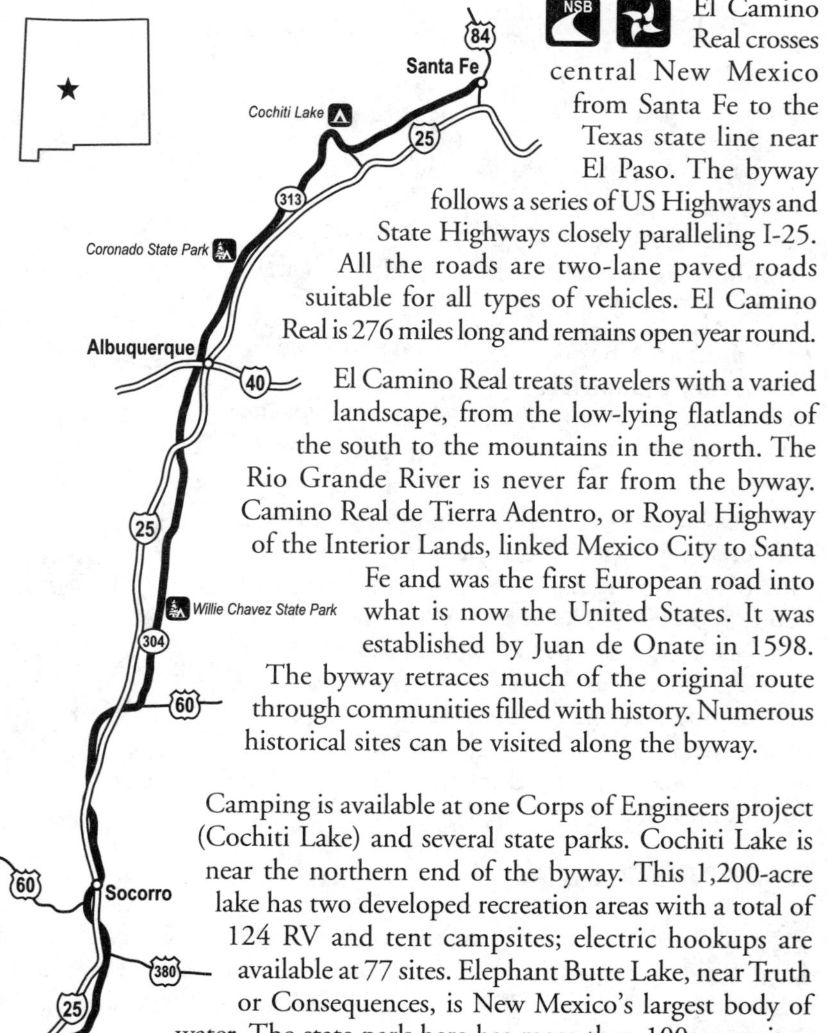

El Camino Real crosses central New Mexico from Santa Fe to the Texas state line near El Paso. The byway follows a series of US Highways and State Highways closely paralleling I-25. All the roads are two-lane paved roads suitable for all types of vehicles. El Camino Real is 276 miles long and remains open year round.

El Camino Real treats travelers with a varied landscape, from the low-lying flatlands of the south to the mountains in the north. The Rio Grande River is never far from the byway. Camino Real de Tierra Adentro, or Royal Highway of the Interior Lands, linked Mexico City to Santa Fe and was the first European road into what is now the United States. It was established by Juan de Onate in 1598. The byway retraces much of the original route through communities filled with history. Numerous historical sites can be visited along the byway.

Camping is available at one Corps of Engineers project (Cochiti Lake) and several state parks. Cochiti Lake is near the northern end of the byway. This 1,200-acre lake has two developed recreation areas with a total of 124 RV and tent campsites; electric hookups are available at 77 sites. Elephant Butte Lake, near Truth or Consequences, is New Mexico's largest body of water. The state park here has more than 100 campsites;

nearly all have electric hookups. South of Elephant Butte Lake is Caballo Lake. The state park on this 11,500-acre lake has 136 developed sites, of which 64 have hookups. A lesser known and used state park is Percha Dam State Park, just south of Caballo Lake. It resides next to the Rio Grande River, which offers anglers good walleye, white bass, and catfish fishing. The park has 29 developed sites, six with electric hookups. The remaining state parks have a total of 72 developed campsites with hookups at 48 sites.

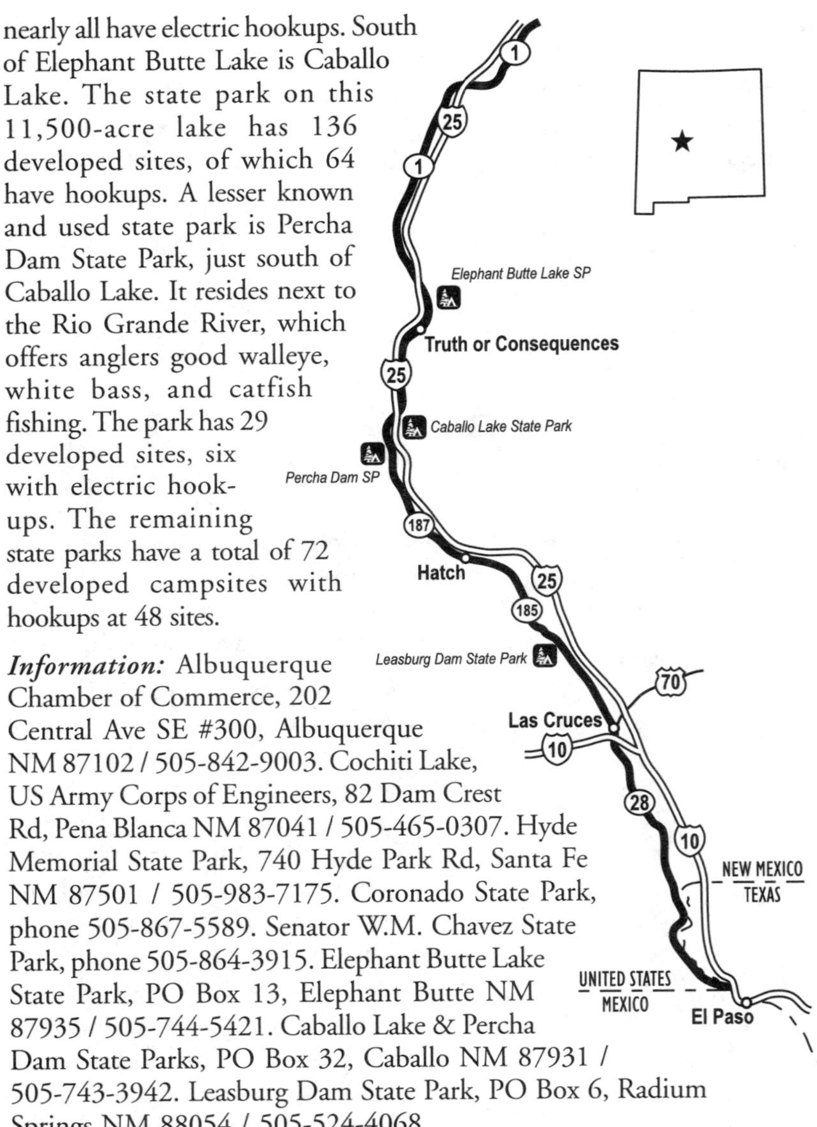

Information: Albuquerque Chamber of Commerce, 202 Central Ave SE #300, Albuquerque NM 87102 / 505-842-9003. Cochiti Lake, US Army Corps of Engineers, 82 Dam Crest Rd, Pena Blanca NM 87041 / 505-465-0307. Hyde Memorial State Park, 740 Hyde Park Rd, Santa Fe NM 87501 / 505-983-7175. Coronado State Park, phone 505-867-5589. Senator W.M. Chavez State Park, phone 505-864-3915. Elephant Butte Lake State Park, PO Box 13, Elephant Butte NM 87935 / 505-744-5421. Caballo Lake & Percha Dam State Parks, PO Box 32, Caballo NM 87931 / 505-743-3942. Leasburg Dam State Park, PO Box 6, Radium Springs NM 88054 / 505-524-4068.

Enchanted Circle

US FS

Enchanted Circle is in north-central New Mexico about 70 miles northeast of Santa Fe. The byway forms a loop drive beginning and ending in Taos. It follows NM 38, NM 522, and US 64 for a total of 84 miles. All the roads are two-lane paved roads suitable for all types of vehicles. Enchanted Circle generally remains open year-round.

Enchanted Circle crosses Carson National Forest forming a circle around the 13,161-foot Wheeler Peak, New Mexico's highest point. The byway climbs the southern portion of the Sangre de Cristo Mountains through forests of spruce and fir, crosses wide mountain valleys and meadows, and follows alongside meandering streams and rivers.

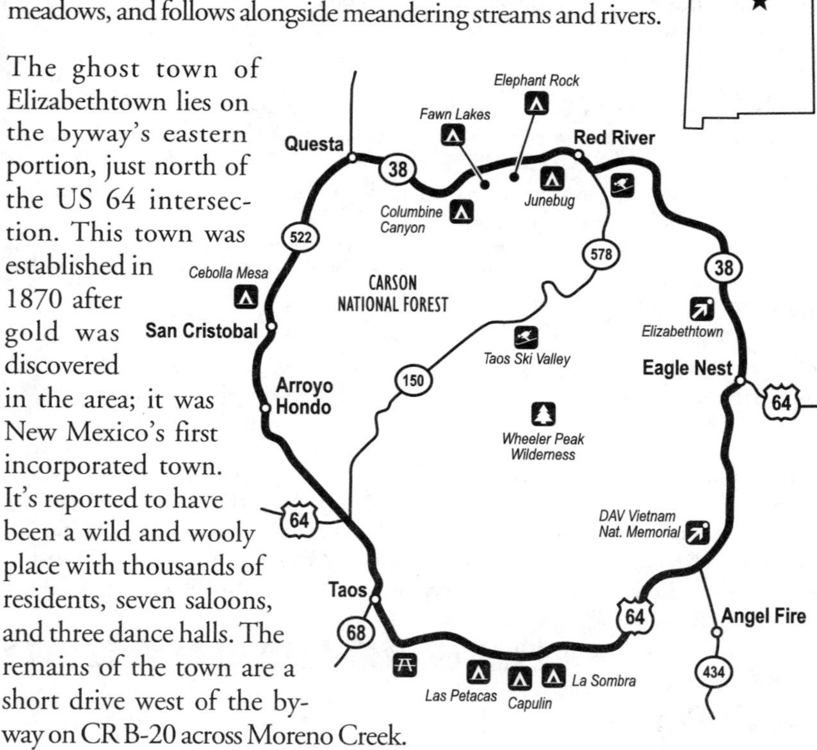

The ghost town of Elizabethtown lies on the byway's eastern portion, just north of the US 64 intersection. This town was established in 1870 after gold was discovered in the area; it was New Mexico's first incorporated town. It's reported to have been a wild and wooly place with thousands of residents, seven saloons, and three dance halls. The remains of the town are a short drive west of the byway on CR B-20 across Moreno Creek.

Farther south of Elizabethtown is another monument to American history. The Vietnam Veterans National Memorial, now operated by the Disabled American Veterans, was originally built by Dr. Victor Westphall in memory of his son who died in the Vietnam War. The memorial is open daily and has special Memorial Day Services each year.

Plenty of opportunities exist for extending your stay along the byway. The national forest developed several campgrounds with numerous shaded sites and picnic tables. Dispersed camping is also permitted nearly anywhere on national forest land.

Information: Carson National Forest, 208 Cruz Alta Rd, Taos NM 87571

/ 505-758-6200. "Angle Fire" Vietnam Veterans Nat'l Memorial, Hwy 64, Angle Fire NM 87710 / 505-377-6900.

Lodging Invitation

San Geronimo Lodge	Phone:	505-751-3776
1101 Witt Road		800-894-4119
Taos, NM 87571	Fax:	505-751-1493
MAIL: 216M Paseo del Pueblo N167	E-mail:	sever12893@aol.com

The San Geronimo Lodge is situated on 2½ acres with spectacular views of Taos Mountain and Kit Carson National Forest. A traditional style adobe hacienda built in 1925, the lodge has spacious common areas, high-beamed ceilings and wood floors. All rooms have handcrafted furniture, down comforters, color cable TV, private bath and telephone. Visa, MC, AMEX, and Discover cards accepted.

Terrace Towers Lodge	Phone:	800-695-6343
712 W. Main		505-754-2962
P.O. Box 149	Fax:	505-754-2989
Red River, NM 87558	Internet:	http://www.redrivernm.com/terracetowers

Terrace Towers Lodge is an all-suites condominium and lodge with 1 and 2 bedroom apartments. Located in the beautiful Sangre de Cristo Mountains within the Enchanted Circle just north of Taos. Super views, quiet and convenient to shops, restaurants, fishing, skiing, and all kinds of mountain activities. Historical sites, Indian culture, southwestern art galleries and museums are just a short drive away. Enjoy Red River's special events throughout the year. Call for a free visitor's guide.

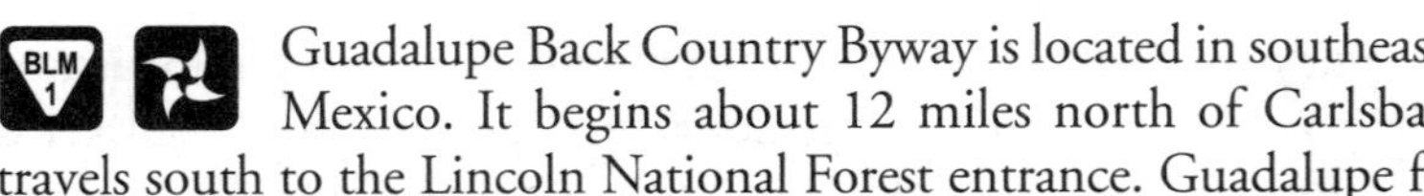

Guadalupe

Guadalupe Back Country Byway is located in southeast New Mexico. It begins about 12 miles north of Carlsbad and travels south to the Lincoln National Forest entrance. Guadalupe follows NM 137, which is a two-lane paved road suitable for all vehicles. The byway is 30 miles long and is open year-round.

Guadalupe ascends nearly 3,000 feet from the Chihuahuan Desert at the beginning of the byway to the Guadalupe Mountains. Opportunities exist for hiking, wildlife viewing, four-wheeling, hunting, and exploring. The area is home to mule deer, pronghorn antelope, hawks and eagles, coyotes, lizards, and rattle snakes. A short side trip from the byway takes you to the scenic Sitting Bull Falls and a picnic area.

Guadalupe Back Country Byway is rich in history. Stone spearheads or dart points have been found in the area that are between 8,000 and 9,000 years old. Various types of pottery have also been found that are associated with the ancient Anasazi Indians. The first ranchers began arriving shortly after the Civil War. West Texas ranchers would also pass through here with their cattle, headed for the railheads in Kansas. Today this area is used for livestock grazing and oil and gas exploration.

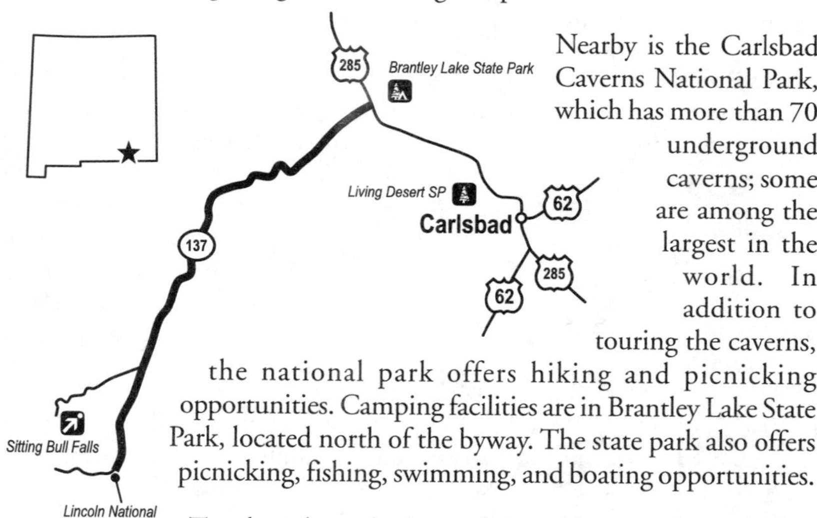

Nearby is the Carlsbad Caverns National Park, which has more than 70 underground caverns; some are among the largest in the world. In addition to touring the caverns, the national park offers hiking and picnicking opportunities. Camping facilities are in Brantley Lake State Park, located north of the byway. The state park also offers picnicking, fishing, swimming, and boating opportunities.

Travelers along the byway may wish to continue driving through Lincoln National Forest to the Dog Canyon Ranger Station in Guadalupe National Park. The national park contains what is considered to be one of the finest examples of an ancient marine fossil reef in the world. The park is also home to Guadalupe Peak, the highest point in Texas at 8,749 feet. A small campground is located near the ranger station. Hiking trails that lead to Guadalupe Peak and wilderness camping are also in the area.

Information: BLM-Carlsbad Field Office, 620 E Greene, Carlsbad NM 88220 / 505-887-6544. Lincoln National Forest, Federal Bldg, 1101 New York Ave, Alamogordo NM 88310 / 505-437-7200. Brantley Lake SP, PO Box 2288, Carlsbad NM 88221 / 505-457-2384. Living Desert SP, PO Box 100, Carlsbad NM 88221 / 505-887-5516. Carlsbad Caverns National Park, 3225 National Parks Hwy, Carlsbad NM 88220 / 505-785-2232.

Inner Loop - Gila Cliff Dwellings

The Inner Loop - Gila Cliff Dwellings scenic byway is in southwest New Mexico about 100 miles northwest of Las

Cruces. It begins in Silver City and heads east to San Lorenzo. It then travels northwest to the Gila Cliff Dwellings National Monument. From here the byway heads south, retracing part of the byway, to end back in Silver City. The byway is 110 miles long and follows NM 15, NM 35, NM 152, and US 180. All the roads are two-lane paved roads. Vehicles over 17 feet long should not attempt NM 15 between Pinos Altos and the junction with NM 35. This portion of the state highway is narrow and has many sharp curves. The byway is open year-round.

This scenic drive travels across the Gila National Forest through a high desert and mountainous landscape, crossing the Continental Divide twice. Located all along the byway are scenic turnouts that provide panoramic views of the surrounding mountains or a nice spot to enjoy a picnic lunch. New Mexico Highway 15 to the Gila Cliff Dwellings NM is enshrouded by the pristine Gila Wilderness.

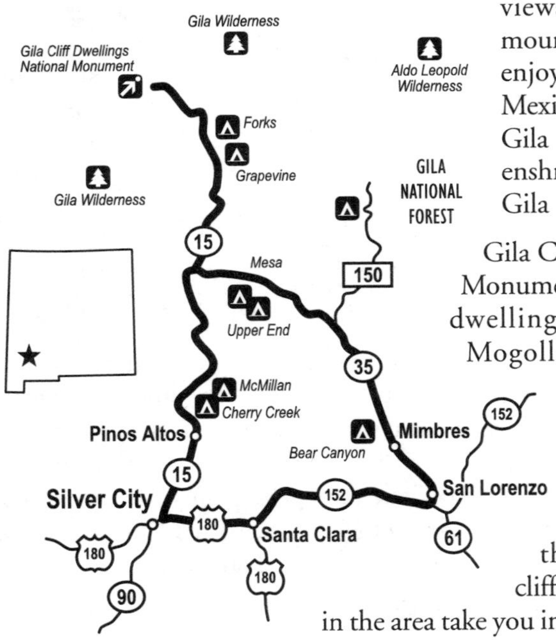

Gila Cliff Dwellings National Monument is the site of six cliff dwellings inhabited by the Mogollans in the late 13th century. Over 40 masonry rooms were built within six caves. A moderately easy trail takes you through these historic cliff dwellings. Hiking trails in the area take you into the Gila Wilderness.

Wildlife observers will want to remain alert for bald eagles flying overhead. Golden eagles and red-tailed hawks can also be seen. In the mountains and valleys of Gila National Forest you'll also find elk, mule deer, and wild turkeys. Black bear also inhabit the area.

There are numerous national forest campgrounds along the byway. Most are set among trees alongside bubbling streams or rivers. Mesa and Upper End Campgrounds are situated on the shores of Lake Roberts. Those interested in a more primitive setting are invited to explore the Gila Wilderness area and may camp anywhere they desire.

Information: Gila National Forest, 3005 E Camino del Bosque, Silver City NM 88061 / 505-388-8201. Gila Cliff Dwellings National Monument, PO Box 100, Silver City NM 88061 / 505-536-9461.

Lodging Invitation

Holiday Motor Hotel
3420 Hwy. 180 East
Silver City, NM 88061

Phone: 505-538-3711
Fax: 505-538-3711
Internet: www.holidayhotel.com

Located within minutes of the Gila National Forest the Holiday Motor Hotel offers 80, recently renovated, modern rooms. Amenities include: cable TV • A/C • heated outdoor pool • disabled persons' rooms • no-smoking rooms • fax and copy service • banquet, meeting and convention facilities • on-premises breakfast, lunch, and fine evening dinning. Guests enjoy easy access to hiking, mountain biking, golf, tennis, and the many art galleries & museums in the area.

Silver City KOA Kampground
11824 Hwy. 180 East
Silver City, NM 88061

Phone: 505-388-3351
800-562-7623 reservations
Fax: 505-388-0461
E-mail: sckoa@zianet.com
Internet: www.koakampgrounds.com

Camp KOA style, cook out and enjoy the great outdoors. At Silver City you can pitch your tent, stay in a Kamping Kabin®, rent their RV, or pull your rig into one of the full-service RV sites. Guests will enjoy the excellent shower and restroom facilities, laundry, TV room, playground and heated pool. Complete sight-seeing information and quality service. Open year-round. Silver City's Best Camping!

Jemez Mountain Trail

Jemez Mountain Trail is in north-central New Mexico just west of Los Alamos. It follows NM 4, NM 126, and US 550 for a total of 132 miles. New Mexico Highway 126 is a narrow, unpaved road. The other highways are two-lane paved roads suitable for all vehicles. New Mexico Highway 4 is heavily used by bicyclists; be on the lookout for them. New Mexico Highway 126 is generally closed in winter; the others remain open year-round.

This scenic byway travels through the Jemez Mountains, alongside clear streams, and across large meadows. The Jemez River flows beside much of the byway along NM 4. Near the byway's eastern end is Bandelier National Monument, which contains numerous cliff houses and pueblo style

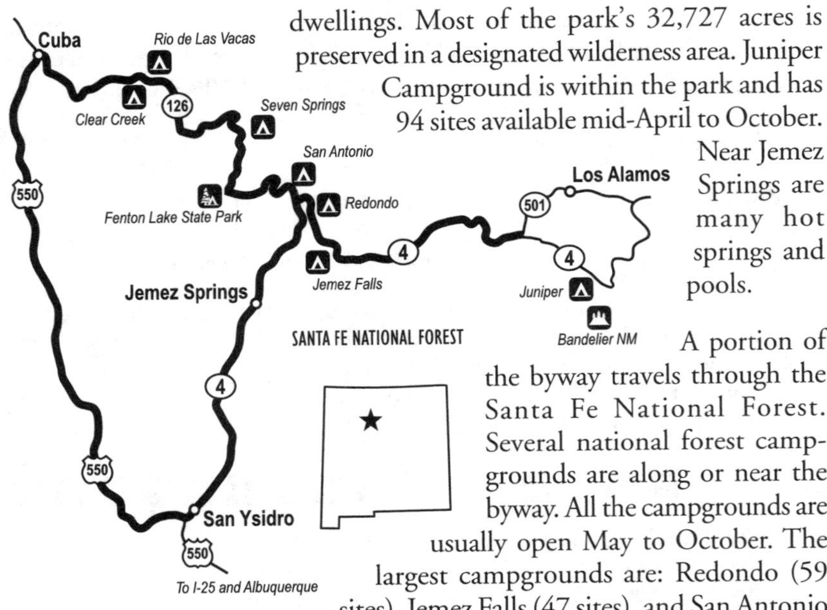

dwellings. Most of the park's 32,727 acres is preserved in a designated wilderness area. Juniper Campground is within the park and has 94 sites available mid-April to October. Near Jemez Springs are many hot springs and pools.

A portion of the byway travels through the Santa Fe National Forest. Several national forest campgrounds are along or near the byway. All the campgrounds are usually open May to October. The largest campgrounds are: Redondo (59 sites), Jemez Falls (47 sites), and San Antonio (36 sites). None of the campgrounds have sites with hookups. Camping is also available in Fenton Lake State Park. It has 40 developed sites on the shores of 35-acre Fenton Lake; six have electric hookups. The state park is open year-round.

Information: County of Sandoval, 243 Camino del Pueblo, Bernalillo NM 87004 / 505-867-8687. Bandelier National Monument, HCR 1 Box 1 Suite 15, Los Alamos NM 87544 / 505-672-0343. Santa Fe National Forest, 1474 Rodeo Rd, Santa Fe NM 87505 / 505-438-7840. Fenton Lake State Park, 455 Fenton Lake, Jemez Springs NM 87025 / 505-829-3630.

Lake Valley

BLM 1 The Lake Valley scenic byway is located in southwestern New Mexico, 50 miles northwest of Las Cruces. It begins south of Caballo at Exit #63 on I-25. It travels west to Hillsboro and then south to Nutt. Lake Valley is 44 miles long and follows NM 27 and NM 152, which are two-lane paved roads suitable for all vehicles. Both state highways usually remain open all year. Several low-water crossings are encountered; it is best to not attempt crossing when water is present.

Travelers may begin their journey on the Lake Valley Back Country Byway by taking the Hillsboro exit from I-25. From here the byway heads west across the desert landscape with views of distant Animas Peak and Black Peak to the north. Before reaching Hillsboro, you'll see the remains of an open copper mine. You may want to spend some time in Hillsboro exploring the historic buildings.

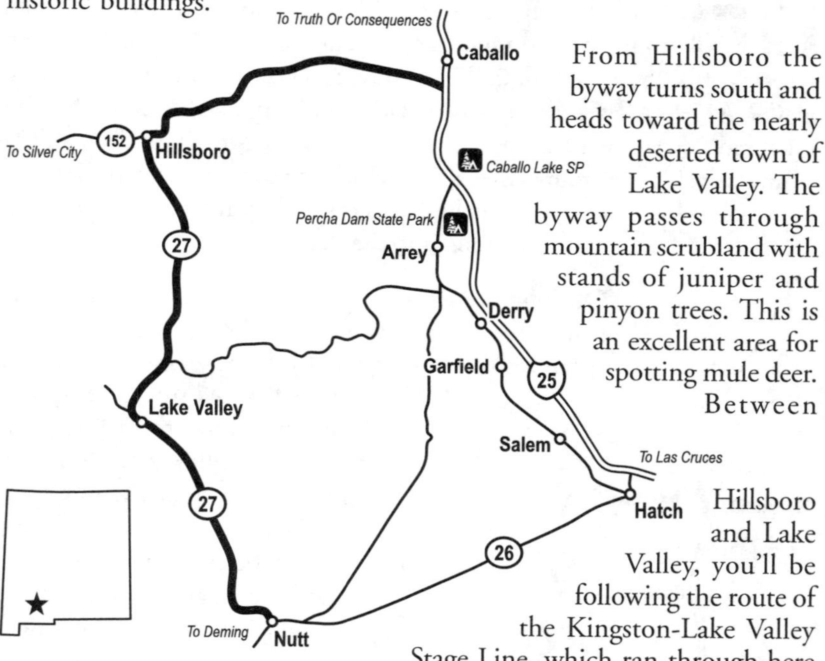

From Hillsboro the byway turns south and heads toward the nearly deserted town of Lake Valley. The byway passes through mountain scrubland with stands of juniper and pinyon trees. This is an excellent area for spotting mule deer. Between Hillsboro and Lake Valley, you'll be following the route of the Kingston-Lake Valley Stage Line, which ran through here during the 1880s. Soldiers were stationed in Hillsboro and Lake Valley to protect settlers from Apache attacks. Lake Valley was once a thriving mining town of over 4,000 inhabitants. The devaluation of silver in 1893 led to its eventual decline. A few historic structures remain, among them is the schoolhouse that is still used by locals for weddings and dances.

Once through Lake Valley the byway continues south with views of Monument Peak and Nutt Mountain. Among the wildlife in this area are antelope, deer, roadrunners, red-tailed hawks, and coyotes. The byway ends in Nutt, originally a stop on the Atchison, Topeka, and Santa Fe Railway.

There are no public campgrounds along the byway, however, two state parks are near the byway's northern terminus. Caballo Lake State Park has 130 sites for tents and recreational vehicles, many with electrical hookups. The Percha Dam State Park has 60 sites, some also with hookups.

Information: BLM-Las Cruces Field Office, 1800 Marquess St, Las Cruces NM 88005 / 505-525-4300. Caballo Lake & Percha Dam State Parks, PO Box 32, Caballo NM 87931 / 505-743-3942.

Quebradas

Quebradas Back Country Byway is approximately 75 miles south of Albuquerque in central New Mexico. Northern access is off I-25 in Escondida. The byway travels southeast to the junction of CR A129, a few miles north of US 380. The 24-mile route follows Quebradas Road, which is a dirt road requiring a two-wheel drive, high-clearance vehicle. A four-wheel drive vehicle is recommended during wet weather. Quebradas is open all year but heavy rain can make portions impassable.

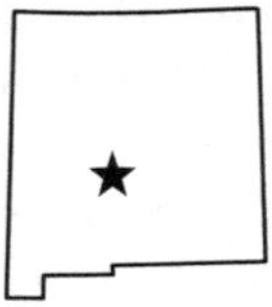

To Albuquerque
25
Escondida
Socorro
25
A 129
San Antonio
380
Bosque del Apache NWR

Quebradas Back Country Byway traverses a ruggedly scenic desert landscape east of the Rio Grande Valley. It crosses the Rio Grande River just east of Escondida. The river valley and surrounding area provides habitat for a variety of wildlife including mule deer, gray fox, coyote, bobcat, opossum, and jack rabbit. Bird watchers should be on the lookout for red-tailed hawk, horned lark, snow goose, and sandhill crane. Occasionally, the endangered whooping crane may also be seen along the river.

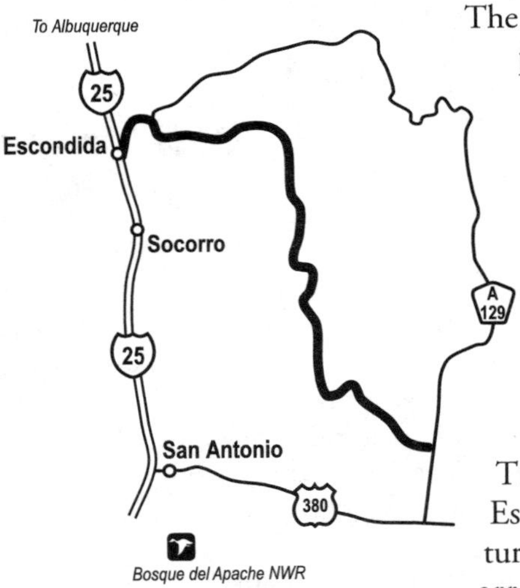

The byway continues east of Escondida for several miles before turning south where it crosses several arroyos that drain into the Rio Grande River. These crossings can contain deep pockets of sand and should not be crossed during or immediately following heavy rain. Loma de las Canas comes into view as you continue driving southward. Nearly vertical, multicolored cliffs and narrow box canyons dominate the view through here. This area provides excellent opportunities for exploring the back country on foot and is popular with hikers and backpackers.

To the south of the byway lies 57,000-acre Bosque del Apache National Wildlife Refuge. Nearly 300 species of birds either inhabit this area or migrate through on a seasonal basis. The whooping crane has also made its presence known in this area.

Although there are no developed public campgrounds along the byway, the Bureau of Land Management permits camping nearly anywhere on BLM-managed land. To the west of the byway is Cibola National Forest, which has developed camping facilities.

Information: BLM-Las Cruces Field Office, 1800 Marquess St, Las Cruces NM 88005 / 505-525-4300. Bosque del Apache NWR, PO Box 1246, Socorro NM 87801 / 505-835-1828.

Sandia Crest Road

Sandia Crest Road is about 23 miles northeast of downtown Albuquerque in central New Mexico. It begins at the intersection of NM 14 and NM 536. The byway heads west across Cibola National Forest and ends near the summit of Sandia Peak. Sandia Crest Road follows NM 536 for 11 miles. The highway is a two-lane paved road suitable for all vehicles; there are some sharp curves. Travelers will need to retrace the route back to NM 165 or NM 14. The highway is usually passable year-round. Winter driving conditions can be hazardous, especially in higher elevations. Chains or snow tires are sometimes required.

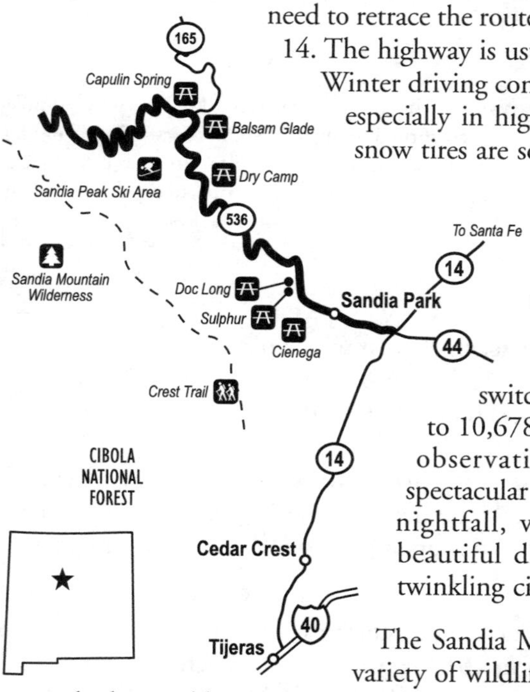

Sandia Crest Road climbs nearly 4,000 feet as it travels through the high desert and dense forests of the Sandia Mountains. The byway switchbacks up the mountain to 10,678-foot Sandia Crest where observation platforms provide spectacular panoramic views. Come nightfall, visitors are treated to a beautiful display of Albuquerque's twinkling city lights.

The Sandia Mountains are home to a variety of wildlife. Careful observers may see mule deer, golden eagles, or bighorn sheep. Mountain lions, bobcats, and black bear also inhabit the area but are rarely seen.

Trailheads along the byway provide access to the Sandia Mountain

Wilderness. This 37,232-acre mountain wilderness offers excellent opportunities for hiking, backpacking, and horseback riding. Crest Trail is a 28-mile hiking trail following the mountain ridgeline from Tijeras Canyon to Placitas.

Many picnic areas along the byway provide a good spot for relaxing a bit and enjoying a lunch or early dinner. No public campgrounds have been developed along the byway, nor is car camping permitted. The nearest public campground is found in Coronado State Park, approximately 20 miles west of the byway. It has 25 campsites, many with electric hookups. Facilities also include showers, drinking water, picnic areas, and a dump station.

Information: Cibola National Forest, 2113 Osuna Rd NE Suite A, Albuquerque NM 87113 / 505-346-2650.

Lodging Invitation

Sandia Mountain Hostel
12234 Hwy. 14 N.
Cedar Crest, NM 87008

Phone: 505-281-4117

Sandia Mountain Hostel is a passive solar building on the Turquoise Trail only 10 miles east of Albuquerque. Located in a peaceful rural setting close to hiking, biking, climbing, and skiing. The Cibola National Forest is across the street and nearby you'll find ghost towns and ancient Indian pueblos. Dorm beds are $12 a night, private rooms are $30 per night.

Santa Fe

US FS

The Santa Fe scenic drive is in north-central New Mexico. It begins in the city of Santa Fe at the corner of Palace and Washington Avenues. It travels northeast to the road's end near the Santa Fe Ski Area. The byway is 15 miles long and follows NM 475, which is a narrow two-lane paved road with sharp curves and steep grades. Caution should be used by all drivers. Travelers will need to retrace the route back to Santa Fe. The byway remains open year-round but delays are possible in winter.

The scenic byway begins near the historic Palace of the Governors. This adobe structure was built in 1610 by the Spanish government and is the oldest continuously occupied public building in the United States. From this point, drive north on Washington Avenue for several blocks and then turn east on Artist Road, which is also NM 475. From this point, the byway begins climbing the Sangre de Cristo Mountains. You first pass through picturesque Tesuque Canyon and then enter dense stands of ponderosa pine, which eventually give way to a mixed conifer and aspen forest near the ski area.

A trailhead for the Winsor Trail is at the byway's end and provides access to the Pecos Wilderness. Numerous other trails are at the campgrounds and picnic areas along the byway. They range in difficulty from a short, easy walk to more strenuous backpacking trails.

Camping areas are abundant along this scenic byway. The national forest maintains three campgrounds. New Mexico State Parks and Recreation Department operates Hyde Memorial State Park for byway travelers. The state park is nearly 400 acres of land completely surrounded by national forest land. There are 45 campsites with picnic tables and fire rings; some sites have electric hookups. Black Canyon Campground is the next largest campground with 41 sites. Hookups are also available at many of its campsites. Big Tesuque and Aspen Basin Campgrounds are a little more primitive but offer a total of 17 campsites with picnic tables. Neither campground has drinking water or hookups.

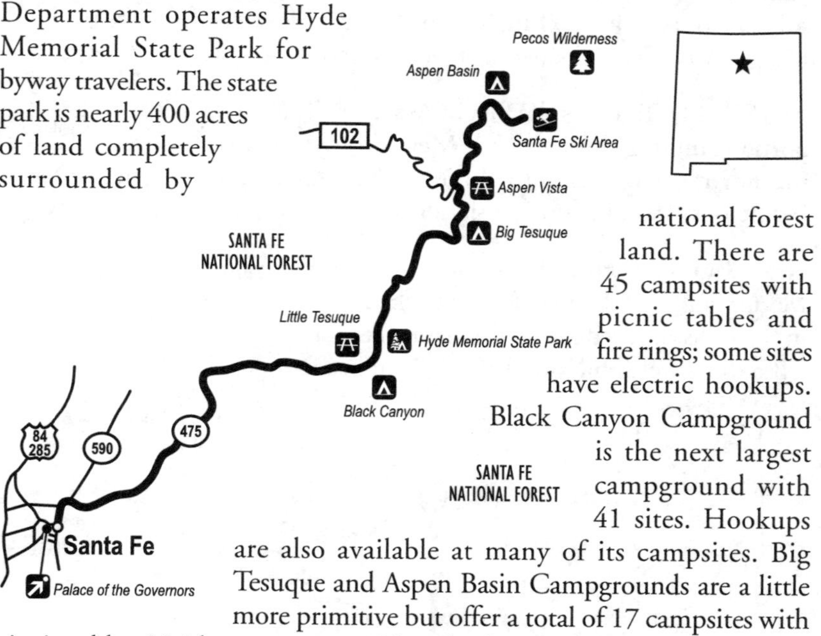

Information: Santa Fe National Forest, 1474 Rodeo Rd, Santa Fe NM 87505 / 505-438-7840. Hyde Memorial State Park, 740 Hyde Park Rd, Santa Fe NM 87501 / 505-983-7175. Santa Fe Ski Area, 1210 Luisa St, Santa Fe NM 87505 / 505-983-8200.

Lodging Invitation

Residence Inn by Marriott
1698 Galisteo St.
Santa Fe, NM 87505

Phone: 505-988-7300
Fax: 505-988-3243

Relax in comfort at Residence Inn — the All Suite hotel. Spacious living room area with fireplace and a fully equipped kitchen. Complimentary deluxe continental breakfast and newspaper daily. Voice mail and extended stay discounts are available. Only minutes (1½ miles) from historic plaza and 18 miles to ski resort.

Santa Fe Trail

Santa Fe Trail is a 300-mile byway traveling throughout northeast New Mexico. The byway follows a series of US Highways and State Highways, all of which are two-lane paved roads suitable for all vehicles. Much of the byway follows the frontage road of I-25. Santa Fe Trail remains open year-round.

The Santa Fe Trail was the first of America's Trans-Mississippi routes. The portion running through New Mexico travels across the grassy plains of the northeast corner into the mountainous region around Santa Fe. Numerous sites of historical significance are located all along the byway.

Near Watrous is Fort Union National Monument. Fort Union was established in 1851 as a guardian of the Santa Fe Trail. Three forts were built during its 40-year history;

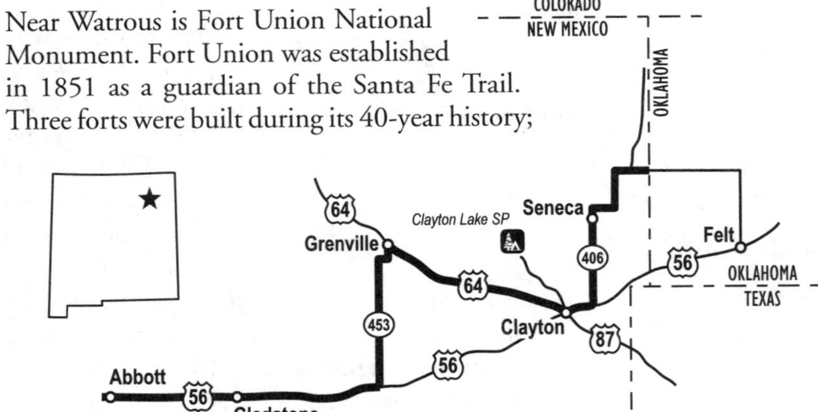

a self-guided tour path takes you among the remains of two. The largest visible network of Santa Fe Trail ruts can be seen here.

East of Santa Fe is Pecos National Historical Park, which preserves the ancient pueblo of Pecos, two Spanish Colonial Missions, Santa Fe Trail sites, and the site of the Civil War Battle of Glorieta Pass. A self-guided trail takes you through Pecos pueblo and the mission ruins.

Public campgrounds are available in four state parks near the byway: Sugarite Canyon, Clayton Lake, Storrie Lake, and Hyde Memorial State

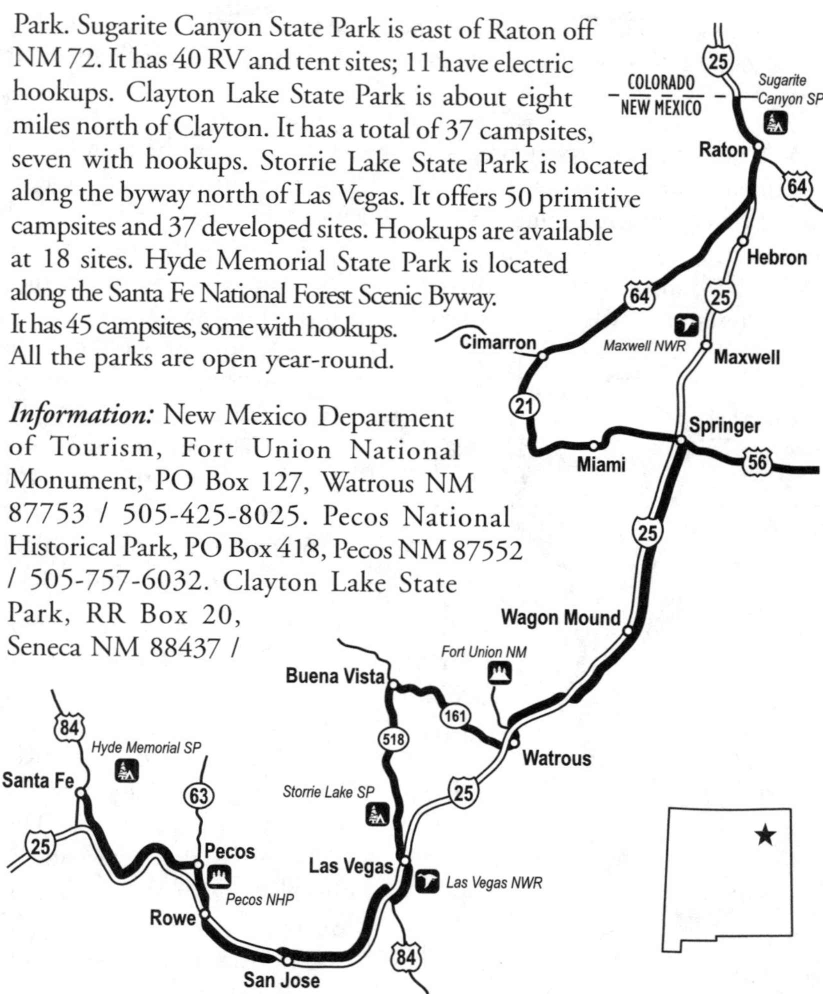

Park. Sugarite Canyon State Park is east of Raton off NM 72. It has 40 RV and tent sites; 11 have electric hookups. Clayton Lake State Park is about eight miles north of Clayton. It has a total of 37 campsites, seven with hookups. Storrie Lake State Park is located along the byway north of Las Vegas. It offers 50 primitive campsites and 37 developed sites. Hookups are available at 18 sites. Hyde Memorial State Park is located along the Santa Fe National Forest Scenic Byway. It has 45 campsites, some with hookups. All the parks are open year-round.

Information: New Mexico Department of Tourism, Fort Union National Monument, PO Box 127, Watrous NM 87753 / 505-425-8025. Pecos National Historical Park, PO Box 418, Pecos NM 87552 / 505-757-6032. Clayton Lake State Park, RR Box 20, Seneca NM 88437 / 505-374-8808. Hyde Memorial State Park, 740 Hyde Park Rd, Santa Fe NM 87501 / 505-983-7175. Storrie Lake State Park, HC 33 Box 109 #2, Las Vegas NM 87701 / 505-425-7278. Sugarite Canyon State Park, HC 63 Box 386, Raton NM 87740 / 505-445-5607.

Sunspot

Sunspot is in south-central New Mexico approximately 85 miles east of Las Cruces. It travels across Lincoln National Forest between Cloudcroft and the Sunspot Solar Observatory. The byway follows NM 6563, which is a two-lane paved road suitable for all vehicles, for a total of 14 miles. New Mexico Highway 6563 is normally open all year.

The Sunspot scenic byway travels along the front rim of the Sacramento Mountains through a mixed forest of Douglas-fir, white fir, Southwestern white pine, ponderosa pine, and aspen. Mule deer, black bears, elk, and the occasional eagle and spotted owl can be seen from the byway. Turnouts along the route provide spectacular views of Tularosa Basin and the shifting sand dunes of nearby White Sands National Monument. On a clear day you can see the space port for the landing of the space shuttle. In fall, the aspen and maple-covered canyons and hillsides to the west of the byway display brilliant colors of yellow, orange, and red.

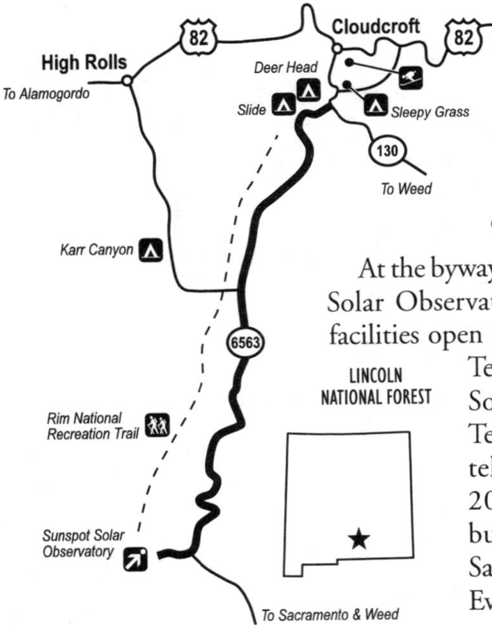

At the byway's southern end is the Sunspot Solar Observatory. There are two research facilities open to the public, Vacuum Tower Telescope and the John W. Evans Solar Facility. Vacuum Tower Telescope is the largest of the telescopes located here. Over 200 feet of this telescope is buried beneath the surface of Sacramento Peak. The John W. Evans Solar Facility is used for studying the sun's surface.

There are several scenic turnouts that not only provide panoramic vistas of the surrounding landscape, but also opportunities for taking a break and enjoying a picnic. Those that enjoy hiking will find 13 miles of the Rim National Recreation Trail running alongside the byway. Many side roads off the byway also invite exploration by the hiker or mountain biker.

Several national forest campgrounds are along or near the byway. They have campsites suitable for RV and tent campers but there are no hookups. All of the campsites have picnic tables and fire rings; some campgrounds have drinking water and restrooms.

Information: Lincoln National Forest, 1101 New York Ave, Alamogordo NM 88310 / 505-437-7200.

Wild Rivers

Wild Rivers is in north-central New Mexico about 25 miles north of Taos and 17 miles south of the Colorado state line. The scenic byway begins in Cerro and travels south alongside the Rio Grande River through the Wild Rivers Recreation Area. It is 13 miles long and follows Wild Rivers Road, which is also known as NM 378. The road is a two-lane paved road suitable for all types of vehicles. Wild Rivers is not maintained during winter; heavy snow may restrict access.

Wild Rivers Back Country Byway is a pleasant drive along the Rio Grande River around the Guadalupe Mountains. The byway crosses a landscape covered with sagebrush and stands of pinyon and juniper. The byway takes you to a point overlooking the confluence of the Rio Grande River and Red River, some 800 feet beneath you. The Guadalupe Mountains rise above the desert floor to the east. A hiking trail can be accessed from the byway that will take you into these rugged mountains. Several scenic overlooks are also provided along the byway that give you the chance to gaze at the river flowing way down below.

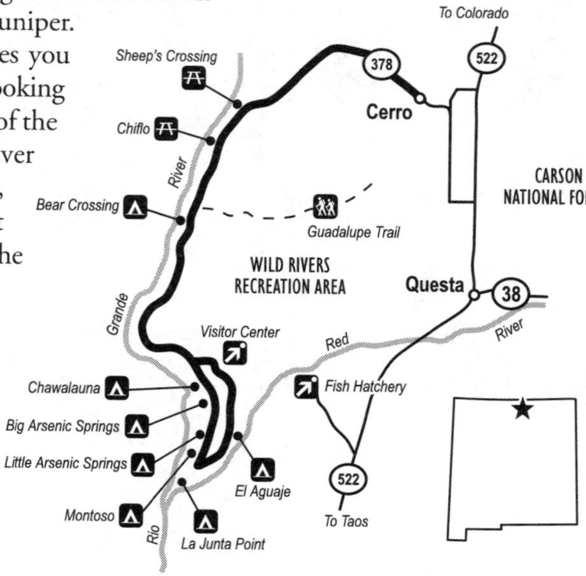

There are trails along the byway that will take you down the gorge to the river's edge. Here you may wish to cast a line in hopes of finding a brown trout attached to the other end. There are campgrounds located along the river's edge if you discover that you need to spend some more time trying to pull the fish from the water.

Those not interested in fishing can spend the day looking for wildlife. There are plenty of species inhabiting the area. Mule deer can often be seen along the roadside foraging among the grass. Red-tailed hawks and turkey vultures may be spotted flying over the canyon rims, almost effortlessly floating upon the wind currents. Cold winter snow forces the beautiful elk from higher elevations to the lower in search of food.

Travelers of the byway will find plenty of opportunities for pitching a tent or parking your RV. Some campgrounds are situated on the rim of the gorge, while others are along the river's edge. Campfire programs are offered from Memorial Day through Labor Day.

Information: BLM-Albuquerque Field Office, 435 Montano Rd NE, Albuquerque NM 87107 / 505-761-8700. Carson National Forest, 208 Cruz Alta Rd, Taos NM 87571 / 505-758-6200.

New York

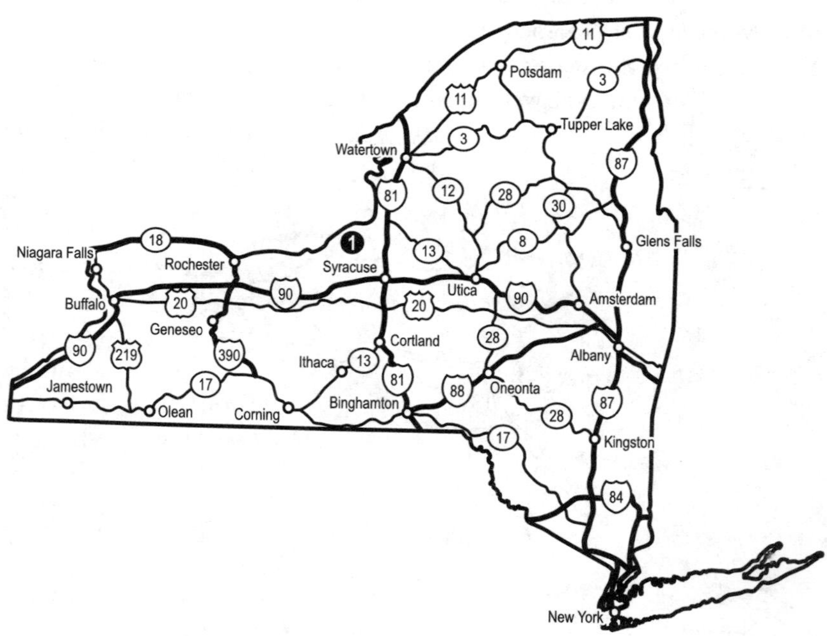

Seaway Trail

Seaway Trail follows the shoreline of Lake Erie and Lake Ontario as it travels from southwest New York to Rooseveltown. The byway is 454 miles long and follows a series of two-lane paved roads that are suitable for all types of vehicles. For detailed directions, please refer to the sidebar "Following the Seaway Trail." The byway is open year-round.

Seaway Trail travels along the shores of New York's Great Lakes, the Niagara River, and Saint Lawrence River, connecting quaint villages, historic sites, picturesque bays, and rolling farmland. The route is part of the National Park Service's National Recreational Trail system and is the longest such trail in the United States. Several scenic overlooks offer spectacular views of the Great Lakes.

During the months of September and October, the Seaway Trail is ablaze with fall colors of red, orange, and gold. Fall foliage tours can be taken by car, boat, floatplane, and train. Farmer's markets and roadside stands offer autumn's harvest of fruits and vegetables, or you may desire to pick your own.

The winter months bring cross-country skiers and snowmobilers to the trail. Miles of well groomed trails are found all along the route. Niagara Falls celebrates the season with its Festival of Lights illuminating the majestic waterfalls. In February, visitors can enjoy a frosty hot air balloon ride at the Thousand Island Winter Balloon Festival in Clayton. Farther north along the trail, the Ogensburg "River Shiver" reenacts its War of 1812 battle history.

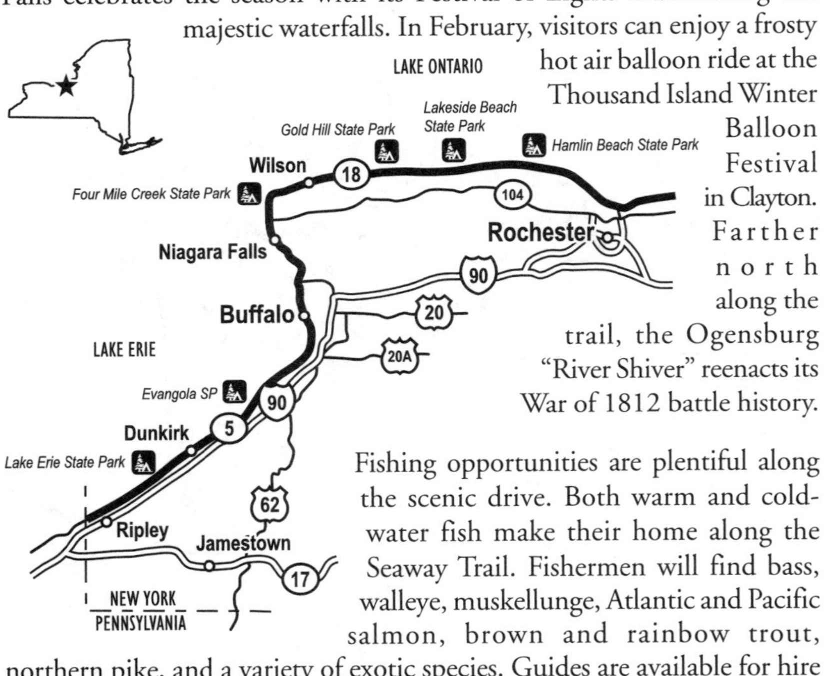

Fishing opportunities are plentiful along the scenic drive. Both warm and cold-water fish make their home along the Seaway Trail. Fishermen will find bass, walleye, muskellunge, Atlantic and Pacific salmon, brown and rainbow trout, northern pike, and a variety of exotic species. Guides are available for hire that will take you on Lake Erie or Lake Ontario.

For those interested in camping, many state parks and privately owned campgrounds along the byway can accommodate all types of camping interests—tents, recreational vehicles, cottages, and cabins. New York's state parks also offer hiking trails and picnic areas in addition to fishing, boating, and swimming opportunities. Some state parks offer interpretive sites of historic significance. History buffs will find 42 historical markers along the route providing information of events that occurred along the trail in the War of 1812. Historic lighthouses can also be found along the drive.

Information: NYS Seaway Trail Inc, PO Box 660, Sackets Harbor NY 13685 / 800-SEAWAY-T. Lake Erie Sp, RD1, Brocton NY 14716 / 716-

792-9214. Evangola SP, 10191 Old Lake Shore Rd, Irving NY 14081 / 716-549-1802. Four Mile Creek SP, Lake Rd, Youngstown NY 14174 / 716-745-3802. Golden Hill SP, 9691 Lower Lake Rd, Barker NY 14102 / 716-795-3885. Lakeside Beach SP, Rt 18, Waterport NY 14571 / 716-682-4888. Hamlin Beach SP, 1 Camp Rd, Hamlin NY 14464 / 716-964-2462. Fair Haven Beach SP, PO Box 16, Fair Haven NY 13064 / 315-947-5205. Selkirk Shores SP, 7101 SR 3, Pulaski NY 13142 / 315-298-5737. Southwick Beach SP, 8119 Southwicks Pl, Henderson NY 13650 / 315-846-5338. Westcott Beach SP, PO Box 339, Sackets Harbor NY 13685 / 315-646-2239. Long Point SP, 4459 Rt 430, Bemus Point NY 14712 / 716-386-2722. Burnham Point SP, 340765 NYS Rt 12E, Cape Vincent NY 13618 / 315-654-2522. Cedar Point SP, 36661 Cedar Point State Park Dr, Clayton NY 13624 / 315-654-2522. Keewaydin SP, PO Box 247, Alexandria Bay NY 13607 / 315-482-3331. Jacques Cartier SP, PO Box 380, Morristown NY 13664 / 315-375-6371. Coles Creek SP, PO Box 442, Waddington NY 13694 / 315-388-5636.

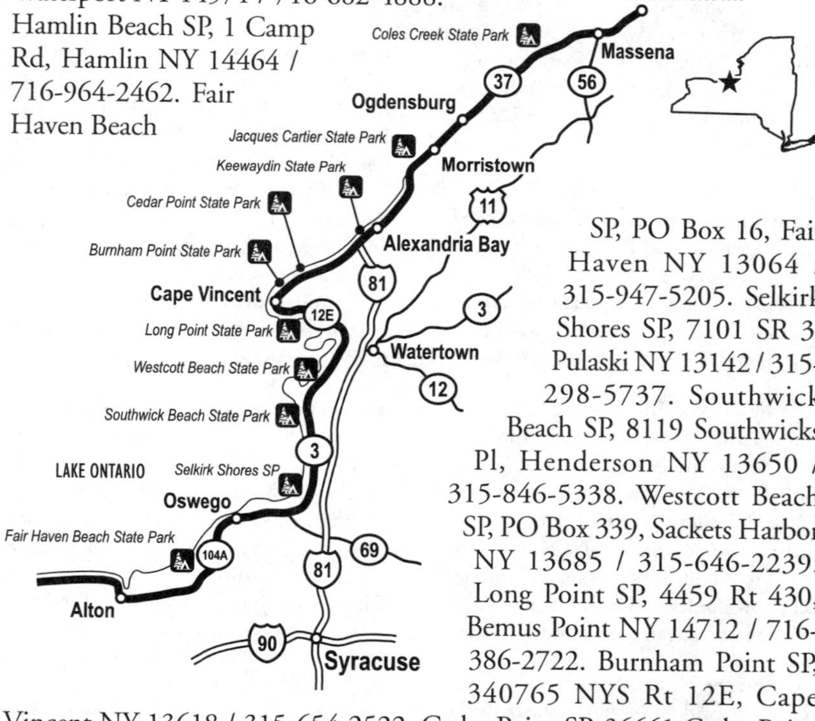

Lodging Invitation

The Vineyard Motel & Restaurant
3929 Vineyard Drive
Dunkirk, NY 14048

Phone: 1-888-DUNKIRK
716-366-4400
Fax: 716-366-3375

The Vineyard Motel offers 39 newly renovated rooms — AAA Approved — and one of western New York's finest restaurants with lounge and coffee shop. Located only 700 yards from I-90 at exit 59, tollbooth.

Following the Seaway Trail

Beginning at the Pennsylvania and New York state line near Ripley, the Seaway Trail follows NY 5 in a northeasterly direction toward the village of Silver Creek, to a point where NY 5 merges with US 20. Continue along NY 5 and US 20 to the community of Irving, where the trail leaves the highway and follows Old Lake Shore Road to the community of Wanakah.

In Wanakah, the byway picks up NY 5 again and continues to Lackawanna. In Lackawanna, follow Buffalo Skyway to the Delaware Avenue exit in Buffalo. Follow Delaware Avenue to Niagara Square. Go around Niagara Square to Niagara Street and follow Nigara Street to River Road.

The byway continues along River Road through the cities of Tonawanda and North Tonawanda to Buffalo Avenue. Follow Buffalo Avenue to the Robert Moses State Parkway. Follow the parkway to the Quay Street exit in Niagara Falls. Follow Quay Street to Rainbow Boulevard and turn left. Rainbow Boulevard is also NY 384. Follow NY 384 to Niagara Street and turn left.

Continue on Niagara Street until you reach Rainbow Bridge. Near Rainbow Bridge, follow NY 104E north to Lewiston and the intersection with NY 18F. Follow NY 18F north through Youngstown until it intersects with NY 18. Follow NY 18 through Roosevelt Beach, Olcott, Ashwood, and Kuckville.

Near Lakeside Beach State Park, the byway leaves NY 18 and follows Lake Ontario State Parkway. Follow the parkway to Irondequoit and Stutson Street. Follow Stutson Street to Saint Paul Boulevard and turn right and then left on Lake Shore Boulevard. Follow Lake Shore Boulevard east to Culver Road and turn right. Follow Culver Road to Empire Boulevard (NY 104) and turn left. Follow NY 104 east to Bay Road and turn left. Follow Bay Road north to Lake Road. Turn right and follow Lake Road east through Pultneyville to Sodus Point.

In Sodus Point, the byway travels south on NY 14 to Alton, where it intersects with Ridge Road. Follow Ridge Road through Resort and Wolcott, where you'll pick up Old Ridge Road and follow it to Red Creek and NY 104A. The Seaway Trail continues north on NY 104A through Fair Haven, Sterling, Southwest Oswego, and Oswego, where it then follows NY 104. Follow NY 104 through the community of Scriba to NY 104B and travel north through Texas to the intersection with NY 3.

Travel north on NY 3 to Baggs Corner and NY 180. Follow NY 180 north through Dexter to NY 12E at Limerick. Follow NY 12E west through Chaumont to Cape Vincent, where the highway then travels east along the Saint Lawrence River. Continue heading east on NY 12E to Clayton and the intersection with NY 12.

In Clayton, travel northeast on NY 12 through Alexandria Bay, Chippewa Bay, and Oak Point to Morristown. Near Morristown, the Seaway Trail picks up NY 37. Follow NY 37 to Ogdensburg.

In Ogdensburg, the byway follows NY 124 onto the state arterial, north on State Street, and east on Washington Street to North Rossell Street. Turn right and follow North Rossell Street to Fort Street and turn left. Follow Ford Street to Proctor Avenue and turn left. Follow Proctor Avenue to NY 812 and follow it south to NY 37.

Once you're back on NY 37, head northeast through Waddington to NY 131. Follow NY 131 until it rejoins NY 37. Travel east on NY 37 to the byway's end in Rooseveltown at the International Bridge.

North Carolina

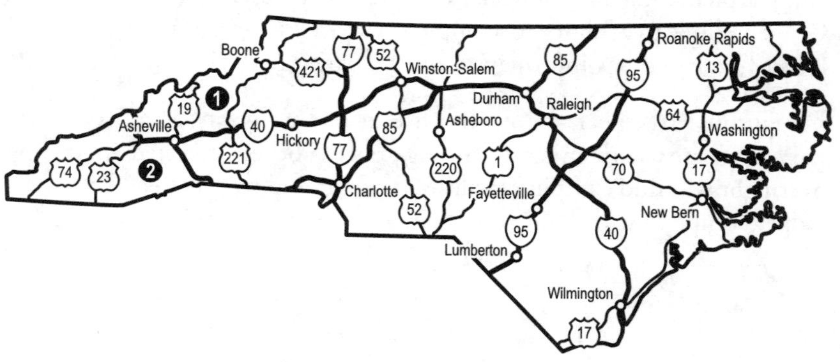

Blue Ridge Parkway

Virginia section see page 304

Blue Ridge Parkway is a 469-mile drive between Shenandoah National Park in Virginia and the Great Smoky Mountains National Park in North Carolina. This 252-mile segment is in western North Carolina and travels between the Virginia state line and Great Smoky Mountains National Park. Blue Ridge Parkway is a two-lane paved road that is suitable for most vehicles. Portions of the byway pass through small tunnels cut into the rock and may prohibit trailer traffic. The byway is generally open year-round but portions may temporarily close during winter.

The Blue Ridge Parkway follows the Appalachian Mountain chain, twisting and turning through the beautiful mountains. From the Shenandoah National Park, the scenic drive travels along the Blue Ridge Mountains for 355 miles. Then, for the remaining 114 miles, it skirts the southern end of the Black Mountains, weaves through the Craggies, the Pisgahs, and the Balsams before finally ending in the Great Smokies. The Blue

Ridge Parkway was authorized in 1933 and became a unit of the National Park Service in 1936.

This portion of the Blue Ridge Parkway is a beautiful drive across western North Carolina. Cumberland Knob is the first stopping point when traveling the route from north to south. This is a good place to walk through fields and woodlands on a loop trail to Cumberland Knob or enjoy a picnic lunch. A longer trail here will take you into Gully Creek Gorge. Allow two hours to complete the walk. A visitor center is also located here and has information on the parkway.

Doughton Park, near the northern end of the byway, is a 7,000-acre recreation area with miles of hiking trails. Those interested in staying overnight will find camping facilities for tents and trailers in addition to a lodge, complete with food service and gasoline. Picnicking facilities can also be found here.

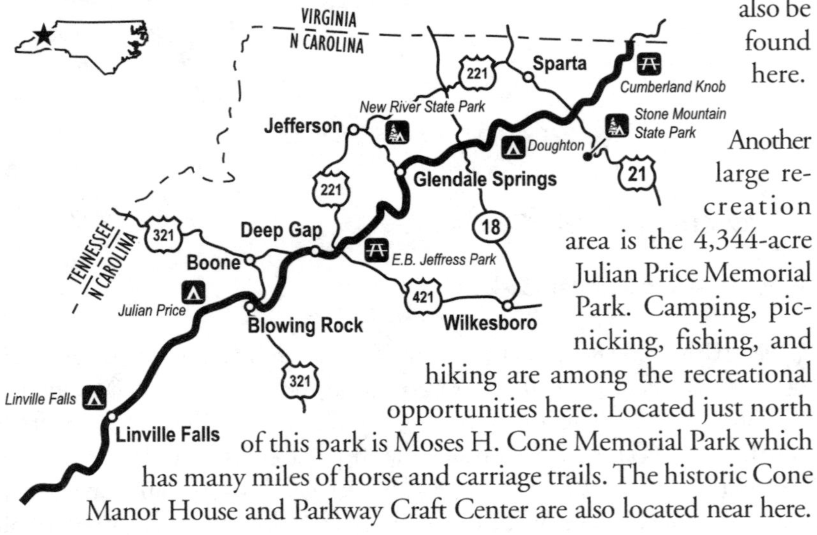

Another large recreation area is the 4,344-acre Julian Price Memorial Park. Camping, picnicking, fishing, and hiking are among the recreational opportunities here. Located just north of this park is Moses H. Cone Memorial Park which has many miles of horse and carriage trails. The historic Cone Manor House and Parkway Craft Center are also located near here.

The National Park Service has also developed several smaller recreation areas along the byway. At Linville Falls Recreation Area, visitors will find a walking trail that leads to scenic overlooks. The falls plummet through a dramatic, rugged gorge; an area that was donated by John D. Rockefeller. A visitor center, campground, and picnic facilities are also available.

Crabtree Meadows is a 250-acre recreation area that is painted a beautiful pink in the spring. A picnic area provides a pleasant setting for enjoying a lunch. Scenic waterfalls are reached by a short hiking trail. There is also camping facilities.

The Blue Ridge Parkway ends at the Great Smoky Mountains National Park, which preserves over 500,000 acres of heavily forested Appalachian Mountain land. For hikers, the Appalachian Trail runs through the park as do numerous other trails. Visitors will also find short, self-guided nature trails. There are ten developed camping areas in the park. The campgrounds have tent sites, limited trailer space, drinking water, fire rings, picnic tables, and restrooms. No hookups or shower facilities are provided.

Fall is a special time of the year to be traveling the Blue Ridge Parkway. Dogwood, sourwood, and blackgum turn a deep red in late September. Tulip-trees and hickories turn bright yellow, sassafras a vivid orange. The various oak trees add russet and maroon while the red maples proudly display their fall colors. All of this vivid color is set against a backdrop of the evergreen Virginia pine, white pine, hemlock, spruce, and fir.

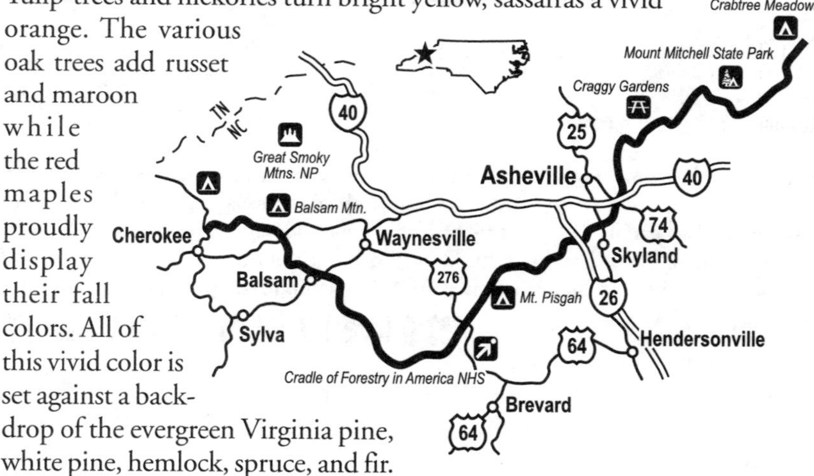

Wildlife is abundant along the route. Woodchucks, chipmunks, raccoon, and opossum are the more commonly seen among the wildlife. White-tailed deer and black bears are also present in the woods.

Information: National Park Service, Blue Ridge Pkwy, One West Pack Square Suite 400, Ashville NC 28801 / 828-298-0398. Pisgah National Forest, National Forests in North Carolina, PO Box 2750, Asheville NC 28802 / 828-257-4200. Mt. Mitchell State Park, Rt 5 Box 700, Burnsville NC 28714 / 828-675-4611. New River State Park, 1477 Wagoner Access Rd, Jefferson NC 28640 / 336-982-2587. Mt. Jefferson State Park, PO Box 48, Jefferson NC 28604 / 336-246-9653. Stone Mtn. State Park, 3042 Frank Pkwy, Roaring Gap NC 28668 / 336-957-8185. Cradle of Forestry in America NHS, 100 S Broad St, Brevard NC 28712 / 828-884-5713. Great Smoky Mountains National Park, 107 Park Headquarters Rd, Gatlinburg TN 37738 / 423-436-1200.

Lodging Invitation

Chestnut Street Inn
176 E. Chestnut St.
Asheville, NC 28801

Phone: 704-285-0705

A beautifully restored c. 1905 Colonial Revival in the heart of Chestnut Hill Historic District. The Chestnut Street Inn features antique furnishings, private baths, large porches, and afternoon "tea and crumpets". In the morning you'll enjoy a sumptuous breakfast served on antique china. A short five minute walk takes you downtown for antiquing, sight-seeing, or dining. Visa • MC • Discover cards accepted.

A/C H

Maple Lodge
152 Sunset Drive
P.O. Box 1236
Blowing Rock, NC 28605

Phone: 704-295-3331

Located one mile off the Blue Ridge Parkway in the heart of a picturesque mountain village. The eleven guest rooms and suites feature private baths, antiques, and goose down comforters. Two parlors with stone fireplace and library. Guests are treated to a full breakfast overlooking a wildflower garden. Only a ½ block from the restaurants, shops, and galleries of Main Street. Smoke-free Inn. AAA 3-Diamond rating. All major credit cards accepted.

A/C H

Oak Park Inn
314 S. Main Street
Waynesville, NC 28786

Phone: 704-456-5328
Fax: 704-456-8126

This quaint and charming renovated Inn awaits your arrival to beautiful downtown Waynesville. Oak Park Inn offers comfortable rooms with your choice of efficiency and two bedroom apartments or golf homes. All rooms have color cable TV, A/C & heat, and free rocking chairs! An easy walk to Main Street shops • boutiques • restaurants • grills • pubs • library • churches • and much more. Golf, skiing, rafting, and the Great Smoky Mountains are all nearby. Best rates in town! Our Inn and staff will have you proclaiming "I wasn't born in Waynesville but I got here as fast as I could".

A/C H

Stone Pillar Bed & Breakfast
P.O. Box 1881
144 Pine St.
Blowing Rock, NC 28605

Phone: 704-295-4141
800-962-9955
Internet: http://blowingrock.com/northcarolina

Nestled in the beautiful mountains of western North Carolina, the Stone Pillar provides a relaxing homelike atmosphere in an historic 1920's house. The decor is a tasteful blend of heirlooms and antiques, accented by a few touches of modern. Open all year, the accommodations include six guests rooms, each with private bath. A full breakfast is created daily in the house kitchen, and served family style. Area activities and attractions include: hiking • skiing • sight-seeing • shopping • dining • antiquing • Grandfather Mountain • the Tweetsie Railroad • or just relaxing on the front porch swing and rocking chairs. Located just off the Blue Ridge Parkway, in Blowing Rock, ½ block from Main St.

Sunset Motel
415 S. Broad St. (on US 64)
Brevard, NC 28712

Phone: 704-884-9106

A North Carolina classic motel. Clean rooms with free local calls, A/C, refrigerators, some with kitchenettes, and a refreshing cross-breeze in most rooms. AAA rated. Near the Cradle of Forestry • Brevard's renowned summer music festival • Pisgah National Forest • and trout fishing streams.

A/C

Forest Heritage

US FS

Forest Heritage is in western North Carolina about 30 miles southwest of Asheville. The byway forms a loop drive through Pisgah National Forest. Byway travelers can begin at the forest visitor center located near the junction of US 64 and NC 280. Forest Heritage is 79 miles long and follows NC 215, US 276, and US 64. The roads are two-lane paved roads suitable for all types of vehicles. The byway is usually open year-round.

Forest Heritage scenic byway crosses the spruce and fir-covered mountains of the Pisgah National Forest. Many beautiful rivers and streams flow alongside the byway. Scenic waterfalls are seen such as Looking Glass Falls, which tumbles 60 feet to the creek below.

Adjacent to Pink Beds Picnic Area is the Cradle of Forestry in America, a National Historic Site commemorating the birthplace of scientific forestry and forestry education in America. The area offers a visitor center with exhibits and historical film, gift shop, snack bar, and two interpretive trails. The one-mile paved Biltmore Forest School Campus Trail leads visitors to reconstructed and restored buildings used by forestry students at the turn of the century. The other trail, Forest Festival Trail, features early 1900s exhibits including a 1915 Climax logging locomotive and a steam-powered sawmill. The historical site is open May through October from 10:00 a.m. to 6:00 p.m.

Campgrounds along the byway provide the perfect spot for staying overnight or longer. Davidson River Campground has 161 sites for tents and RVs. It is recommended that reservations for a campsite be made at least two weeks in advance. Sunburst is a smaller camp-ground situated on the banks of the West Fork of the Pigeon River; there are ten sites available. The White Pine camping area is a group campground that can accommodate groups of 25 or less.

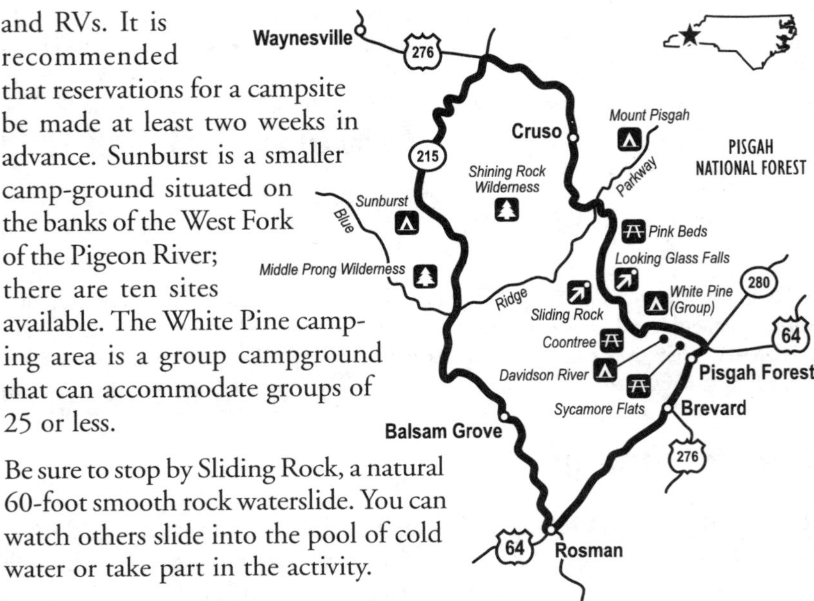

Be sure to stop by Sliding Rock, a natural 60-foot smooth rock waterslide. You can watch others slide into the pool of cold water or take part in the activity.

Information: Pisgah National Forest, Pisgah Ranger District, 1001 Pisgah Hwy, Pisgah Forest NC 28768 / 828-877-3350.

Lodging Invitation

Oak Park Inn
314 S. Main Street
Waynesville, NC 28786

Phone: 704-456-5328
Fax: 704-456-8126

This quaint and charming renovated Inn awaits your arrival to beautiful downtown Waynesville. Oak Park Inn offers comfortable rooms with your choice of efficiency and two bedroom apartments or golf homes. All rooms have color cable TV, A/C & heat, and free rocking chairs! An easy walk to Main Street shops • boutiques • restaurants • grills • pubs • library • churches • and much more. Golf, skiing, rafting, and the Great Smoky Mountains are all nearby. Best rates in town! Our Inn and staff will have you proclaiming "I wasn't born in Waynesville but I got here as fast as I could".

Sunset Motel
415 S. Broad St. (on US 64)
Brevard, NC 28712

Phone: 704-884-9106

A North Carolina classic motel. Clean rooms with free local calls, A/C, refrigerators, some with kitchenettes, and a refreshing cross-breeze in most rooms. AAA rated. Near the Cradle of Forestry • Brevard's renowned summer music festival • Pisgah National Forest • and trout fishing streams.

Ohio

1 Covered Bridge, *216*
2 Ohio River Scenic Route, *217*

Covered Bridge

Covered Bridge scenic byway is in southeast Ohio east of Marietta. The byway begins at the junction of OH 7 and OH 26. It follows OH 26 northeasterly to Woodsfield. The highway is a narrow, two-lane paved road suitable for most vehicles. Covered Bridge is 47 miles long and is open all year.

The Covered Bridge scenic drive winds through the pretty hills and valleys of southeastern Ohio across Wayne National Forest. Little Muskingum River flows alongside much of the byway and provides good fishing and canoeing. Wildlife that may be seen along the byway includes white-tailed deer, turkeys, beavers, red foxes, raccoons, and minks. This scenic byway is especially beautiful in fall when the route is covered with brilliant colors of red, orange, and yellow. Before traveling the byway, pick up a brochure from the Forest Service office in Marietta. It highlights ten points of interest along the way.

Ohio once boasted of 2,000 covered bridges, more than any other state. You'll come across three of these historical bridges. These bridges were covered with a roof, not to protect travelers from the elements of weather, but to keep the main structural timbers dry. If left exposed to rain, the timber would quickly rot.

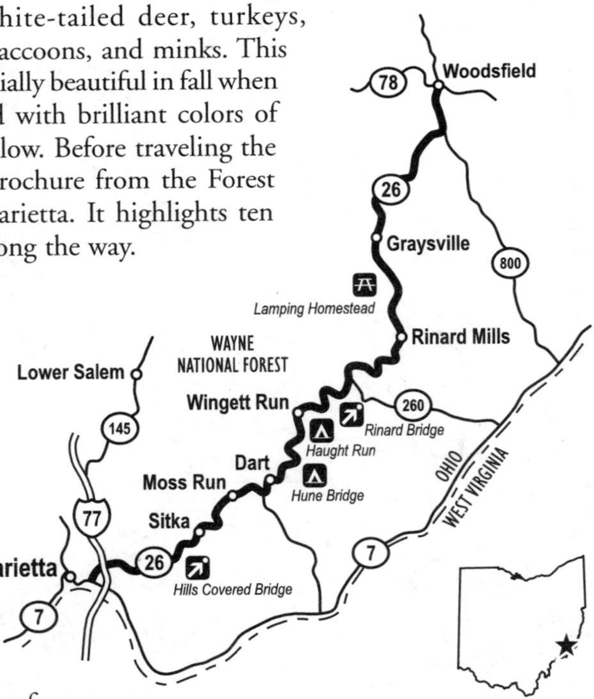

There are two national forest campgrounds on the byway: Hune Bridge and Haught Run. The Hune Bridge area has only two campsites with picnic tables; Haught Run has three. No drinking water is available at either campground.

The many rivers and streams within the national forest provide excellent opportunities for fishing. Anglers will find a large variety of fish including largemouth bass, smallmouth bass, bluegill, catfish, and crappie. The rivers also provide pleasant canoe trips. Outfitters can provide you with all that you need to enjoy a leisurely float.

If you feel like stretching your legs a bit, you can catch the North Country National Scenic Trail from the byway. This portion of the trail winds through the national forest between Woodsfield and Hune Covered Bridge.

Information: Wayne National Forest, Marietta Field Office, Rt 1 Box 132, Marietta OH 45750 / 740-373-9055.

Ohio River Scenic Route

Ohio River Scenic Route crosses southern Ohio for 452 miles. It primarily follows US 50, US 52, and OH 7 from the Indiana state line to the Pennsylvania state line. The roads are primarily two-lane paved roads suitable for all vehicles. In eastern Ohio, OH 7 is a four-lane divided highway. Ohio River Scenic Route is generally open year-round.

Ohio River Scenic Route cuts across southern Ohio through hardwood forests and rocky hillsides. The byway passes through numerous historical towns and historical sites. In Steubenville is the restored Fort Steuben, a 1780s fort built under the command of Captain John Francis Hamtramck to protect the early land surveyors. The birthplace of Ulysses S. Grant is along the byway in Point Pleasant near Neville. The site contains the restored three-room cottage where the 18th President of the United States was born.

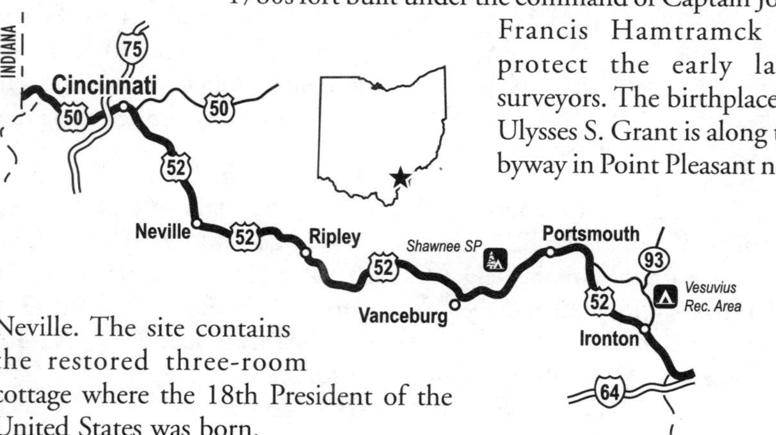

In addition to history lessons, the Ohio River Scenic Route offers opportunities for outdoor recreation. A portion of the byway crosses Wayne National Forest, where visitors will find trails, picnic areas, and camping

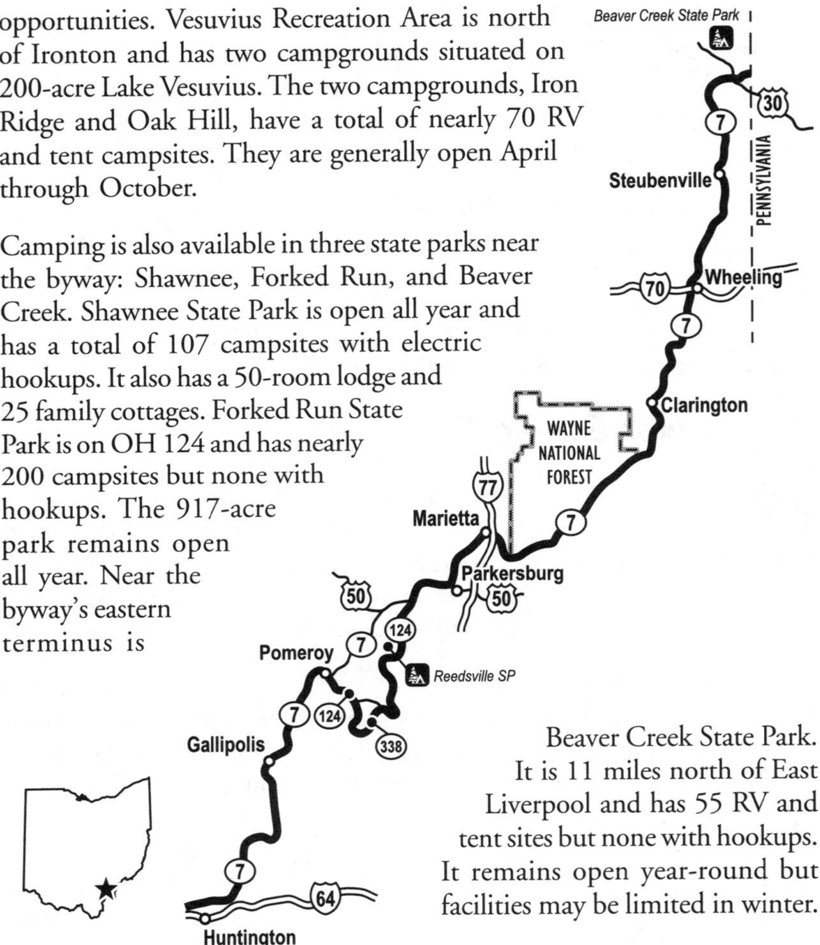

opportunities. Vesuvius Recreation Area is north of Ironton and has two campgrounds situated on 200-acre Lake Vesuvius. The two campgrounds, Iron Ridge and Oak Hill, have a total of nearly 70 RV and tent campsites. They are generally open April through October.

Camping is also available in three state parks near the byway: Shawnee, Forked Run, and Beaver Creek. Shawnee State Park is open all year and has a total of 107 campsites with electric hookups. It also has a 50-room lodge and 25 family cottages. Forked Run State Park is on OH 124 and has nearly 200 campsites but none with hookups. The 917-acre park remains open all year. Near the byway's eastern terminus is Beaver Creek State Park. It is 11 miles north of East Liverpool and has 55 RV and tent sites but none with hookups. It remains open year-round but facilities may be limited in winter.

Information: Ohio River Trails Inc., PO Box 300, Moscow OH 45153 / 513-553-1500. Wayne National Forest, 219 Columbus Rd, Athens OH 45701 / 740-592-0200. Wayne National Forest, Marietta Field Office, Rt 1 Box 132, Marietta OH 45750 / 740-373-9055. Beaver Creek State Park, 12021 Echo Dell Rd, East Liverpool OH 43920 / 330-385-3091. Forked Run State Park, PO Box 127, Reedsville OH 45772 / 740-378-6206. Shawnee State Park, 4404 State Route 125, Portsmouth OH 45663 / 740-858-6652.

Oklahoma

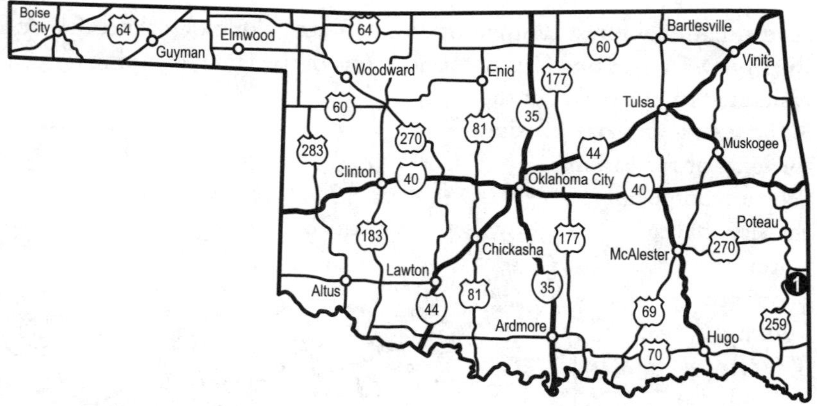

Talimena

The Talimena scenic byway is in southeast Oklahoma and southwest Arkansas. It follows OK 1 and AR 88 for 54 miles between Talihina, Oklahoma and Mena, Arkansas. Both state highways are two-lane paved roads with some steep grades and sharp curves. All types of vehicles can safely drive the byway. Temporary closure is possible during winter, otherwise the byway remains open year-round.

Talimena scenic byway rides atop the forested Ouachita Mountains, one of America's oldest land masses. These mountains are unique because they stretch east to west rather than north and south. The byway also cuts through the 26,445-acre Winding Stair Mountain National Recreation Area. Several scenic turnouts are located along the route providing beautiful panoramic views of the surrounding wilderness. Numerous side roads invite the traveler to further explore these heavily forested mountains. Wildflowers in spring proudly display their colors while autumn, not to be outdone, also puts on its own beautiful display.

The byway offers nearly unlimited opportunities for outdoor recreation. Wilderness areas adjacent to the byway offer seclusion for hikers, backpackers, and horseback riders. Also popular with the hiker or backpacker is the Ouachita National Recreation Trail, which can be accessed from the byway.

Several national forest campgrounds are located along or a short drive off the byway. Cedar Lake Campground is one of the larger camping areas. It is situated on the shores of the 90-acre lake and has 98 sites for tents or recreational vehicles. Some of the sites have water and electric hookups. The campground also has drinking water, restrooms, a boat ramp, shower facilities, hiking trails, fishing, and swimming. Hundreds of miles of horseback riding trails are also in the area. Billy Creek Campground is a short drive off the byway and has 11 units. Winding Stair Campground is located along the byway and has 26 campsites with picnic tables. Drinking water and restrooms are also provided.

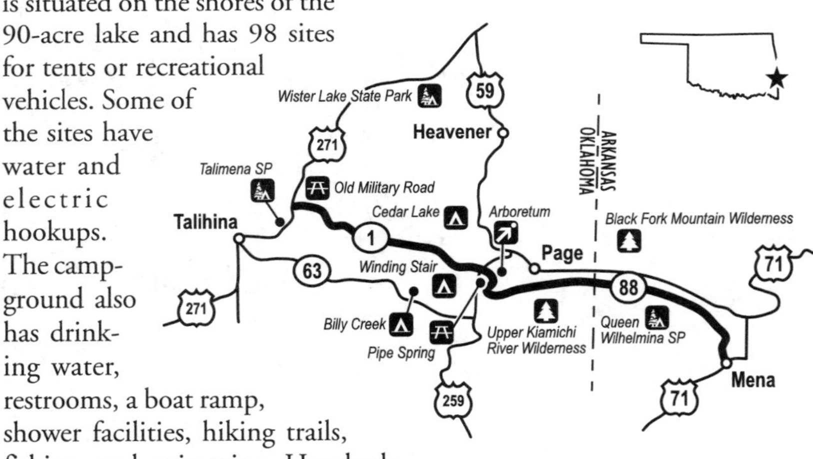

Information: Ouachita National Forest, PO Box 1270, Hot Springs AR 71902 / 501-321-5202. Talimena State Park, PO Box 318, Talihina OK 74571 / 918-567-2052. Queen Wilhelmina State Park, 3877 Hwy 88 W, Mena AR 71953 / 501-394-2863

Oregon

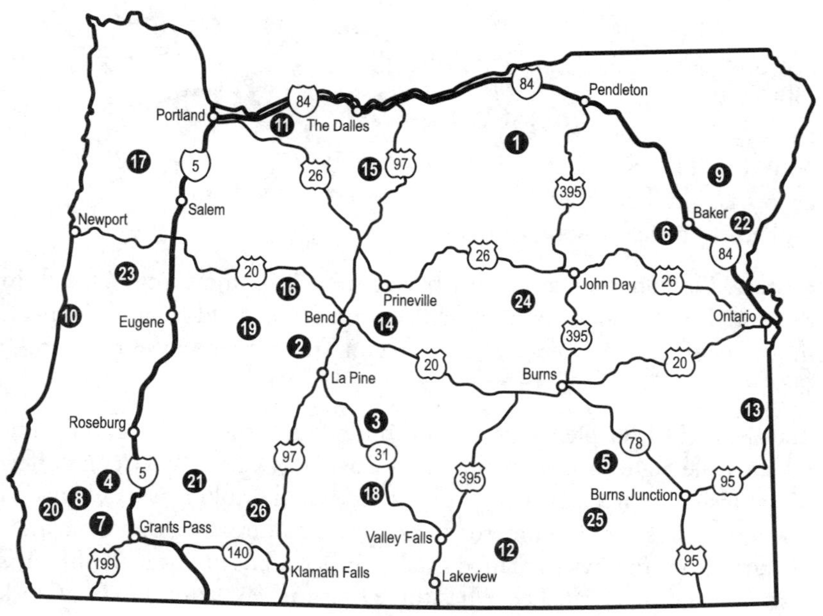

84
Pendleton
Portland
11
The Dalles
1
17
5
26
15
97
9
395
Salem
Newport
Baker
22
6
84
23
20
16
26
John Day
26
Prineville
24
Ontario
10
Eugene
19
Bend
14
395
2
20
La Pine
Burns
20
3
13
Roseburg
78
97
31
395
5
5
4
21
95
Burns Junction
8
20
18
26
7
25
Grants Pass
Valley Falls
140
12
199
Klamath Falls
Lakeview
95

Blue Mountain

The Blue Mountain byway is in northeast Oregon. It begins east of Arlington at Exit #147 on I-84 and travels southeast to the junction with FSR 73. Blue Mountain is 130 miles long and follows OR 74, FSR 52, and FSR 53. The roads are two-lane paved roads suitable for all types of vehicles. Oregon Highway 74 is generally open year-round; the Forest Service Roads are open May through mid-November.

The Blue Mountain byway begins on the southern bank of the mighty Columbia River and climbs south through rolling grassland alongside the tumbling waters of Willow Creek. The landscape changes dramatically as you climb up the Blue Mountains through forests of pine and fir, separated by valleys and meadows covered with wildflowers. Wildlife observers will want to be looking for white-tailed deer and bighorn sheep. Other wildlife includes mountain lions, black bears, an occasional bald eagle, and numerous species of songbirds.

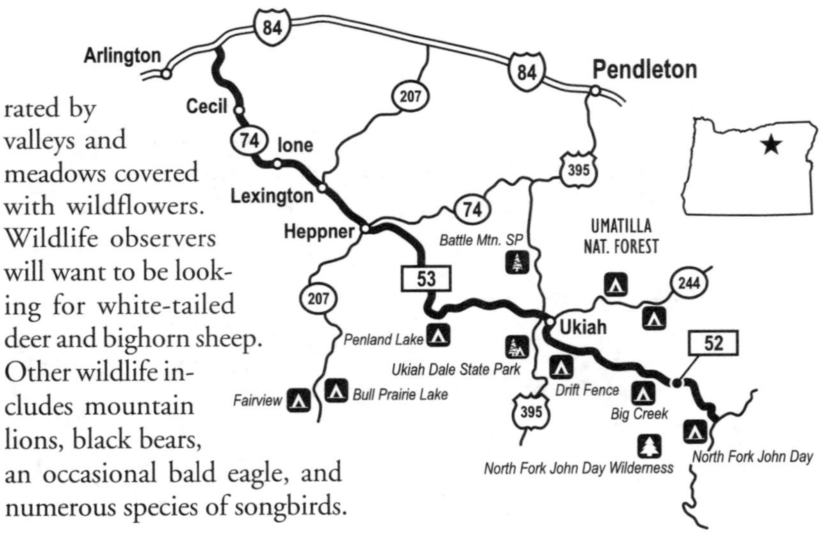

Historic Oregon Trail crosses the byway near the community of Cecil. In the mid-1800s wagon trains wore deep ruts in the land as more pioneers moved westward. Evidence of the Oregon Trail wagon wheel ruts can be seen near Wells Spring, 13 miles east of Cecil.

Travelers will find plenty of opportunities for outdoor recreation. The Ukiah-Dale State Park is situated on the banks of Camas Creek and offers 25 campsites for tents. It also has picnic tables and drinking water. Umatilla National Forest offers numerous campgrounds directly along or a short distance from the byway. Three small campgrounds are near the byway's eastern terminus. Drift Fence has three sites for tent camping, Big Creek has two. There are five sites suitable for either tents or recreational vehicles at the North Fork John Day Campground. None of the campgrounds have drinking water.

Information: Umatilla National Forest, 2517 SW Hailey Ave., Pendleton OR 97801 / 541-278-3716. Oregon Parks & Recreation Dept., 1115 Commercial St NE, Salem OR 97310/ 800-551-6949.

Cascade Lakes Highway

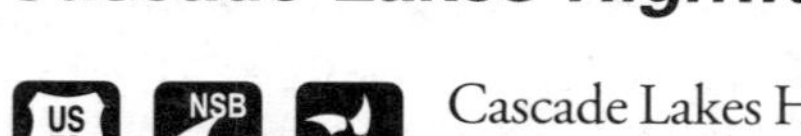

Cascade Lakes Highway is in central Oregon. It begins in Bend at the intersection of Galveston Avenue and 14th Street. From there, it travels west and south to the intersection with OR 58. Cascade Lakes Highway is 79 miles long and follows CR 46, which is a two-lane paved road suitable for all vehicles. The portion from Bend to Mount Bachelor Ski and Summer Resort is usually open year-round; the rest is closed in winter.

The scenic byway travels through the Deschutes National Forest offering magnificent views of snow-covered Cascade Mountain peaks. It travels through dense forests of pine and fir, skirting the shores of numerous mountain lakes. Wildlife observers will want to be on the lookout for mule deer, bald eagles, and a variety of hawks. The area is also inhabited by black bear.

Three Sisters Wilderness is 200,000 acres of preserved wilderness northeast of the byway. This pristine wilderness area offers over 100 alpine lakes for excellent fishing opportunities. It is also home to Collier Glacier, Oregon's largest glacier, which is located on the North Sister mountain peak. Trails are found along the byway that guide you into this unspoiled wilderness area. Since the wilderness is closed to all forms of motorized transportation, it is an excellent area for those seeking solitude, whether on foot or horseback.

Those interested in pitching a tent or parking an RV should not have any problem finding a spot as their are hundreds of campsites available. Most of the national forest campgrounds have drinking water and restrooms available. Some have shower facilities, however, none have electrical hookups. Boat ramps at many of the campgrounds provide access to the lakes. La Pine State Recreation Area offers 145 campsites, 95 with full hookups and 50 with electric. The recreation area also has drinking water, shower facilities, a dump station, and hiking trails.

Information: Bend Visitor Center and C of C, 63085 N Hwy 97, Bend OR 97701 / 541-382-3221 or 800-905-2362. Deschutes National Forest, 1645 Hwy 20 E, Bend OR 97701 / 541-388-2715. Oregon Parks & Recreation Dept., 1115 Commercial St NE, Salem OR 97310/ 800-551-6949.

Lodging Invitation

Shilo Inn Suites Hotel - Bend	Phone:	541-389-9600
3105 O.B. Riley Road		800-222-2244
Bend, OR 97701-7527	Fax:	541-382-4310

This full-service resort features a fine dining restaurant & lounge located along the banks of the scenic Deschutes River. All 151 guestrooms and suites are complete with microwave • refrigerator • coffee maker • ironing unit • and satellite TV with premium channels. VCR and movie rentals are available to guests. Facilities include a sauna, steam room, fitness center, and indoor/outdoor pools & spas. Amenities include free local calls, USA Today newspaper, complimentary full breakfast buffet and courtesy airport and Mt. Bachelor shuttle. Guests will enjoy the nearby golf courses and shopping at the factory outlet stores.

Christmas Valley

Christmas Valley is in south-central Oregon about 60 miles south of Bend. The byway follows a series of county roads and BLM Road 6109C for a total of 102 miles. The roads are a combination of paved and gravel roads suitable for most passenger cars. BLM Road 6109C requires a high-clearance or four-wheel drive vehicle. Some sections of the byway are closed in winter. Sections may also become impassable after periods of heavy rain from March through May.

Christmas Valley Back Country Byway travels across the high desert landscape covered with sagebrush and shifting sand dunes. A unique feature to this desert landscape, however, is the isolated forest of pine trees. The Lost Forest area preserves a 9,000-acre stand of ponderosa pine growing among the high desert land-scape common to this part of Oregon. This stand of ponderosa pine is about 35 miles east of the nearest ponderosa pine forest.

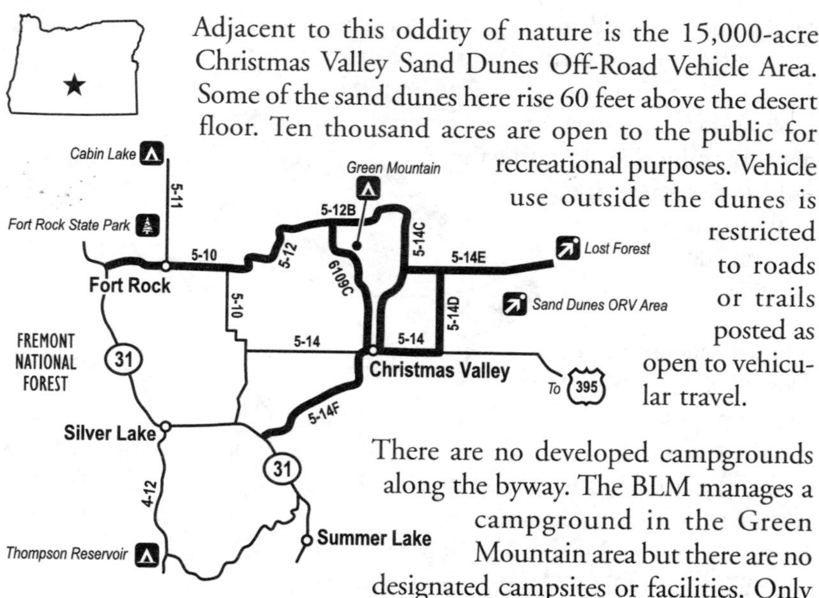

Adjacent to this oddity of nature is the 15,000-acre Christmas Valley Sand Dunes Off-Road Vehicle Area. Some of the sand dunes here rise 60 feet above the desert floor. Ten thousand acres are open to the public for recreational purposes. Vehicle use outside the dunes is restricted to roads or trails posted as open to vehicular travel.

There are no developed campgrounds along the byway. The BLM manages a campground in the Green Mountain area but there are no designated campsites or facilities. Only picnic tables are provided. About ten miles north of Fort Rock is the Deschutes National Forest and Cabin Lake Campground. It has 14 campsites on five acres and drinking water. South of the byway is Thompson Reservoir and the Fremont National Forest. Two campgrounds with a total of 32 sites and drinking water are on the lake.

Information: BLM-Lakeview District Office, 1000 S 9th St, Lakeview OR 97630 / 541-947-2177. Fremont National Forest, HC 10 Box 337, 1300 South G St, Lakeview OR 97630 / 541-947-2151. Oregon Parks & Recreation Dept., 1115 Commercial St NE, Salem OR 97310/ 800-551-6949.

Cow Creek

BLM 1 Cow Creek scenic byway is in southwest Oregon about 25 miles north of Grants Pass. The byway forms an open loop drive west of I-5 between Glendale and Riddle. Southern access from I-5 is Exit #80; northern access is Exit #103. The byway follows Cow Creek Road, which is a two-lane paved road suitable for all vehicles. Cow Creek is 45 miles long and remains open year-round.

The cool waters of Cow Creek flow alongside the byway as it makes its way through a mixed conifer forest. Railroad tracks of the historic Oregon & California Railroad also accompany you for most of the byway. Rugged rock bluffs, railroad bridges, tunnels, and retaining walls are among some of the views offered to the byway traveler. The railroad tracks, tunnels, and bridges are now used by Southern Pacific Railroad. Wildlife observers will want to be looking for osprey nests along the creek as well as mule deer. In spring the wildflowers proudly make their presence known along the byway.

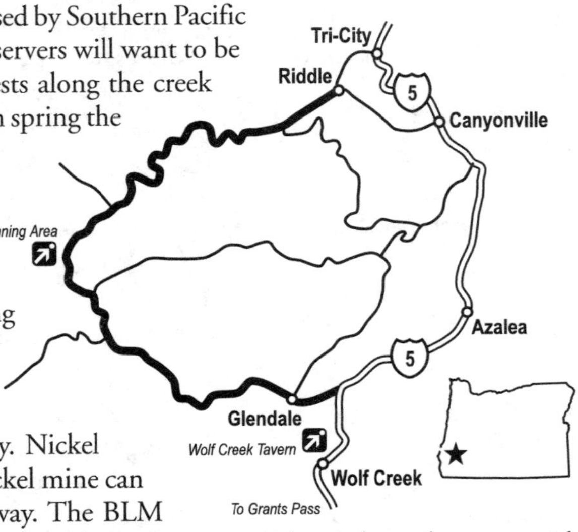

The area encompassing Cow Creek has long been a popular mining area, and still is to this day. Nickel Mountain with its nickel mine can be seen from the byway. The BLM maintains a recreational gold panning area midway along the route with day-use facilities including picnic tables and restrooms.

Although there are no developed campgrounds along the byway, the BLM permits camping nearly anywhere on public lands. Private land may surround public land, so it is best to obtain detailed maps showing the boundaries before choosing your campsite. Public campgrounds can be found along nearby scenic byways and in the nearby Siskiyou National Forest.

Information: BLM-Medford District Office, 3040 Biddle Rd, Medford OR 97504 / 541-770-2411. Siskiyou National Forest, 200 NE Greenfield Rd, Grants Pass OR 97526 / 541-471-6500.

Diamond Loop

Diamond Loop Back Country Byway is located in southeast Oregon 40 miles southeast of Burns. The byway's northern terminus is off OR 78 in New Princeton. It travels south to Frenchglen with a side trip through Diamond. The 64-mile route follows a series of county and state secondary roads, which are a combination of paved and gravel roads. Diamond Loop can be driven in a normal passenger car. Large RVs and vehicles pulling trailers should check with the BLM about current road conditions. The byway usually remains open year-round, though the graveled portions can be difficult during and after inclement weather.

Diamond Loop travels through a patchwork of high desert terrains, from mountain vistas and sagebrush-covered hills to red rimrock canyons and grassy marshes and valleys. Numerous species of wildlife can be seen including wild horses, mule deer, pronghorn antelope, hawks, and eagles. For viewing wild horses, the best place is the Kiger Mustang Viewing Area, located approximately 14 miles east of Diamond. The road to this area requires a high-clearance vehicle and is passable only in dry weather.

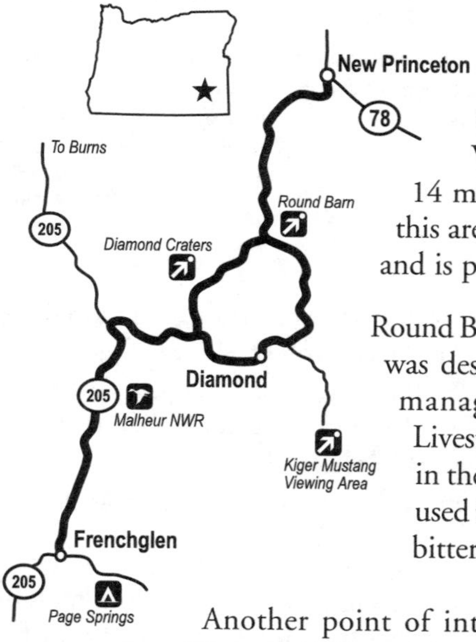

Round Barn on the northern end of the loop was designed and built by Peter French, manager of the historic Frenchglen Livestock Company. The barn was built in the late 1870s or early 1880s and was used to break horses during the long and bitter cold Oregon winters.

Another point of interest found along the byway is Diamond Craters, an outstanding natural area. This 17,000-acre area displays some of the most diverse volcanic features in America. A self-guided tour identifies the craters, cinder cones, and lave tubes found in the area. Malheur National Wildlife Refuge, managed by the U.S. Fish and Wildlife Service, was dedicated in 1908 by President Theodore Roosevelt. The area is popular with birdwatchers as there are over 200 species in the area.

There are no developed camping areas along the byway, however, dispersed camping is permitted on public lands. Check with the local office for more information and maps before setting up camp. Campgrounds can be found along the Steens Mountain scenic byway, which is to the south of this byway.

Information: BLM-Burns District Office, HC 74-12533 Hwy 20 W, Hines OR 97738 / 541-573-4400. Malheur NWR, PO Box 245, Princeton OR 97721 / 541-493-2612.

Lodging Invitation

McCoy Creek Inn
HC 72, Box 11
Diamond, OR 97722

Phone: 541-493-2131
Fax: 541-493-2131

At the base of Steens Mountain in the heart of country rich with history lies the McCoy Creek Ranch. The turn-of-the-century home has been carefully restored and renovated to give old-fashioned ambience without giving up modern convenience. The three bedrooms in the main house as well as the bunkhouse are beautifully furnished and have private baths. Guests can enjoy the breathtaking scenery of Steens Mountain recreation area, a stroll along McCoy Creek, a relaxing soak in the hot tub, or a hike over the rim onto the gentle north face of the Steens to watch the sun set. Children are welcome at the inn.

Elkhorn Drive

US FS

Elkhorn Drive is in northeast Oregon. It forms a loop drive beginning and ending in Baker City. The byway follows OR 7, CR 24, FSR 73, CR 1146, and US 30 for a total of 106 miles. The roads are two-lane paved roads suitable for all vehicles. Most of Elkhorn Drive is open all year. The portion between Granite and Anthony Lake is not plowed during winter and is closed mid-November through mid-June.

The Elkhorn Drive cuts through dense forests of ponderosa pine, Douglas-fir, and Engelmann spruce as it winds through the Elkhorn Mountains of the Wallowa-Whitman National Forest. The byway passes beautiful mountain lakes and rivers, all providing excellent fishing opportunities. Gold was discovered in this area in 1862 by five ex-Confederate soldiers. Visitors may wish to pan for gold near the Deer Creek Campground or McCulley Fork Campground at the areas set aside for this purpose.

Be sure to take some time and ride the rails of the historic Sumpter Valley Railroad. A five-mile section of the original tracks have been restored between Sumpter and the McEwen Station. The ten-mile round trip ride is powered by a steam locomotive. The narrow-gauge train operates on weekends and holidays throughout the summer.

Those interested in hiking or just taking a walk will find numerous trails along the byway. Hikers can access the Elkhorn Crest National Recreation

Trail, which is a 22½-mile trail following the ridge top of the Elkhorn Mountains. Other shorter trails can be found that lead to placid mountain lakes and secluded spots.

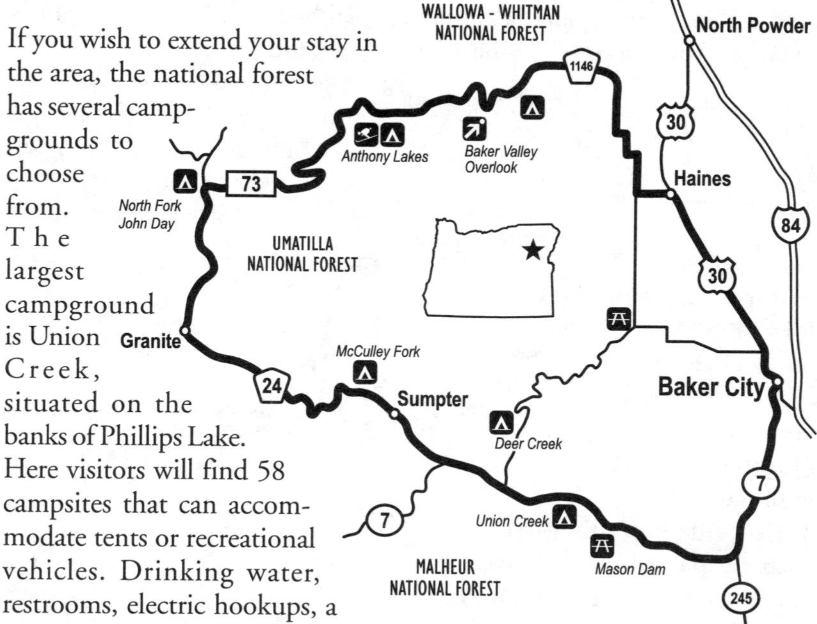

If you wish to extend your stay in the area, the national forest has several campgrounds to choose from. The largest campground is Union Creek, situated on the banks of Phillips Lake. Here visitors will find 58 campsites that can accommodate tents or recreational vehicles. Drinking water, restrooms, electric hookups, a boat ramp, and swimming area are among the facilities. Deer Creek Campground is a small six-site campground for tent campers. The Anthony Lakes area offers four campgrounds with a total of 56 sites.

Information: Wallowa-Whitman National Forest, Baker Ranger District, 3165 10th St, Baker City OR 97814 / 541-523-4476. Umatilla National Forest, 2517 SW Hailey Ave, Pendleton OR 97801 / 541-278-3716. Malheur National Forest, PO Box 909, John Day OR 97845 / 541-575-3000.

Galice - Hellgate

BLM 1 Galice - Hellgate is in southwest Oregon about four miles northwest of Grants Pass. Travelers can access the byway from I-5 at Exit #61. The byway travels west to the Siskiyou National Forest. A small segment travels north to Grave Creek, which is the beginning of the Grave Creek to Marial Back Country Byway. Galice - Hellgate is 39 miles long and follows Merlin-Galice Road, Hellgate Road, BLM 34-8-36, and FSR 23. The roads vary from single-lane to two-lane paved roads, which are suitable for passenger vehicles. Forest Service Road 23 is closed in winter; the rest of the byway remains open all year.

The Galice - Hellgate byway begins off I-5 and travels through forested hills and open pastures filled with grazing cattle, until it reaches the Rogue River. Here the landscape changes dramatically as the National Wild and Scenic River cuts through a rugged canyon bordered by forested slopes. In Galice, you can continue the drive for eight miles north with the Rogue River keeping you company. If you decide to head west, you'll begin climbing away from the river canyon into the heavily forested Siskiyou Mountains.

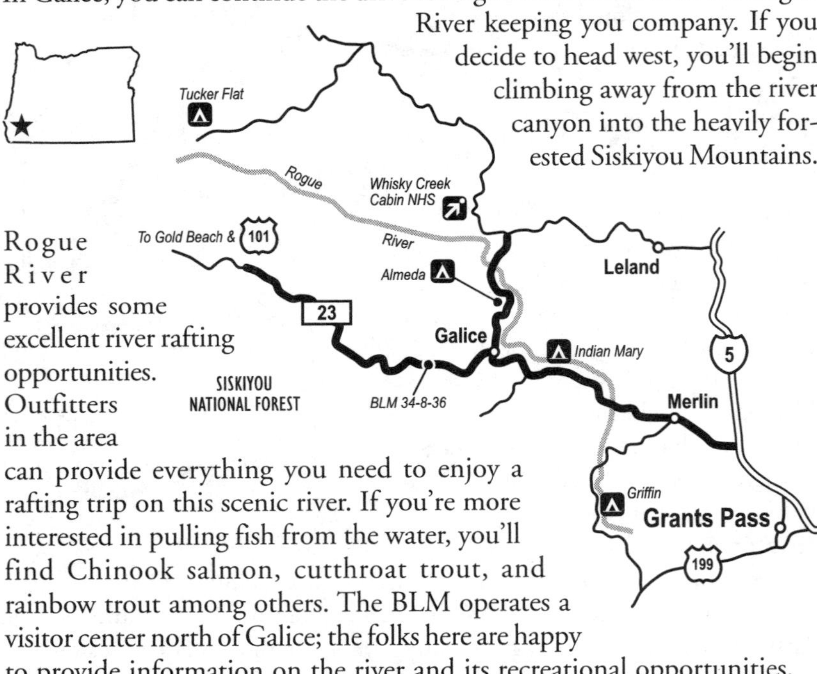

Rogue River provides some excellent river rafting opportunities. Outfitters in the area can provide everything you need to enjoy a rafting trip on this scenic river. If you're more interested in pulling fish from the water, you'll find Chinook salmon, cutthroat trout, and rainbow trout among others. The BLM operates a visitor center north of Galice; the folks here are happy to provide information on the river and its recreational opportunities.

There are two developed campgrounds along the byway, both situated on the banks of the river. Indian Mary Campground provides 95 sites with picnic tables, drinking water, full hookups, shower facilities, and access to the river. The Almeda Park is smaller with 25 campsites, drinking water, and a boat ramp.

Information: BLM-Medford District Office, 3040 Biddle Rd, Medford OR 97504 / 541-770-2411. Siskiyou National Forest, 200 NE Greenfield Rd, Grants Pass OR 97526 / 541-471-6500.

Lodging Invitation

Shilo Inn - Grants Pass	Phone:	541-479-8391
1880 NW 6th Street		800-222-2244
Grants Pass, OR 97526-1038	Fax:	541-474-7344

This newly remodeled Shilo Inn is conveniently located off I-5 just two miles from city center. All 70 guestrooms feature a satellite TV with premium channels. VCR and movie rentals are available at the front desk. Facilities include an outdoor heated pool for use during the warmer seasons as well as a year-round sauna and steam room. Amenities include free local calls, USA Today newspaper, continental breakfast, and Grants Pass Airport shuttle. Meeting space is available for up to 25 people. A restaurant is located adjacent to the motel.

Grave Creek to Marial

Grave Creek to Marial is in southwest Oregon about 28 miles northwest of Grants Pass. The byway can be reached from the Cow Creek scenic byway or the Galice - Hellgate byway. It begins at Grave Creek and travels northwest to the road's end in Marial. The 33-mile route follows Mount Reuben (BLM 34-8-1), Kelsey Mule, and Marial Roads, which are a combination of single-lane paved and gravel roads suitable for passenger cars. Motorhomes and vehicles pulling trailers should not attempt the byway. All the roads are closed in winter.

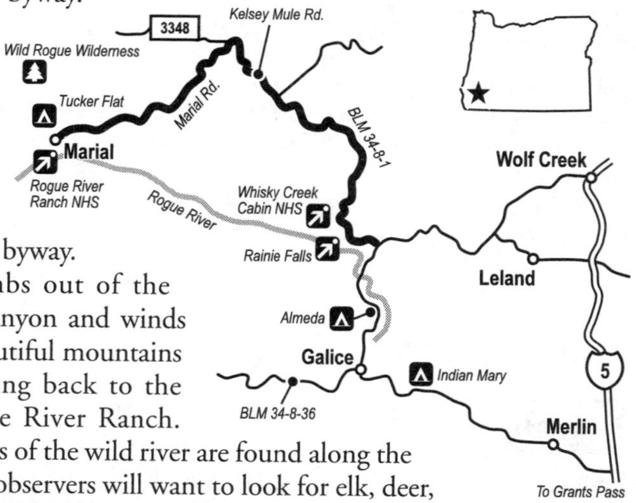

This byway is an excellent extension of the Galice - Hellgate byway. The route climbs out of the Rogue River Canyon and winds through the beautiful mountains before descending back to the river and Rogue River Ranch. Spectacular views of the wild river are found along the byway. Wildlife observers will want to look for elk, deer, and wild turkeys. Black bears also inhabit the area.

Near the beginning of this byway is a hiking trail that takes you to the scenic Rainie Falls. Also nearby is the trailhead to the Rogue River National Recreation Trail. Hikers and backpackers can take the trail along the banks of the river from Grave Creek to Marial, a distance of 24 miles. The trail continues south from Marial for an additional 16 miles to Illahe, crossing the Siskiyou National Forest.

Historic Rogue River Ranch lies at the end of the byway. It has a history dating back to the late 1800s when all that existed was a one-room "sugar pine shake" cabin. In the years that followed, the pioneer Billings family added more buildings including a barn and a trading post. The ranch was sold to the Bureau of Land Management in 1970 and now operates a museum depicting the ranch's history.

Camping is available at the Tucker Flat Campground, which offers ten sites. Be prepared to bring your own water or draw from Mule Creek. Be sure to purify the water from the creek before consuming.

Information: BLM-Medford District Office, 3040 Biddle Rd, Medford OR 97504 / 541-770-2411. Siskiyou National Forest, 200 NE Greenfield Rd, Grants Pass OR 97526 / 541-471-6500.

Lodging Invitation

Shilo Inn - Grants Pass	Phone:	541-479-8391
1880 NW 6th Street		800-222-2244
Grants Pass, OR 97526-1038	Fax:	541-474-7344

This newly remodeled Shilo Inn is conveniently located off I-5 just two miles from city center. All 70 guestrooms feature a satellite TV with premium channels. VCR and movie rentals are available at the front desk. Facilities include an outdoor heated pool for use during the warmer seasons as well as a year-round sauna and steam room. Amenities include free local calls, USA Today newspaper, continental breakfast, and Grants Pass Airport shuttle. Meeting space is available for up to 25 people. A restaurant is located adjacent to the motel.

A/C

Hells Canyon

US FS

Located in northeast Oregon, the byway forms an open loop drive east of I-84 with access points in Baker City and La Grande. Hells Canyon is 314 miles long and follows a series of state highways and national forest roads. The main loop follows OR 82, OR 86, and FSR 39, which are two-lane paved roads suitable for all vehicles. The spur roads are OR 350, FSR 454, FSR 3955, FSR 3965, and FSR 4240. These roads vary from two-lane paved roads to gravel roads. They are suitable for passenger vehicles but large RVs and vehicles pulling trailers may experience difficulty in turning around. Portions of the byway close temporarily during winter, otherwise Hells Canyon remains open all year.

Hells Canyon scenic byway takes travelers through the forested mountains and valleys of the Wallowa-Whitman National Forest to the scenic splendor of Hells Canyon National Recreation Area. This 652,488-acre recreation area protects the free-flowing Snake River in Hells Canyon and its surrounding landscape.

The byway offers access to numerous opportunities for outdoor recreation. Nearly a thousand miles of trails can be found in the National Recreation Area alone. Some trails are easy to travel providing quiet walks while others are difficult to find and a challenge to the experienced hiker.

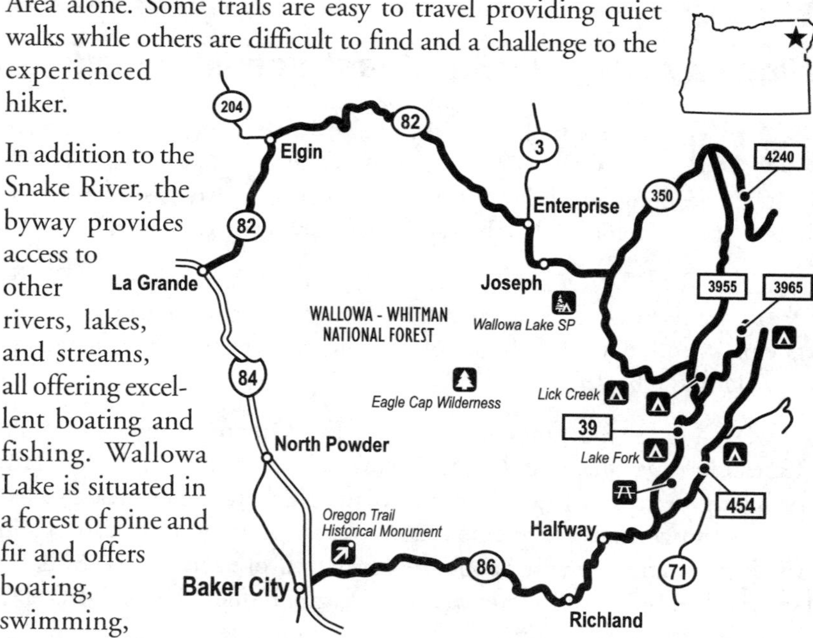

In addition to the Snake River, the byway provides access to other rivers, lakes, and streams, all offering excellent boating and fishing. Wallowa Lake is situated in a forest of pine and fir and offers boating, swimming, skiing, and fishing opportunities. The state park here has 210 campsites, 121 with full hookups and 89 for tent campers. Hiking trails provide access to the 200,416-acre Eagle Cap Wilderness.

Information: Wallow-Whitman National Forest, 1550 Dewey Ave, Baker City OR 97814 / 541-523-6391. Hells Canyon NRA, Wallowa Valley Ranger District, 88401 Hwy 82, Enterprise OR 97828 / 541-426-5546. Oregon Parks & Recreation Dept., 1115 Commercial St NE, Salem OR 97310/ 800-551-6949.

Lodging Invitation

Shilo Inn - Troy Wilderness Retreat	Phone:	541-828-7741
84570 Bartlett Road		800-222-2244
Enterprise, OR 97828-0085	Fax:	541-828-7891

At the Troy Wilderness Retreat you'll enjoy rustic cabins, lodge rooms and RV spaces located in the pristine Wallowa Mountains where the Wenaha River meets the Grande Ronde River. The facilities include a beautiful rustic restaurant and a country store where hunting licences and game tags can be purchased as well as basic necessities. Other facilities include a fuel service station, bath house, laundromat, game room, meat cooler, and recreation room with pool table. Your mountain vacation or hunting & fishing excursion can be an experience of a lifetime at the Shilo Inn - Troy Wilderness Retreat.

Highway 101 - Pacific Coast Scenic Byway

This scenic byway is a journey along Oregon's coast from the California state line to Washington's state line. The byway is 363 miles long and follows US 101, which is a two-lane paved road suitable for all vehicles. The byway is generally open year-round.

Travelers of this byway are rewarded with spectacular views of the Pacific Ocean, sandy beaches, rugged cliffs, and dense forests. There are many state parks with day use facilities for enjoying the scenery while picnicking or walking the beach.

Between North Bend and Florence is the Oregon Dunes National Recreation Area where sand dunes average 250 feet high. There are trails for hiking, horseback riding, and off-road vehicle use. The area also has several campgrounds and picnic areas. A visitor center is in Reedsport and has displays and a movie about the formation of sand dunes. Midway between Reedsport and Florence is the Oregon Dunes Overlook that has dune observation platforms, picnic areas, hiking trails, and restrooms.

A portion of the byway travels through the Siuslaw National Forest. South of Tillamook is the Sand Lake Recreation Area, which has three public campgrounds. A total of 240 RV and tent campsites are available. Between Waldport and Florence are four more national forest campgrounds: Tillicum Beach, Cape Perpetua, Rock Creek, and Sutton Creek. Tillicum Beach is open year-round and has 60 campsites. Cape Perpetua is open mid-May through September and has 38 sites. Rock Creek has 16 RV and tent sites available mid-May through September. Sutton Creek is also open mid-May through September and has 80 campsites; 20 have electric hookups. Besides camping, the national forest also offers numerous picnic areas, hiking and equestrian trails, and great spots for fishing.

Information: Oregon Tourism Commission, 775 Summer St NE, Salem OR 97310 / 503-986-0007 or 800-547-7842. Bay Area C of C Visitor Bureau, PO Box 210, Coos Bay OR 97420 / 800-824-8486. Siuslaw

National Forest, PO Box 1148, Corvallis OR 97339 / 541-750-7000. Oregon Parks & Recreation Dept., 1115 Commercial St NE, Salem OR 97310/ 800-551-6949.

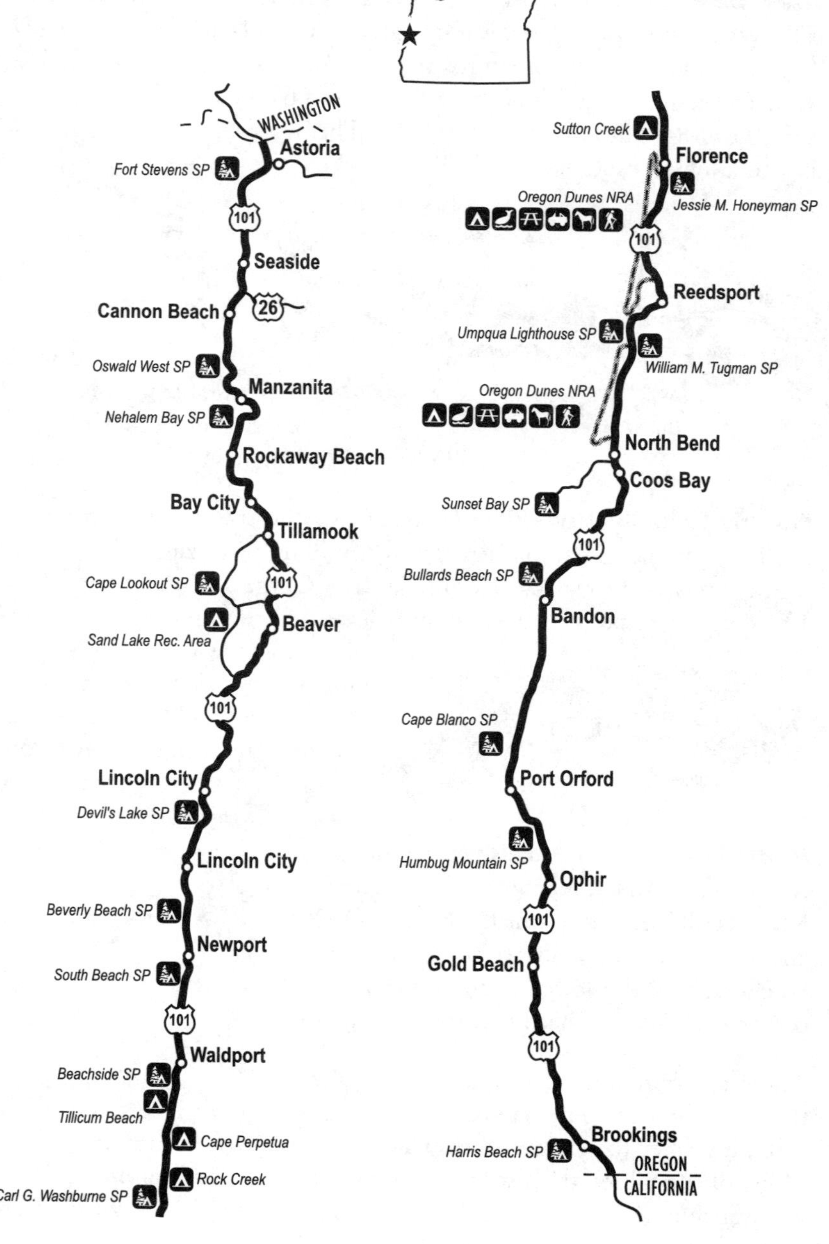

Historic Columbia River Highway

Historic Columbia River Highway is in northwest Oregon, east of Portland. The byway is divided into two segments. The western portion begins near Troutdale at Exit #18 on I-84 and follows Crown Point Highway for approximately 21 miles. It rejoins I-84 at Exit #35. The eastern segment begins at I-84 Exit #69 and follows US 30 to I-84 Exit #83 near The Dalles. The byway is a total of 37 miles long and follows two-lane paved roads suitable for all types of vehicles. Historic Columbia River Highway usually remains open year-round.

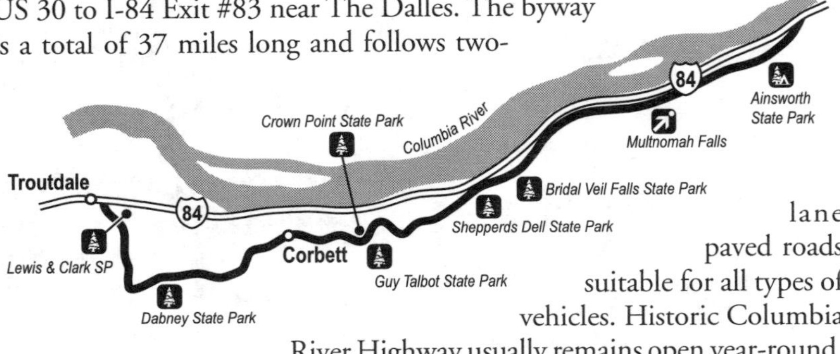

Historic Columbia River Highway rewards the traveler with beautiful overlooks of the Columbia River and tumbling waterfalls. The western segment travels through the Columbia River Gorge National Scenic Area. The gorge is a spectacular river canyon cutting the only sea-level route through the Cascade Mountains. Perhaps the highlight of this segment of the byway is Multnomah Falls, which drops 620 feet.

A paved one-mile trail takes you to the top of the falls. Nearby is the historic Multnomah Falls Lodge, which was built in 1925 and is on the National Register of Historic Places. Inside the lodge is an information center, a restaurant, snack bar, and gift shop.

There are numerous state parks along the byway. Most have only day-use facilities such as hiking trails and picnic areas, but offer the chance to stop and enjoy the rich beauty of the area. Many of the hiking trails will guide you to waterfalls. Camping facilities are available in Ainsworth and Memaloose State Parks. Ainsworth State

Park is on the western segment of the byway and has 45 RV sites with electric, water, and sewage hookups. The park is usually open March through October. Memaloose State Park is off I-84 eleven miles west of The Dalles. It is open April through October and has 43 RV sites and 67 tent sites.

Information: Columbia River Gorge National Scenic Area, 902 Wasco Ave #2000, Hood River OR 97031 / 541-386-2333.

Lakeview to Steens

Lakeview to Steens is in southeast Oregon and begins five miles north of Lakeview. It travels northeast to the junction with OR 205, south of Frenchglen. The 90-mile byway follows OR 140, CR 3-13, and CR 3-12. Oregon Highway 140 and CR 3-13 are two-lane paved roads suitable for all vehicles. Country Road 3-12 is a gravel road that requires a high-clearance vehicle. Vehicles pulling trailers are not recommended on this portion. Lakeview to Steens is usually open all year, but severe winter storms can result in rough driving conditions or temporary closure.

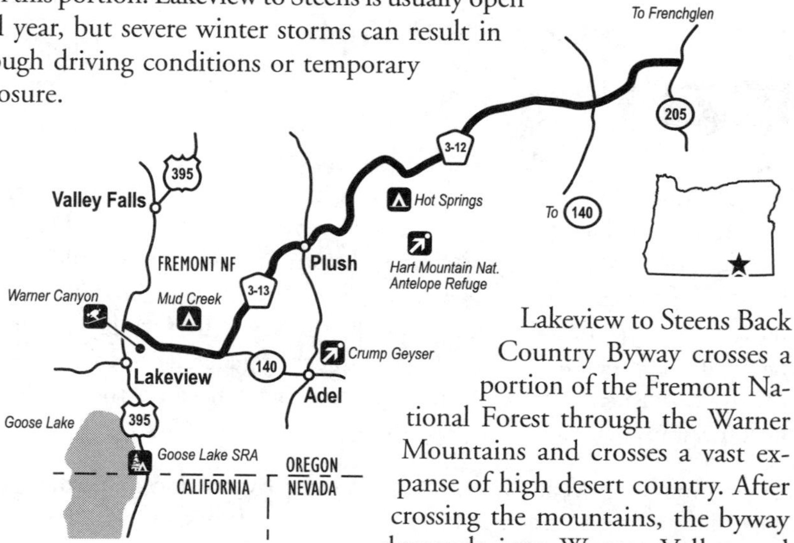

Lakeview to Steens Back Country Byway crosses a portion of the Fremont National Forest through the Warner Mountains and crosses a vast expanse of high desert country. After crossing the mountains, the byway descends into Warner Valley and crosses the Warner Wetlands. Spring and fall brings hundreds of migrating birds to this area including cranes, herons, egrets, ducks, and swans. The route then climbs the escarpment of Hart Mountain through the Hart Mountain National Antelope Refuge. In addition to herds of pronghorn antelope, the refuge provides habitat for sage grouse, burrowing owls, and coyotes in the lower elevations and mule deer, bighorn sheep, and prairie falcons in higher elevations.

Developed recreational facilities are nearly nonexistent along the byway. A primitive campground is located in the antelope refuge a few miles south of the refuge headquarters. Dispersed camping is permitted nearly anywhere on land managed by the Bureau of Land Management. Check with the district office in Lakeview regarding any private land that may exist along the byway before choosing your campsite.

Fremont National Forest offers Mud Creek Campground, which has eight campsites and drinking water. The campground is a few miles north of OR 140. About fifteen miles south of Lakeview off US 395 is Goose Lake State Recreation Area. Visitors will find 48 campsites with electric hookups. The park also has shower facilities, picnic areas, and a trailer dump station.

Information: BLM-Lakeview District Office, 1000 S 9th St, Lakeview OR 97630 / 541-947-2177. Fremont National Forest, HC 10 Box 337, 1300 South G St, Lakeview OR 97630 / 541-947-2151. Oregon Parks & Recreation Dept., 1115 Commercial St NE, Salem OR 97310/ 800-551-6949.

Leslie Gulch - Succor Creek

This scenic byway is 100 miles southeast of Baker City in eastern Oregon, near the Idaho state line. The 52-mile byway follows Succor Creek Road and Leslie Gulch Road, which are a combination of dirt and gravel roads. A high-clearance, two-wheel drive vehicle is recommended to travel the entire byway. Large RVs and vehicles pulling trailers are strongly discouraged from traveling Leslie Gulch Road because of its sustained 11 percent grade. The byway is also steep and narrow within Succor Creek Canyon, the segment through the state recreation area. Leslie Gulch - Succor Creek is generally open mid-April through October. Severe summer rainstorms can cause the byway to become impassable.

Leslie Gulch - Succor Creek Back Country Byway travels through the beautifully rugged landscape of eastern Oregon. It first crosses sagebrush-covered hills and then descends into the rugged canyon carved by Succor Creek. The byway then climbs back out of Succor Creek Canyon to rolling stretches of open landscape. The side trip on Leslie Gulch Road is a neat drive through a narrow and winding canyon of steep cliffs and towering rock spires. This road ends on the bank of 53-mile long Lake Owyhee.

Those interested in staying awhile will find camping areas courtesy of the BLM and the State of Oregon. Located along the byway is Succor Creek

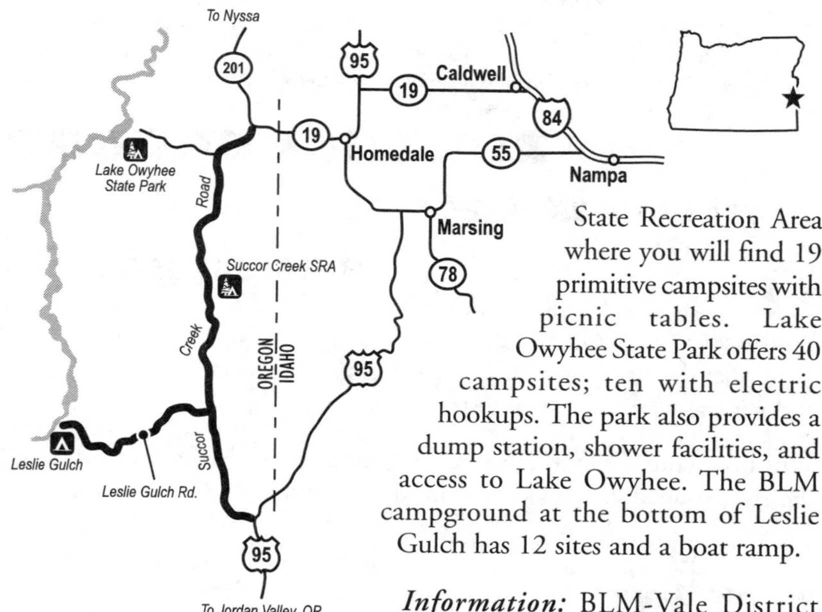

State Recreation Area where you will find 19 primitive campsites with picnic tables. Lake Owyhee State Park offers 40 campsites; ten with electric hookups. The park also provides a dump station, shower facilities, and access to Lake Owyhee. The BLM campground at the bottom of Leslie Gulch has 12 sites and a boat ramp.

Information: BLM-Vale District Office, 100 Oregon St, Vale OR 97918 / 541-473-3144. Oregon Parks & Recreation Dept., 1115 Commercial St NE, Salem OR 97310/ 800-551-6949.

Lodging Invitation

Shilo Inn - Nampa Boulevard	Phone:	208-466-8993
617 Nampa Boulevard		800-222-2244
Nampa, ID 83687-3065	Fax:	208-465-3239

Conveniently located off I-84, this motel is one of two Shilo Inns available to travelers in the Nampa area. All 61 guestrooms feature a microwave • refrigerator • and satellite TV with premium channels. VCR and movie rentals are available to guests. Facilities include an outdoor heated pool, indoor spa, sauna, steam room and guest laundromat. Amenities include free local calls, continental breakfast, USA Today newspaper and shuttle to both Nampa & Boise Airports. Meeting space for up to 25 people is available. A restaurant is located adjacent to the motel.

Shilo Inn - Nampa Suites	Phone:	208-465-3250
1401 Shilo Drive		800-222-2244
Nampa, ID 83687-3065	Fax:	208-465-5929

Located only 5 miles from city center, this larger of the two Shilo Inns in the Nampa area offers travelers 83 guestrooms. The mini-suites provide guests with a microwave • refrigerator • wet bar • and satellite TV with premium channels. VCR and movie rentals are also available. Facilities include a 24-hour indoor pool, spa, sauna, steam room, fitness center and guest laundromat. Amenities include free local calls, USA Today newspaper and shuttle to both Nampa and Boise Airports. Meeting space is available. O'Callahan's Restaurant & Lounge is located on premises.

Lower Crooked River

Lower Crooked River is in central Oregon about 35 miles east of Bend. The 43-mile byway follows OR 27 between Prineville and Brothers. Oregon Highway 27 is a two-lane paved road for 21 miles from Prineville; the rest is gravel. The road is suitable for all types of vehicles and generally remains open year-round.

This back country byway begins in Prineville and heads south through the steep-walled canyon carved by the Crooked River. The river flows alongside the byway until you reach Prineville Reservoir, formed by the construction of Arthur R. Bowman dam on the river. The segment of river along the byway is a National Wild and Scenic River. The river, besides being scenic, provides excellent fishing for native rainbow trout. Wildlife seen along this stretch of the byway includes deer, coyotes, and numerous birds of prey. Black bear inhabit the area as do bald eagles during winter.

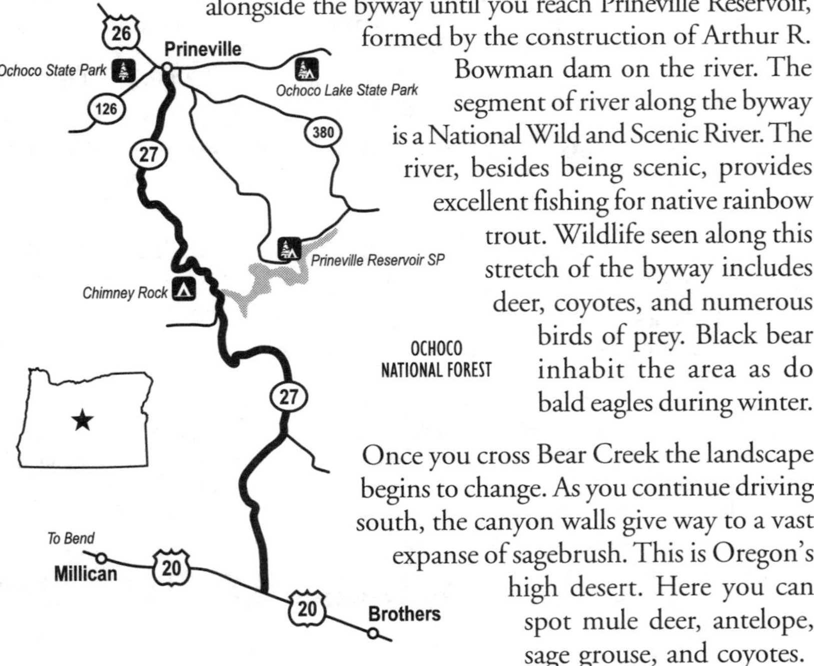

Once you cross Bear Creek the landscape begins to change. As you continue driving south, the canyon walls give way to a vast expanse of sagebrush. This is Oregon's high desert. Here you can spot mule deer, antelope, sage grouse, and coyotes.

There are several primitive BLM campgrounds along the byway in addition to the Chimney Rock Campground, which offers 16 campsites with picnic tables. Although not located directly along the byway, there are two state parks that offer camping facilities. Ochoco State Park has 22 primitive sites situated on the shore of Ochoco Lake. Prineville Reservoir State Park is more developed and has 22 sites with full hookups and 48 sites for tent campers. Shower facilities and a swimming beach are among the facilities available here.

Information: BLM-Prineville District Office, 3050 NE Third St, Prineville OR 97754 / 541-416-6700. Ochoco National Forest, 3160 NE Third St, Prineville OR 97754 / 541-416-6500. Oregon Parks & Recreation Dept., 1115 Commercial St NE, Salem OR 97310/ 800-551-6949.

Lower Deschutes River

Lower Deschutes River scenic byway is 40 miles south of The Dalles in north-central Oregon. Travelers can begin in Maupin and travel north for 28 miles or south for eight miles. The byway follows Deschutes River Road for a total of 36 miles. The road is an old railroad grade that is mostly unpaved. Only nine miles of the byway is paved. Most vehicles can complete the byway; those pulling trailers are discouraged from traveling the route south of Maupin. Also, there are some narrow, sharp curves along the unpaved portion. Lower Deschutes River is generally open all year.

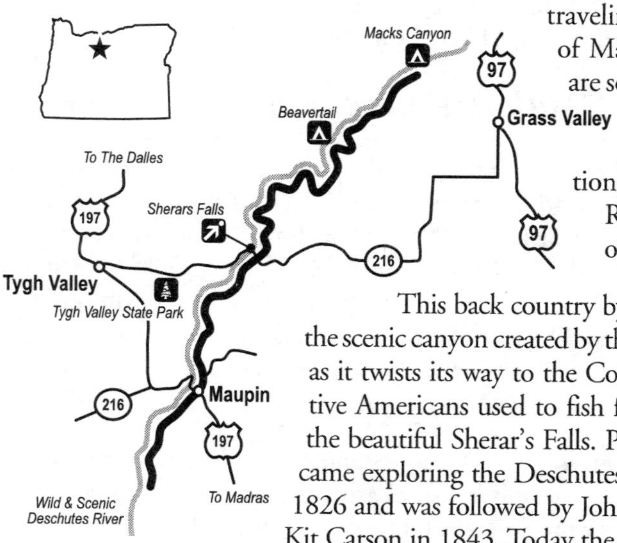

This back country byway cuts through the scenic canyon created by the Deschutes River as it twists its way to the Columbia River. Native Americans used to fish for salmon here at the beautiful Sherar's Falls. Peter Skene Ogden came exploring the Deschutes River Canyon in 1826 and was followed by John C. Fremont and Kit Carson in 1843. Today the river is part of the National Wild and Scenic River System and is used by rafters for its challenging white-water rapids. There are several good spots along the byway for watching these rafters or you may decide you'd like to float the river yourself.

If you're not interested in floating the river, then perhaps you would like to spend some time trying to pull rainbow trout, steelhead, or Chinook salmon from the river. Or you may be interested in finding a quiet, secluded spot to read and enjoy a picnic lunch. There's a variety of wildlife to be looking for, too. The watchful eye may catch glimpses of mule deer, osprey, or the great blue heron.

There are two developed and numerous primitive campgrounds along the byway for those interested in extending their stay. The two developed campgrounds are Beavertail and Macks Canyon. Beavertail Campground has 20 campsites with picnic tables and fire rings. Macks Canyon Campground offers 16 sites, also with picnic tables and fire rings. Drinking water and pit toilets are provided in both campgrounds. Both also provide boat access to the river. A small fee is charged for the use of each campground. The remains of a prehistoric pithouse village can be seen at the Macks Canyon recreation area.

This back country byway is heavily used by outdoor recreationists during spring and summer months. Exercise caution while driving the byway.

Information: BLM-Prineville District Office, 3050 NE Third St, Prineville OR 97754 / 541-416-6700. Oregon Parks & Recreation Dept., 1115 Commercial St NE, Salem OR 97310/ 800-551-6949.

McKenzie - Santiam Pass Loop

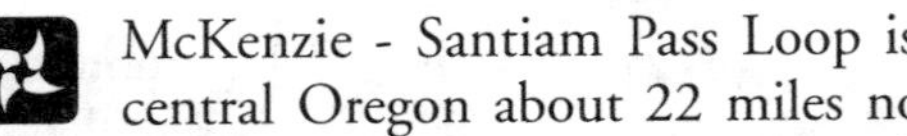

McKenzie - Santiam Pass Loop is located in west-central Oregon about 22 miles northwest of Bend. The byway begins in Sisters on US 20 and forms a loop drive back to Sisters. It follows OR 126, OR 242, and US 20 for a total of 82 miles. The roads are two-lane paved roads suitable for all vehicles. Motorhomes over 22 feet long and vehicles pulling trailers are discouraged from traveling OR 242. US Highway 20 and OR 126 normally remain open year-round; OR 242 is closed November to early July.

This scenic drive crosses the Deschutes and Willamette National Forests through ponderosa pine and stands of aspen, across Oregon's high desert landscape, and skirts the shores of numerous mountain lakes. Scenic vistas along the byway provide beautiful views of the Three Sisters mountain peaks as well as the surrounding wilderness. Mount Washington, standing proudly at 7,794 feet, may also be seen at times from the byway.

Flowing alongside OR 126 is the McKenzie River. The McKenzie River National Recreation Trail also follows the banks of the river. Several scenic waterfalls reward the hiker and offer a nice place to take a break and relax a bit. There are numerous access points along this part of the byway. There's a half-mile trail off OR 242 that leads to the beautiful Proxy Falls. Both the upper and lower falls drop about 200 feet over moss-covered cliffs. The Pacific Crest National Scenic Trail can also be accessed from the byway. Several other trails provide opportunities for a short stroll or a long day hike.

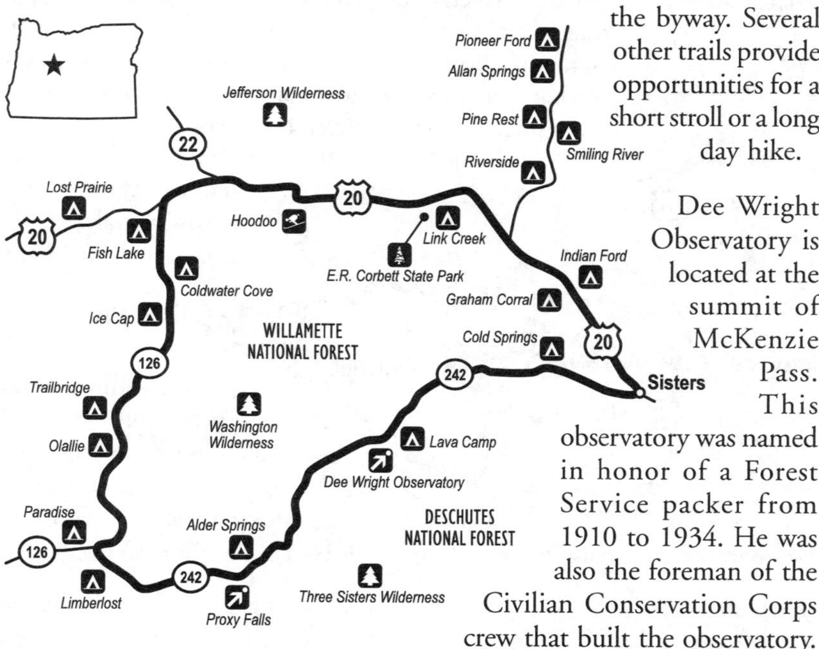

Dee Wright Observatory is located at the summit of McKenzie Pass. This observatory was named in honor of a Forest Service packer from 1910 to 1934. He was also the foreman of the Civilian Conservation Corps crew that built the observatory. Views from the observatory include Mount Hood, Mount Washington, Mount Jefferson, and Three Fingered Jack as well as the Three Sisters. The Lava River Trail is an interpretive trail beginning at the observatory and winds through interesting volcanic features.

Information: Willamette National Forest, McKenzie Ranger Station, 57600 McKenzie Hwy, MeKenzie Bridge OR 97413 / 541-822-3381. Deschutes National Forest, 1645 Hwy 20 E, Bend OR 97701 / 541-388-2715. Oregon Parks & Recreation Dept., 1115 Commercial St NE, Salem OR 97310/ 800-551-6949.

Nestucca River

BLM 1 Nestucca River is in northwest Oregon about 32 miles north of Salem. It begins in Carlton and travels west to Beaver on US 101. The byway is 45 miles long and follows Meadow Lake Road, Nestucca Access Road, and Blaine Road. The roads are two-lane paved roads suitable for all vehicles; a small segment is unpaved. Eleven miles are officially designated a Back Country Byway. Nestucca River generally remains open year-round; snow and ice may occasionally close some portions.

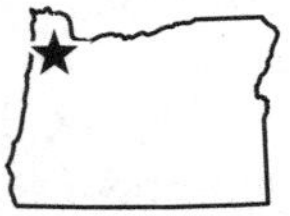

Nestucca River Back Country Byway travels through Oregon's old growth forest where Douglas firs reach heights of 200 feet and over 400 years old. It also cuts through the moss-covered canyon walls carved by the Nestucca River. The byway is kept company by the tumbling waters of this scenic river for most of its length. Wildflowers growing alongside the byway provide a diversity of colors throughout much of the year. Wildlife observers need to be on the lookout for elk and deer, which are common to the area. The byway traveler may also catch a glimpse of a bald eagle flying overhead.

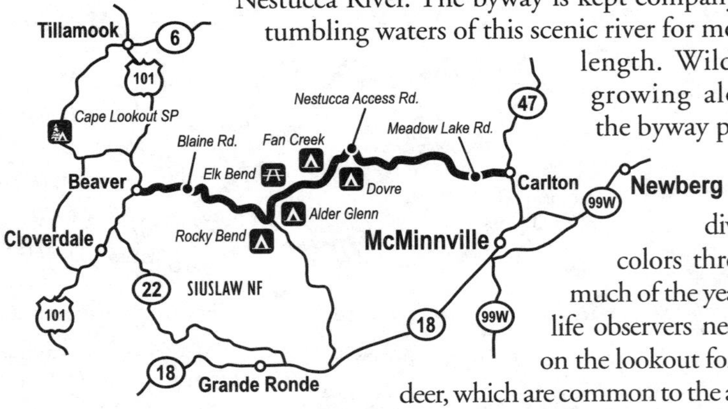

There are four BLM operated recreation areas and one Siuslaw National Forest campground along the byway. Dovre Campground offers ten campsites with picnic tables and fire rings. Fan Creek Campground has 12 sites and Alder Glen has 11, each with picnic tables. Elk Bend is primarily a day use area but does offer four campsites. West of the Alder Glen recreation area, the byway enters Siuslaw National Forest. Here, visitors will find the 12-site Rocky Bend Campground. This is the only campground where drinking water is not available. The campgrounds are situated on the banks of Nestucca River and provide excellent places for fishing or swimming.

Information: BLM-Salem District Office, 1717 Fabry Rd SE, Salem OR 97306 / 503-375-5646. Siuslaw National Forest, PO Box 1148, Corvallis OR 97339 / 541-750-7000. Oregon Parks & Recreation Dept., 1115 Commercial St NE, Salem OR 97310/ 800-551-6949.

Lodging Invitation

Sandlake Country Inn	Phone:	503-965-6745
8505 Galloway Road	Fax:	503-965-7425
Cloverdale, OR 97112		

Sshhh... Sandlake Country Inn is a secret hideaway on the awesome Oregon Coast. A private, peaceful place for making memories. This 1894 shipwreck-timbered farmhouse on the Oregon Historic Registry is tucked into a bower of old roses. You'll enjoy hummingbirds, Mozart, cookies at midnight, fireplaces, whirlpools for two, honeymoon cottage, breakfast "en suite", and vintage movies. Four rooms with private baths • full breakfast • no smoking. From Beaver travel north on US 101 approximately 2 miles to Sandlake Road. Travel west on Sandlake Road to Galloway Road, 5½ miles. Turn right (west) on Galloway Road.

Shilo Inn - Newberg	Phone:	503-537-0303
501 Sitka Avenue		800-222-2244
Newberg, OR 97132-1304	Fax:	503-537-0442

Conveniently located off highway 99 in the heart of Oregon's wine country, this Shilo Inn offers 60 mini-suites complete with microwave, refrigerator and satellite TV with premium channels. VCR and movie rentals are available to guests. Facilities include an outdoor pool for use during the warmer seasons and a year-round 24-hour indoor spa, sauna, steam room, fitness center and guest laundromat. Amenities include free local calls, continental breakfast, USA Today newspaper and McMinnville Airport shuttle. Meeting space is available for up to 50 people. A restaurant is located adjacent to the motel.

Shilo Inn - Tillamook	Phone:	503-842-7971
2515 N. Main		800-222-2244
Tillamook, OR 97141-9216	Fax:	503-842-7960

Conveniently located on the Wilson River — the perfect retreat for the avid fishing enthusiast. Shilo Inn offers the traveler 100 guestrooms and a fine dining restaurant & lounge. The mini-suites are fully equipped with a microwave • refrigerator • wet bar • and satellite TV with premium channels. VCR and movie rentals are also available. Facilities include a 24-hour indoor pool, spa, sauna, steam room, fitness center, guest laundromat and fish cleaning room. Amenities include free local calls, USA Today newspaper and Tillamook Airport shuttle. Meeting space is available.

Outback Scenic Byway

Outback Scenic Byway begins near La Pine in central Oregon. It follows OR 31 and US 395 south to New Pine Creek. A small segment follows CR 5-10 to Fort Rock. The roads are two-lane paved roads suitable for all vehicles. Outback Scenic Byway is 165 miles long and remains open year-round.

Oregon's Outback Scenic Byway travels through a diverse landscape, from lush green forests to arid desert. A portion of the byway travels through

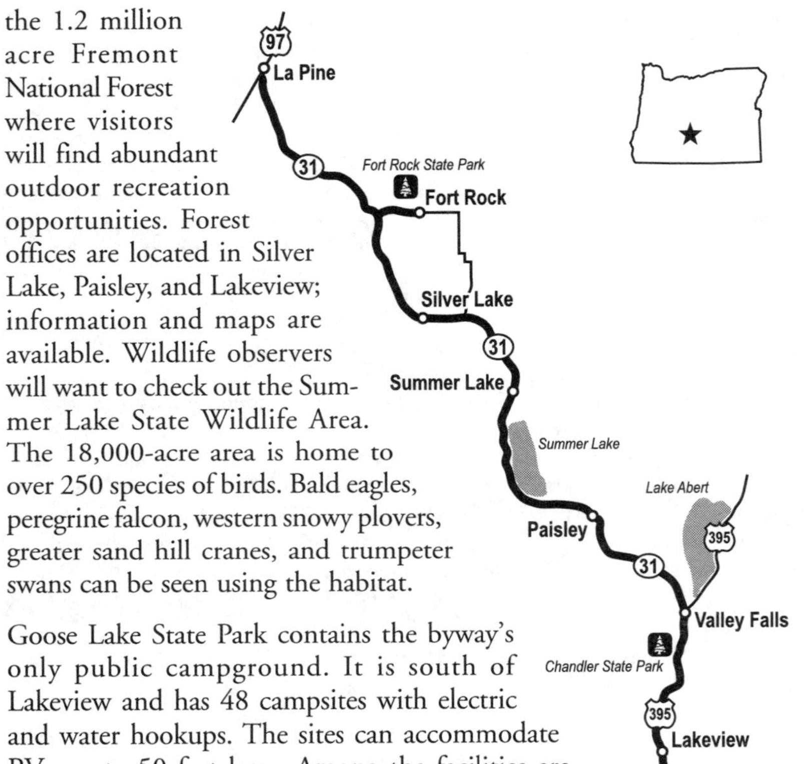

the 1.2 million acre Fremont National Forest where visitors will find abundant outdoor recreation opportunities. Forest offices are located in Silver Lake, Paisley, and Lakeview; information and maps are available. Wildlife observers will want to check out the Summer Lake State Wildlife Area. The 18,000-acre area is home to over 250 species of birds. Bald eagles, peregrine falcon, western snowy plovers, greater sand hill cranes, and trumpeter swans can be seen using the habitat.

Goose Lake State Park contains the byway's only public campground. It is south of Lakeview and has 48 campsites with electric and water hookups. The sites can accommodate RVs up to 50 feet long. Among the facilities are restrooms, a dump station, drinking water, and showers. The park is usually open April to October. Fremont National Forest contains numerous public campgrounds but none are located directly on the byway.

Information: Lake County C of C, 126 North E St, Lakeview OR 97630 / 541-947-6040. Fremont National Forest, HC 10 Box 337, 1300 South G St, Lakeview OR 97630 / 541-947-2151. Oregon Parks & Recreation Dept., 1115 Commercial St NE, Salem OR 97310/ 800-551-6949.

Robert Aufderheide Memorial Drive

US FS Robert Aufderheide Memorial Drive is in west-central Oregon about 40 miles east of Eugene. It begins just east of Blue River and travels south to Westfir. The byway is 65 miles long and follows FSR 19, which is a two-lane paved road suitable for all vehicles. Travelers can pick up an audio cassette tape of the tour from ranger stations in Blue River or

Oakridge. The tape is free and is returned when you complete the drive. Robert Aufderheide Memorial Drive is generally open April through October.

Robert Aufderheide Memorial Drive is named in honor of a man who devoted 24 years of his life to forestry. Robert Aufderheide was the Supervisor of Willamette National Forest from 1954 until his death in 1959.

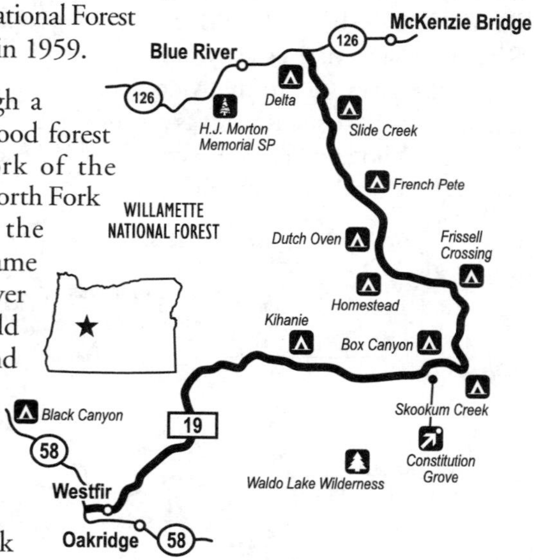

The byway travels through a mixed conifer and hardwood forest alongside the South Fork of the McKenzie River and the North Fork of the Middle Fork of the Willamette River, a long name but a scenic river. This river is part of the National Wild and Scenic River System and provides good opportunities for catching rainbow and cutthroat trout.

Those interested in hiking, backpacking, or horseback riding will find a lot of trails along the byway. There's the Waldo Wilderness Trail that takes you into Waldo Wilderness. Another trail is called the Grasshopper Trail and takes you through the Chucksney Roadless Area, not a designated wilderness but offers seclusion just the same. There is a self-guided trail in the area of Constitution Grove that will guide you among a grove of trees over 200 years old.

Travelers of the byway could easily spend a week or longer here. The national forest has developed numerous campgrounds with hundreds of campsites to choose from. Most of the campgrounds are situated on the banks of pretty meandering rivers and streams. Plan on finding a spot and staying awhile.

Information: Willamette National Forest, 211 E 7th Ave, Eugene OR 97401 / 541-465-6521. Oregon Parks & Recreation Dept., 1115 Commercial St NE, Salem OR 97310/ 800-551-6949.

Rogue - Coquille

US FS Rogue - Coquille is in southwest Oregon approximately 25 miles southeast of Coos Bay. It is 83 miles long and follows OR 242, CR 219, CR 595, and FSR 33. The roads are two-lane paved roads suitable for all types of vehicles and are usually open all year.

Rogue - Coquille National Forest Scenic Byway travels alongside the Wild and Scenic Rogue River between Gold Beach and Agness, then leaves the river to climb over the gentle divide and descend into the Coquille River Basin. Here the byway begins to follow the course dictated by the Coquille River through a narrow canyon rimmed with high cliffs. The river canyon eventually gives way to the wide open valley near Powers to the byway's northern end. Rogue River was one of eight rivers initially included in the National Wild and Scenic Rivers Act of 1968 and is popular with anglers, river rafters, and photographers.

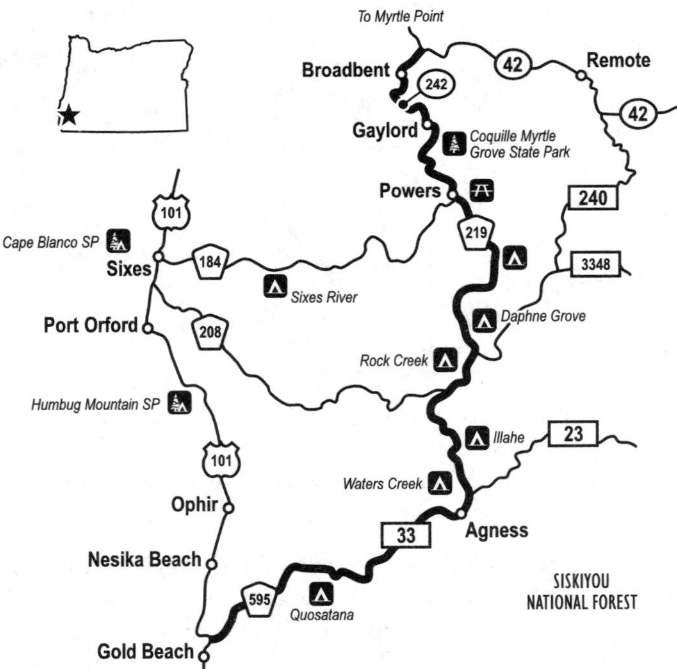

There are numerous pullouts along the byway that provide beautiful panoramic vistas of the forest's rivers and surrounding mountains. These places are always good spots for enjoying a picnic, taking photos, or looking for wildlife. Siskiyou National Forest supports a variety of wildlife including deer, bobcats, mountain lions, bald eagles, and river otters. You'll also find hiking trails at some turnouts that invite you to explore the forest. There are some short hiking trails that reward you with a cascading waterfall.

There are several national forest campgrounds along the byway that provide the perfect spot for an overnight stay. To the west of the byway are state parks with hundreds of developed campsites.

Near the byway's southern terminus is Battle Rock, located at the mouth of Lobster Creek. This was the site of a bloody battle between settlers and Native Americans living in the Rogue River corridor in the 1800s. Nearly all the Indians involved in the battle lost their lives.

Information: Siskiyou National Forest, 200 NE Greenfield Rd, Grants Pass OR 97526 / 541-471-6500. Oregon Parks & Recreation Dept., 1115 Commercial St NE, Salem OR 97310/ 800-551-6949.

Rogue Umpqua / North Umpqua River

This scenic byway is in southwest Oregon 70 miles south of Eugene. It begins in Roseburg and travels east to Diamond Lake; it then heads south to Gold Hill. The byway follows OR 62, OR 138, OR 230, and OR 234, which are two-lane paved roads suitable for all vehicles. It is 172 miles long and remains open year-round.

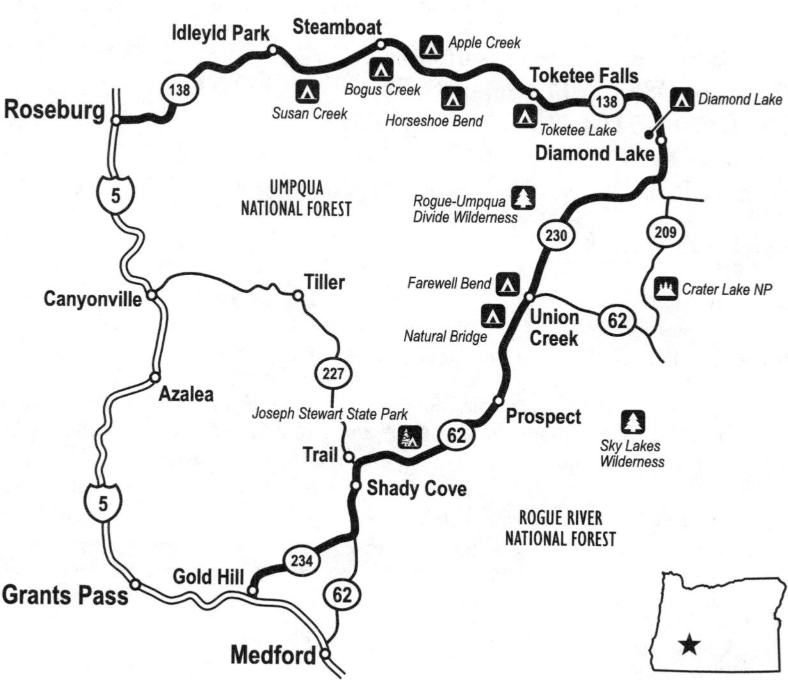

This scenic drive takes the traveler through a diverse landscape, from rural countryside dotted with farms and open pastures to thick forests of Douglas fir and lodgepole pine. Wildflowers bloom along the byway making their colorful presence known. Travelers are also treated to views of the beautiful Cascade Mountains, meandering mountain streams, and scenic cascading waterfalls.

The byway provides nearly unlimited opportunities for outdoor recreation. There are hiking trails ranging from short easy walks to pretty waterfalls to longer, more arduous trails that are enjoyed by experienced hikers and backpackers. Wilderness areas surrounding the byway provide opportunities for hiking or horseback riding to secluded places.

Numerous campgrounds are provided along the entire length of the route by the Bureau of Land Management, National Forest Service, Corps of Engineers, and the State of Oregon. You're bound to find a campsite that interests you, whether you seek a primitive, secluded site or one that is highly developed.

The byway winds along two National Wild and Scenic Rivers, the North Umpqua and Upper Rogue. These rivers, and the many others found within the forest, provide excellent fishing and rafting opportunities.

Information: Rogue River National Forest, 333 W 8th St, Medford OR 97501 / 541-858-2200. Umpqua National Forest, PO Box 1008, Roseburg OR 97470 / 541-672-6601. Oregon Parks & Recreation Dept., 1115 Commercial St NE, Salem OR 97310/ 800-551-6949. Crater Lake National Park, PO Box 7, Crater Lake OR 97604 / 541-594-2211.

Lodging Invitation

Budget 16 Motel
1067 NE Stephens St.
Roseburg, OR 97470

Phone: 541-673-5556
800-414-1648 reservations
Fax: 541-673-7942

One of Roseburg's most reasonable motels. Amenities include: clean rooms • outdoor pool • free cable TV • in-room phones • A/C • and complimentary coffee. Within walking distance to many restaurants. Close to shopping & area attractions. Reasonable daily and weekly rates. Located on Business Loop Hwy. 99 (Stephens Street) between exits 124 and 125 of Interstate 5. For reservations please call 800-414-1648. Visa, MC, AMEX, and Discover cards accepted.

A/C H

Mountain Country RV Park
117 Elk Ridge Lane
Idleyld Park, OR 97447

Phone: 541-498-2454
Fax: 541-498-2454

Open year round, the Mountain Country RV Park offers campers spectacular scenery and an abundance of nearby recreational opportunities. Facilities include: 25 sites • full hook-ups • 20/30/50 amp • phone • laundry • restrooms • showers • video rentals • horseshoes and volleyball area. Food, gas and supplies are available next door. Area activities include world-class fly fishing and white water on the North Umpqua River, rafting, kayaking, trails, skiing, hot springs and waterfalls. Daily, weekly, and monthly rates, tenters welcome. Visa, MC, Discover & AMEX credit cards accepted. Located 47 miles east of Roseburg on Hwy. 138 at milepost 47.

Snake River / Morman Basin

BLM 1 BLM 2 Snake River / Mormon Basin is in northeast Oregon. It forms a loop drive beginning and ending in Baker City. The 150-mile byway follows OR 7, OR 86, OR 245, and a series of county roads marked with byway signs. The roads are a combination of paved, gravel, and narrow dirt roads. A high-clearance vehicle is needed to travel the entire route. Large RVs and vehicles pulling trailers should not attempt to complete the byway. Portions of the byway may become impassable during winter or after periods of heavy rain.

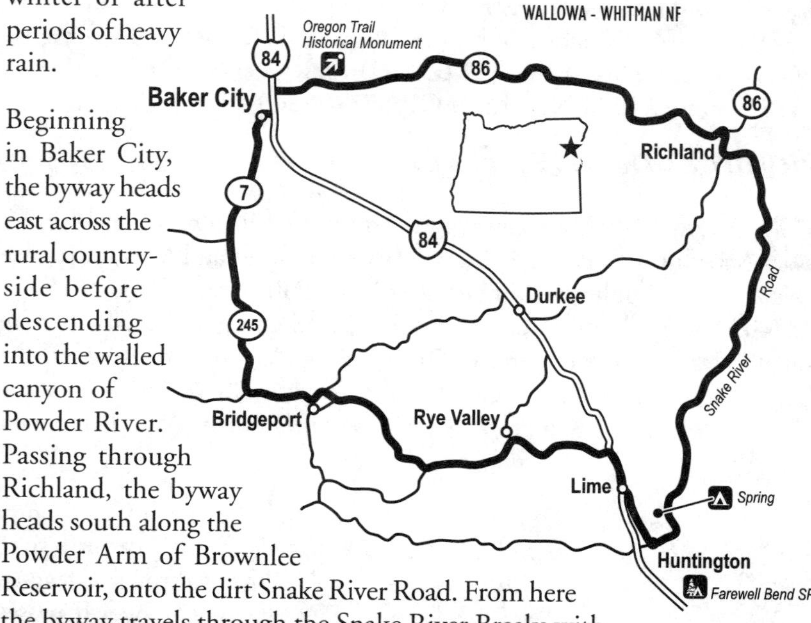

Beginning in Baker City, the byway heads east across the rural countryside before descending into the walled canyon of Powder River. Passing through Richland, the byway heads south along the Powder Arm of Brownlee Reservoir, onto the dirt Snake River Road. From here the byway travels through the Snake River Breaks with Snake River flowing alongside. The byway comes across the BLM Spring Recreation Site where you can pitch a tent and take in the scenery or continue driving. This campground does not have any designated campsites, but picnic tables and drinking water are available.

Continue driving north on old Highway 30 and then I-84 for a few short miles. Take the Rye Valley exit and head west. Through this portion of the byway you're kept company by the waters of Dixie Creek as you travel through rangeland into pinyon juniper country. In Rye Valley the byway narrows and begins climbing the heavily forested slopes of ponderosa pine, juniper, and Douglas fir to the crest of Mormon Basin.

At a four-way intersection, the byway heads northwest up Glengarry Gulch alongside Clarks Creek through aspen, pine, and juniper forests. Cottonwood Creek will join Clarks Creek as you continue. Shortly, you'll begin heading west along the Burnt River through Bridgeport Valley until you link up with OR 245.

You'll want to head north on OR 245 where you will enter the Wallowa-Whitman National Forest, taking numerous hairpin turns until you come to the OR 7 junction. Continue north on OR 7 through pine, aspen, and fir until you return to Baker City.

Information: BLM-Vale District Office, 100 Oregon St, Vale OR 97918 / 541-473-3144. Wallowa-Whitman National Forest, 1550 Dewey Ave, Baker City OR 97814 / 541-523-6391. Oregon Parks & Recreation Dept., 1115 Commercial St NE, Salem OR 97310/ 800-551-6949.

South Fork Alsea River

BLM 1 South Fork Alsea River is in northwest Oregon about 30 miles northwest of Eugene. It travels between Alpine and Alsea, a distance of 19 miles. It follows Alpine Road, South Fork Access Road, and CR 48200. The roads are a combination of paved and gravel roads that are suitable for all types of vehicles. Travelers should be on the lookout for logging trucks in the area. Eleven miles are officially designated a Back Country Byway. The byway's roads are maintained throughout the year.

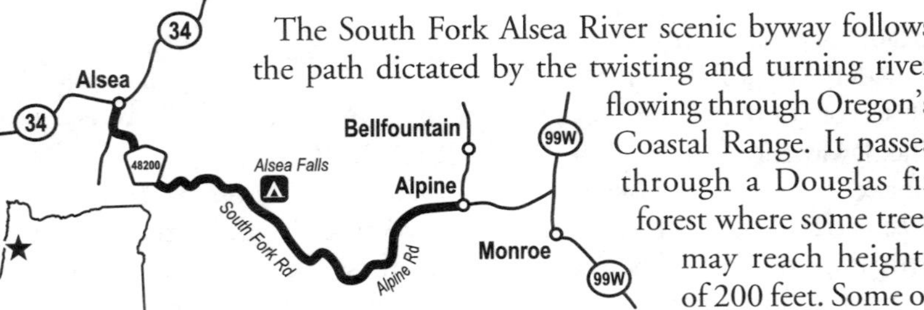

The South Fork Alsea River scenic byway follows the path dictated by the twisting and turning river flowing through Oregon's Coastal Range. It passes through a Douglas fir forest where some trees may reach heights of 200 feet. Some of these old-growth trees have attained the honorable age of 400 years or more. From mid-summer through autumn, red vine maples proudly display their color. The competing wildflowers bloom much of the year and need not beg for your attention.

The beautiful waterfalls of the South Fork of the Alsea River is perhaps the byway's main attraction. Here the water tumbles over a 20-foot series of rock steps to the pool formed below. Visitors will find a 16-site BLM campground here, all with picnic tables and fire rings. Drinking water and comfort stations are also provided. Take some time and spend a few days relaxing here. A trail nearby will lead you to the base of the waterfalls, a nice spot for reading a book or enjoying a picnic. Anglers can spend their days attempting to pull coho salmon, Chinook salmon, steelhead, or cutthroat trout from the river. Wildlife observers can enjoy the byway in search of deer or elk. Black bears and bobcats also inhabit the area but are not seen very often.

To the south of the byway is a Corps of Engineers project, Fern Ridge Lake. There are day use parks surrounding the lake that offer swimming beaches and picnic areas. There's also a campground situated on the south shore that has campsites with hookups, drinking water, restrooms, a swimming beach, and a boat ramp. The lake is also a popular spot for sailboating, waterskiing, and fishing.

Information: BLM-Salem District Office, 1717 Fabry Rd SE, Salem OR 97306 / 503-375-5646. Siuslaw National Forest, PO Box 1148, Corvallis OR 97339 / 541-750-7000.

South Fork John Day River

The South Fork John Day River byway is in central Oregon about 140 miles south of Pendleton. It begins in Dayville at the intersection of Park Avenue and South Fork John Day Road. It travels south to the Malheur National Forest entrance, a few miles south of Izee. The byway is 50 miles long and follows CR 68 and South Fork John Day Road. Most of the byway is a gravel road, varying from a single lane to two lanes. South of Izee the road is paved. Sections of the byway may become impassable during winter or spring, otherwise it remains open all year.

The byway takes travelers through a scenic river canyon, along hillsides covered with sagebrush, juniper, and scattered stands of ponderosa pine. The canyon narrows as the byway climbs into higher elevations where the sagebrush and juniper landscape gives way to ponderosa pine and the occasional Douglas fir and white fir. Willows, shrubs, and hardwood trees line the banks of the river.

The byway passes Murderer's Creek Wildhorse Management Area about ten miles south of Dayville. This 150,000-acre area is home to approximately 100 wild horses. It is also an excellent area for viewing mule deer, elk, and bighorn sheep. Other wildlife found in the area are black bear, coyotes, eagles, and hawks.

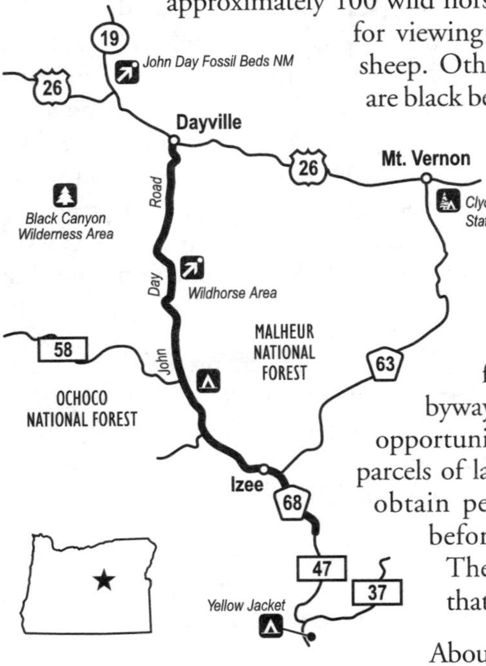

The South Fork of the John Day River flows alongside the byway from start to finish. This part of the river is a National Wild and Scenic River, preserving its free-flowing waters. All along the byway anglers are provided excellent opportunities for trout fishing. Private parcels of land do exist along the byway; obtain permission from land owners before crossing private property. The BLM has maps of the area that show public and private land.

About 23 miles south of Dayville is a primitive campground with sites for tents and recreational vehicles. There are no facilities available. Camping is also permitted nearly anywhere along the byway on BLM land.

Information: BLM-Prineville District Office, 3050 NE Third St, Prineville OR 97754 / 541-416-6700. Malheur National Forest, PO Box 909, John Day OR 97845 / 541-575-3000. Ochoco National Forest, 3160 NE Third St, Prineville OR 97754 / 541-416-6500. Oregon Parks & Recreation Dept., 1115 Commercial St NE, Salem OR 97310/ 800-551-6949. John Day Fossil Beds NM, HCR 82 Box 126, Kimberly OR 97848 / 541-987-2333.

Steens Mountain

Steens Mountain byway is in southeast Oregon approximately 60 miles south of Burns. The 66-mile route begins in Frenchglen and follows Steens Mountain Loop Road and OR 205 back to Frenchglen. Oregon Highway 205 is a two-lane paved road; the rest is gravel. Portions are narrow, rough, and steep and require a high-clearance vehicle. Motorhomes and vehicles pulling trailers are discouraged from traveling the byway. Steens Mountain is usually open mid-July through October. There are five gates at various elevations that control access during wet or snowy conditions. The lower gates are usually open by May; the upper gates open around mid-July.

Steens Mountain Back Country Byway travels across Oregon's high desert country and up through the ruggedly beautiful Steens Mountain. Several scenic overlooks along the byway provide spectacular views of Kiger Gorge, wild horses, and the vast expanse of the sagebrush-covered Alvord Desert. In almost every season of the year wildflowers bloom, elegantly displaying their brilliant colors of purple, yellow, and pink.

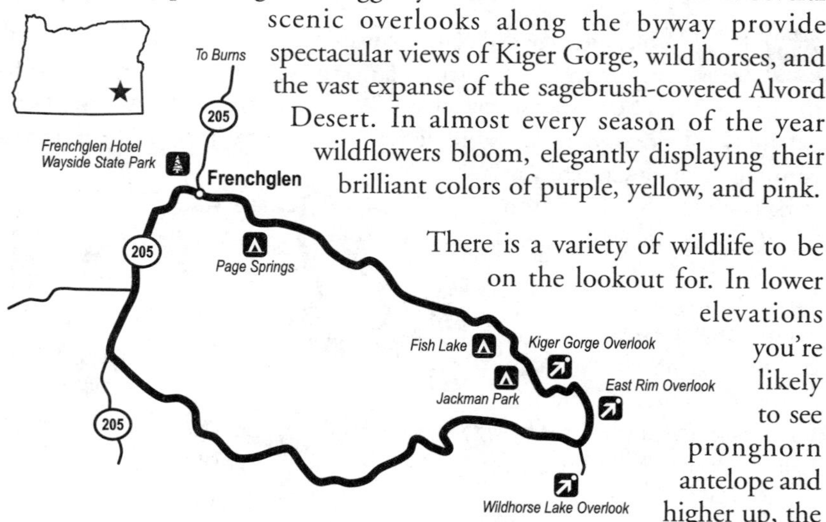

There is a variety of wildlife to be on the lookout for. In lower elevations you're likely to see pronghorn antelope and higher up, the majestic bighorn sheep. Mule deer and Rocky Mountain elk are most likely seen near cover and water in the evening and early morning. Overhead, the byway traveler will want to be searching for golden eagles, hawks, and falcons.

There are three BLM campgrounds on the byway: Page Springs, Fish Lake, and Jackman Park. Page Springs Campground is the first campground encountered east of Frenchglen. There are 30 sites with picnic tables and fire rings. Fish Lake Campground provides 24 campsites with picnic tables and grills. The lake is stocked with cutthroat and rainbow trout. Jackman Park Campground has six sites. Drinking water and comfort stations are available in each camping area.

Frenchglen was named for Peter French and his father-in-law, Dr. Hugh Glen. Frenchglen was originally known as P Station and was part of French's

P Ranch. The remains of Mr. French's former headquarters for his cattle ranch can be seen about one mile east of Frenchglen. The historic Frenchglen Hotel, built in 1924, is listed on the National Register of Historic Places and is owned by the State of Oregon. The hotel still accepts guests from March through November.

Information: BLM-Burns District Office, HC74-12533 Hwy 20 W, Hines OR 97738 / 541-573-4400. Oregon Parks & Recreation Dept., 1115 Commercial St NE, Salem OR 97310/ 800-551-6949.

Volcanic Legacy Scenic Byway

Volcanic Legacy Scenic Byway is in south-central Oregon. It begins on US 97 at the California state line and travels north for 140 miles. The byway follows US 97, OR 140, OR 62, and OR 138. All are two-lane paved roads suitable for all types of vehicles. The portion running through Crater Lake National Park is closed by snow from mid-October to mid-June.

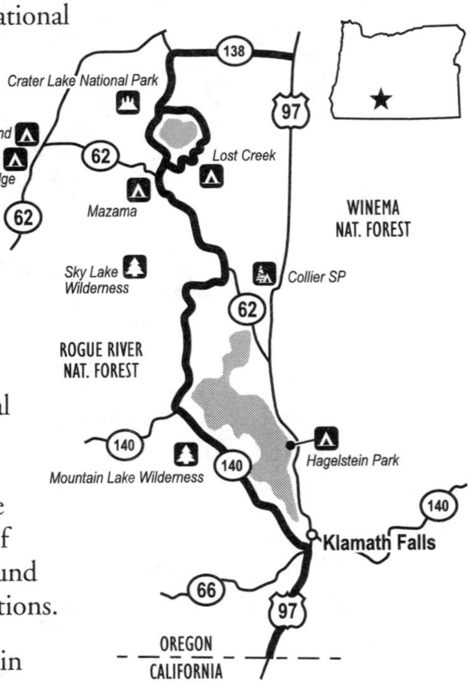

Volcanic Legacy Scenic Byway takes travelers along the shores of Upper Klamath Lake and through Crater Lake National Park. It crosses the desert landscape of Klamath Basin and evergreen forests surrounding the national park. Upper Klamath Lake is Oregon's largest fresh-water lake; it has a surface area of more than 90,000 acres. Thousands of migrating birds can be seen around the lake during peak fall migrations.

Crater Lake National Park's main attraction is six-mile long Crater Lake. The lake is 1,932 feet deep and is surrounded by lava cliffs that rise 500 to 2,000 feet. Over 50 miles of trails exist within the park, including 33 miles of the Pacific Crest National Scenic Trail. Some trails lead to the summit of high points above the lake while others bring you closer to the lake. There are two campgrounds within the national park: Lost Creek and Mazama. Lost Creek has 16 tent-only campsites. Mazama has nearly 200 sites, restrooms, showers, laundry facilities, and a dump station. There are no hookups in either campground. A 71-room lodge is also in the park.

Other public campgrounds are available along or near the byway. Hagelstein Park is a county-operated park that has ten campsites on Upper Klamath Lake. Collier State Park is 30 miles north of Klamath Falls on US 97 and has 50 sites with complete hookups. It is open mid-April through October.

Information: Klamath County Department of Tourism, 1451 Main St., Klamath Falls OR 97601 / 541-884-0666 or 800-445-6728. Crater Lake National Park, PO Box 7, Crater Lake OR 97604 / 541-594-2211. Rogue River National Forest, 333 W 8th St, Medford OR 97501 / 541-858-2200. Oregon Parks & Recreation Dept., 1115 Commercial St NE, Salem OR 97310/ 800-551-6949.

PENNSYLVANIA

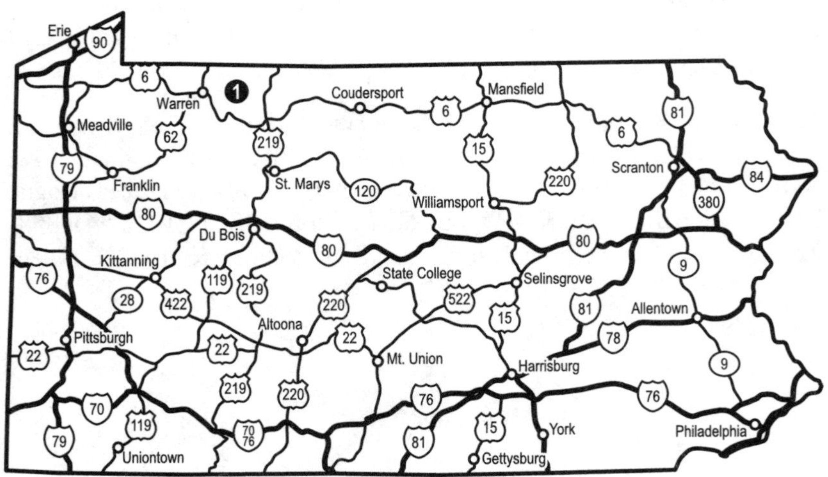

Longhouse

Longhouse scenic drive is in northwest Pennsylvania 15 miles east of Warren. It is 29 miles long and follows PA 59, PA 321, and FSR 262. The roads are two-lane paved roads suitable for all vehicles. Forest Service Road 262 is closed by snow from mid-December through March. The rest of the byway usually remains open year-round.

Longhouse scenic byway travels through the hardwood forests of Allegheny National Forest as it makes its way around the Kinzua Arm of Allegheny Reservoir. Scenic turnouts along the route provide beautiful vistas of the forest's valleys, rugged rock outcrops, and the lake's blue waters. Fall paints the byway in brilliant colors of red, orange, and gold.

Allegheny Reservoir is a 12,080-acre lake formed by the construction of a dam on Allegheny River. The dam was constructed by the Corps of Engineers. The lake provides excellent opportunities for fishing, swimming, boating, and waterskiing.

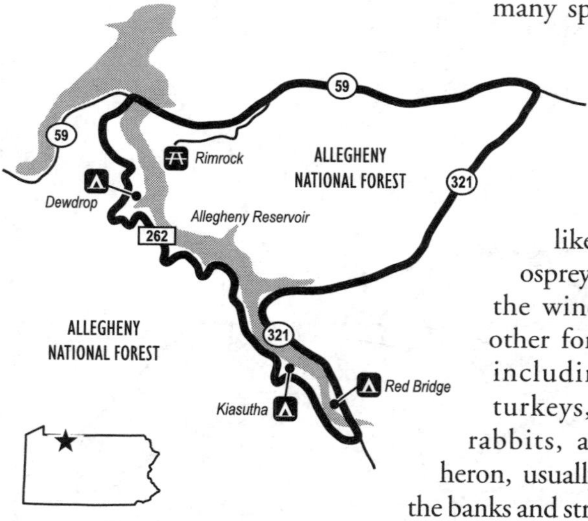

Wildlife observers will delight in the many species inhabiting the area. The best time for viewing white-tailed deer is early in the morning or evening. If you look above, you're likely to spot an eagle, osprey, or hawk riding on the wind currents. There's other forms of wildlife here including black bears, turkeys, an abundance of rabbits, and the great blue heron, usually seen fishing along the banks and streams of the reservoir.

Those interested in camping will find three developed national forest campgrounds. Red Bridge Campground offers 55 campsites with picnic tables and grills. Drinking water, restrooms, a dump station, shower facilities, and a playground are also provided. Kiasutha Campground is a little larger and has 90 sites for tents and RVs, drinking water, restrooms, a boat ramp, showers, trailer dump station, and playground equipment. The third camping area is the Dewdrop Campground with 74 sites, drinking water, restrooms, dump station, playground, and boat access to the lake. None of the campgrounds have hookups.

Information: Allegheny National Forest, Bradford Ranger District, Star Rt 1 Box 88, Bradford PA 16701 / 814-362-4613.

South Carolina

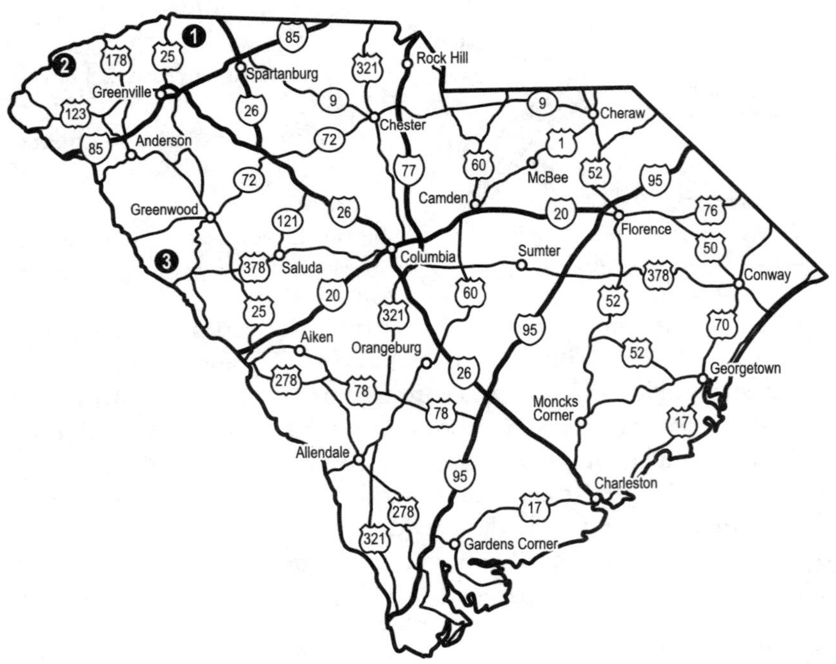

Cherokee Foothills Scenic Byway

Cherokee Foothills Scenic Byway crosses northwest South Carolina. Travelers can access the byway from I-85 at Exit #1 and follow SC 11 east to Gaffney or rejoin I-85 at Exit #92. South Carolina Highway 11 is a two-lane paved road suitable for all vehicles. The byway is about 120 miles long and usually remains open year-round.

Cherokee Foothills Scenic Byway travels across the heavily forested foothills of the Blue Ridge Mountains. The byway crosses numerous small streams and rivers. More than 50 scenic waterfalls can be accessed from the route. Anglers may wish to spend some time at Lake Hartwell or Lake Keowee near the byway's western end. Among the fish inhabiting the lakes are bass, bluegill, catfish, and crappie.

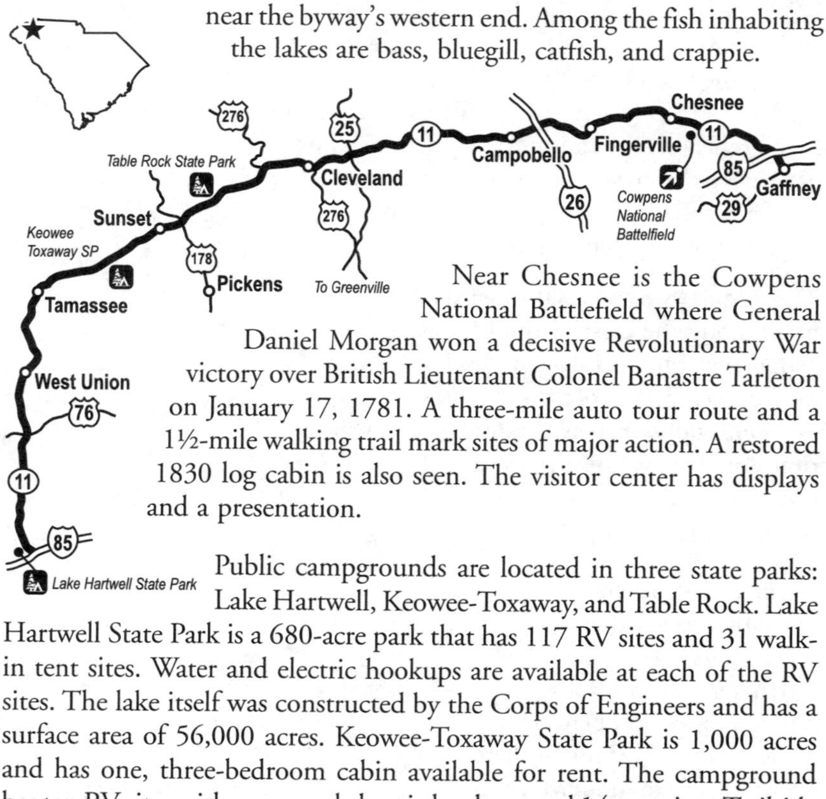

Near Chesnee is the Cowpens National Battlefield where General Daniel Morgan won a decisive Revolutionary War victory over British Lieutenant Colonel Banastre Tarleton on January 17, 1781. A three-mile auto tour route and a 1½-mile walking trail mark sites of major action. A restored 1830 log cabin is also seen. The visitor center has displays and a presentation.

Public campgrounds are located in three state parks: Lake Hartwell, Keowee-Toxaway, and Table Rock. Lake Hartwell State Park is a 680-acre park that has 117 RV sites and 31 walk-in tent sites. Water and electric hookups are available at each of the RV sites. The lake itself was constructed by the Corps of Engineers and has a surface area of 56,000 acres. Keowee-Toxaway State Park is 1,000 acres and has one, three-bedroom cabin available for rent. The campground has ten RV sites with water and electric hookups and 14 tent sites. Trailside camping is permitted at designated sites on the Raven Rock Hiking Trail, which is a strenuous four mile loop. Table Rock State Park lies east of Sunset and has 100 RV and tent sites with water and electric hookups. The park also has 14 cabins, a restaurant, and gift shop.

Information: Discover Upcountry Carolina Association, 864-233-2690 or 800-849-4766. Lake Hartwell State Park, 19138-A South Hwy 11, Fair Play SC 29643 / 864-972-3352. Keowee-Toxaway State Park, 108 Residence Dr, Sunset SC 29685 / 864-868-2605. Table Rock State Park, 158 E Ellison, Pickens SC 29671 / 864-878-9813. Jones Gap State Park, 303 Jones Gap Rd, Marietta GA 29661 / 864-836-3647. Devils Fork State Park, 161 Holcombe Cir, Salem SC 29676 / 864-944-2639. Cowpens National Battlefield, PO Box 308, Chesnee SC 29323 / 864-461-2828.

Oscar Wigington

Oscar Wigington is in northwest South Carolina about 53 miles west of Greenville. It begins at the intersection with SC 28 and travels north to the North Carolina state line. A spur road heads east and ends at the junction with SC 130. The byway is 20 miles long and follows SC 107 and SC 413. Both state highways are two-lane paved roads suitable for all vehicles. Icy conditions may exist in winter, otherwise the byway is open year-round. Fourteen miles are officially designated a National Forest Scenic Byway.

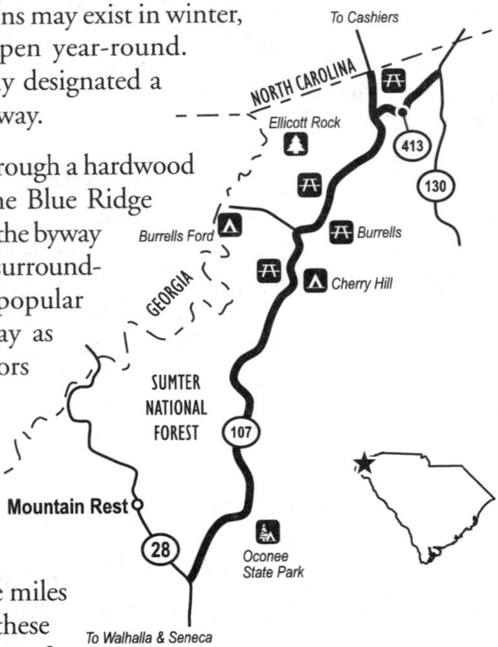

The scenic byway winds through a hardwood forest along the crest of the Blue Ridge Mountains. Turnouts along the byway provide scenic vistas of the surrounding mountains. Fall is a popular time for driving the byway as the area is ablaze with colors of orange, red, and gold.

Hikers, backpackers, and horseback riders will be interested in the 9,015-acre Ellicott Rock Wilderness Area. There are miles of trails running through these beautiful mountains. Maps of the wilderness area and its trails are available from the Andrew Pickens Ranger District in Walhalla. Other trails throughout the forest provide opportunities for short walks to longer day hikes.

The Chattooga River crosses the national forest and is in fact the boundary line between Georgia and South Carolina. Portions of this scenic river have been designated a National Wild and Scenic River. The river offers white-water rapids for those interested in floating. Outfitters can provide you with all you need to enjoy a float trip down this wild and scenic river. Anglers will find the river provides enjoyable trout fishing.

Those interested in camping will find one national forest campground directly along the byway. This campground has 22 tree-shaded sites with picnic tables. Drinking water, restrooms, and shower facilities are also provided. Oconee State Park is near the southern end of the byway and has 140 sites with water and electrical hookups.

Information: Francis Marion & Sumter National Forests, 4931 Broad River Rd, Columbia SC 29212 / 803-561-4000. Oconee State Park, 624 State Park Rd, Mountain Rest SC 29664 / 864-638-5353.

Savannah River Scenic Highway

NSB Savannah River Scenic Highway is in western South Carolina. It begins near Augusta, Georgia at the South Carolina state line and travels north to Westminster. The byway is 110 miles long and follows SC 28, SC 81, SC 181, SC 187, and SC 24. All the roads are two-lane paved roads suitable for all types of vehicles. Savannah River Scenic Highway is open year-round.

Savannah River Scenic Highway is a pleasant drive through the uplands of western South Carolina. It travels alongside the Savannah River. Actually, three dams constructed on the river have created three beautiful lakes. Thurmond Lake is a 71,000-acre lake along the byway's southern end. Near the middle is Richard B. Russell Lake, which has a surface area over 26,000 acres. On the northern end of the byway is Hartwell Lake, a beautiful 56,000-acre lake. Avid fishermen will want to spend some time on these lakes attempting to catch bass, bluegill, catfish, and crappie.

The byway provides access to a large number of campgrounds. Five are managed by the State of South Carolina. Sadlers Creek State Park is on Hartwell Lake and has 37 RV and tent sites with water and electric hookups. Calhoun Falls State Recreation Area is on Russell Lake. It has 100 sites for tents and RVs; some sites have hookups. Hickory Knob, Baker Creek, and Hamilton Branch State Parks are on Thurmond Lake and have a total of more than 300 RV and tent sites. Nearly all of the campsites have water and electric hookups.

There are seven Corps of Engineers campgrounds along or near the byway. Coneross and Twin Lakes are on Hartwell Lake. Coneross Campground has a total of 104 sites; 67 with water and electric hookups. Twin Lakes has a total of 102 sites; 73 have hookups. There are five Corps-managed campgrounds on Thurmond Lake: Mount Carmel, Leroy's Ferry, Hawe Creek, Modoc, and Petersburg. Mount Carmel Campground is remote and quiet. It has 21 sites with hookups and 22 without. Leroy's Ferry offers ten primitive campsites. Hawe Creek Campground has 28 sites with water and electric hookups. Modoc has 31 sites with hookups and 17 without. Petersburg is the largest Corps campground on Thurmond Lake and is about six miles west of Clarks Hill. It has 93 RV and tent campsites; most have water and electric hookups.

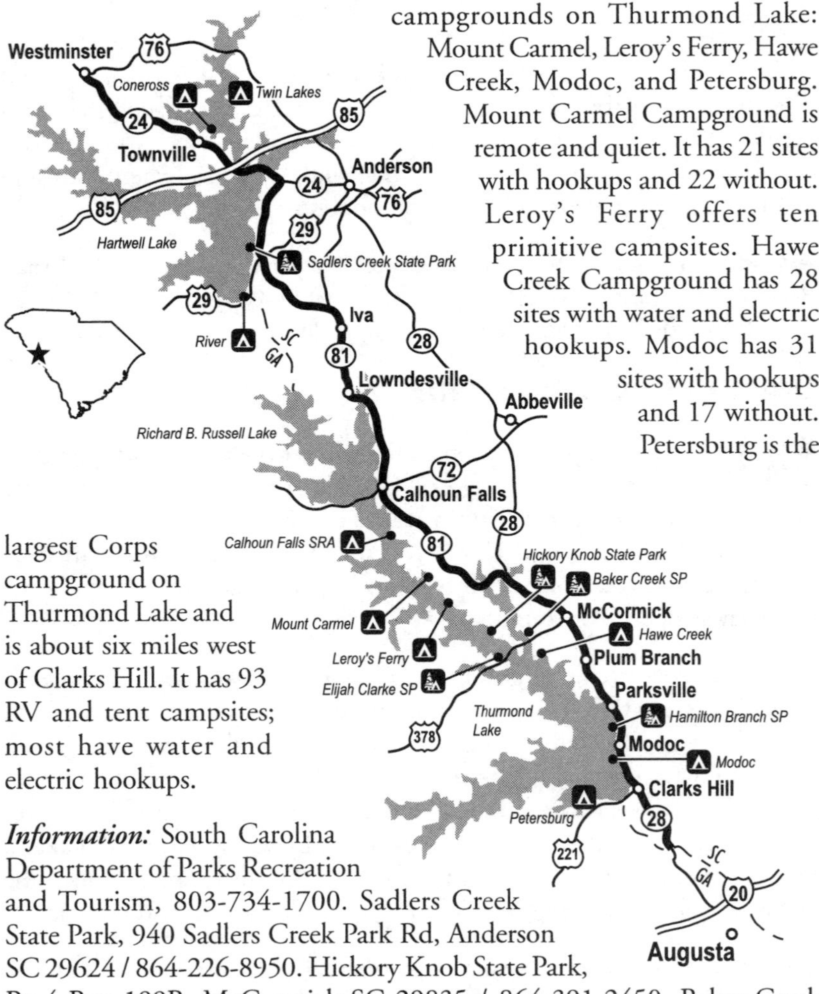

Information: South Carolina Department of Parks Recreation and Tourism, 803-734-1700. Sadlers Creek State Park, 940 Sadlers Creek Park Rd, Anderson SC 29624 / 864-226-8950. Hickory Knob State Park, Rt 4 Box 199B, McCormick SC 29835 / 864-391-2450. Baker Creek State Park, Rt 3 Box 50, McCormick SC 29835 / 864-443-2457. Hamilton Branch State Park, Rt 1 Box 97, Plum Branch SC 29845 / 864-333-2223. Calhoun Falls State Park, 246 Maintenance Shop Rd, Calhoun Falls SC 29628 / 864-447-8267. Elijah Clark State Park, 2959 McCormick Hwy, Lincolnton GA 30817 / 706-359-3458. US Army Corps of Engineers, Savannah District, PO Box 889, Savannah GA 31402 / 912-652-5822.

South Dakota

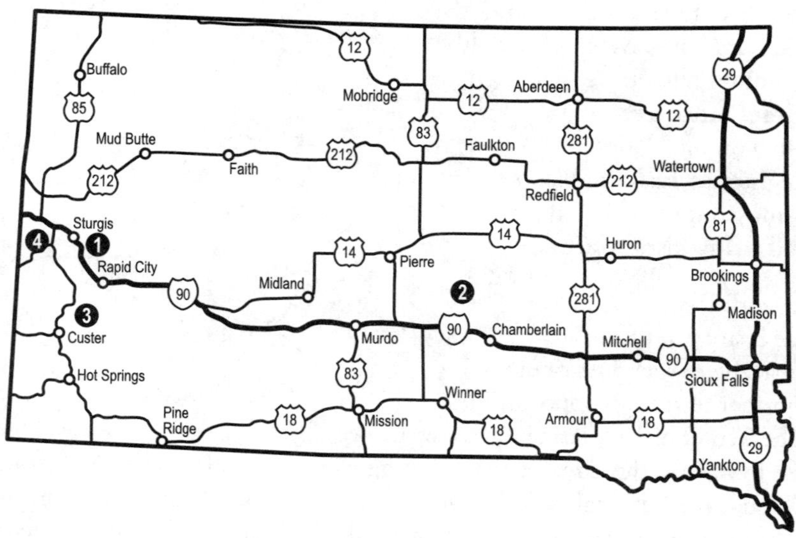

Fort Meade

BLM 1 The Fort Meade byway is located in west-central South Dakota, just east of Sturgis. It begins at the intersection with SD 34 and travels south to I-90. The byway is a short five-mile route that follows Fort Meade Road, which is a two-lane gravel road suitable for all vehicles. The byway remains open year-round.

The Fort Meade Back Country Byway travels through rolling hills covered with ponderosa pine to the historic calvary post of Fort Meade. Historically, this region of the Black Hills was home to Sioux, Cheyenne, and Arapahoe Indian tribes. Settlement of this area by pioneers generated disputes among the Native Americans and newcomers. By 1878, these conflicts prompted the government to establish this military post situated between Fort Laramie and the Montana forts. Many of the old buildings remain intact and are listed on the National Register of Historic Places. A museum contains exhibits and many historic artifacts.

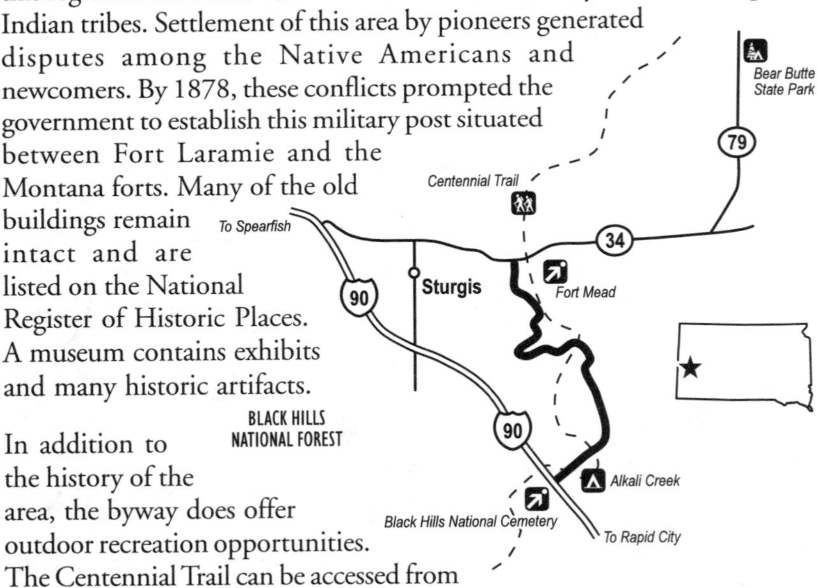

In addition to the history of the area, the byway does offer outdoor recreation opportunities. The Centennial Trail can be accessed from the byway for those interested in hiking. This 111-mile trail extends from Wind Cave National Park to Black Butte State Park, about 12 miles north of the byway. Alkali Creek flows alongside the trail near the southern end of the byway.

Those interested in camping will find a six-site BLM campground near the southern terminus. A separate campground for riders and their horses is located adjacent to Alkali Creek Campground. Additional public campgrounds can be found in the Black Hills National Forest to the south. To the north of the byway is Black Butte State Park. There are fifteen sites for tents and recreational vehicles, however, no hookups are provided.

Information: BLM-South Dakota Field Office, 310 Roundup St, Belle

Fourche SD 57717 / 605-892-2526. Black Hills National Forest, RR 2 Box 200, Custer SD 57730 / 605-673-2251. Bear Butte State Park, PO Box 688, Sturgis SD 57785 / 605-347-5240.

Native American Scenic Byway

Native American Scenic Byway travels between Pierre and Chamberlain in central South Dakota. The 100-mile byway follows SD 50, BIA 4, SD 47, BIA 5, BIA 10, and SD 1806. The roads are two-lane paved roads suitable for all vehicles. Native American Scenic Byway is usually open all year.

Native American Scenic Byway crosses the Crow Creek and Lower Brule Sioux Indian Reservations. It travels across South Dakota's high plains and the hills and bluffs alongside the Missouri River. Dams constructed by the Corps of Engineers created two scenic lakes on the river: Lake Francis Case and Lake Sharpe. Among the wildlife inhabiting the area are deer, eagles, and large numbers of waterfowl. Anglers will find catfish, walleye, pike, bass, crappie, and sunfish in both lakes.

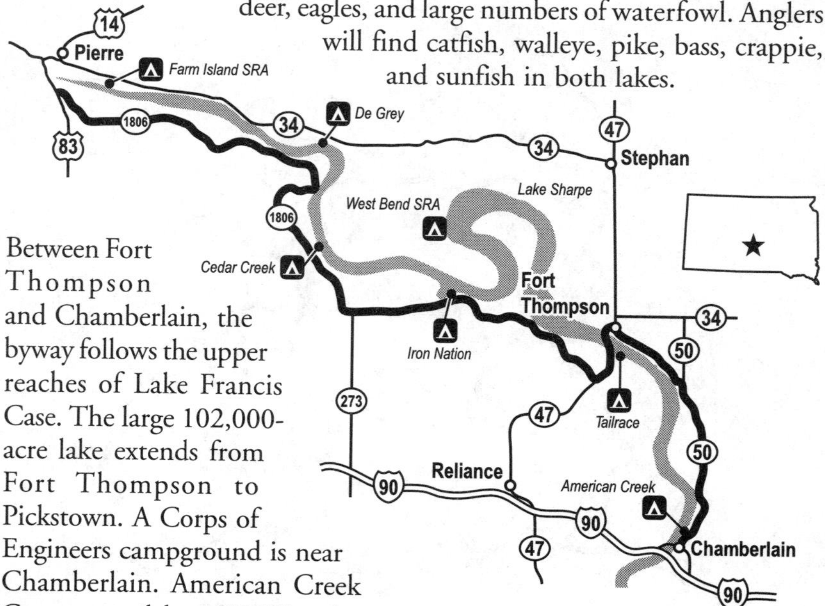

Between Fort Thompson and Chamberlain, the byway follows the upper reaches of Lake Francis Case. The large 102,000-acre lake extends from Fort Thompson to Pickstown. A Corps of Engineers campground is near Chamberlain. American Creek Campground has 60 RV and tent campsites with electric hookups. From Fort Thompson to Pierre, the byway travels alongside Lake Sharpe. The 61,000-acre lake offers numerous campgrounds and picnic areas. Three campgrounds can be accessed from the byway: Tailrace, Iron Nation, and Cedar Creek. Tailrace has 72 campsites with hookups; Iron Nation also has 72 sites with hookups and 12 without.

Information: South Dakota Department of Tourism, 711 E Wells Ave, Pierre SD 57501 / 605-773-3301. Lower Brule Sioux Tribe, Tourism/ Public Relations, Convention Center, PO Box 187, Lower Brule SD 57548 / 605-473-5399. Farm Island and West Bend State Recreation Areas, 1301 Farm Island Rd, Pierre SD 57501 / 605-224-5605.

Peter Norbeck

Peter Norbeck is in southwest South Dakota about 20 miles southwest of Rapid City. The byway forms a 70-mile loop as it follows SD 87, SD 89, SD 244, and US 16A. All the highways are two-lane paved roads suitable for most vehicles. Large RVs and vehicles pulling trailers may want to inquire locally before attempting to travel US 16A and SD 87. These routes have many curves and narrow tunnels along with short radius pig-tailed bridges. South Dakota Highway 87 and sections of US 16A are closed by snow from December through March.

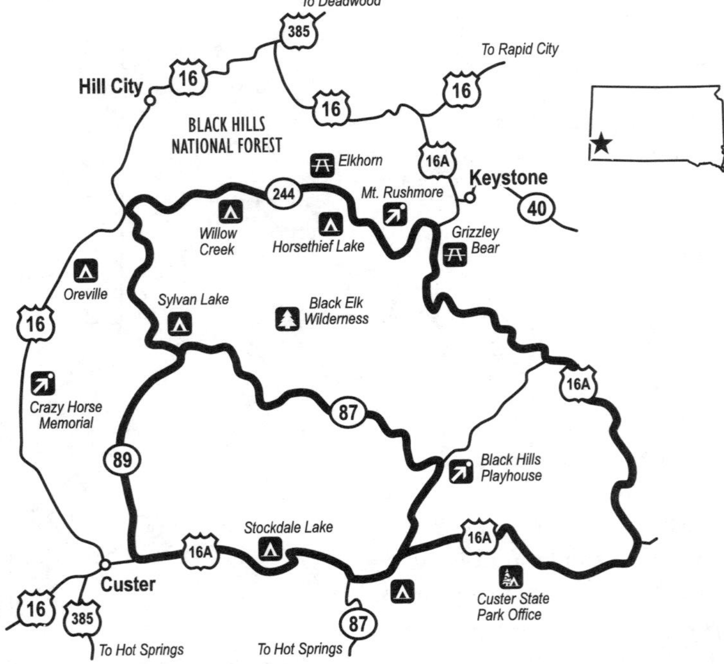

The Peter Norbeck scenic byway travels through forests of pine, spruce, and groves of aspen as it twists and turns through the beautiful Black Hills. Overlooks along the byway provide spectacular vistas of the surrounding mountains and rugged rock outcrops.

Wildlife observers will be thrilled at the variety of wildlife found here. The American bison, lots of them, can be seen in the area of Custer State Park. Bighorn sheep, pronghorn antelope, wild burros, and prairie dogs can also be seen in the park. Other wildlife frequently seen along the byway includes white-tailed deer, mule deer, and wild turkeys. Rocky Mountain elk, coyotes, red fox, and bobcats also inhabit the area but are seen less frequently. Bird watchers will want to be on the lookout for golden eagles, hawks, woodpeckers, wrens, warblers, and swallows. Bald eagles can be seen from late fall to early spring.

Hikers, backpackers, and horseback riders will find miles of trails within the 9,824-acre Black Elk Wilderness. Some of the hiking trails lead to the summit of 7,242-foot Harney Peak for spectacular panoramic views of the Black Hills. There are numerous other trails accessed along the byway.

Those interested in extending their stay will find numerous public campgrounds. The 73,000-acre Custer State Park offers over 300 campsites in several campgrounds along the byway. The state park also offers resorts for those seeking a little more comfort.

Information: Black Hills National Forest, RR 2 Box 200, Custer SD 57730 / 605-673-2251. South Dakota Department of Transportation, US 385 Box 431, Custer SD 57730 / 605-673-4948. Custer State Park, HC83 Box 70, Custer SD 57730 / 605-255-4515. Mount Rushmore National Memorial, PO Box 268, Keystone SD 57751 / 605-574-2523.

Spearfish Canyon Highway

US FS

Spearfish Canyon Highway is in west-central South Dakota approximately 47 miles northwest of Rapid City. It begins in Spearfish and travels south to US 85, a distance of 20 miles. The byway follows US 14A, which is a two-lane paved road suitable for all types of vehicles. Spearfish Canyon Highway is generally open year-round.

Crossing the Black Hills National Forest, the Spearfish Canyon Highway takes you through a narrow canyon created by the tumbling waters of adjacent Spearfish Creek. The byway twists and turns, following the path dictated by the creek. Spruce, pine, aspen, birch, and oak trees cover much of the hillsides, with limestone cliffs piercing the sky above the forested slopes. In fall the canyon explodes with color as the aspens, birch, and oak prepare for the coming of winter.

Wildlife observers will want to be searching the canyon for white-tailed deer or mule deer. Occasionally raccoons can be seen climbing or wandering among the trees. Overhead, eagles or hawks may be seen riding on the wind currents. Numerous songbirds fill the canyon with their music.

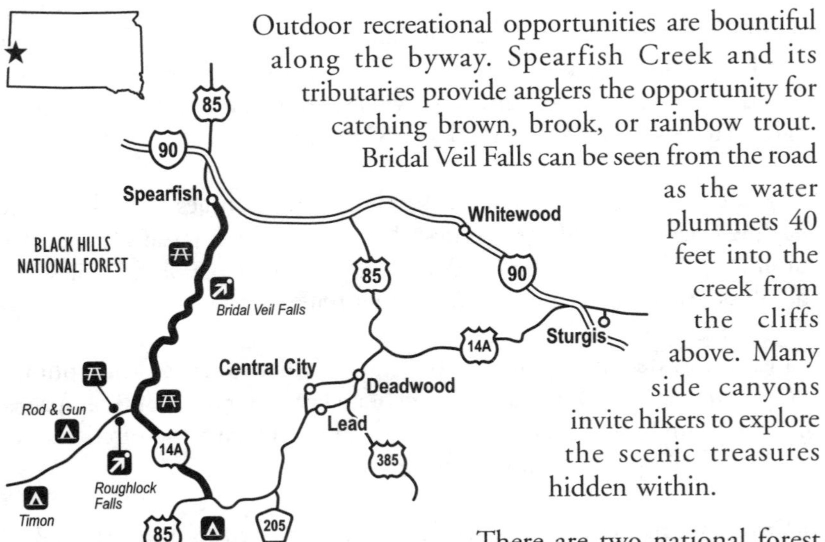

Outdoor recreational opportunities are bountiful along the byway. Spearfish Creek and its tributaries provide anglers the opportunity for catching brown, brook, or rainbow trout. Bridal Veil Falls can be seen from the road as the water plummets 40 feet into the creek from the cliffs above. Many side canyons invite hikers to explore the scenic treasures hidden within.

There are two national forest campgrounds located off the byway down FSR 222. Rod and Gun has seven campsites scattered along the banks of Little Spearfish Creek. Timon Campground also has seven sites situated along the creek. Near the byway's southern end is Hanna Campground, which has 13 campsites.

Information: Black Hills National Forest, Spearfish Ranger District, 2014 N Main St, Spearfish SD 57783 / 605-642-4622.

Lodging Invitation

TENNESSEE

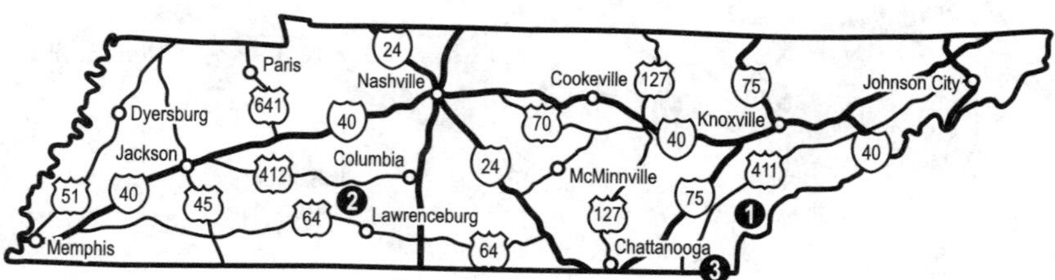

Cherohala Skyway

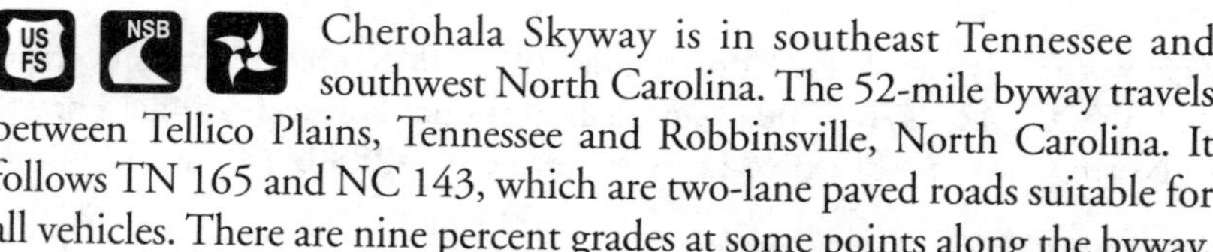

Cherohala Skyway is in southeast Tennessee and southwest North Carolina. The 52-mile byway travels between Tellico Plains, Tennessee and Robbinsville, North Carolina. It follows TN 165 and NC 143, which are two-lane paved roads suitable for all vehicles. There are nine percent grades at some points along the byway. Cherohala Skyway is usually open year-round.

Cherohala Skyway travels across the mountains, valleys, and dense forests of the Cherokee and Nantahala National Forests. Several scenic overlooks provide beautiful views of the surrounding mountains. Santeetlah Overlook is the byway's highest point at 5,390 feet. Wildlife observers will want to be on the lookout for deer, which are best seen in early morning or evening. Among other wildlife inhabiting the area are bears, wild boars, and the northern flying squirrel. From Tellico Plains, the byway is accompanied by Tellico River, which is a popular river for trout fishing, canoeing, and kayaking. A short side trip on FSR 221 (Tellico River Road) leads to the scenic Bald River Falls.

Numerous trails can be accessed from the byway. They vary in length from three to eight miles and are rated from easy to strenuous. Trails that lead to Slickrock Wilderness are also accessed along the byway. These trails are for experienced hikers as they tend to be primitive, rugged, and steep.

Several public campgrounds are accessed along the byway. Indian Boundary has 120 campsites that can accommodate tents or RVs up to 22 feet. The park also has a 90-acre lake, picnic area, swimming area, and bicycle trails.

Bicycles are available for rent at the Ketoowah Interpretive Center. On the North Carolina side is Horse Cove Campground, which has 17 sites that can accommodate RVs up to 22 feet long. Other campgrounds can be reached by wandering off the byway.

Information: Cherokee National Forest, 2800 N Ocoee St, Cleveland TN 37320 / 423-476-9700. Nantahala National Forest, National Forests in North Carolina, PO Box 2750, Asheville NC 28802 / 828-257-4200.

Natchez Trace Parkway

Alabama section see page 9 / Mississippi portion see page 150

This historic route generally follows the old Indian trace, or trail, between Nashville, Tennessee and Natchez, Mississippi. This portion of the byway travels 103 miles across central Tennessee from Pasquo to the Alabama state line. The parkway is a two-lane paved road suitable for all vehicles and remains open year-round.

Once trekked by Indians and trampled into a rough road by traders, trappers, and missionaries, the Natchez Trace Parkway is now a scenic 445-mile route traveling from Natchez, Mississippi to Nashville, Tennessee. In the late 1700s and early 1800s, "Kaintucks," as the river merchants were called, would float downriver on flatboats loaded with their merchandise to be sold in New Orleans. Since there wasn't any practical way to return by river, the boats were dismantled and the lumber sold. The Natchez Trace would be the only pathway home.

At that time, the Trace was a dangerous path to take. Travelers waded through swamps and swam streams and fended off attacks by wild animals and poisonous snakes. It was also necessary to keep an eye open for murderous bandits and Indian attacks. The terrain of the trace was rough, too. A broken leg of a lone traveler would often mean certain death. The dangers of the route earned the Trace the nickname "Devil's Backbone." Modern-day travelers don't have these dangers to face as they travel this historic route.

On the parkway's northern end lies the historic city of Nashville, which was incorporated in 1806. Early in the 19th century, Nashville became a bustling river port known for shipping cotton. During the Civil War, Nashville was a strategic military post for the Confederacy, but was captured by Union troops in 1862. The Confederates unsuccessfully attempted to retake the city in the Battle of Nashville in December of 1864. Today Nashville is known as "Music City USA," the place to be for country-and-western musicians and fans.

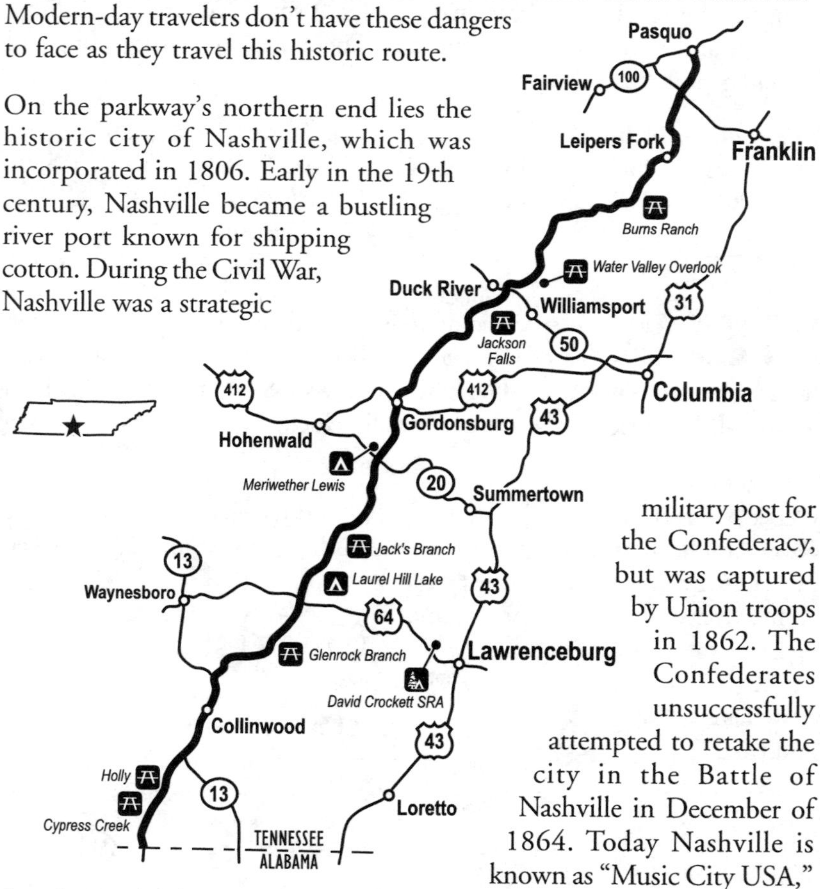

There are many parks developed by the National Park Service along the route. Most of the parks provide picnic facilities and nature trails; some of the trails follow the original Natchez Trace. Camping is available at Meriwether Lewis Park. This park is the site of Grinder's Inn where Meriwether Lewis, the noted member of the Lewis and Clark expedition, died of gunshot wounds in 1809. A monument designed as a broken shaft marks his grave. There are 32 campsites for tents or recreational vehicles. A pioneer cemetery, exhibit room, and picnic tables are also found here.

Another option for camping is not too far from the parkway, the David Crockett State Park near Lawrenceburg. The state park offers over 100 campsites for tents and recreational vehicles. A small lake provides fishing, boating, and swimming opportunities. There are also nature trails and bicycling trails.

Information: National Park Service, Natchez Trace Pkwy, 2680 Natchez Trace Pkwy, Tupelo MS 38804 / 662-680-4027. David Crockett State Park, PO Box 398, Lawrenceburg TN 38464 / 931-762-9408.

Ocoee

The Ocoee scenic drive is in southeast Tennessee about ten miles east of Cleveland. It begins in Ocoee and travels east for 29 miles to Ducktown. The byway follows US 64 and FSR 77, which are two-lane paved roads suitable for all vehicles. Ocoee is usually open year-round.

Ocoee winds across Cherokee National Forest through the beautiful Ocoee River Gorge. It is accompanied by the rushing waters of Ocoee River, popular with white-water rafters. Several scenic overlooks provide panoramic vistas of the surrounding forested mountains and Lake Ocoee.

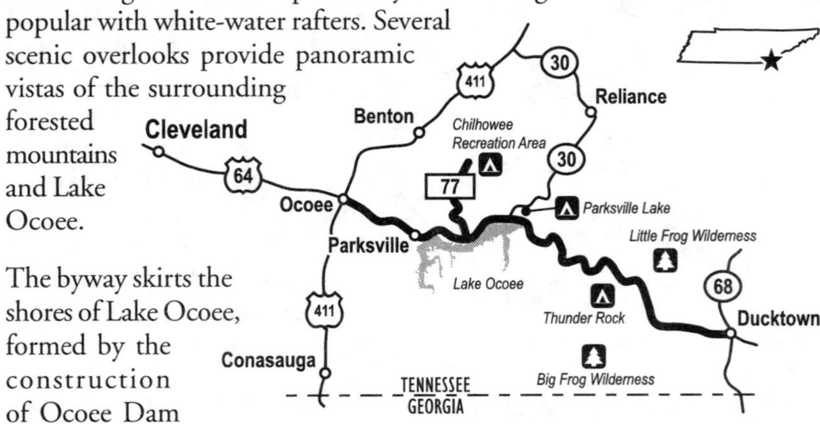

The byway skirts the shores of Lake Ocoee, formed by the construction of Ocoee Dam on the Ocoee River. This 1,950-acre lake is nestled among the forested mountains with Sugarloaf Peak standing proudly nearby. Several turnouts are along this portion of the byway providing scenic views of the lake. Parksville Beach and Mac Point Swimming Area provide visitors a chance to relax and go for a dip. A visitor center located nearby has maps and brochures.

There are numerous trails accessed along the byway; horse trails, bicycling trails, nature trails, and longer hiking trails. Two wilderness areas are near the byway's eastern end. Both Little Frog and Big Frog Wilderness Areas provide opportunities for hiking to secluded spots.

The side trip up FSR 77 is a steady climb up Chilhowee Mountain. From here, panoramic views extend beyond Lake Ocoee, across the Tennessee Valley to the distant Cumberland Mountains. The large recreation area here offers a 68-site campground, a seven-acre lake with swimming beach, and picnic areas. Those wishing to camp will find two other campgrounds in addition to the Chilhowee Recreation Area. Parksville Lake has 32 sites that can accommodate tents or RVs. Thunder Rock is a smaller campground with only six sites with picnic tables and grills. Drinking water and comfort stations are available in both camping areas.

Information: Cherokee National Forest, 2800 N Ocoee St NW, Cleveland TN 37320 / 423-476-9700.

Lodging Invitation

Lake Ocoee Inn & Marina	Phone:	423-338-2064
Rt. 1, Box 347		800-272-7238
Benton, TN 37307	Fax:	423-338-9514

Lake Ocoee Inn is located in the Cherokee National Forest providing beautiful views of Lake Ocoee and the surrounding mountains. Guests can choose to stay in cabins, located right on the water with a dock and kitchen facilities, or a rustic motel room located near their celebrated restaurant. At the marina you can rent a canoe, pontoon boat, fishing boat, water skis and knee boards. For those seeking a little more excitement you can take a whitewater rafting trip with Ocoee Inn Rafting. Nearby attractions and activities include: museum • trout fishing • swimming holes • hiking trails • horseback riding • and picnic areas. Located on U.S. Hwy. 64 (Ocoee Scenic Byway), east of State Hwy. 30.

UTAH

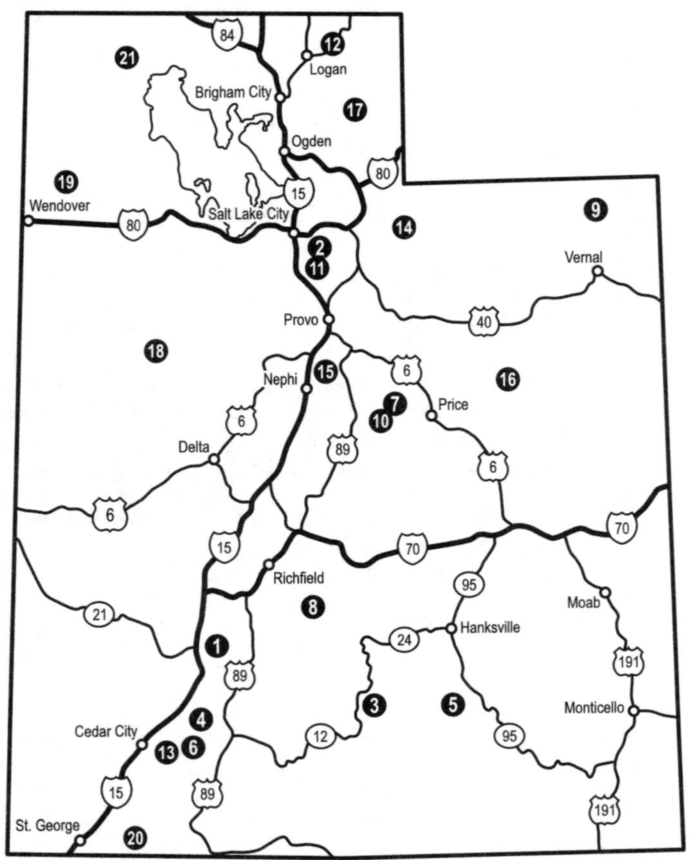

84
21
12
Logan
Brigham City
17
Ogden
80
19
15
Wendover
80
Salt Lake City
14
9
2
11
Vernal
Provo
40
18
6
16
Nephi
15
7
Price
10
6
89
Delta
6
6
70
15
70
Richfield
95
8
Moab
21
Hanksville
24
1
191
89
3
5
Monticello
4
12
95
Cedar City
13
6
15
89
191
St. George
20

Beaver Canyon

Beaver Canyon is in southwest Utah about 50 miles northeast of Cedar City. The byway begins off I-15 in Beaver and travels east on UT 153 to Junction, a distance of about 40 miles. From Beaver to the Elk Meadows Ski Area, UT 153 is a two-lane paved road suitable for all vehicles. This portion remains open year-round. From the ski area to Junction, UT 153 is an unpaved, dry-weather-only road and is usually closed in winter.

Travelers of this scenic byway are treated to the scenic Beaver Canyon. From Beaver, the byway begins climbing through the forested canyon filled with pine, aspen, and maple. The byway climbs the western slopes of the Tushar Mountains. Several scenic turnouts provide panoramic vistas of the surrounding mountains. Beaver River flows alongside for much of your scenic journey.

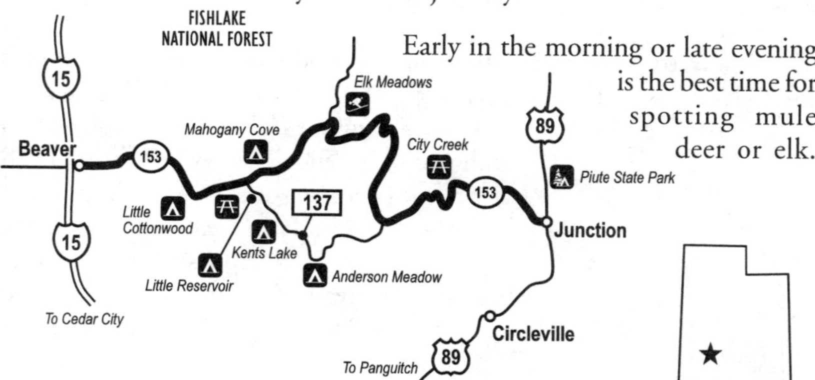

Early in the morning or late evening is the best time for spotting mule deer or elk. Wild turkeys can also be seen occasionally. Overhead you may catch glimpses of eagles, hawks, or falcons. Other wildlife inhabiting the national forest includes moose, mountain goat, bobcat, and mountain lion.

There are two national forest campgrounds along the byway and three a short side trip up FSR 137. The first campground you come across is situated on the banks of the river. This is the Little Cottonwood Campground. There are fourteen sites here, with two barrier-free sites. Farther up the byway is Mahogany Cove Campground. There are seven campsites here set among mountain mahogany and pinyon pine.

About one mile up FSR 137 is Little Reservoir and its campground with eight sites. Little Reservoir is stocked with rainbow and brown trout. Four miles farther along is Kents Lake Campground with seventeen sites surrounding the lake. Continue on another four miles and you'll come across the Anderson Meadow Campground. This campground is at an elevation of 9,350 feet and has ten campsites and good fishing in the nearby reservoir.

Information: Fishlake National Forest, Beaver Ranger District, 575 S Main, Beaver UT 84713 / 435-438-2436. Piute State Park, PO Box 43, Antimony UT 84712 / 435-624-3268.

Big Cottonwood Canyon

Big Cottonwood Canyon is in north-central Utah about 13 miles south of downtown Salt Lake City. It begins in Cottonwood Heights at the intersection of Wasatch Boulevard and UT 190. It heads east for 15 miles and ends in Brighton. Utha Highway 190 is a two-lane paved road suitable for all types of vehicles. Delays are possible in winter and snow tires or chains may be required November through April.

The byway treats visitors with beautiful mountain scenery as it climbs through thick stands of fir, aspen, Engelmann spruce, and lodgepole pine. Big Cottonwood Creek flows alongside the byway and will remain with you to the end. The byway is surrounded by two wilderness areas, Mount Olympus to the north and Twin Peaks to the south. Several scenic turnouts along the way provide breathtaking views into these two pristine mountain wilderness areas.

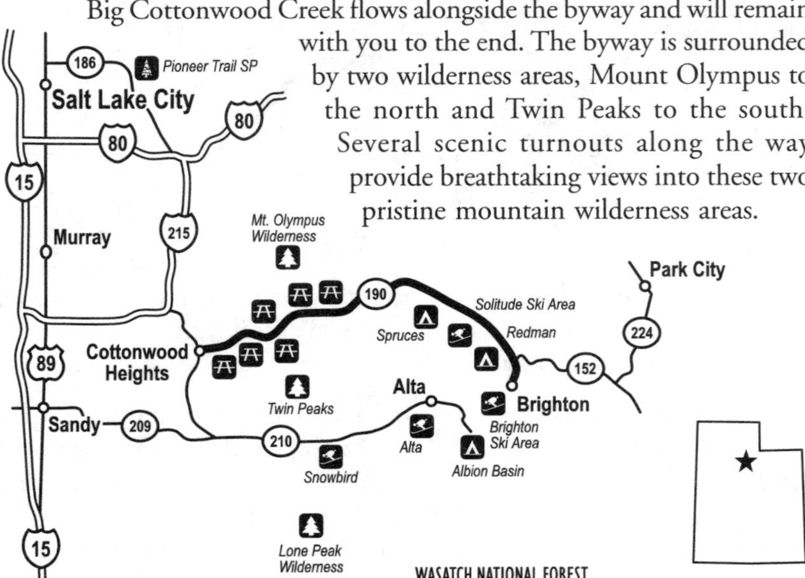

Wildlife observers will delight in the variety of species found along the byway. If you look closely, you may catch glimpses of elk or mule deer foraging among the woods. Moose also inhabit the region but are not seen as often. Other wildlife calling the area home are bobcats, mountain lions, coyotes, beavers, and the snowshoe hare. Birdwatchers will want to be looking for golden eagles, hawks, and a large variety of songbirds.

During warmer months, byway travelers enjoy picnicking, camping, hiking, and bicycling. At Birches Picnic Area you can see a water flume clinging to the canyon wall. Winter sport enthusiasts come to this area in search of snowmobiling, downhill skiing, and cross-country skiing. Those interested in hiking will find trails that wind deep into the surrounding wilderness areas. The Doughnut Falls Trail will take you to an unusual waterfall where the waters of Mill D South Fork tumble through a hole in the rock. Those interested in camping will find two along the byway. Spruces Campground has 97 campsites for tents and RVs. Redman Campground is set at an elevation of 8,300 feet and offers 38 sites.

Information: Wasatch-Cache National Forest, 8236 Federal Bldg, 125 S State St, Salt Lake City UT 84138 / 801-524-3900.

Boulder Mountain Highway

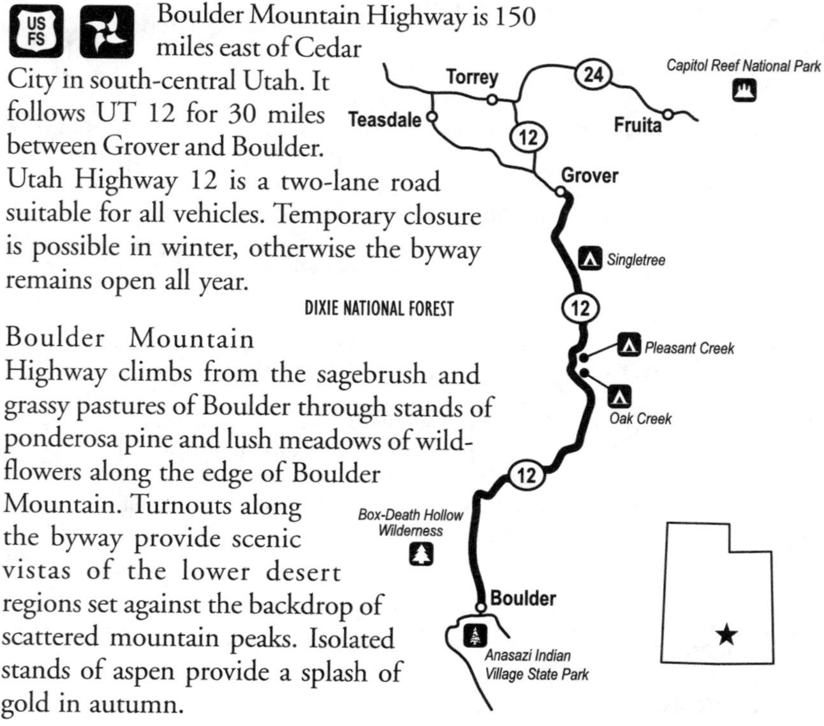

Boulder Mountain Highway is 150 miles east of Cedar City in south-central Utah. It follows UT 12 for 30 miles between Grover and Boulder. Utah Highway 12 is a two-lane road suitable for all vehicles. Temporary closure is possible in winter, otherwise the byway remains open all year.

Boulder Mountain Highway climbs from the sagebrush and grassy pastures of Boulder through stands of ponderosa pine and lush meadows of wildflowers along the edge of Boulder Mountain. Turnouts along the byway provide scenic vistas of the lower desert regions set against the backdrop of scattered mountain peaks. Isolated stands of aspen provide a splash of gold in autumn.

Near the byway's southern end is the Anasazi Indian Village State Park. The park depicts the cultural aspects of the Anasazi Indian that once inhabited this region. Native American artifacts dating back to the 11th century can be seen as well as a full-scale replica of a dwelling believed to have existed here. A self-guided trail takes you to the site of on-going excavations. Other trails along the byway lead to scenic lakes for fishing or enjoying a picnic lunch. There are three national forest campgrounds located along the byway. Oak Creek Campground has eight sites situated on the creek. You'll also find fishing and hiking opportunities here. Farther north of this campground is Pleasant Creek Campground with eighteen sites. Singletree Campground is the largest of the three with twenty-six sites.

Information: Dixie National Forest, 82 N 100 E, Cedar City UT 84720 / 435-865-3700. Capitol Reef National Park, HC70 Box 15, Torrey UT 84775 / 435-425-3791. Anasazi Indian Village State Park, PO Box 1429, Boulder UT 84716 / 435-335-7308.

Lodging Invitation

Boulder View Inn	Phone:	801-425-3800
385 West Main (Hwy. 24)	Fax:	801-425-3366
P.O. Box 750237	E-mail:	cptlreef@color-country.net
Torrey, UT 84775		

Boulder View Inn, located 1 mile from scenic Highway 12, welcomes travelers to a new 12 room unit with king & queen beds. Your stay includes a free continental breakfast. Guests enjoy a beautiful view of red ledges. A restaurant is located across the street. Only 4 miles from Capitol Reef National Park. Best Rates. AAA and AARP discounts. For reservations, call 24-hours a day, 800-444-3980. Visa, MC, Discover, and AMEX cards accepted.

Cactus Hill Ranch Motel	Phone:	801-425-3578
830 S. 1000 E.		800-507-2624 reservations
Teasdale, UT 84773	Fax:	801-425-3578

A beautiful location only minutes away from Boulder Mountain Highway (Hwy. 12) and Capitol Reef National Park. Available accommodations include a new 5-unit motel and one cabin on their 100 acre ranch. It's time to relax and enjoy the beauty and serenity of being "off the beaten path." Reasonable rates • free coffee • AAA & AARP discounts. Take the Teasdale exit off Hwy. 12 northwest of Grover. Located 2 miles south of Teasdale.

Cockscomb Inn & Cottage B & B	Phone:	801-425-3511
97 S. State St.		800-530-1038
P.O. Box B	Fax:	801-425-3511 (call first)
Teasdale, UT 84773		

The Cockscomb Inn offers charming comfortable rooms in a turn of the century farm house in the small picturesque town of Teasdale. Guests enjoy: queen beds • private baths • spacious living room / dining room • summer patio / barbecue • and excellent full breakfasts. A fully equipped one bedroom private cottage is also available. Only minutes away from Capitol Reef National Park, Boulder Mountain (gateway to the new Grand Staircase National Monument), Thousand Lakes and Fishlake Recreation Areas. Take the Teasdale exit off Hwy. 12 northwest of Grover.

Thousand Lakes RV Park
1050 W. Hwy. 24
P.O. Box 750070
Torrey, UT 84775

Phone: 435-425-3500
800-355-8995 reservations

A beautiful location with large areas of grass and trees near Capitol Reef National Park. Cabins, tent, and large pull-thru sites with full hook-ups. Clean showers and restrooms • pavilion • laundry facilities • mini mart & gift shop • western dinners. Rates: $11 to $17. AAA—Good Sam—Senior Citizen discounts. Open April 1 through October 25. Visa, MC, and Discover cards accepted.

Brian Head - Panguitch Lake

US FS

The Brian Head - Panguitch Lake scenic byway is located in southwest Utah. It begins in Parowan and travels south to the Cedar Breaks National Monument where it then travels northeast to Panguitch. The 55-mile route follows UT 143, a two-lane paved road suitable for all vehicles. The byway is usually open year-round.

From Parowan the byway climbs through Parowan Canyon to Utah's highest incorporated city of Brian Head. Nearby is 11,305-foot Brian Head Peak. From here the byway cuts through the northeastern corner of Cedar Breaks National Monument, turns northeasterly and continues on to pass the shores of Panguitch Lake before descending into the town of Panguitch. The waters of Parowan Creek will guide you from Parowan to Brian Head, tempting the angler to pull over and attempt to catch a rainbow trout or two. Autumn is a good time to drive the byway as aspen leaves display their colors of gold.

Those wishing to prolong their stay in the area will find several public campgrounds. Vermillion Castle Campground is located a short distance east of the byway. There are 16 sites, suitable for tents and RVs up to 24 feet long, sitting on the banks of Bowery Creek among Douglas fir and pinyon pines. Drinking water and flush toilets are available.

Panguitch Lake is in a sagebrush basin with aspen and pine trees covering the surrounding hillsides. The lake is stocked with rainbow and brown trout. There are two campgrounds nearby, Panguitch Lake North and Panguitch Lake South. The northern campground has 49 sites suitable for tents and RVs, drinking water, flush toilets, and a dump station. The southern campground has 18 sites for tent campers only. Drinking water is not available, but there are comfort stations.

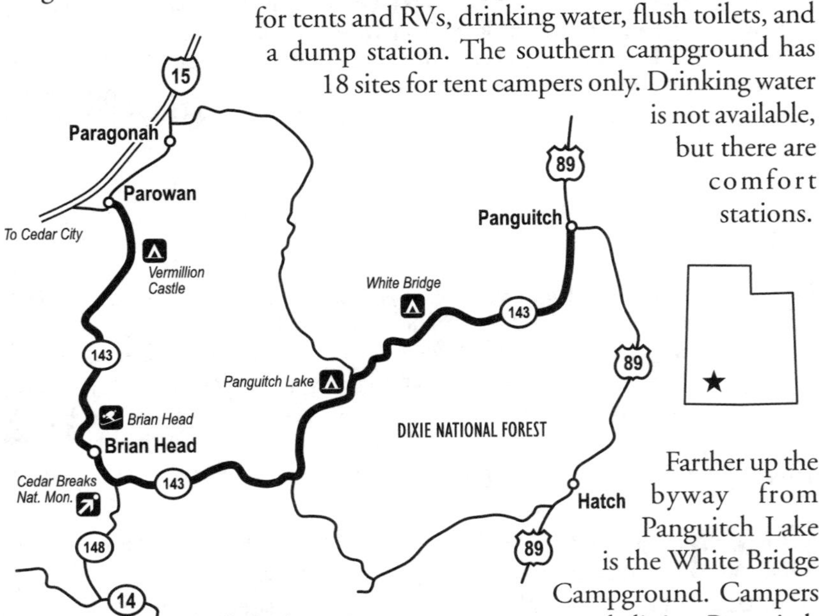

Farther up the byway from Panguitch Lake is the White Bridge Campground. Campers will find 28 sites among cottonwoods lining Panguitch Creek that are suitable for tents and recreational vehicles up to 24 feet. Drinking water and flush toilets are also provided.

Information: Dixie National Forest, 82 N 100 E, Cedar City UT 84720 / 435-865-3700. Cedar Breaks National Monument, 2390 W Hwy 56 - Suite 11, Cedar City UT 84720 / 435-586-9451.

Bull Creek Pass

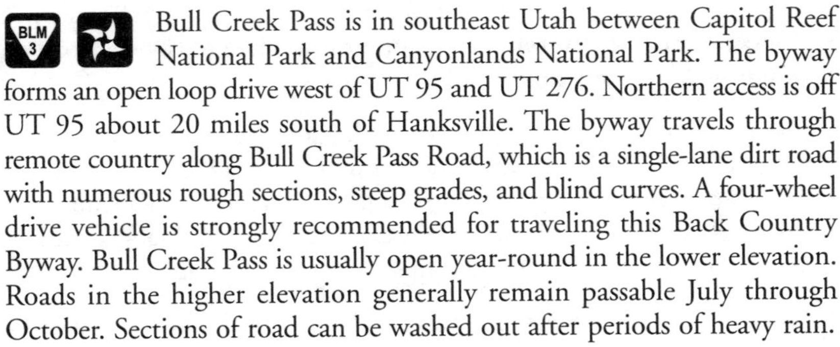

Bull Creek Pass is in southeast Utah between Capitol Reef National Park and Canyonlands National Park. The byway forms an open loop drive west of UT 95 and UT 276. Northern access is off UT 95 about 20 miles south of Hanksville. The byway travels through remote country along Bull Creek Pass Road, which is a single-lane dirt road with numerous rough sections, steep grades, and blind curves. A four-wheel drive vehicle is strongly recommended for traveling this Back Country Byway. Bull Creek Pass is usually open year-round in the lower elevation. Roads in the higher elevation generally remain passable July through October. Sections of road can be washed out after periods of heavy rain.

Bull Creek Pass travels from the desert floor at an elevation around 5,000 feet to Bull Creek Pass in the Henry Mountains, a height of 10,485 feet above sea level. The view from the pass is truly spectacular. To the west you'll see Waterpocket Fold, Circle Cliffs, and Boulder Mountain. In the east are tributaries of the Dirty Devil River, Canyonlands National Park, and the distant Abajo Mountains. The Henry Mountains were the last to be explored and named in continental United States.

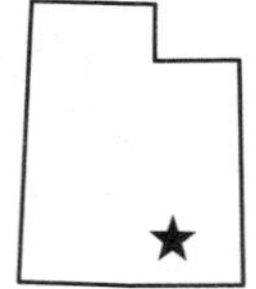

As you travel this byway, you'll come across the remains of Eagle City on Cresent Creek. Eagle City was founded in the 1890s after gold was discovered in nearby Bromide Basin. The town once boasted of a hotel, two saloons, a dance hall, three stores, and a post office. By 1900 the gold boom went bust and the town was deserted.

There are three developed campgrounds along or near the byway that are maintained by the BLM. Lonesome Beaver Campground has five sites with picnic tables and fire rings. McMillan Springs has ten sites and Starr Springs has twelve. All the campgrounds have drinking water and vault toilets. There are also two primitive campgrounds along the byway. Camping is also permitted nearly anywhere along BLM lands. Check with the BLM office in Hanksville for more information.

Information: BLM-Richfield Field Office, 150 E 900 N, Richfield UT 84701 / 435-896-1500. BLM-Henry Mountain Field Station, PO Box 99, Hanksville UT 84734 / 435-542-3461.

Cedar Breaks

Cedar Breaks is 14 miles east of Cedar City in southwest Utah. The short six-mile byway follows UT 148 alongside Cedar Breaks National Monument between UT 14 and UT 143. Utah Highway 148 is a two-lane paved road suitable for all types of vehicles. Cedar Breaks is closed during winter.

The Cedar Breaks scenic byway takes travelers through the stunningly beautiful Cedar Breaks National Monument. Turnouts along the byway provide panoramic views of this nature-made amphitheater. Byway travelers are treated to forests of pine, fir, spruce, aspen, and mountain meadows filled with wildflowers. The colorful display of wildflowers reaches its peak during July and August. In September, the aspen trees turn a bright gold. Byway travelers are most likely to encounter mule deer grazing in the meadows every morning and evening.

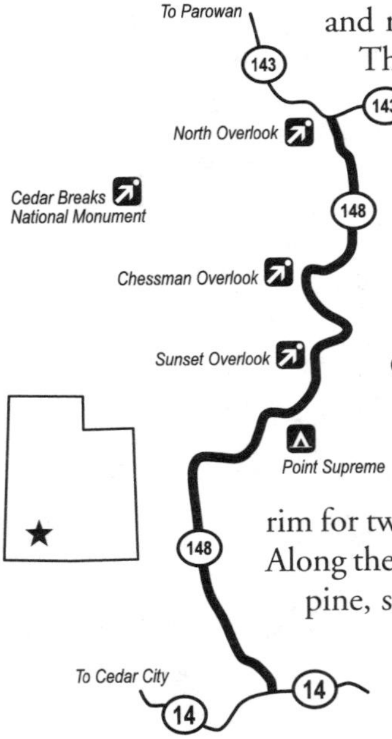

The visitor center near Point Supreme Campground offers exhibits on the plants and animals of the area as well as the formation of the amphitheater. Wasatch Ramparts Trail begins here and follows the rim for two miles, taking you to panoramic overlooks. Along the trail at Spectra Point is a stand of bristlecone pine, some trees being over 1,500 years old.

About midway along the scenic drive is the Alpine Pond Trail. This is a short, easy, self-guided trail that guides you to Alpine Pond where wildflowers grow along the shore. A stand of bristlecone pine is near the Chessman Ridge Overlook.

A campground and picnic area is located near Point Supreme. The campground offers 30 sites for tents and recreational vehicles. Drinking water and comfort stations are among the facilities available.

Information: Dixie National Forest, 82 N 100 E, Cedar City UT 84720 / 435-865-3700. Cedar Breaks National Monument, 2390 W Hwy 56 - Suite 11, Cedar City UT 84720 / 435-586-9451.

Eccles Canyon

Eccles Canyon is 50 miles southeast of Provo in central Utah. It begins south of Scofield and follows UT 264 west to the junction with UT 31, a distance of 16 miles. Utah Highway 264 is a two-lane paved road suitable for all vehicles. It usually remains open year-round, but chains or snow tires may be required at times from October to April.

Eccles Canyon scenic byway travels across 10,000 foot Wasatch Plateau offering beautiful panoramic vistas of the Manti-La Sal National Forest. It then descends 2,500 feet to enter Eccles Canyon. The meandering waters of Upper Huntington Creek will greet you midway along this route and will accompany you for several miles. Wildflowers growing in the meadows provide a colorful display set against the backdrop of the evergreens.

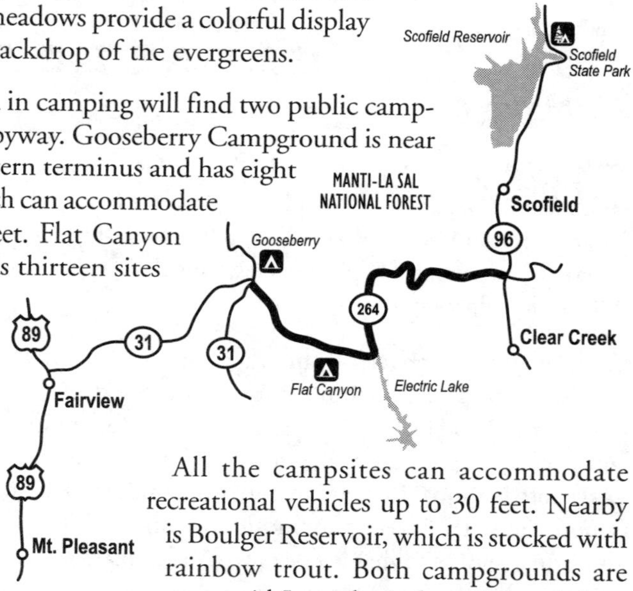

Those interested in camping will find two public campgrounds on the byway. Gooseberry Campground is near the byway's western terminus and has eight sites, two of which can accommodate RVs up to 25 feet. Flat Canyon Campground has thirteen sites set among Engelmann spruce and subalpine fir.

All the campsites can accommodate recreational vehicles up to 30 feet. Nearby is Boulger Reservoir, which is stocked with rainbow trout. Both campgrounds are open mid-June through mid-September.

To the north of the byway's eastern end is Scofield State Park. There are 134 campsites here, most suitable for tent campers only. Drinking water, restrooms, and showers are among the facilities. The park also offers miles of groomed snowmobile and cross-country skiing trails for winter sport enthusiasts.

Information: Manti-La Sal National Forest, 599 W Price River Dr., Price UT 84501 / 435-637-2817. Scofield State Park, PO Box 166, Price UT 84501 / 435-448-9449.

Lodging Invitation

Larsen House Bed & Breakfast	Phone:	435-462-9337
298 South State St.		800-848-5263
Mt. Pleasant, UT 84647	Fax:	435-462-2362

At the Larsen House, beautiful antiques blend with an elegant restored Victorian Mansion. Each room is tastefully decorated with its own special charm. Handsomely carved bannister • winding staircase • hand rubbed Cherrywood fireplace • and a massive stained-glass window dominates the entrance hall. Two rooms will include whirlpool tubs and warm toasty fireplaces. For more privacy, a honeymoon cottage is available. Guests enjoy relaxing in the parlor while they sip their favorite beverage, read a good book, and admire the original hand-painted mural on the ceiling. The homemade breakfast is becoming world famous — as good as Mom used to make! Your friendly innkeepers go to great lengths to live up to their motto: "You'll feel Right at home with us".

Fishlake

Fishlake is in south-central Utah about 30 miles southeast of Richfeld. The 16-mile byway follows UT 25 between UT 24 and Fremont River Road (FSR 036). Utah Highway 25 is a two-lane paved road suitable for all vehicles, Fishlake is open all year; use extra caution in winter.

Fishlake takes the traveler from a sagebrush and juniper landscape through stands of aspen, Engelmann spruce, and white fir. A portion of the byway follows the shoreline of Fish Lake, a beautiful mountain lake that is nearly six miles long and two miles wide. Lakeshore National Recreation Trail surrounds the lake and is popular with hikers and mountain bikers. The watchful eye of wildlife observers will most likely see mule deer foraging among the forest. Elk, moose, and mountain lions also make their home here but are not commonly seen. Osprey, golden eagles, and hawks can be seen riding the wind currents above, especially around the lake.

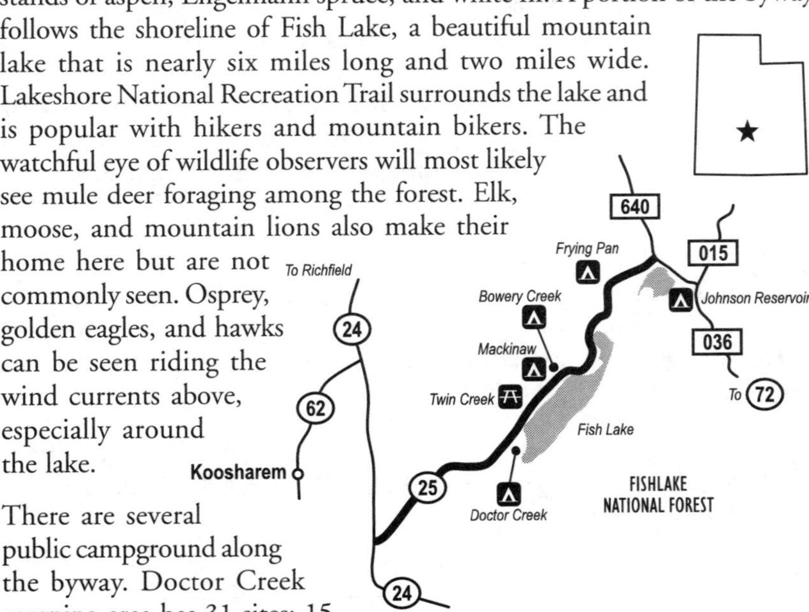

There are several public campground along the byway. Doctor Creek camping area has 31 sites; 15 that can accommodate RVs up to 22 feet long. Mackinaw Campground has 68 sites suitable for tent campers and recreational vehicles up to 22 feet. Bowery Creek Campground has 43 RV and tent sites. All the campsites here have hookups and can accommodate RVs up to 22 feet. The Frying Pan camping area has 12 sites suitable for tents and RVs.

Many of the campgrounds are situated on picturesque Fish Lake, a natural lake surrounded by rolling mountains. Anglers will find rainbow and brown trout among other species. Johnson Reservoir is a smaller lake but also provides good fishing opportunities.

Information: Fishlake National Forest, 115 E 900 N, Richfield UT 84701 / 435-896-9233.

Flaming Gorge - Uinta's

The Flaming Gorge - Uinta's scenic byway is in northeast Utah. It begins in Vernal and travels north to Manila. The 67-mile route follows US 191 and UT 44 across Ashley National Forest. Both are two-lane paved roads suitable for all vehicles and usually remain open year-round. Caution is needed when traveling the byway in winter, especially in the higher elevations.

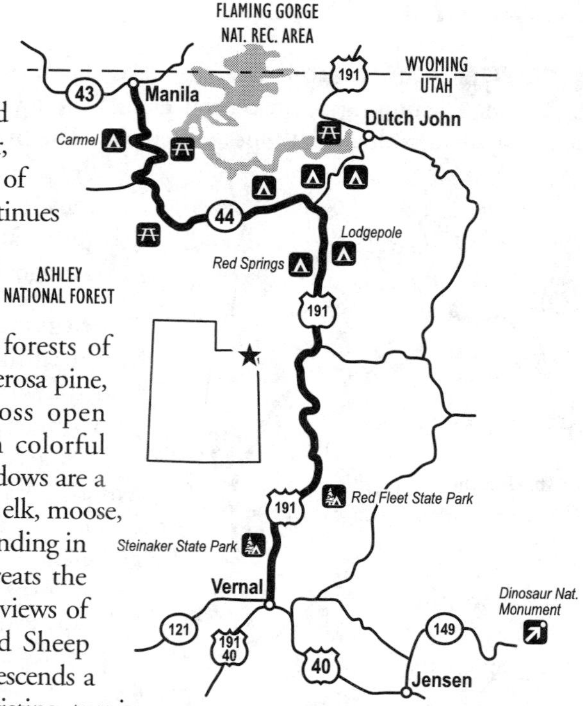

Beginning in Vernal, the byway climbs through sculptured layers of sandstone and steep slopes of juniper, pinyon, and patches of aspen. The byway continues its winding course, climbing the eastern flank of the Uinta Mountains through forests of lodgepole pine, ponderosa pine, and aspen and across open meadows filled with colorful wildflowers. The meadows are a good area for spotting elk, moose, or mule deer. Before ending in Manila, the byway treats the visitor with beautiful views of Sheep Creek Bay and Sheep Creek Canyon as it descends a steep cliff along the twisting, turning road. Wildlife observers will want to keep one eye on the road and the other in search of bighorn sheep through this area. Visitors can obtain maps and brochures at the national forest offices in either Vernal or Manila.

Flaming Gorge National Recreation Area, near the northern end of the byway, is loaded with outdoor recreation opportunities. Flaming Gorge Reservoir is a 91-mile lake formed when the Bureau of Reclamation constructed a dam on Green River. The huge lake extends into Wyoming and offers excellent boating and fishing opportunities. Fishermen will find lake trout, rainbow trout, smallmouth bass, and Kokanee salmon. Boat ramps provide access to the lake and can be found in many of the campgrounds surrounding the lake.

Information: Ashley National Forest, 355 N Vernal Ave, Vernal UT 84078 / 435-789-1181. Dinosaur National Monument, 4545 E US Hwy 40, Dinosaur CO 81610 / 970-374-3000. Flaming Gorge NRA, PO Box 278, Manila UT 84046 / 435-784-3445. Steinaker State Park, 4335 N Hwy 191, Vernal UT 84078 / 435-789-4432. Red Fleet State Park, 8750 N Hwy 191, Vernal UT 84078 / 435-789-4432.

Huntington Canyon

Huntington Canyon travels between Fairview and Huntington in central Utah. It follows UT 31, a two-lane paved road suitable for all types of vehicles. The byway is 48 miles long and remains open year-round. Snow tires or chains may be required at times from October through April.

Beginning in Fairview, the byway climbs through Fairview Canyon with Cottonwood Creek flowing nearby. Cottonwood Creek accompanies you until it passes beneath the byway through the Narrows Tunnel. Douglas fir, Engelmann spruce, and patches of aspen cover the steep slopes. The byway turns south and skirts the shores of three picturesque lakes; good trout fishing may be found here. The byway continues its descent through Huntington Canyon and is now accompanied by Huntington Creek. You'll end your scenic journey across the Wasatch Plateau in the community of Huntington.

There are several camping areas along the byway, many situated on the banks of bubbling creeks. Gooseberry is a short drive north of the byway and offers eight campsites. Old Folks Flat also offers eight sites set among spruce and fir trees. The campsites can accommodate tents or recreational vehicles up to 30 feet. Forks of Huntington Campground lies on the banks of Huntington Creek and has six tent-only campsites. A hiking trail accessed here will take you along Left Fork Creek. Bear Creek is a county-maintained campground with twenty sites for tents and recreational vehicles. Two miles east of Huntington is a state park with twenty-two sites, some with hookups.

Information: Manti-La Sal National Forest, 599 W Price River Dr., Price UT 84501 / 435-637-2817. Huntington State Park, PO Box 1343, Huntington UT 84528 / 435-687-2491.

Lodging Invitation

Larsen House Bed & Breakfast
298 South State St.
Mt. Pleasant, UT 84647

Phone: 435-462-9337
800-848-5263
Fax: 435-462-2362

At the Larsen House, beautiful antiques blend with an elegant restored Victorian Mansion. Each room is tastefully decorated with its own special charm. Handsomely carved bannister • winding staircase • hand rubbed Cherrywood fireplace • and a massive stained-glass window dominates the entrance hall. Two rooms will include whirlpool tubs and warm toasty fireplaces. For more privacy, a honeymoon cottage is available. Guests enjoy relaxing in the parlor while they sip their favorite beverage, read a good book, and admire the original hand-painted mural on the ceiling. The homemade breakfast is becoming world famous — as good as Mom used to make! Your friendly innkeepers go to great lengths to live up to their motto: "You'll feel Right at home with us".

Little Cottonwood Canyon

Little Cottonwood Canyon is 18 miles south of downtown Salt Lake City in north-central Utah. It begins at the junction of UT 209 and UT 210 and travels east to the road's end, three miles east of Alta. The 12-mile route follows UT 210, which is a narrow two-lane paved road to Alta and thereafter is graveled. All types of vehicles can safely drive the byway. The paved portion is open year-round; the graveled section is closed November through May.

Little Cottonwood Canyon is a scenic journey through the narrow, sheer-walled canyon of Little Cottonwood Creek. Near the mouth of the canyon is a site where Mormon pioneers quarried huge granite blocks used to construct the Salt Lake Temple. Today, the canyon is used by those in pursuit of outdoor recreation. The area attracts downhill and cross-country skiers during winter and hikers, campers, and photographers during warmer months. A beautiful display of colorful wildflowers reward byway travelers that reach the end of the road.

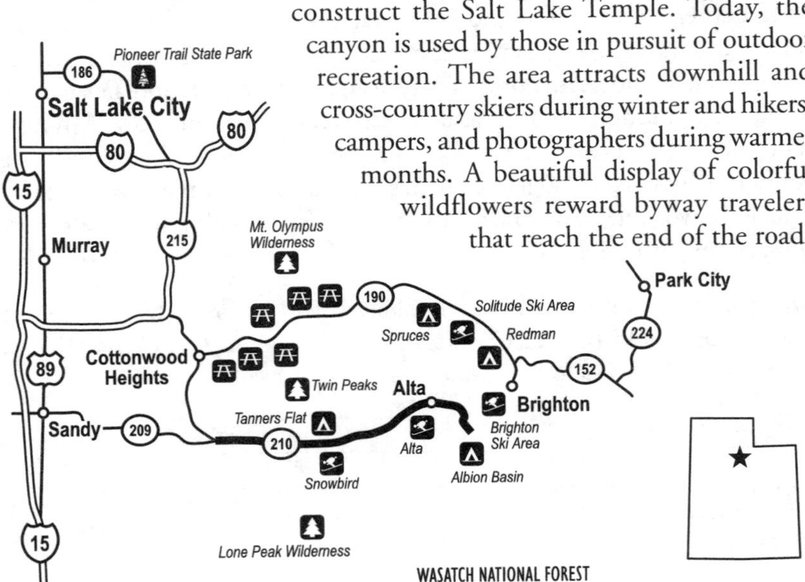

Wildlife observers will want to be on the lookout for mule deer, elk, and moose. Golden eagles and hawks can sometimes be seen riding the wind currents above the canyon walls. If you decide to camp among the stars, hooting of the great horned owl may break the nighttime silence. During the day, numerous songbirds will be heard speaking to one another in a language known only to them. Other wildlife inhabiting the area but rarely seen includes coyotes, mountain lions, and bobcats.

For a breathtaking view of the surrounding mountains and wilderness areas, be sure to take the Snowbird Tram to the top of 11,000-foot Hidden Peak. There are two wilderness areas along the byway. Twin Peaks Wilderness to the north protects 11,796 acres of the rugged landscape and separates Big Cottonwood Canyon from Little Cottonwood Canyon. To the south is 30,088-acre Lone Peak Wilderness. Both wilderness areas invite back country exploration for experienced hikers. Tanners Flat Campground has 36 sites suitable for tents and RVs. Albion Basin Campground is set 9,500 feet above sea level and has 21 campsites.

Information: Wasatch-Cache National Forest, 8236 Federal Bldg, 125 S State St, Salt Lake City UT 84138 / 801-524-3900.

Logan Canyon Highway

Logan Canyon Highway travels between Logan and Garden City in northern Utah. It follows US 89 for 40 miles. US Highway 89 is a two-lane paved road suitable for all vehicles. It usually remains open year-round. Caution is needed when traveling in winter, especially in the higher elevations.

The byway takes travelers through a beautiful canyon carved by the clear waters of Logan Creek. The creek accompanies you for most of the byway's journey eastward from Logan. You're likely to see many anglers along the creek attempting to pull trout from its water. The nearly vertical limestone walls and rock formations contain fossils that speak much of the geological history of the canyon. The byway begins in Logan at an elevation of 4,525 feet and climbs to Bear Lake Summit, nearly 7,800 feet, then quickly descends through a series of switchbacks to end in Garden City.

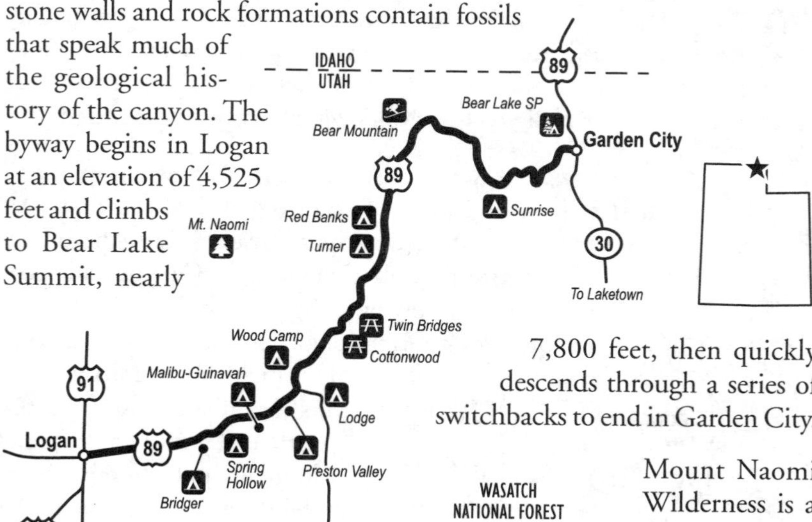

Mount Naomi Wilderness is a 44,964-acre wilderness area, home to the region's tallest peak at 9,980 feet. A side trip west of the byway near Turner Campground leads to scenic Tony Grove Lake. From here you can hike a nearly five-mile trail to White Pine Lake within the wilderness area. Limber Pine Trail is a one-mile loop at Bear Lake Summit near Sunrise Campground. It is a pleasant walk with scenic vistas of Bear Lake ten miles away. Another one-mile trail near the Cottonwood Picnic Area will take you to Logan Canyon's Wind Caves. The caves offer an outstanding example of a series of arches and rooms formed by wind and ice erosion.

Malibu-Guinavah is the largest campground offering 40 sites for tents and RVs up to 25 feet long. Sunrise is the next largest and has 27 campsites. Bridger, Lodge, and Turner Campgrounds each have ten sites with picnic tables and fire rings. Twelve campsites for tents and RVs await the byway traveler in Red Banks and Spring Hollow Campgrounds. Preston Valley offers eight sites while Wood Camp has six. All the campgrounds can accommodate RVs up to 20 feet except Malibu-Guinavah. The campgrounds have a seven day length of stay limit.

Information: Wasatch-Cache National Forest, 8236 Federal Bldg, 125 S State St, Salt Lake City UT 84138 / 801-524-3900. Bear Lake State Park, PO Box 184, Garden City UT 84028 / 435-946-3343.

Markaguant

Markaguant is in southwest Utah. It begins in Cedar City and heads east across Dixie National Forest to Long Valley Junction. The byway is 40 miles long and follows UT 14, a two-lane paved road suitable for all vehicles. Markaguant is open year-round.

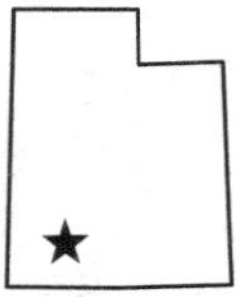

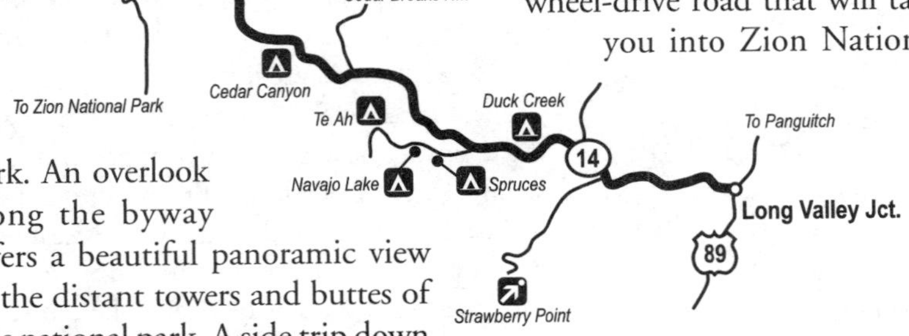

The byway begins in historic Cedar City where pioneers first arrived in 1851 and soon established the first iron refinery west of the Mississippi. Heading east, the byway begins its steep climb through Cedar Canyon with Coal Creek quietly flowing alongside. The stunning, multi-colored rock formations of Cedar Breaks National Monument come into view as you continue eastward. To the south is 10,000-foot Cedar Mountain and a bumpy, four-wheel-drive road that will take you into Zion National Park. An overlook along the byway offers a beautiful panoramic view of the distant towers and buttes of this national park. A side trip down Strawberry Point Road will take you to spectacular views of southern Utah extending into Zion National Park. Nearing completion of your scenic journey across the forested Markaguant Plateau, the byway descends into Long Valley Junction.

Situated along the byway is the 3½-mile long Navajo Lake, popular with the trout fisher. There are also three national forest campgrounds here. Spruces Campground has 28 campsites with picnic tables. Navajo Lake Campground also offers 28 campsites for tents and RVs up to 24 feet long. There are 42 sites available in the Te-Ah Campground. All the campgrounds have drinking water, flush toilets, and boat access to the lake. Visitors can stay at any one site for up to two weeks.

Two more national forest campgrounds are along the byway: Cedar Canyon and Duck Creek. Cedar Canyon, the smaller of the two, has 19 sites with picnic tables. The campsites can accommodate tents and RVs up to 24 feet long. Duck Creek has 79 sites for tents and RVs up to 35 feet long.

Information: Dixie National Forest, 82 N 100 E, Cedar City UT 84720 / 435-865-3700. Cedar Breaks National Monument, 2390 W Hwy 56 - Suite 11, Cedar City UT 84720 / 435-586-9451. Iron Mission State Park, 585 N Main St, Cedar City UT 84720 / 435-586-9290.

Mirror Lake

US FS

Mirror Lake is 45 miles east of Salt Lake City in north-central Utah. The byway begins in Kamas and travels northeast to the Wyoming state line, a distance of 65 miles. It follows UT 150, which is a two-lane paved road suitable for all vehicles. Mirror Lake is open Memorial Day to mid-October. A portion of the byway is groomed in winter for snowmobile use.

Byway travelers can begin their scenic journey in Kamas, which is 6,437 feet above sea level. Traveling east you'll pass through stands of pinyon pines and juniper with Beaver Creek flowing nearby. As the byway begins to climb, the pinyon-juniper landscape gives way to lodgepole pine and aspen. You'll leave Beaver Creek and begin following the course set by the Provo River. The byway continues to climb until you reach Bald Mountain Pass at 10,715 feet. Overlooks nearby provide beautiful views of Bald Mountain, just west of you, and the vast wilderness of high mountain peaks to the east. The byway then begins its descent to end at the Wyoming state line, all the while providing spectacular views of the surrounding landscape.

A two-mile trail accessed near Bald Mountain Pass will take you to the top of Bald Mountain. The panoramic view from this mountain peak is breathtaking. Another short walking trail, this one paved, will take you to the Provo River Falls Overlook. Trails near Lost Creek Campground will lead you among many alpine lakes. The ten-mile Notch Mountain Trail will leave the byway from this area, take you along beautiful mountain lakes, and return to the byway at Bald Mountain Pass.

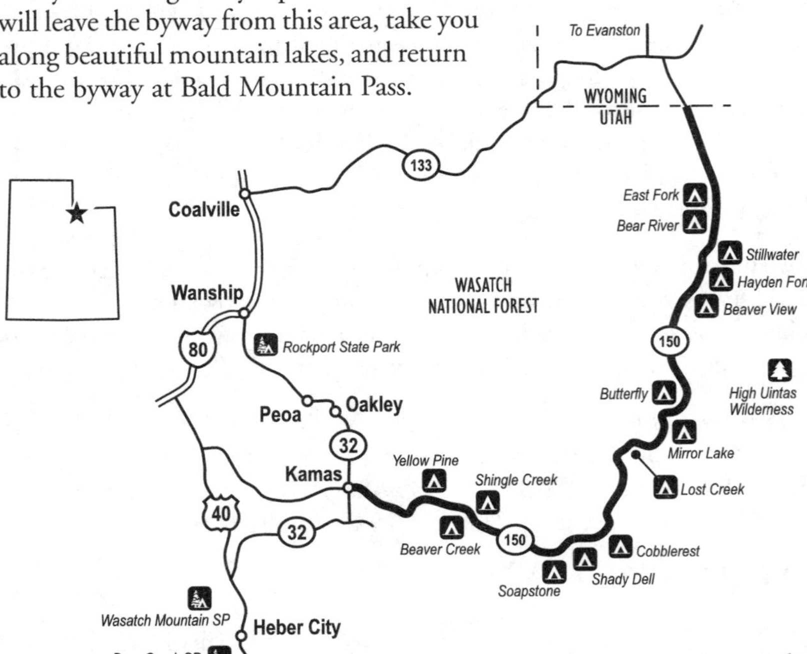

If you're interested in staying overnight, there are over twenty campgrounds to choose from with a total of nearly 700 sites. The campgrounds are generally open from Memorial Day through September. All the campgrounds can accommodate tents or RVs. Most provide drinking water and comfort stations; none have hookups.

Information: Wasatch-Cache National Forest, 8236 Federal Bldg, 125 S State St, Salt Lake City UT 84138 / 801-524-3900. Rockport State Park, 9040 N UT 302, Peoa UT 84061 / 435-336-2241. Wasatch Mountain State Park, PO Box 10, Midway UT 84049 / 435-654-1791. Deer Creek State Park, PO Box 257, Midway UT 84049 / 435-654-0171.

Nebo Loop

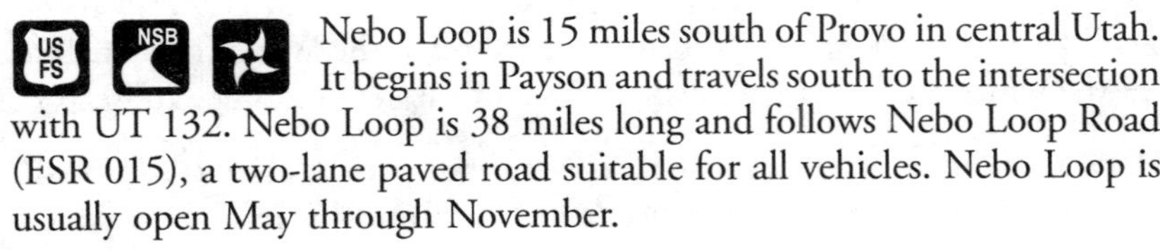

Nebo Loop is 15 miles south of Provo in central Utah. It begins in Payson and travels south to the intersection with UT 132. Nebo Loop is 38 miles long and follows Nebo Loop Road (FSR 015), a two-lane paved road suitable for all vehicles. Nebo Loop is usually open May through November.

The Nebo Loop scenic drive climbs over 9,000 feet in elevation through beautiful mountain scenery. Scenic overlooks along the byway provide vistas of 11,877-foot Mount Nebo and 10,931-foot Bald Mountain. Colorful canyons lined with maples, oaks, and stands of aspen are passed, beseeching the hiker to come and explore. These trees provide beautiful fall colors and stand out among the spruce, fir, and pine. Displaying its own brilliant color of red is the sandstone rock formation known as the Devil's Kitchen. An overlook constructed along the byway provides visitors the chance to photograph this ruggedly beautiful work of nature.

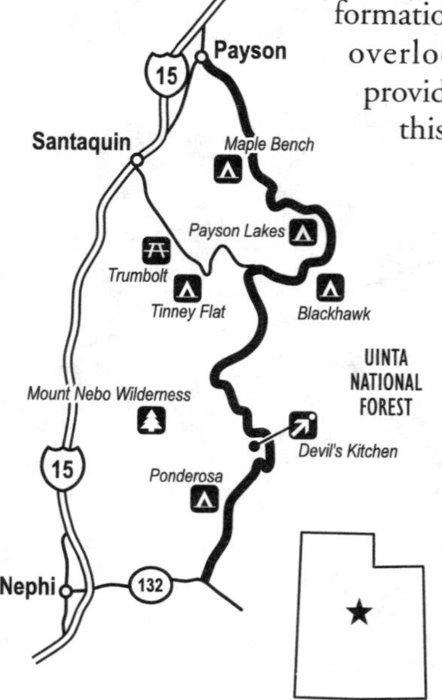

Mount Nebo Wilderness lies to the west of this scenic route. Hikers, backpackers, and horseback riders will find hundreds of miles of trails running through the 28,170-acre area. Trailheads can be found at various points along the byway that lead you into the wilderness. Some guide you to the top of Mount Nebo. Shorter trails can also be found for those interested in just taking a stroll. As you walk the trails, be sure to look for mule deer, elk, or moose grazing around lakes.

There are several campgrounds along the byway. Payson Lakes is the largest with 100 units available. The campground has barrier-free facilities for the handicapped. All the sites have picnic tables, grills, and access to drinking water. Blackhawk Campground is the next largest with 38 sites. Ponderosa Campground has 22 sites; Maple Bench offers ten sites set among Rocky Mountain maples.

Information: Uinta National Forest, 88 W 100 N, Provo UT 84601 / 801-342-5100.

Nine Mile Canyon

Nine Mile Canyon is in east-central Utah about 80 miles southeast of Provo. Southern access is east of Wellington off US 6; northern access is west of Myton off US 40. The byway is 78 miles long and follows Nine Mile Canyon Road, primarily a two-lane gravel and dirt road. The first 12 miles from Wellington is paved. Large RVs and vehicles pulling trailers are discouraged from completing the byway because of steep grades and sharp curves. A four-wheel drive vehicle is recommended for exploring the side roads. Nine Mile Canyon can usually be driven year-round, however, sections may become impassable after heavy rain.

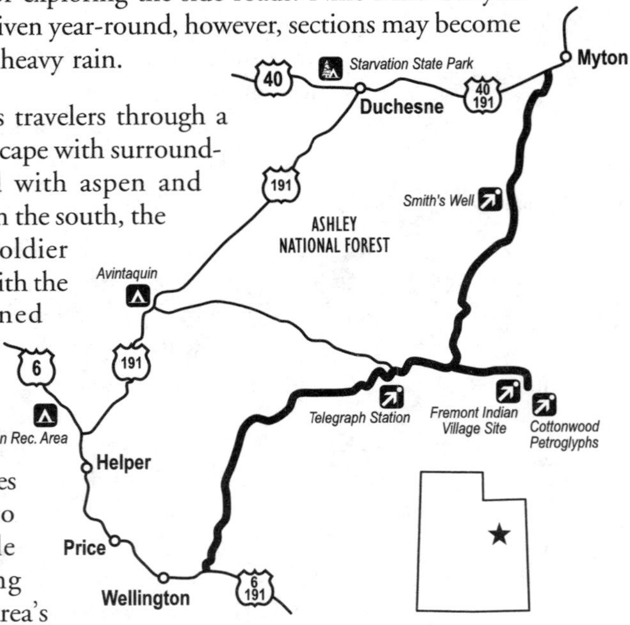

The byway takes travelers through a high desert landscape with surrounding hills dotted with aspen and Douglas fir. From the south, the byway enters Soldier Creek Canyon with the cottonwood-lined Soldier Creek meandering nearby. The byway then leaves Soldier Creek to enter Nine Mile Canyon offering glimpses of this area's history. The Fremont Indians once inhabited the region, leaving behind petroglyphs and pictographs on the canyon walls. After the Civil War, the military built a major supply road through here to Myton. A stone structure at Telegraph Station served as a home and telegraph office between Price and Duchesne. Telegraph wire was strung on metal poles that still stand along the byway. Farther into the canyon, byway travelers can see the remains of a Fremont Indian village on the terrace above the road. Small boulders indicate where structures once stood.

Once you've completed your exploration of Nine Mile Canyon, continue driving north on the byway. Leaving the canyon, you'll come across the site of a stage stop once operated by Owen Smith. Mr. Smith and his family constructed nine buildings including a restaurant, blacksmith shop, and a small hotel to serve the needs of passengers on the Myton to Price stage line. From here the byway once again crosses sagebrush covered hills to its end near Myton.

Information: BLM-Moab Field Office, 82 E Dogwood Suite M, Moab

UT 84532 / 435-259-2100. Ashley National Forest, 355 N Vernal Ave, Vernal UT 84078 / 435-789-1181. Starvation State Park, PO Box 584, Duchesne UT 84021 / 435-738-2326.

Ogden River

Ogden River scenic byway travels across the Wasatch-Cache National Forest in northern Utah. It follows UT 39 between Ogden and Woodruff, a distance of 60 miles. Utah Highway 39 is a two-lane paved road suitable for all vehicles and is generally open late April to mid-December. The portion that crosses the national forest is groomed in winter for snowmobile use. Thirty-three miles are officially designated a National Forest Scenic Byway.

The scenic byway travels through narrow Ogden Canyon, around the shores of Pineview Reservoir, and climbs to Monte Cristo Summit. From the summit, the byway begins its descent to end in the community of Woodruff. Spectacular views of Monte Cristo Peak come into view as the byway traveler approaches the summit. Travelers are taken through a diverse landscape; from sagebrush covered hills in lower elevations to forests of Engelmann spruce, Douglas fir, and stands of aspen.

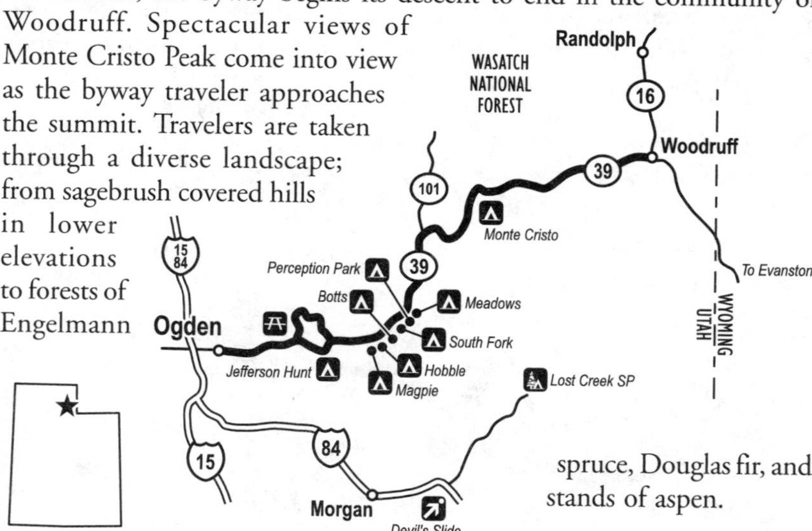

The Ogden River scenic drive travels alongside cottonwood-lined rivers where mule deer and elk can be seen. The best time to spot these graceful animals are early morning or evening. Occasionally, beavers can also be seen working dutifully, building or repairing their dams. Bald eagles can occasionally be seen around Pineview Reservoir. Other wildlife inhabiting the area but not commonly seen includes moose, bobcats, mountain lions, and coyotes.

There are several national forest campgrounds with a total of more than

200 campsites. All have picnic tables, drinking water, and comfort stations available. Most are open from mid-May through October.

Information: Wasatch-Cache National Forest, 8236 Federal Bldg, 125 S State St, Salt Lake City UT 84138 / 801-524-3900. Ft. Buenaventura State Park, 2450 A Ave, Ogden UT 84401 / 801-621-4808. Lost Creek State Park, 5535 S Hwy 66, Morgan UT 84050 / 801-829-6866.

Pony Express

Pony Express is in west-central Utah beginning about 30 miles south of Salt Lake City. It travels between Lehi and Ibapah and follows UT 73 and Pony Express Road, which is marked with stone pillars. Utah Highway 73 is a two-lane paved road suitable for all vehicles. The rest of the byway is a gravel and dirt road requiring a two-wheel drive, high-clearance vehicle. Periods of heavy rain can cause flash flooding and wash out sections of the road. Travelers in a motorhome or pulling a trailer should inquire with the BLM about current road conditions. The BLM has designated 133 miles, from Fairfield to Ibapah, a Type II Back Country Byway.

Byway visitors will be retracing the path followed by the historic Pony Express Trail. This mail route lasted only eighteen months from April 1860 to October 1861. The trail was made obsolete when the first transcontinental telegraph system was completed. The byway travels across the arid desert landscape of the Great Salt Lake Desert. No gas is available between Faust and Ibapah.

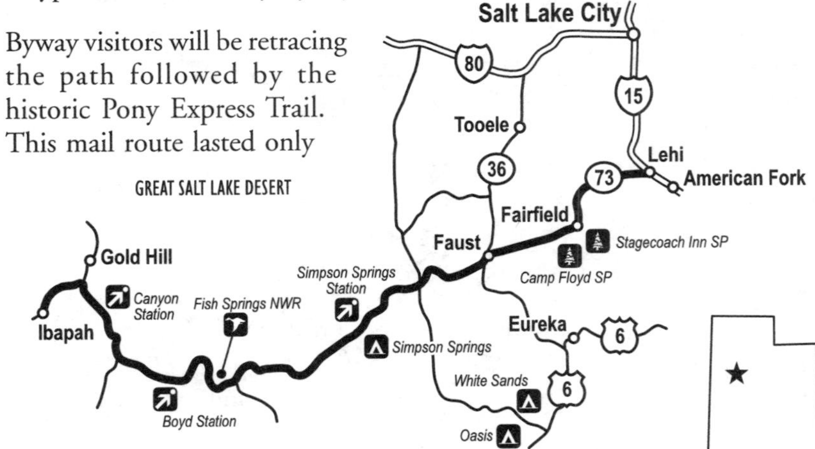

Visitors may wish to begin their journey back in time at the Stage Coach Inn State Park. The adobe inn, built in 1858, was an overnight stop for riders of the Pony Express Trail. Nearby is Camp Floyd State Park, which was originally established in 1858 as a military post.

The Simpson Springs Station was one of the most dependable watering points in this desert region. A stone building has been restored and closely resembles the original that was built around 1860. A BLM campground is located just east of the station and has fourteen campsites. Boyd Station has only a rock wall remaining from the building that once housed the station keeper, a spare rider, and a blacksmith. Canyon Station was originally located northwest of the present site and consisted of a log house, a stable, and a dugout where meals were served.

Information: BLM-Richfield Field Office, 150 E 900 N, Richfield UT 84701 / 435-896-1500. Stagecoach Inn State Park, PO Box 446, Riverton UT 84065 / 801-768-8932. Camp Floyd State Park, PO Box 446, Riverton UT 84065 / 801-768-8932.

Silver Island Mountains

Silver Island Mountains byway is 120 miles west of Salt Lake City in northwest Utah. It begins north of Wendover and is accessed from Exit #4 on I-80. It forms a loop drive of 54 miles and follows Silver Island Mountains Road, a graded gravel and dirt road that requires a two-wheel drive, high-clearance vehicle. Travelers in large RVs or pulling a trailer should inquire with the BLM about any vehicle limitations and current road conditions. Portions of the byway become muddy after periods of rain, otherwise it remains open year-round.

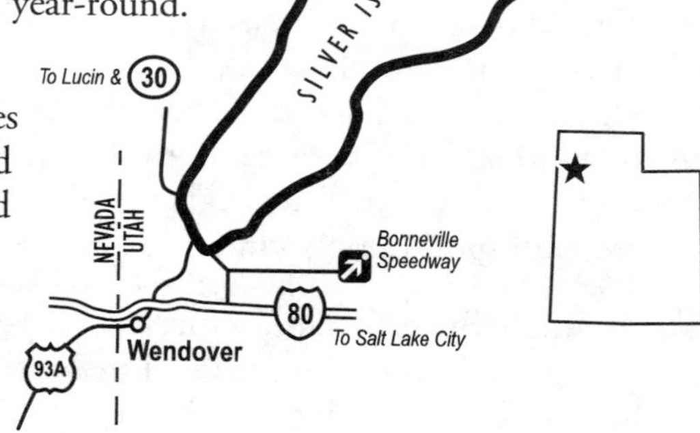

Silver Island Mountains Back Country Byway takes travelers around the rugged and isolated Silver Island Mountains. The byway is surrounded by the vast expanse of the Bonneville Salt Flats; deposits of salt and minerals left behind by the evaporated and ancient Lake Bonneville. Views can often become distorted with distances running together or becoming disguised in the heat.

Numerous side roads will take you into the rugged mountains for exploring. A four-wheel drive vehicle is a must if you wish to drive into the mountains. The mountains do, however, provide excellent opportunities for hikers. These bumpy roads also provide challenges to experienced mountain bikers.

The Silver Island Mountains have seen mountain men, explorers, and wagon trains cross its peaks and valleys. Pilot Peak, eleven miles to the northwest, was named by John C. Fremont in 1845. This mountain peak became a beacon for later travelers passing through the area. The Donner-Reed Party attempted this route on their way to California but abandoned their wagons in the soft mud east of here. You can see part of their fateful route near Donner-Reed Pass.

By the 1930s, Bonneville Salt Flats had become known as the place to be for setting world land speed records. Some of the surrounding mountain peaks are named for famous racers associated with the salt flats.

Information: BLM-Salt Lake Field Office, 2370 S 2300 W, Salt Lake City UT 84119 / 801-977-4300.

Smithsonian Butte

Smithsonian Butte is in southwest Utah 40 miles northeast of Saint George. The short nine-mile route follows Smithsonian Butte County Road between Rockville and UT 59. The county road is a graded dirt road suitable for most vehicles. Because of sharp curves and a half-mile of steep grade, large RVs and vehicles pulling trailers are discouraged from traveling the byway. Smithsonian Butte can usually be completed under dry conditions and should not be attempted after rain or snowfall. The road on the north-facing slope of Smithsonian Butte can remain covered with snow during winter.

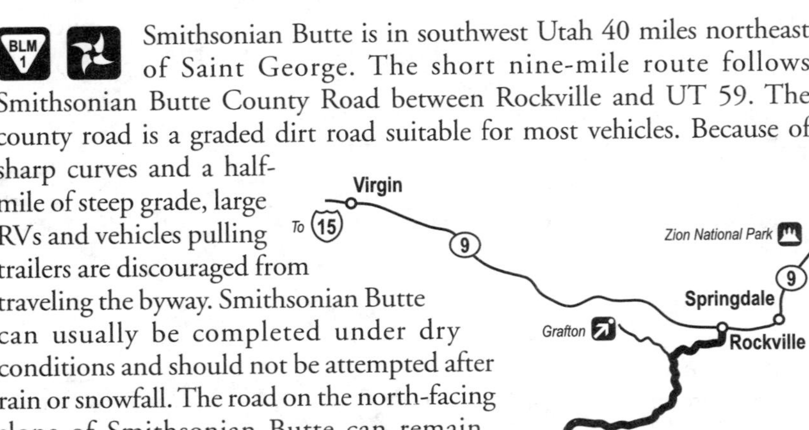

Smithsonian Butte Back Country Byway is best driven from south to north for the spectacular views into Zion National Park. Be cautious, the turn onto the byway from NM 59 is tight. Once you're on the byway heading north, you are treated to views of Smithsonian Butte ahead of you. To the east is Canaan Mountain and the Vermilion Cliffs. Nearly three miles into your scenic journey you'll reach Grafton Wash Canyon. From here you can see the distant Pine Valley Mountains to the northwest; you have reached the byway's highest point at 4,920 feet.

The byway begins heading east, winding across Wire Mesa. Soon you begin the steep descent from Wire Mesa into Horse Valley Wash. Before you is a spectacular view of the Virgin River Valley. Be cautious, though, because this portion of the road descends 800 feet in a little more than a half mile.

Once you've safely descended from Wire Mesa, you'll come to a junction. You can turn left (west) and visit the ghost town of Grafton or head east and end your scenic experience in Rockville. The present site of Grafton was settled in 1862 after the original town was washed away in the big flood of 1859. The town was abandoned in the early 1900s.

Information: BLM-Cedar City Field Office, 176 East DL Sargent Dr, Cedar City UT 84720 / 435-586-2401. Zion National Park, Springdale UT 84767 / 435-772-3256.

Lodging Invitation

Transcontinental Railroad

BLM 2

Transcontinental Railroad is 30 miles west of Brigham City in northwest Utah. It begins south of Promontory near Golden Spike National Historic Site and travels west to Lucin. The byway is 90 miles long and follows Transcontinental Railroad Road, which is a narrow gravel and dirt road. It requires a two-wheel drive, high-clearance vehicle to complete. Vehicles longer than 30 feet are discouraged from traveling the byway. Inquire locally about current road conditions. Portions of the byway may become impassable after heavy rain, otherwise it remains open all year.

This back country byway takes travelers across the abandoned Central Pacific Railroad grade through the old town sites of Kelton, Terrace, and Watercress. The landscape today looks much the same as it did in 1869 when Central Pacific's tracks met Union Pacific's rails. The Golden Spike National Historic Site preserves the site where these two railroads joined their rails with a gold spike on May 10, 1869. A visitor center offers movies and exhibits of this historic event. Take your time to stop and read the more than 30 interpretive sites along the byway. Byway travelers will come across original trestles and culverts as well as remains of two railroad communities and several workers' camps.

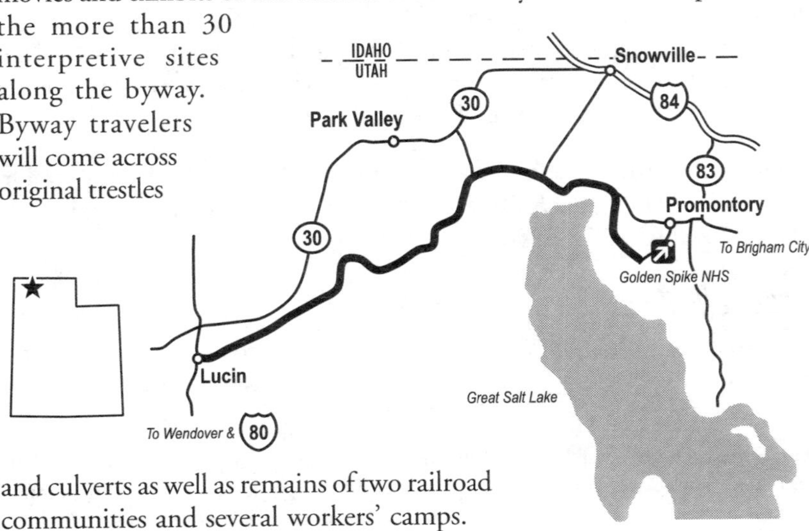

The byway crosses the northern reaches of the Great Salt Lake Desert. The eastern portion provides broad vistas of the northern end of Great Salt Lake. As you travel the western segment of the byway, you are rewarded with views of the Pilot, Newfoundland, Grouse Creek, and Raft River mountain ranges. Please be cautious as you travel this byway as portions of it may be used by bicyclists. Also, there are no services along the byway. Gasoline is available in Snowville, Brigham City, and Wendover.

Information: BLM-Salt Lake Field Office, 2370 S 2300 W, Salt Lake City UT 84119 / 801-977-4300. Sawtooth National Forest, 2647 Kimberly Rd E, Twin Falls ID 83301 / 208-737-3200. Golden Spike NHS, PO Box 897, Brigham City UT 84302 / 435-471-2209.

VIRGINIA

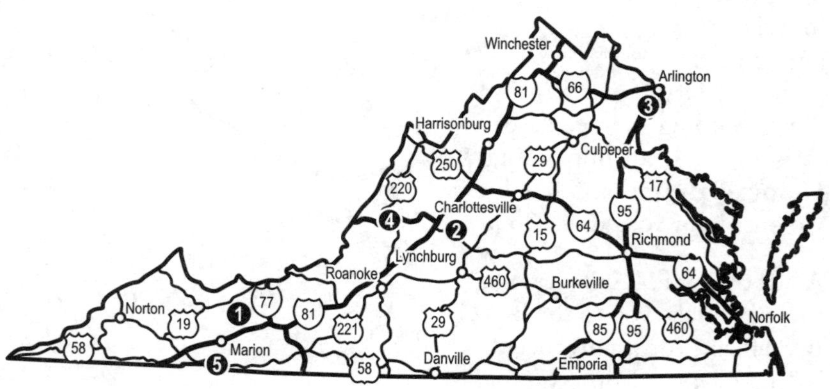

Big Walker Mountain

US FS Big Walker Mountain is 90 miles west of Roanoke in southwest Virginia. It begins west of Bland at the junction of I-77 and US 52. It follows US 52 and VA 717 for a total of 16 miles and reconnects with I-77. The two-lane paved roads remain open year-round and are suitable for all types of vehicles.

Big Walker Mountain takes the traveler through forests of oak, hickory, and white pine as it ascends Big Walker Mountain. In spring colorful wildflowers bloom, beseeching your admiration. Flowering trees compete with the wildflowers, adding their own dash of color to the landscape. In fall the byway is painted in beautiful colors of red and gold. Among the trees within the mountains, one finds a diversity of wildlife. White-tailed deer can sometimes be seen along the byway, usually in the early morning or evening. Wild turkeys tend to be more secretive, but they occasionally allow themselves to be seen. The numerous songbirds inhabiting the area joyfully sing their songs of welcome to visitors. Meandering creeks along the byway add to the symphony with their bubbling and gurgling sounds.

Once atop Big Walker Mountain, visitors will find a privately-owned 100-foot tower open to tourists for a small fee. The view from here is spectacular, encompassing the surrounding densely-forested mountains and wide open valleys. An historical marker here tells the story of Mary Tynes warning the people of Wytheville of an impending Union Calvary raid led by Colonel John Toland in 1863.

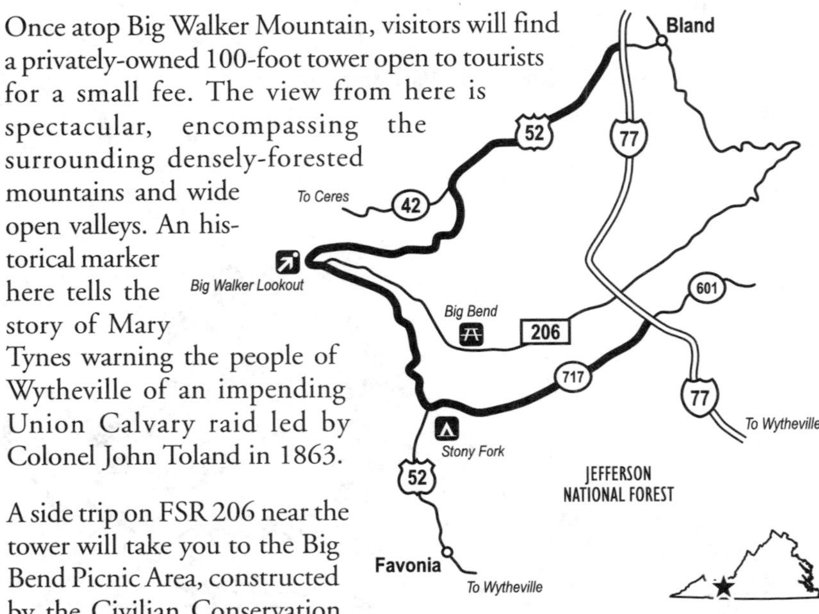

A side trip on FSR 206 near the tower will take you to the Big Bend Picnic Area, constructed by the Civilian Conservation Corps in the 1930s. Set amidst orchard grass under a canopy of oaks, the picnic site offers vistas of the ridge and valley terrain to the south. This is a good spot to take a break and breathe in the surrounding landscape.

A national forest campground is located on the banks of East Fork of the Stony Fork Creek off VA 717. Stony Fork Campground offers 53 sites for tents and recreational vehicles. Drinking water, comfort stations, and a dump station are among the facilities available. A 1½-mile nature trail guides you among the trees and flowers.

Information: Jefferson National Forest, 5162 Valleypointe Pkwy, Roanoke VA 24019 / 540-265-5100.

Blue Ridge Parkway

North Carolina portion see page 209

NP Blue Ridge Parkway is a 469-mile drive between Shenandoah and Great Smoky Mountains National Parks. This portion is in western Virginia; it travels between Shenandoah NP and the North Carolina state line. The byway is 217 miles long and is a two-lane paved road suitable for all types of vehicles. Portions may close from November to mid-April, otherwise the byway remains open year-round.

The Blue Ridge Parkway follows the Appalachian Mountain chain, twisting and turning through the beautiful mountains. From Shenandoah National Park, the scenic drive travels along the Blue Ridge Mountains for 355 miles. Then, for the remaining 114 miles, it skirts the southern end of the Black Mountains, weaves through the Craggies, the Pisgahs, and the Balsams before finally ending in the Great Smokies. The Parkway was authorized in 1933 and became a unit of the National Park Service in 1936.

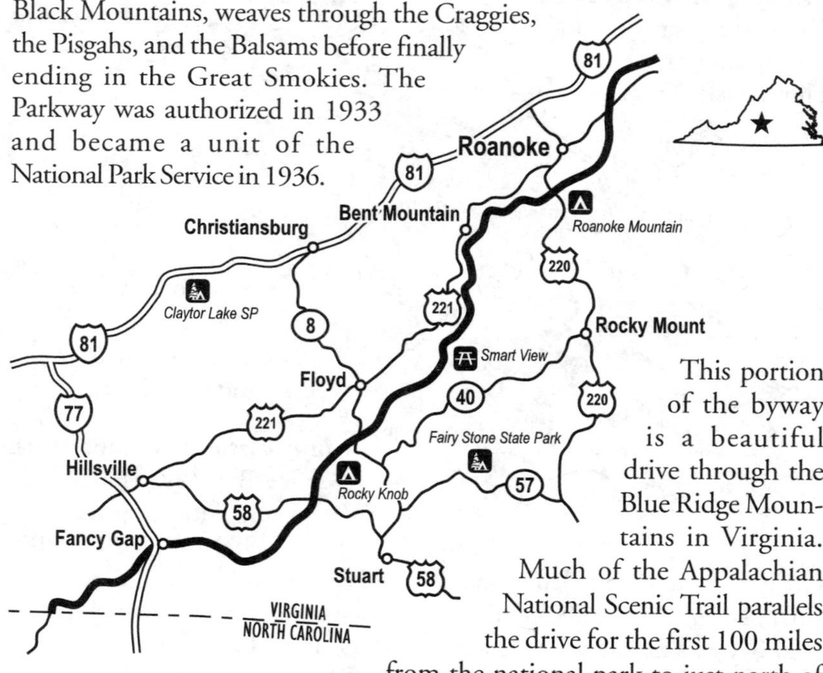

This portion of the byway is a beautiful drive through the Blue Ridge Mountains in Virginia. Much of the Appalachian National Scenic Trail parallels the drive for the first 100 miles from the national park to just north of Roanoke. Access points to this 2,147-mile trail are located along the byway.

Waynesboro, Virginia is the starting point of the byway when traveling north to south. To the north lies the vast Shenandoah National Park and Skyline Drive, which winds 105 miles through the park. To the south is the Blue Ridge Parkway and George Washington National Forest. The national forest covers more than a million acres of mountains and valleys in Virginia and West Virginia. Sherando Lake is a national forest recreation area that offers camping, fishing, boating, hiking, picnicking, and swimming opportunities. Farther south lies the Jefferson National Forest. Numerous camping and picnicking areas are situated around the Cave Mountain Lake area.

The National Park Service also provides numerous areas for camping and picnicking. Otter Creek, Peaks of Otter, and Rocky Knob are just a few examples. In addition to tent and trailer campsites, Peaks of Otter and Rocky Knob also offer lodging. Food service and gasoline are also available in Peaks of Otter. Several picnic areas with scenic vistas of the surrounding mountains are in Humpback Rocks and James River recreation areas. Many of the parks also have visitor centers where you can obtain detailed brochures and maps of the Blue Ridge Parkway.

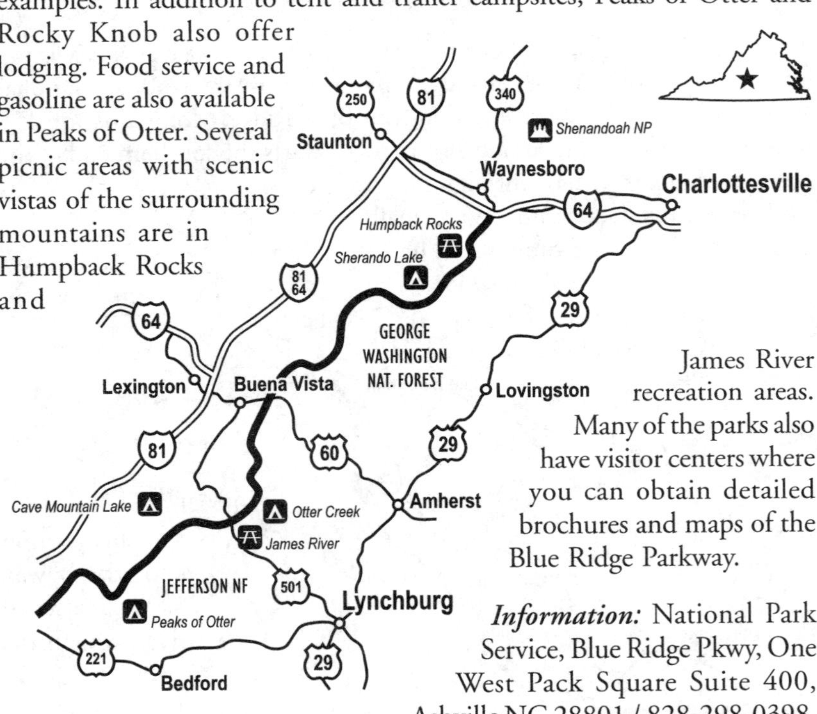

Information: National Park Service, Blue Ridge Pkwy, One West Pack Square Suite 400, Ashville NC 28801 / 828-298-0398. George Washington & Jefferson National Forests, 5162 Valleypointe Pkwy, Roanoke VA 24019 / 540-265-5100. Shenandoah National Park, 3655 US Hwy 211 E, Luray VA 22835 / 540-999-3500. Fairy Stone State Park, 907 Fairystone Lake Dr, Stuart VA 24171 / 540-930-2424.

George Washington Memorial Parkway

Maryland section see page 135

George Washington Memorial Parkway is in northeast Virginia and south-central Maryland. Portions of the scenic drive pass through Washington, D.C. This portion begins in Mount Vernon and travels north to I-495. The byway is 24 miles long and is primarily a four-lane divided highway suitable for all vehicles. In Alexandria, the byway follows Washington Street. George Washington Memorial Parkway is generally open year-round.

The parkway preserves the natural scenery along the Potomac River, connecting historic sites from Mount Vernon to the Great Falls of the Potomac. Many historic sites are complemented by the scenic countryside. The banks of Potomac River are covered with willows, elders, and birches. Fall brings vibrant colors to the parkway as the red maples, oaks, sumacs, and hickories proudly display their autumn attire.

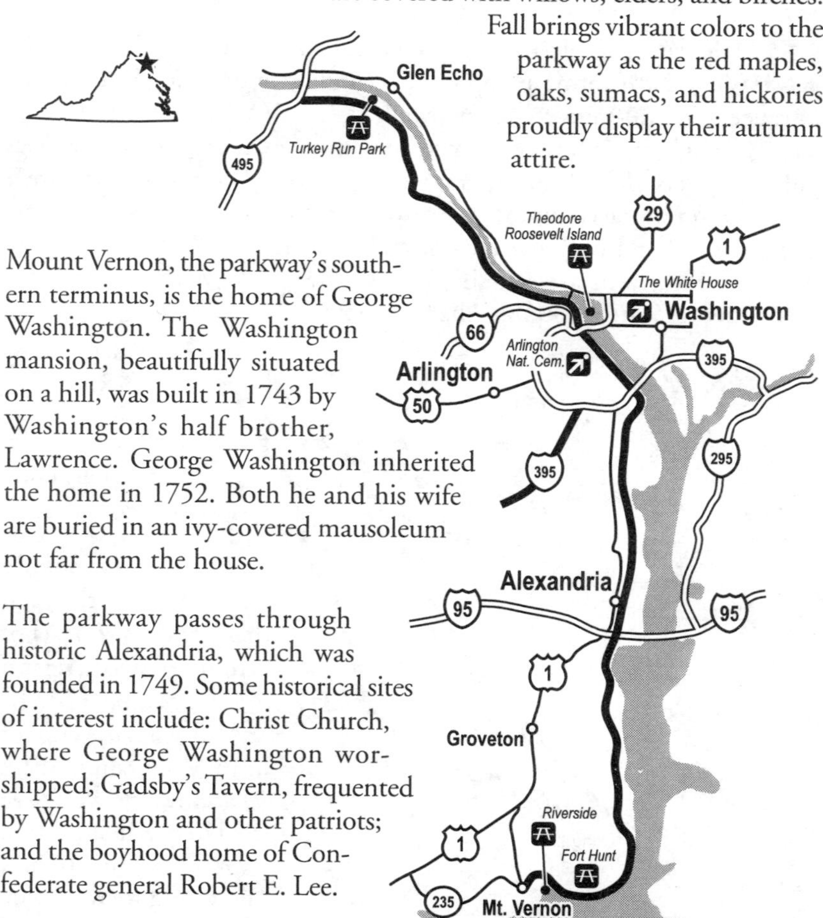

Mount Vernon, the parkway's southern terminus, is the home of George Washington. The Washington mansion, beautifully situated on a hill, was built in 1743 by Washington's half brother, Lawrence. George Washington inherited the home in 1752. Both he and his wife are buried in an ivy-covered mausoleum not far from the house.

The parkway passes through historic Alexandria, which was founded in 1749. Some historical sites of interest include: Christ Church, where George Washington worshipped; Gadsby's Tavern, frequented by Washington and other patriots; and the boyhood home of Confederate general Robert E. Lee.

Besides being an historical route, the byway also offers recreational opportunities. Dyke Marsh is home to over 250 species of birds and is a nice spot for fishing or hiking. Fort Hunt Park offers 156 acres for picnicking, hiking, or bicycling. A boat ramp can be found in Daingerfield Island as well as picnicking facilities.

Information: George Washington Memorial Pkwy, Turkey Run Park, McLean VA 22101 / 703-289-2500. *For information on the various parks and historical sites in the District of Columbia area contact:* National Capital

Parks, National Capital Region, 1100 Ohio Dr SW, Washington DC 20242 / 202-619-7000.

Highlands Scenic Tour

US FS Highlands Scenic Tour is 50 miles northwest of Roanoke in central Virginia. It forms a loop drive beginning and ending in Longdale Furnace. The 20-mile route follows VA 770, VA 850, and FSR 447. Virginia Highway 770 is a narrow road with steep, hairpin turns; vehicles pulling trailers should not attempt this portion. The other roads are a combination of paved and gravel roads suitable for all vehicles. Virginia Highway 770 and FSR 447 are not maintained during winter and are usually impassable December to March. Virginia Highway 850 is generally open year-round.

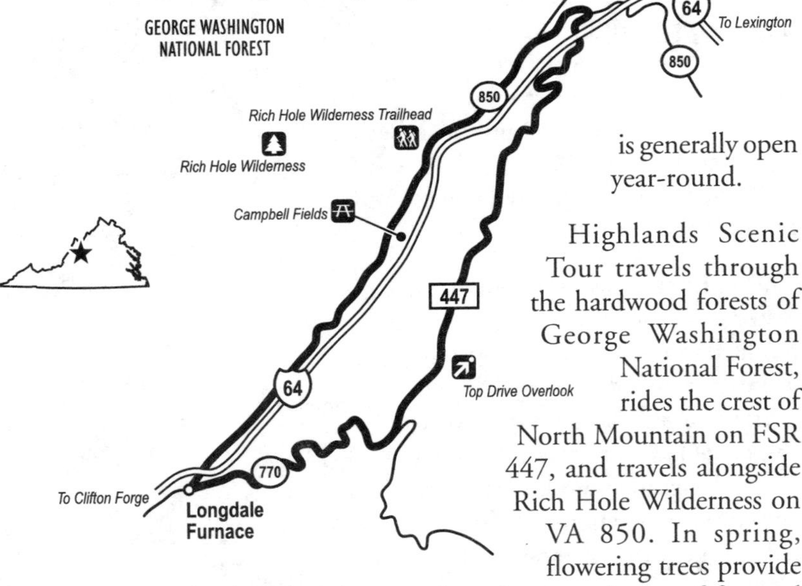

Highlands Scenic Tour travels through the hardwood forests of George Washington National Forest, rides the crest of North Mountain on FSR 447, and travels alongside Rich Hole Wilderness on VA 850. In spring, flowering trees provide beautiful colors of red and pink set against the green leaves of forested hillsides. The trees are given their chance to show off their colors when autumn arrives. If you can look beyond the colorful display, chances are pretty good that you may see white-tailed deer. Perhaps unnoticed by the deer are the numerous songbirds serenading the mountains in thanksgiving for the beautiful habitat. Other wildlife living peacefully among others are black bears, wild turkeys, ruffed grouse, and squirrels. Red-tailed hawks can also be seen soaring overhead.

To the west of the byway is 6,450-acre Rich Hole Wilderness. Visitors may want to take some time to walk the six-mile, moderately strenuous trail running through the wilderness area. The trail takes you along the North Fork of the Simpson Creek through stands of poplar, oak, and hickory. If interested, you can spend some time trying to pull brook and rainbow trout from the creek.

Large RVs and vehicles pulling trailers will want to plan their trip so they travel south on FSR 447. There is a large turnaround point at Top Drive Overlook so these vehicles can avoid the steep switchbacks of VA 770. This portion of the byway provides beautiful views of the Allegheny Highlands in the southwest and the Blue Ridge Mountains to the east.

Information: George Washington National Forest, 5162 Valleypointe Pkwy, Roanoke VA 24019 / 540-265-5100.

Mount Rogers

Mount Rogers is 30 miles east of Bristol in southwest Virginia. It begins in Damascus and follows US 58 east to Volney. Another segment follows VA 603 between Konnarock and Trout Dale. Both highways are two-lane paved roads; US 58 is not recommended for vehicles longer than 35 feet. The byway is 56 miles long and usually remains open all year.

The Mount Rogers scenic byway winds through hardwood forests and rural countryside as it crosses Jefferson National Forest and Mount Rogers National Recreation Area. Mount Rogers stands proudly at 5,729 above sea level and can be seen at various points along the drive. It also has the honor of being Virginia's highest point.

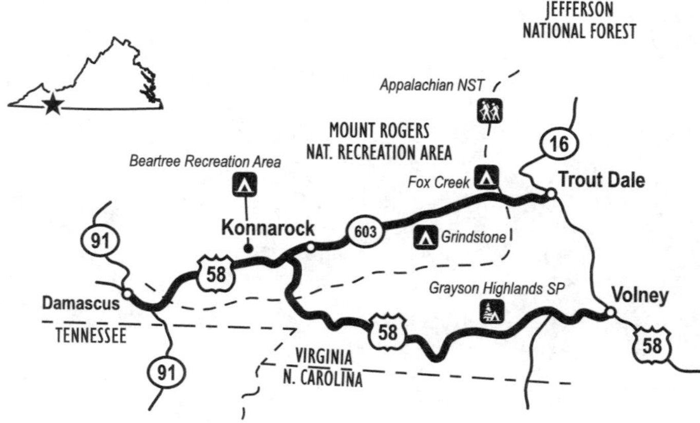

Mount Rogers National Recreation Area encompasses 114,000 acres and is part of the Jefferson National Forest. Visitors will find numerous opportunities for outdoor recreation. Mount Rogers National Recreation Trail is found here as is the Appalachian National Scenic Trail. Enjoy walking a short distance on either of these trails or plan a more extensive backpacking adventure. Either way, you'll be treated to hardwood forests, numerous songbirds, and trickling streams. You might even spot a deer or two. Altogether there is over 400 miles of trail available to the hiker, mountain biker, backpacker, and horseback rider.

Those interested in a more passive activity will find numerous places to pull over and enjoy a good book or picnic. Grayson Highlands State Park is also a good place to find lots of picnic areas. The 4,754-acre park also offers camping opportunities. There are nearly 100 campsites available to tent campers and RVers. It also has comfort stations, shower facilities, and hookups at some campsites. Jefferson National Forest also has several campgrounds but none of the sites have hookups.

Information: Jefferson National Forest, Mt. Rogers NRA, 3714 Hwy 16, Marion VA 24354 / 540-783-5196. Grayson Highlands State Park, 829 Grayson Highland Ln, Mouth of Wilson VA 24363 / 540-579-7092. Mt Rogers NRA, 3714 Hwy 16, Marion VA 24354 / 540-783-5196.

Washington

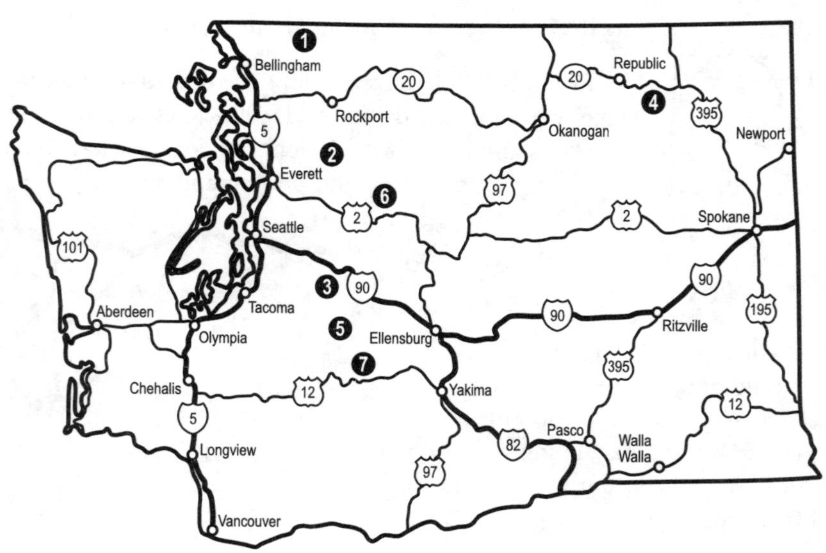

Bellingham
20
Republic
Rockport
395
Newport
5
Okanogan
Everett
97
2
Seattle
2
Spokane
101
90
90
Aberdeen
Tacoma
90
195
Olympia
Ellensburg
Ritzville
395
Chehalis
12
Yakima
12
5
Pasco
Walla Walla
82
Longview
97
Vancouver

Mount Baker Highway

Mount Baker Highway is 35 miles east of Bellingham in northwest Washington. It begins in Glacier and travels east to the road's end at Artist Point. The byway is 24 miles long and follows WA 542, a two-lane paved road suitable for all vehicles. Portions of the byway are subject to closure by snow from November to mid-July.

Travelers of Mount Baker Highway are treated to beautiful mountain scenery as you cross Mount Baker National Forest. You'll climb through the narrow valley of Nooksack River to the rugged timberline of the North Cascades. Artist Point is the destination. From there you're treated to spectacular views of Mount Baker and the wilderness that encompasses the mountain peak. North Fork of the Nooksack River flows alongside the byway for much of your journey. Be sure to take in one of the prettiest gifts the river has to offer, thundering Nooksack Falls.

Mount Baker Wilderness envelops the mountain peak for which it is named and nearly 118,000 acres of mountain streams and lakes. It is a haven for hikers, backpackers, horseback riders, and photographers. There are a lot of trails accessed from the byway that will guide you through this pristine land. There's also several trails that provide the hiking novice a pleasurable and easy-going walk. In winter, cross-country ski enthusiasts will find miles of groomed trails.

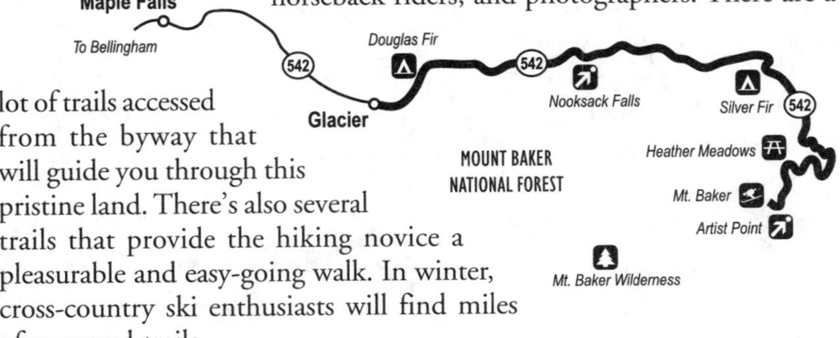

Two national forest campgrounds are on the byway: Douglas Fir and Silver Fir. Douglas Fir Campground is east of Glacier and has 30 campsites situated under Douglas fir and cedar trees on the banks of Nooksack River. Farther east is Silver Fir Campground, which has 21 RV and tent campsites. A picnic area built by the Civilian Conservation Corps is also in the campground. Drinking water and comfort stations are available in both campgrounds. There are no hookups.

Information: Mt. Baker-Snoqualmie National Forest, 21905 64th Ave W, Mountlake Terrace WA 98043 / 425-775-9702.

Mountain Loop Highway

Mountain Loop Highway is in northwest Washington about 35 miles north of Seattle. The byway follows FSR 20 between Granite Falls and Darrington, a distance of 55 miles. From Granite Falls to Barlow Pass, the byway is a two-lane paved road. From Barlow Pass to the confluence of Sauk and Whitechuck rivers, a distance of 14 miles, the road is primarily a single-lane gravel road. The rest of the byway into Darrington is a two-lane paved road. The roads are suitable for all types of vehicles. Mountain Loop Highway is open year-round from Granite Falls to Silverton; the remaining portion is not maintained in winter.

Mountain Loop Highway travels through the heart of Mount Baker-Snoqualmie National Forest. The byway first travels across rural countryside dotted with farmland before climbing into dense forests. Scenic turnouts along the route provide views of the surrounding wilderness. Flowing alongside the byway from Granite Falls to Barlow Pass is South Fork of the Stillaguamish River. Once beyond the pass, South Fork of the Sauk River accompanies you until it reaches its parent river near Bedal Campground. From here on out its the Sauk River you'll see flowing beside you.

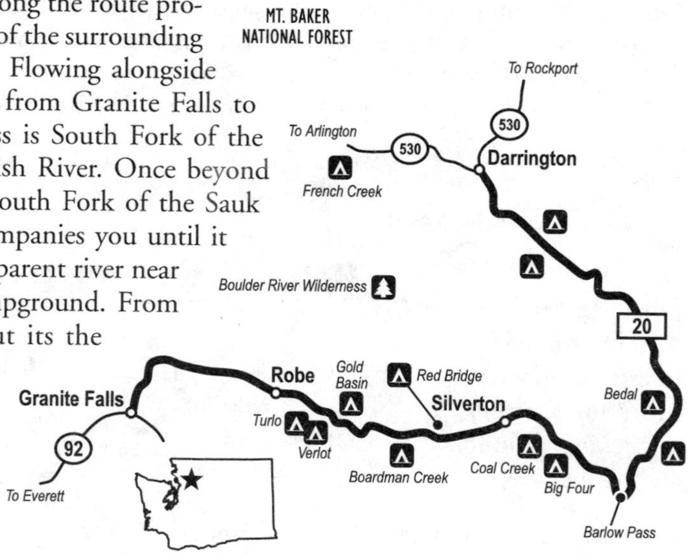

Opportunities for outdoor recreation are abundant. Several trails can be accessed from the byway. Many lead to the seclusion found in Boulder River Wilderness. Other trails take you to scenic viewpoints of the surrounding mountains. Numerous public campgrounds invite the byway traveler to stay awhile. Verlot Campground has 26 campsites among trees near the Stillaguamish River. Gold Basin Campground has 94 sites; Turlo has 19. All three campgrounds have drinking water and comfort stations but no hookups. At Boardman Creek Campground, you'll find 18 sites along the river. There's good fishing for trout here. Nearby Red Bridge Campground has 16 sites. All the campgrounds are open May through September.

Information: Mt. Baker-Snoqualmie National Forest, 21905 64th Ave W, Mountlake Terrace WA 98043 / 425-775-9702.

Mountains to Sound Greenway

NSB Mountains to Sound Greenway is in west-central Washington. It follows I-90 between Eastgate, which is just east of Seattle, and Ellensburg. The byway is about 100 miles long and remains open year-round. Use of chains or snow tires are generally required in winter over Snoqualmie Pass.

Mountains to Sound Greenway takes the traveler from Puget Sound to the forested mountains of Wenatchee and Snoqualmie National Forests. It crosses 3,022-foot Snoqualmie Pass, travels alongside beautiful mountain lakes, and provides access to abundant outdoor recreation possibilities. Although it follows the Interstate, several exits provide access to the national forests and opportunities for camping, picnicking, fishing, and hiking.

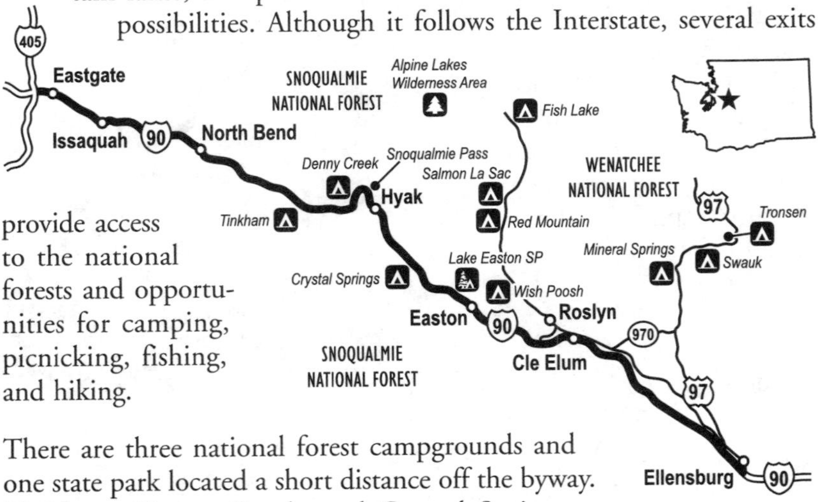

There are three national forest campgrounds and one state park located a short distance off the byway. Tinkham, Denny Creek, and Crystal Springs are national forest campgrounds. They are generally open May through September and have an RV length limit of 22 feet. Hookups are not provided at any of the national forest campgrounds. Tinkham has 48 RV and tent sites; Denny Creek has 33; Crystal Springs has 25 sites. Lake Easton State Park is near the town of Easton. It has 45 campsites with complete hookups and 92 without. The park provides access to nearly 40 miles of trails for hiking, backpacking, and cross-country skiing in winter.

Alpine Lakes Wilderness Area lies north of the byway. It preserves 394,000 acres of Cascade Mountain wilderness and contains nearly 700 small mountain lakes. Hikers and backpackers will find over 600 miles of trails running through the area, including the Pacific Crest National Scenic Trail. Byway travelers can exit I-90 at either Exit #80 or Exit #84 and travel north through Roslyn to the road's end at the wilderness boundary. Numerous national forest campgrounds are located along this side trip, which follows Cle Elum Valley Road.

Information: Washington Department of Trade and Economic Development, 360-753-5601. Wenatchee National Forest, Cle Elum Ranger District, 803 W 2nd St, Cle Elum WA 98922 / 509-674-4411. Snoqualmie National Forest, North Bend Ranger District, 42404 SE North Bend Way, North Bend WA 98045 / 425-888-1421. Washington State Parks & Recreation Commission, Information Center: 800-233-0321.

Sherman Pass

Sherman Pass is 80 miles northwest of Spokane in northeast Washington. The byway follows WA 20 between Kettle Falls and Republic. Washington Highway 20 is a two-lane paved road suitable for all vehicles. The byway is 40 miles long and is usually open year-round; delays are possible in winter.

Sherman Pass National Forest Scenic Byway begins in Republic and takes you across the heavily forested Kettle River Range. The byway steadily climbs from Republic, crosses Sherman Pass at 5,575 feet above sea level, and then descends to Kettle Falls. Frequent turnouts are provided along the byway so you can stop and take in the beautiful scenery. The waters of O'Brien Creek will accompany you for much of the way to Sherman Pass. Once you cross the pass, Sherman Creek will guide you along the byway until it meets the Columbia River. You're pretty much on your own after that but, not to worry, it isn't difficult finding Kettle Falls. This same route

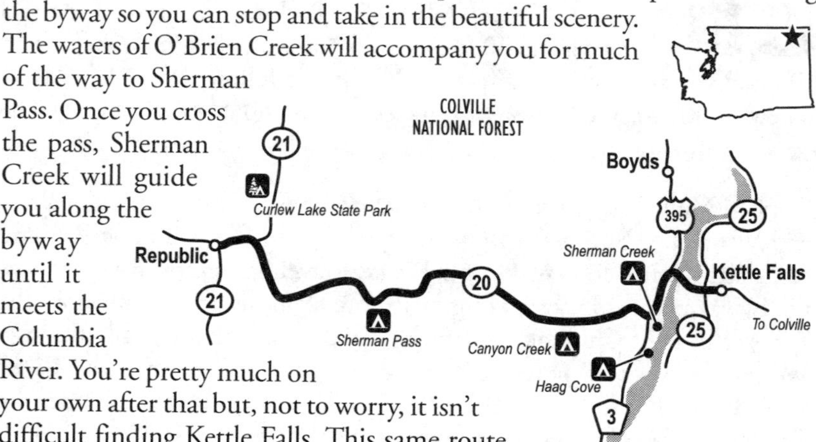

was used by Native Americans long ago as they made their way to the Columbia River for fishing purposes. The trail later became a wagon route for miners. The route is now popular with byway travelers and bicycle riders.

Wildlife observers will be pleased to find many species inhabiting the area. Mule deer and white-tailed deer can be seen, especially in the morning or evening. Other wildlife one might enjoy seeing but not want to get close to is the black bear, coyote, or mountain lion. If you stop at one of the overlooks along the byway, the many songbirds in the area would be happy to sing a tune or two for you.

If you want to take some time to explore the area a bit, there are many trails that would be pleased to provide you access. Kettle Crest National Recreation Trail is one that invites the byway traveler. It can be accessed near the top of Sherman Pass. Other trails will take you among lodgepole pine, subalpine fir, and Douglas fir.

There are two national forest campgrounds located directly along the byway. Sherman Pass Campground has nine sites and an interpretive trail. Canyon Creek Campground has twelve sites. Other campgrounds can be found a short distance off the byway.

Information: Colville National Forest, 765 S Main St, Colville WA 99114 / 509-684-7000. Curlew Lake State Park, 974 Curlew Lake State Park Rd, Republic WA 99166 / 509-775-3592.

Stephen Mather Memorial Parkway

Stephen Mather Memorial Parkway is in west-central Washington 40 miles southeast of Seattle. It begins in Enumclaw and travels southeast to Naches. It follows WA 410, a two-lane paved road suitable for all vehicles, and is about 90 miles long. The byway is usually open year-round; temporary closure is possible in winter.

Stephen Mather Memorial Parkway travels across portions of Snoqualmie and Wenatchee National Forests. It crosses 5,430-foot Chinook Pass and alongside Mount Rainier National Park. Traveling east from Enumclaw, the byway climbs through old growth forests and is accompanied by the White River. At Chinook Pass the byway descends dramatically through Wenatchee National Forest and is accompanied by the American River. From Cliffdell, the Naches River flows beside the byway as you enter the fertile agricultural valley of Yakima County.

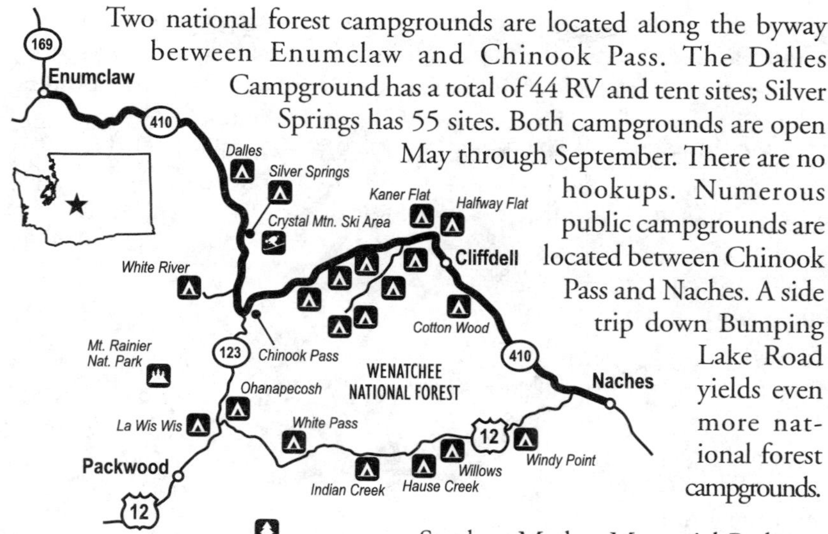

Two national forest campgrounds are located along the byway between Enumclaw and Chinook Pass. The Dalles Campground has a total of 44 RV and tent sites; Silver Springs has 55 sites. Both campgrounds are open May through September. There are no hookups. Numerous public campgrounds are located between Chinook Pass and Naches. A side trip down Bumping Lake Road yields even more national forest campgrounds.

Stephen Mather Memorial Parkway also provides access to Mount Rainier National Park, which contains Washington's highest peak. Mount Rainier is 14,410 feet high and supports the largest glacial system in the lower 48 states. There are 27 named glacier encompassing 35 square miles. The park has six campgrounds with a total of 600 campsites. Two hotels, both listed on the National Register of Historic Places, are also within the park.

Information: Yakima Chamber of Commerce, 509-248-2021. Mount Rainier National Park, Tahoma Woods Star Route, Ashford WA 98304 / 360-569-2211. Snoqualmie National Forest, White River Ranger District, 853 Roosevelt Ave E, Enumclaw WA 98022 / 360-825-6585. Wenatchee National Forest, Naches Ranger District, 10061 Highway 12, Naches WA 98937 / 509-653-2205. Washington State Parks & Recreation Commission, Information Center: 800-233-0321.

Stevens Pass

US FS

Stevens Pass is in west-central Washington about 40 miles northeast of Seattle. It follows US 2 between Gold Bar and Leavenworth, a distance of 70 miles. US Highway 2 is a two-lane paved road suitable for all types of vehicles. Winter driving conditions in higher elevations require extra caution, otherwise the byway remains open year-round.

This drive takes travelers across densely forested Snoqualmie and Wenatchee National Forests as it crosses 4,061-foot Stevens Pass. The byway begins climbing the western slopes of the Cascade Mountains from Gold Bar to its climax at the pass and then descends into Leavenworth. The rushing South Fork of the Skykomish River, with its many cascading waterfalls, flows alongside from Gold Bar to Deception Creek Campground. At that point the Tye River will take over and show you the way to Stevens Pass. Tye River has a couple of scenic waterfalls to show off, too. Beyond the pass, Nason Creek will accompany you to WA 207, just north of Winton.

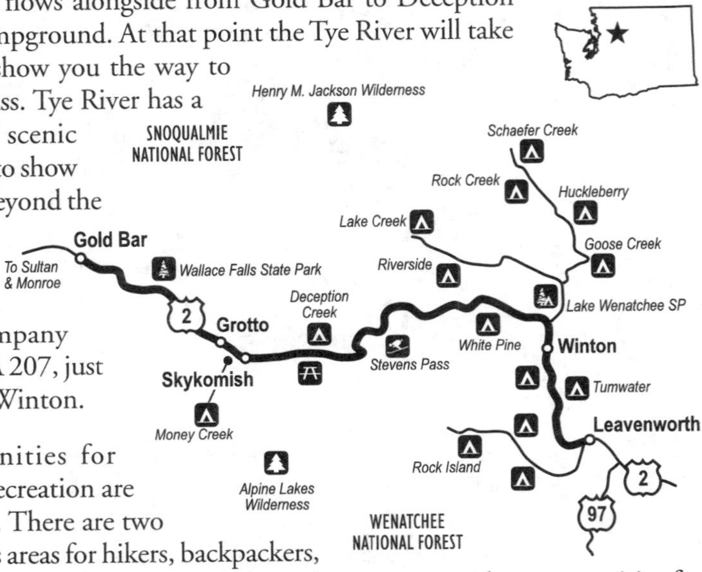

Opportunities for outdoor recreation are abundant. There are two wilderness areas for hikers, backpackers, and horseback riders. Many rivers and streams provide opportunities for spending an afternoon trying to pull fish from the water. The national forest has constructed several campgrounds that provide just the right spot for pitching a tent or parking your RV. Wildlife observers can spend their time seeking the many species inhabiting the area.

Information: Mt. Baker-Snoqualmie National Forest, 21905 64th Ave W, Mountlake Terrace WA 98043 / 425-775-9702. Washington State Parks & Recreation Commission, Information Center: 800-233-0321.

Lodging Invitation

AlpenRose Inn
500 Alpine Place
Leavenworth, WA 98826

Phone: 509-548-3000
800-582-2474

This small European Inn offers 15 individualized decorated rooms with fireplaces, some with balconies, and jacuzzi suites. Within walking distance to Bavarian town of Leavenworth. Your stay includes a full breakfast and delicious dessert in the evening. Close to hiking, golf, and cross country skiing. Amenities include cable TV • phones • swimming pool • hot tub • and large decks. AAA ◆◆◆. Age restriction, non-smoking, and no pets.

Enzian Inn
590 Hwy. 2
Leavenworth, WA 98826

Phone: 509-548-5269
800-223-8511
Fax: 509-548-5269

One of Leavenworth's most authentic and beautiful Bavarian Inns. The 104 guest rooms are complete with imported European furnishings and cozy down comforters. Elegant suites with canopy bed, spa, and fireplace. You'll enjoy complimentary breakfast buffet • indoor & outdoor pools • hot tubs • racquetball court • ping pong table • exercise room • x-country ski equipment • and 18 hole championship putting course.

A/C H

SkyRiver Inn
333 River Drive East
P.O. Box 280
Skykomish, WA 98288

Phone: 360-677-2261
800-367-8194 (WA)

For riverside lodging in the heart of the Cascades, SkyRiver Inn offers travelers a quiet, scenic location on the Skykomish River. Guests enjoy immediate access to river across well kept lawn, surrounded by trees and mountains. Close to whitewater rafting and Stevens Pass skiing. Major credit cards accepted.

A/C

White Pass

US FS

White Pass is in west-central Washington about 20 miles northwest of Yakima. It follows US 12, a two-lane paved road suitable for all vehicles, between Naches and Packwood. The byway is 58 miles long and generally remains open year-round. Traveling the byway in winter requires caution, especially in higher elevations.

White Pass scenic byway travels across the Gifford Pinchot and Wenatchee National Forests. It winds through a mixed conifer forest, beautiful meadows ablaze with wildflowers, and passes pristine lakes and cascading waterfalls. The byway crosses 4,500 foot White Pass where the Pacific Crest National Scenic Trail may be accessed. Several scenic turnouts and overlooks provide visitors with beautiful views of the surrounding wilderness. They also provide good opportunities for spotting deer, elk, eagles, hawks, or osprey.

Rimrock Lake and the numerous other lakes along the byway offer excellent fishing and boating opportunities. The rivers that feed the lakes also offer good fishing and rafting. Situated along the banks are campgrounds and picnic areas.

Near the byway's western end is Mount Rainier National Park. Within the park is Washington's highest peak, 14,410-foot-high Mount Rainier.

This beautiful mountain peak is a dormant volcano supporting the largest glacial system in the lower 48 states. There are 27 named glaciers encompassing 35 square miles. Wonderland Trail is a 93-mile hiking trail that completely circles the mountain peak. To walk the entire trail takes anywhere between 10 and 14 days. Those interested in camping will find over 600 campsites within the park.

Information: Wenatchee National Forest, 215 Melody Ln, Wenatchee WA 98801 / 509-662-4335. Gifford Pinchot National Forest, 10600 NE 51st Cir, Vancouver WA 98682 / 360-891-5000. Mt. Baker-Snoqualmie National Forest, 21905 64th Ave W, Mountlake Terrace WA 98043 / 425-775-9702. Mt. Rainier National Park, Tahoma Woods Star Route, Ashford WA 98304 / 360-569-2211.

Lodging Invitation

Game Ridge Motel & Lodge
27350 U.S. Hwy. 12
Rimrock, WA 98937

Phone: 800-301-9354
509-672-2212
Fax: 509-672-2242

Located on White Pass Highway (Hwy. 12) the *eastern gateway* to Mt. Rainier National Park and Mt. St. Helens National Volcanic Monument. Nestled on the banks of the Tieton River in the beautiful Wenatchee National Forest. Excellent hiking, climbing, hunting, stream fishing and white water rafting are just outside the motel, with lake fishing, waterskiing and windsurfing on nearby Rimrock Lake. You'll enjoy: cabins with private hot tubs • heated pool • riverside hot tub and steam room • fireside recreation room • TV's • Bar-B-Ques • horseshoes • excellent cross-country and downhill skiing • RV spaces • all facilities nearby • group, senior, and weekly rates • and friendly service.

West Virginia

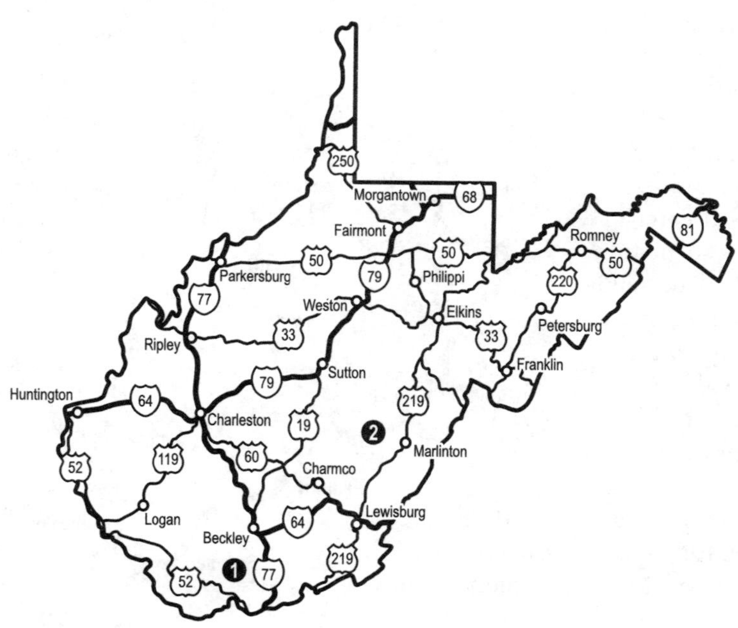

Coal Heritage Trail

Coal Heritage Trail is in southern West Virginia. It begins in Beckley and travels south to Bluefield. The byway is nearly 100 miles long and follows WV 16 and US 52, which are two-lane paved roads suitable for all vehicles. Coal Heritage Trail generally remains open all year.

Coal Heritage Trail travels across the mountains and valleys of southern West Virginia, an area rich in coal mining history. In Beckley, byway travelers can visit the Exhibition Coal Mine, located in the New River City Park. Working equipment and displays demonstrate mining techniques in an old mine. Guided tours of the underground mine are given daily April through September. The byway winds past numerous historical structures of the coal camp life including coal mines, railroad yards, and miners' homes.

Because this byway does not travel through public land, camping opportunities are limited. Twin Falls Resort State Park is north of Mullens off WV 97. It has a 50-site campground; 25 sites have electric hookups. The campground is generally open April through October. A 20-room lodge and 13 secluded cottages are also in the park. Nine hiking and mountain biking trails are within the park, one that leads to two scenic waterfalls: Marsh Fork Falls and Black Fork Falls. Visitors can also see a restored 1800s-style pioneer home.

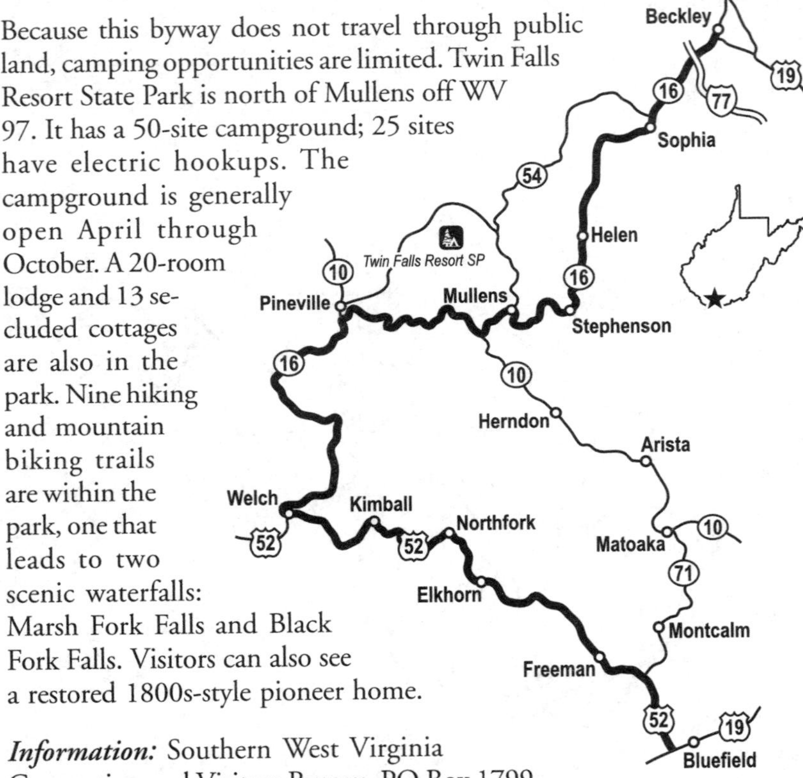

Information: Southern West Virginia Convention and Visitors Bureau, PO Box 1799, Beckley WV 25802 / 304-252-2244 or 800-847-4898. Twin Falls Resort State Park, PO Box 1023, Mullens WV 25882 / 304-294-4000. Pinnacle Rock State Park, PO Box 704, Bluefield WV 24701 / 304-589-5307.

Highland Scenic Byway

Highland Scenic Byway is in east-central West Virginia about 25 miles east of Summersville. It begins in Richwood and travels east to US 219, a distance of 43 miles. The byway follows WV 39 and WV 150, two-lane paved roads suitable for all vehicles. West Virginia Highway 150 is not maintained during winter and is normally closed early December to March.

Highland Scenic Byway travels through the mountainous terrain of the Allegheny Highlands and Plateau. The byway climbs over 2,000 feet from Richwood to the crest of Black Mountain at 4,556 feet. Your scenic journey will take you through hardwood forests of yellow poplar, beech, maples, cherry, and oak trees with wildflowers growing alongside the road. The sparkling North Fork of the Cherry River will accompany you for the first part of your trip from Richwood. Three waterfalls at Falls of Hills Creek gracefully tumble over rock outcrops. A three-quarter-mile trail will guide you to these beautiful falls. The trail to the first waterfall is paved and barrier-free.

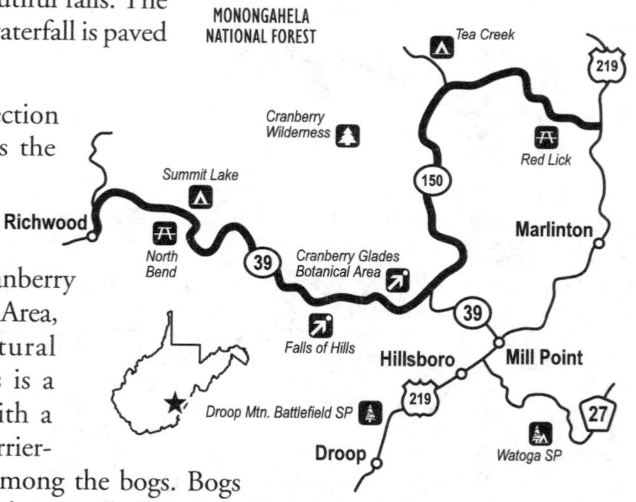

Near the intersection with WV 150 is the Cranberry Mountain Visitor Center. Nearby is the Cranberry Glades Botanical Area, a National Natural Landmark. This is a 750-acre area with a half-mile long barrier-free boardwalk among the bogs. Bogs are acidic wetlands typically found in Canada and the northern United States. Guided tours are conducted on weekends throughout summer. West Virginia Highway 150 travels north alongside 35,864-acre Cranberry Wilderness. Trails accessed along this portion of the byway will take you through the heart of this mountain wilderness area.

Monongahela National Forest offers two camping areas along the byway with more throughout the forest. Summit Lake Campground is situated on the shoreline of a 42-acre lake and has 33 campsites. Anglers will find trout in the lake and many rivers throughout the national forest. Tea Creek Campground has 35 campsites for tents and recreational vehicles. Miles of hiking trails can also be accessed from here.

Information: Monongahela National Forest, Gauley Ranger District, PO Box 110, Richwood WV 26261 / 304-846-2695. Droop Mountain Battlefield State Park, HC64 Box 189, Hillsboro WV 24946 / 304-653-4254. Watoga State Park, Star Route 1 Box 252, Marlington WV 24954 / 304-799-4087.

Wisconsin

Superior
2
Ashland
53
63
1
Hayward
Trego
51
Eagle River
2
Rhinelander
8
Pembine
63
Ladysmith
8
Crandon
8
45
141
Clear Lake
51
Antigo
Marinette
53
Wausau
94
Ellsworth
Eau Clair
Clintonville
10
10
Green Bay
Stevens Point
45
41
10
Black River Falls
Appleton
94
151
Tomah
43
90
51
La Crosse
90
94
Fond Du Lac
Portage
Readstown
12
151
41
14
61
Madison
94
Milwaukee
18
Dodgeville
14
90
12
43
Lancaster
94
Beloit

Great Divide Highway

Great Divide Highway is about 40 miles south of Ashland in northern Wisconsin. It begins about 13 miles south of Mellen and travels west across Chequamegon National Forest. It officially ends at the national forest boundary. Great Divide Highway is 29 miles long and follows WI 77, a two-lane paved road suitable for all vehicles. The byway is generally open year-round.

Great Divide Highway travels through forests of northern hardwoods and mixed conifer. It also treats travelers to meadows filled with wildflowers and wetlands where waterfowl congregate. The byway winds through the hills of the Penokee Range, its ridgelands forming the Great Divide that separates water flowing north to Lake Superior from water flowing south to the Mississippi River. White-tailed deer, black bear, and timber wolves inhabit the forested regions while loons, beavers, and bald eagles can be seen around the byway's many lakes. Scenic overlooks along the route provide panoramic vistas of the surrounding highlands.

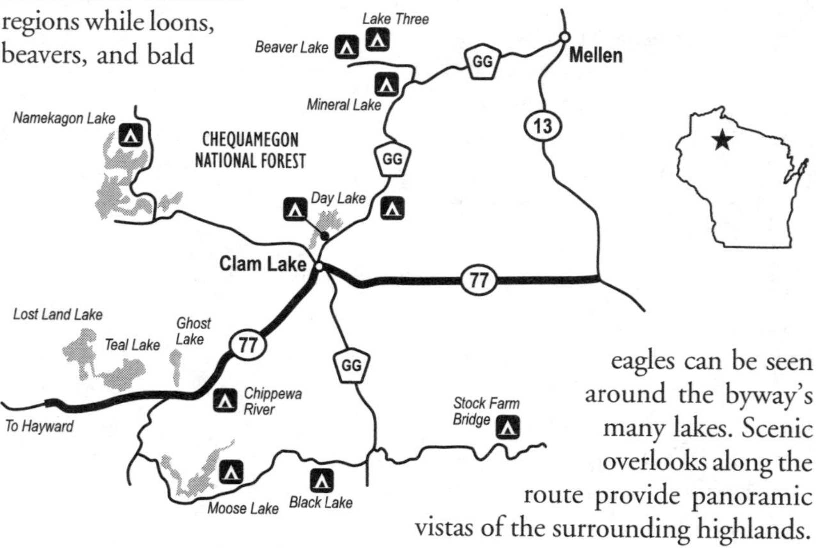

The numerous lakes and rivers surrounding the byway make for great muskellunge, northern pike, bass, walleye, and trout fishing. Portions of the Namekagon River flowing from Namekagon Lake are part of the National Wild and Scenic River System. The river provides some Class II and III rapids for those wishing to tackle the river.

Side roads may tempt you to do some exploring. If you do, you'll be rewarded with many beautiful "hidden" lakes, rivers, and streams. You'll find campgrounds on the shores of many lakes and perfect places for pulling over and enjoying a picnic. This vast network of forest roads also makes for good mountain biking. In winter you're likely to see cross-country skiers and snowmobilers utilizing the miles of groomed trails.

There are two national forest campgrounds along the byway. Day Lake is the largest and is about one mile north of Clam Lake. It has 66 campsites for tents and recreational vehicles. The Chippewa River camping area offers 11 sites and boat access to the river. There are no hookups at either campground.

Information: Chequamegon National Forest, 1170 Fourth Ave S, Park Falls WI 54552 / 715-762-2461.

Heritage Drive

US FS Heritage Drive is 20 miles northeast of Rhineland in northern Wisconsin. The byway begins in Three Lakes and travels north to WI 70. A spur road travels east to Franklin and Butternut Lakes. Heritage Drive is 21 miles long and follows WI 32, FSR 2178 (Military Road), and FSR 2181 (Butternut Lake Road). The roads are narrow, two-lane paved roads suitable for all vehicles. The byway's roads are usually open all year.

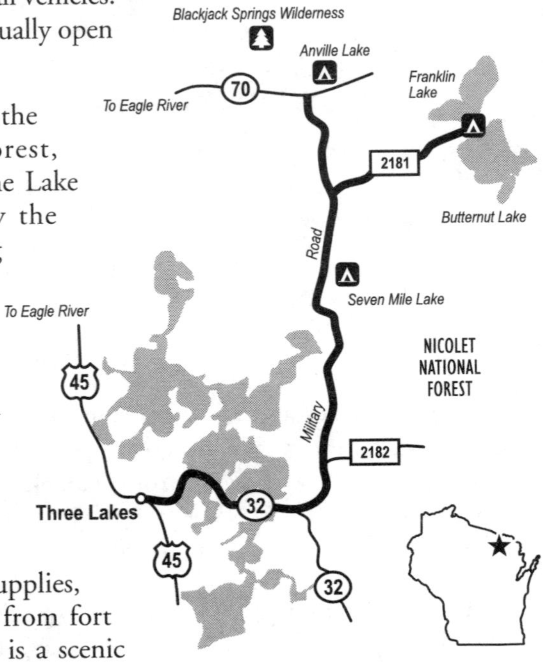

Heritage Drive crosses the Nicolet National Forest, following portions of the Lake Superior Trail used by the Menominee for trading with the Winnebago and Ojibwa Indians. By 1861 the trail was improved a bit and used as a mail route. Shortly following the trail's initial service as a mail route, the military improved the trail to a roadway transporting supplies, ammunition, and mail from fort to fort. Today the road is a scenic byway through old-growth pine and northern hardwoods, and is used to access outdoor recreation activities.

In 1937 the Civilian Conservation Corps constructed eight stone buildings in the area of Franklin Lake Campground. One building has been renovated into an interpretive center where exhibits provide information on the area's geology and history. The campground and its historic stone structures are listed on the National Register of Historic Places. Visitors will find 81 campsites suitable for tents and RVs up to 22 feet long. A nature trail and swimming area are also found here. The lake yields good walleye and bass fishing.

Seven Mile Lake Campground sits on a bluff overlooking the lake. The campground is two miles northeast of the byway on FSR 2435. It has 27 RV and tent campsites. There is boat access to the lake, a swimming area, and good musky, walleye, and bass fishing. A two-mile hiking trail heads east and circles two wetland lakes.

Anvil Lake Campground lies just to the east of the byway's northern terminus. There are 18 campsites with picnic tables and fire rings. Drinking water, a swimming area, and boat access are among the facilities available. Anglers will find walleye and bass inhabiting the lake.

Information: Nicolet National Forest, Eagle River Ranger District, PO Box 1809, Eagle River WI 54521 / 715-479-2827.

Wyoming

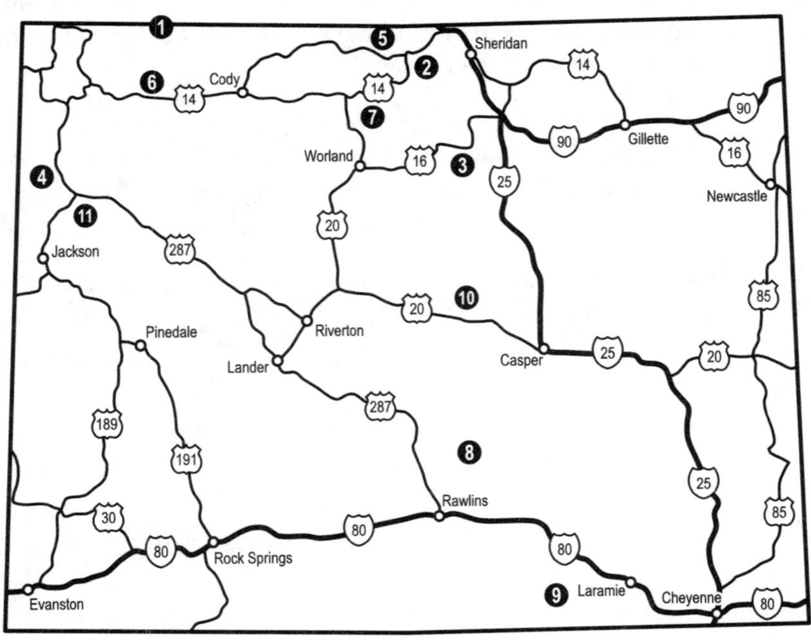

Sheridan
Cody
Worland
Gillette
Newcastle
Jackson
Pinedale
Riverton
Lander
Casper
Rawlins
Rock Springs
Evanston
Laramie
Cheyenne

Beartooth Highway

Beartooth Highway is in northwest Wyoming and southern Montana. It begins in Red Lodge, Montana and travels southwest to Yellowstone National Park. The byway follows US 212 for 68 miles. US Highway 212 is a two-lane paved road suitable for all vehicles. Beartooth Highway is usually open late May through mid-October. Portions of the route are groomed in winter for snowmobile use.

The route takes travelers on a scenic journey across the beautiful Beartooth Mountains. It travels through portions of Custer and Gallatin National Forests in Montana and Shoshone National Forest in Wyoming. A primitive trail was once all that connected the mining towns of Red Lodge and Cooke City until the Civilian Conservation Corps constructed a road between 1932 and 1936. Now travelers can enjoy the spectacular scenery as they climb the switchbacks of this byway to 10,947-foot Beartooth Pass. The forests

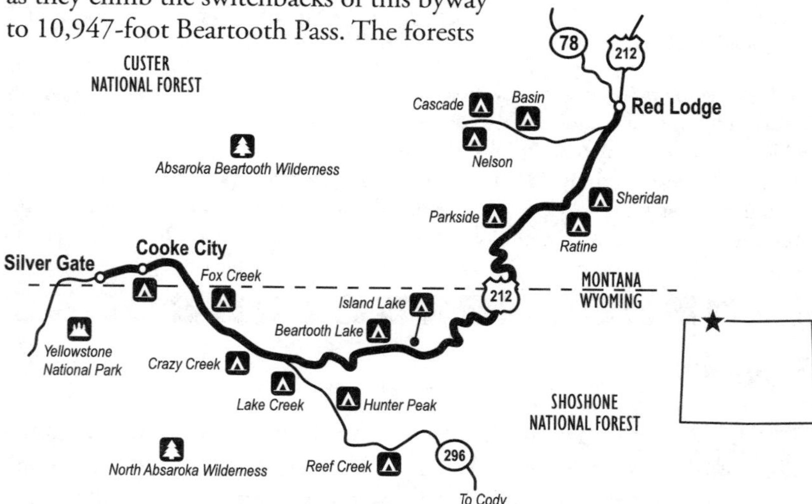

consist of Engelmann spruce, Douglas fir, lodgepole pine, and aspen. Aspen leaves turn a beautiful golden color in fall, making this an even more beautiful drive.

The national forests are home to a wide variety of wildlife. Byway travelers are likely to see elk or mule deer foraging along the roadside, especially in early morning or evening. Moose can sometimes be seen among the willows along lakes and streams. Black and grizzly bears also inhabit the area but are rarely seen. Birdwatchers will need to keep an eye on the sky for hawks, golden eagles, and prairie falcons.

Campers have nearly 200 sites in all from which to choose. Each campsite has a picnic table and fire ring for those nights under stars around a campfire. All the campgrounds have drinking water and comfort stations. The lower elevation campgrounds are usually open by Memorial Day. Campgrounds higher up may not open until mid to late June, depending on snow conditions.

Information: Shoshone National Forest, Clarks Fork Ranger District, 203A Yellowstone Ave, Cody WY 82414 / 307-527-6921. Custer National Forest, Beartooth Ranger District, HC 49 Box 3420, Red Lodge MT 59068 / 406-446-2103. Yellowstone National Park, PO Box 168, Yellowstone WY 82190 / 307-344-7381.

Lodging Invitation

Red Lodging
16½ N. Broadway
P.O. Box 1477
Red Lodge, MT 59068

Phone: 406-446-1272
800-6-RED LODGE (800-673-3563)
Fax: 406-446-4647
Internet: www.redlodging.com

Red Lodging offers you the convenience, privacy and comforts of home. You'll enjoy the finest in fully furnished residential vacation lodging in the heart of Beartooth Country and Red Lodge, Montana. Beautiful Victorian homes • modern condos • creekside cabins • stone fireplaces • hot tubs • private scenic ponds • creekside fishing • antique decors • golf course access • and much more. These are special homes for special vacations in the most undiscovered resort community in the Rocky Mountains. Some homes sleep up to ten people. Personalized customer service. Single nights available during non-peak periods.

Bighorn

Bighorn scenic byway is in north-central Wyoming 21 miles west of Sheridan. It follows US 14 between Dayton and Shell, a distance of 58 miles. US Highway 14 is a two-lane paved road suitable for all vehicles. Temporary closure by snow is possible in winter, otherwise the byway remains open year-round. Forty miles are officially designated a National Forest Scenic Byway.

From Dayton, the Bighorn National Forest Scenic Byway begins at an elevation of 3,926 feet and climbs to over 9,000 feet at Granite Pass. Between these two points, the byway twists and turns up switchbacks as it makes the ascent up the Bighorn Mountains. From Granite Pass, the byway begins its descent of nearly 5,000 feet to pass through Shell Canyon and the byway's end in Shell. Accompanying you for this portion of the byway are the babbling waters of Granite and Shell Creeks. All along the byway wildflowers display their beautiful colors from spring to autumn. Joyful songbirds sing, telling you of the marvelous scenery they live among. Byway travelers will pass through forests of ponderosa pine, alpine fir, Engelmann spruce, and lodgepole pine in addition to wide open grassy meadows and valleys.

Wildlife observers will delight in small and large creatures that inhabit the area. Of the smaller variety are porcupines, gophers, and beavers. Mule deer and white-tailed deer may be seen with elk grazing along rivers and streams or among the grasses of open meadows. Moose, black bears, bobcats, and coyotes also inhabit the area but are more secretive. Bighorn sheep have been transplanted into the area and may also be spotted occasionally. Anglers may want to spend some time trying to pull rainbow, brown, and brook trout from the forest's many rivers and streams.

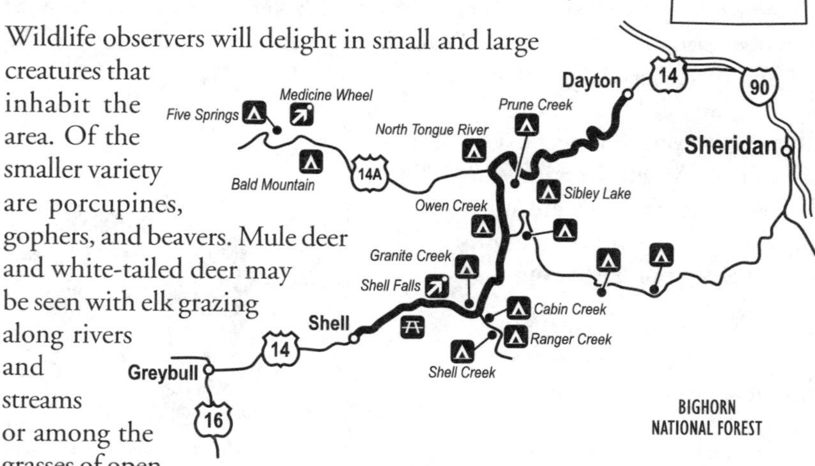

Be sure to stop and view the beautiful Shell Falls. Walking trails provide closer examination of the waterfalls. An information center here has some information on the area. Stay awhile and read a good book, talk with others, or enjoy a picnic. By all means, take some pictures!

Information: Bighorn National Forest, 1969 S Sheridan Ave, Sheridan WY 82801 / 307-672-0751.

Cloud Peak Skyway

Cloud Peak Skyway is 35 miles south of Sheridan in north-central Wyoming. It begins in Buffalo and travels west to Ten Sleep. The byway is 67 miles long and follows US 16, a two-lane paved road suitable for all vehicles. Temporary closure by snow is possible in winter, otherwise the byway is open all year. Wyoming has officially designated 47 miles as a state scenic byway. The US Forest Service designated 43 miles as a National Forest Scenic Byway.

Cloud Peak Skyway begins at an elevation of 4,645 feet in Buffalo and heads west across the forested Bighorn Mountains. It crosses Powder River Pass at an elevation of 9,666 feet and then drops down through Ten Sleep Canyon to end in Ten Sleep at 4,206 feet. Several viewpoints provide expansive vistas into Cloud Peak Wilderness and the surrounding mountain scenery. Wildlife observers need to be looking for mule deer or elk among the rivers and grassy meadows. Wildflowers bloom from spring through autumn, providing a splash of color against the green of ponderosa pine.

If you're interested in hiking, backpacking, or horseback riding, you're in the right place. To the north of the byway lies the pristine land of the vast Cloud Peak Wilderness. The area protects 195,000 acres of the Bighorn Mountains. Trails leading into this beautiful wilderness can be accessed from the byway. Hikers and backpackers will find trails that will take them several days to hike.

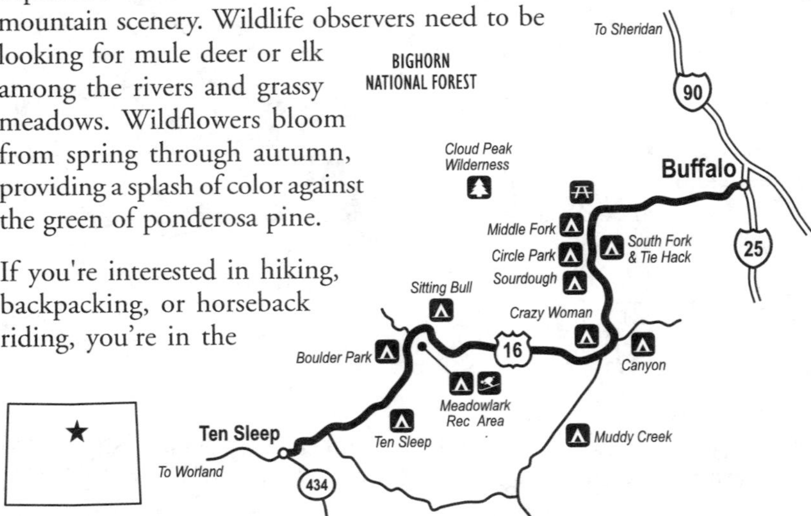

Those less interested in hiking the back country but want to enjoy an evening around a campfire can do so at the many campgrounds found along the byway. Meadowlark Recreation Area offers over 100 campsites in five nearby campgrounds. The lake here is popular during summer with anglers and boaters. Middle Fork, Circle Park, South Fork, and Tie Hacks Campgrounds provide a total of 43 sites. Trailheads found here can take you into the wilderness area.

Information: Bighorn National Forest, 1969 S Sheridan Ave, Sheridan WY 82801 / 307-672-0751.

Lodging Invitation

Mountain View Inn
585 Fort Street
Buffalo, WY 82834

Phone: 307-684-2881 / 307-684-5443
E-mail: jgampetr@wyoming.com
Internet: www.buffalowyoming.com/mtview

Guests choose the Mountain View Inn for its authentic log cabins, quiet shaded picnic grounds and friendly Western atmosphere. Choose from individual queen bed cabins and double room family cabins, some with kitchenettes. Camping, hiking and backpacking opportunities for every level of expertise abound. Lake and stream trout fishing is excellent, while not over-crowded. Within walking distance of the museum, Buffalo's town center, the park, swimming pool, tennis courts, nature trail and golf course. RV hookups • laundry • shower facilities • and tent sites are also available.

A/C H

John D. Rockefeller Jr. Memorial Parkway

NP US FS

John D. Rockefeller, Jr. Memorial Parkway is in northwest Wyoming. It follows US 89 between Grant Village and Moose, a distance of 82 miles. US Highway 89 is a two-lane paved road suitable for all vehicles. The highway north of Flagg Ranch is not maintained during winter; access to Yellowstone National Park is by snowmobile or commercial snow coach. The portion from Moran Junction to Moose is also part of the Wyoming Centennial byway.

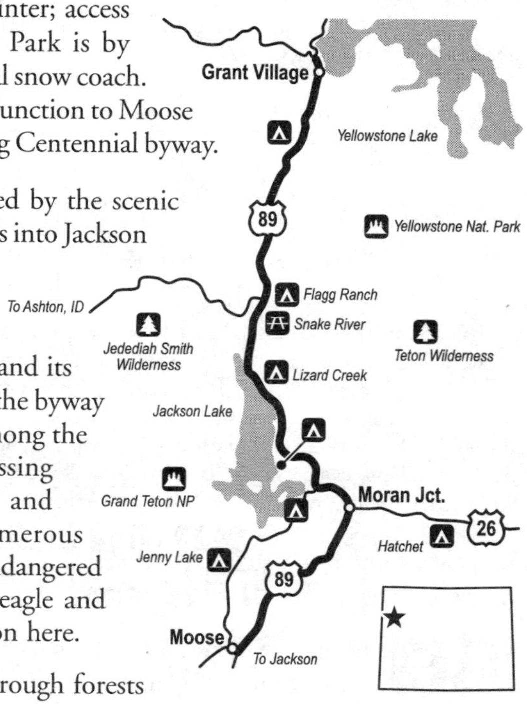

The byway is accompanied by the scenic Snake River, which empties into Jackson Lake. Cutthroat trout, brown and brook trout, mackinaw, and whitefish are abundant in the river and its tributaries. Visitors along the byway may see moose feeding among the willows; elk and deer passing through the open forest; and beavers working the numerous creeks. Threatened and endangered species, such as the bald eagle and grizzly bear, find protection here.

The scenic drive winds through forests

of lodgepole pine, spruce, fir, and aspen. Wet meadows and willow thickets line the rivers while wildflowers and grasses cover the open hillsides during summer. Several scenic overlooks provide views of majestic the Teton Range of the Rocky Mountains. A 24,000-acre parcel of land is also known as the John D. Rockefeller, Jr. Memorial Parkway. This land area connects the two national parks and was dedicated in 1972 to recognize Mr. Rockefeller's generosity in making significant contributions to several national parks across the country, including Acadia, Great Smoky Mountains, Virgin Islands, and the Blue Ridge Parkway.

There are several trails that can be accessed along the drive. Some are short self-guided trails while others are long, strenuous paths that will take you deep into the national park and surrounding national forests. Wilderness areas offer the sweet silence of seclusion and two of these primitive and rugged areas can only be reached by hiking trails. Several camping areas are also along this route. Some recreation areas offer such amenities as restaurants, lodging, and grocery stores.

Information: John D. Rockefeller Jr. Memorial Pkwy, c/o Grand Teton National Park, PO Drawer 170, Moose WY 83012 / 307-543-2401. Bridger-Teton National Forest, PO Box 1888, Jackson WY 83001 / 307-739-5500. Yellowstone National Park, PO Box 168, Yellowstone WY 82190 / 307-344-7381.

Lodging Invitation

Dornan's Spur Ranch Cabins
10 Moose St.
P.O. Box 39
Moose, WY 83012

Phone: 307-733-2522
Fax: 307-733-3544
E-mail: spur@sisna.com
Internet: http://www.sisna.com/jackson/dornan/spur1.htm

Dornan's Spur Ranch Cabins is located just inside Grand Teton National Park next to the Snake River providing great views of the Teton Mountains. Accommodations include 8 one-bedroom and 4 two-bedroom housekeeping cabins with full kitchens. A grocery store, gift shop, wine shop, deli, sports shop and restaurant are all located on-site. Other services available include: scenic or whitewater float trips • sportswear and equipment shop for climbing, hiking, camping, and cross-country skiing • fishing tackle shop with guided fishing trips • rentals of mountain bikes and canoes. No pets—No TV's—No smoking.

Medicine Wheel Passage

Medicine Wheel Passage is 47 miles west of Sheridan in north-central Wyoming. It follows a 27-mile segment of US

14A, a two-lane paved road suitable for all vehicles. Medicine Wheel Passage is usually open May to mid-November.

The Medicine Wheel Passage scenic byway provides an alternate route for those traveling the Bighorn scenic byway. It also provides an excuse to complete the other scenic drive and then make your way around to drive this byway. As with the sister scenic byway, Medicine Wheel takes you through the beautiful scenery known as the Bighorn Mountains. The mountains are covered with lodgepole pine, alpine fir, Engelmann spruce, and ponderosa pine.

A large parking area adjacent to the byway at Bald Mountain provides breathtaking views of the northern Bighorn Mountains. Be sure you have enough film in your camera. This area marks the center of gold mining activity during the late 1880s. To the northeast are the remains of Bald Mountain City, a gold mining ghost town.

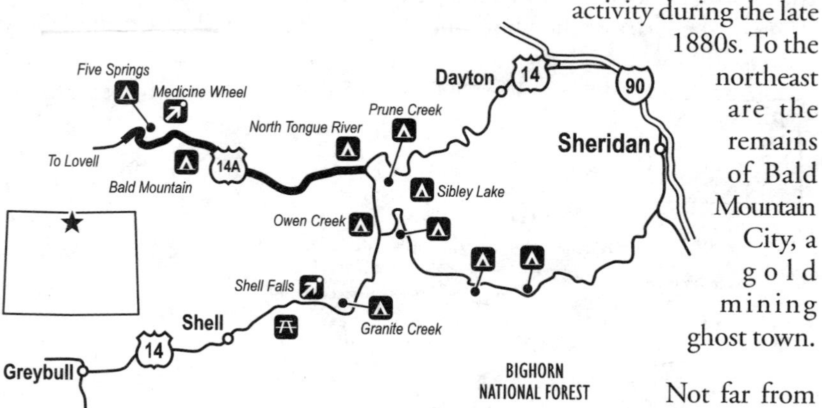

Not far from the Bald Mountain overlook is Medicine Wheel National Historic Landmark. Believed to have been built by prehistoric Indians, this giant wheel is made of limestone slabs and boulders. It measures 245 feet in circumference. This wheel is recognized by Native Americans as a sacred site. The reason for its construction remains a mystery. If you want to continue exploring this area, find FSR 11/14. It will take you to the trailhead for Bucking Mule Falls National Recreation Trail. The trail is eleven miles long but the first three will take you to a viewpoint of the thundering Bucking Mule Falls.

Camping opportunities along this stretch of US 14A are not as extensive as its sister byway, the Bighorn. North Tongue has eleven sites while Bald Mountain provides fifteen.

Information: Bighorn National Forest, 1969 S Sheridan Ave, Sheridan WY 82801 / 307-672-0751.

North Fork Highway

North Fork Highway is in northwest Wyoming about 20 miles west of Cody. If follows US 14 (also US 16 and US 20) between Wapiti and Pahaska. The 30-mile byway is a two-lane paved road that is suitable for all types of vehicles. US Highway 14 is usually open all year. West of Pahaska, US 14 enters Yellowstone National Park; this road is closed mid-November through March. It is groomed for snowmobiling and cross-country skiing. North Fork Highway is also known as the Buffalo Bill Cody scenic byway.

North Fork Highway travels through the beautiful Shoshone Canyon where the North Fork of the Shoshone River flows nearby. The route travels through the heart of the Shoshone National Forest and is surrounded by two wilderness areas. The canyon is a narrow valley with extremely steep slopes and vertical cliffs, giving the visitor a feeling of being embraced by the surrounding mountains.

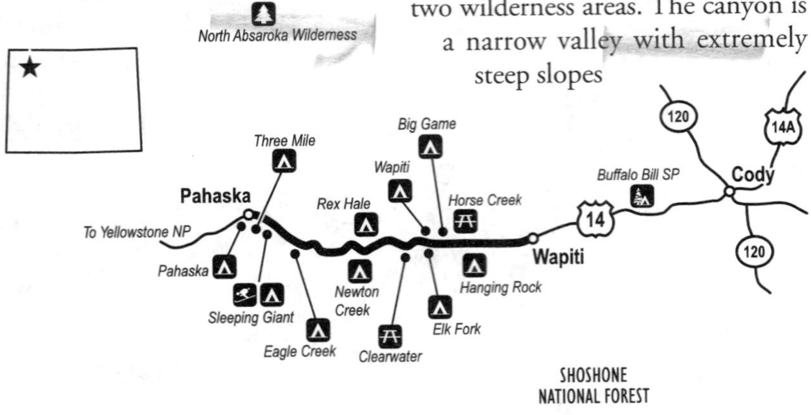

Wildlife observers will want to be on the lookout for mule deer and elk that can sometimes be seen grazing in the meadows or along the river. Moose, bighorn sheep, black bear, and the mighty grizzly bear are also inhabitants of the area. The North Fork is believed to have one of the highest concentrations of grizzly bears in the lower 48 states.

There are numerous trails along the byway that invite the traveler to explore. Many will lead into the wilderness areas lying to the north and south of the byway. To the north is 350,488-acre North Absaroka Wilderness. To your south is the huge 704,529-acre Washakie Wilderness. Both of these wilderness areas provide excellent opportunities for those seeking solitude. You don't have to be a seasoned hiker or backpacker to enjoy short segments of the trails. For those that are equipped to handle the wilderness, the trails are your gateway to a wonderland of beautiful mountains and wildlife in its most natural setting.

Those interested in sleeping under the stars will find a lot of campgrounds along the byway. Altogether, there are over 200 campsites. All of them but Deer Creek Campground is situated on the banks of the river.

Information: Shoshone National Forest, 808 Meadow Lane Ave., Cody WY 82414 / 307-527-6241. Buffalo Bill State Park, 47 Lakeside Rd, Cody WY 82414 / 307-587-9227. Yellowstone National Park, PO Box 168, Yellowstone WY 82190 / 307-344-7381.

Red Gulch / Alkali

Red Gulch / Alkali is ten miles east of Greybull in north-central Wyoming. It is 32 miles long and follows the Red Gulch / Alkali Road, which is a gravel and dirt road. The byway requires a two-wheel drive, high-clearance vehicle to complete. It is open May through October but can become impassable after periods of rain.

Travelers of the Red Gulch / Alkali Back Country Byway will find themselves winding through the foothills of the beautiful Bighorn Mountains. It's easy to see how the byway was named when you travel this back country route. The reddish color of the Chugwater

formation is seen to the east with the Bighorn Mountains as a backdrop. The landscape is composed mostly of sagebrush that provides habitat for the sage grouse. The sage grouse will proudly display their showy plumage at dawn in early spring for those traveling that time of year. If you're traveling this byway in the fall, be on the lookout for mule deer or elk that make their way down from higher elevations for the coming winter. You may also encounter a gold eagle or peregrine falcon soaring overhead.

As you travel along the byway you may notice stacks of stone piled upon each other. Some of these were constructed by Native Americans to mark trail routes, hunting areas, or other important features of the landscape. Others may have been constructed by sheepherders to mark bed grounds and springs or simply out of boredom.

Although there are no developed campgrounds along the byway, the Bureau of Land Management permits dispersed camping nearly anywhere on public land. It is best, however, to obtain maps from the BLM before setting up camp as there may be private property nearby. The Medicine Lodge Archaeological Site, just east of the southern end of the byway, has camping facilities. You can also see Native American petroglyphs here.

Information: BLM-Worland Field Office, 101 S 23rd St, Worland WY 82401 / 307-347-5100.

Seminoe to Alcova

BLM 1 Seminoe to Alcova is 32 miles southwest of Casper in south-central Wyoming. The byway is 64 miles long and follows CR 351 and CR 407. The gravel roads vary from single-lane to two lanes and are suitable for most vehicles. Motorhomes and vehicles pulling trailers are discouraged from traveling the portion from Semino State Park to Miracle Mile. Seminoe to Alcova is usually open May to early December.

Seminoe to Alcova Back Country Byway takes travelers across a desert landscape between the Seminoe Mountains in the west and Shirley Mountains rising in the east. Portions of the byway travel along the banks of the North Platte River, which has brought life to the Seminoe and Pathfinder Reservoirs. Byway travelers will cross the river in an area known as Miracle Mile. This stretch of the North Platte River is renowned as a blue-ribbon trout stream.

Travelers are most likely to see pronghorn antelope and mule deer grazing

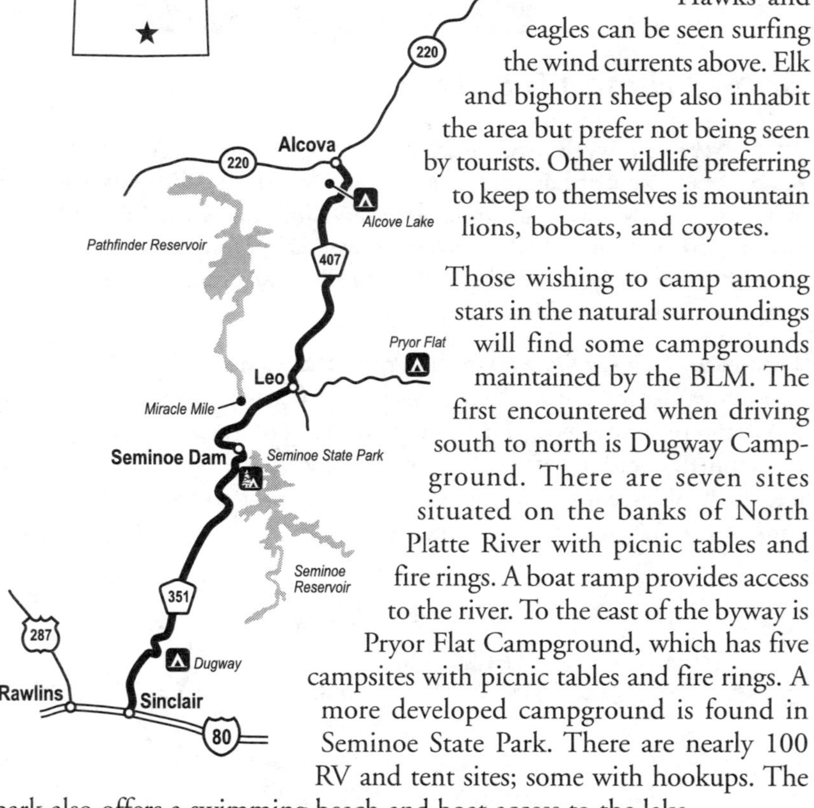

along the roadside. Hawks and eagles can be seen surfing the wind currents above. Elk and bighorn sheep also inhabit the area but prefer not being seen by tourists. Other wildlife preferring to keep to themselves is mountain lions, bobcats, and coyotes.

Those wishing to camp among stars in the natural surroundings will find some campgrounds maintained by the BLM. The first encountered when driving south to north is Dugway Campground. There are seven sites situated on the banks of North Platte River with picnic tables and fire rings. A boat ramp provides access to the river. To the east of the byway is Pryor Flat Campground, which has five campsites with picnic tables and fire rings. A more developed campground is found in Seminoe State Park. There are nearly 100 RV and tent sites; some with hookups. The park also offers a swimming beach and boat access to the lake.

Information: BLM-Rawlins Field Office, 1300 N Third St, Rawlins WY 82301 / 307-328-4200. Seminoe State Park, CR 351 Seminoe Dam Rt., Sinclair WY 82334 / 307-320-3013.

Lodging Invitation

Royal Inn Motel	Phone:	307-234-3501
Aries Car Rental & Western Union	Fax:	307-234-7340
440 East "A" Street		
Casper, WY 82601		

The Royal Inn Motel offers travelers a convenient location in the business district of downtown Casper. Located in a well lighted quiet area — accommodations include 37 rooms, 3 with kitchenettes, and an outside swimming pool. Complimentary coffee in the morning. Nearby, guests will find theaters, banks, restaurants, airport, and post office. Only 15 minutes from Casper Mountain Ski Area. Reasonable rates. All major credit cards welcome. From I-25 travel south on Centre Street, turn left on "A" Street.

Snowy Range Highway

Snowy Range Highway is in southern Wyoming 30 miles west of Laramie. It begins in Centennial and travels west to WY 230. The byway is 40 miles long and follows WY 130, a two-lane paved road suitable for all vehicles. Snowy Range Highway is open late May through early November. Thirty miles are officially designated a National Forest Scenic Byway.

The Snowy Range Highway travels across the Medicine Bow Mountains, also known as the Snowy Range, through forests of Engelmann Spruce, subalpine fir, and aspen. The byway climbs more than 2,000 feet from Centennial at 8,076 feet to Snowy Range Pass, an elevation of 10,847 feet. It then descends from the pass, skirts the shores of several lakes, and ends at the national forest boundary west of Ryan Park. At the top of

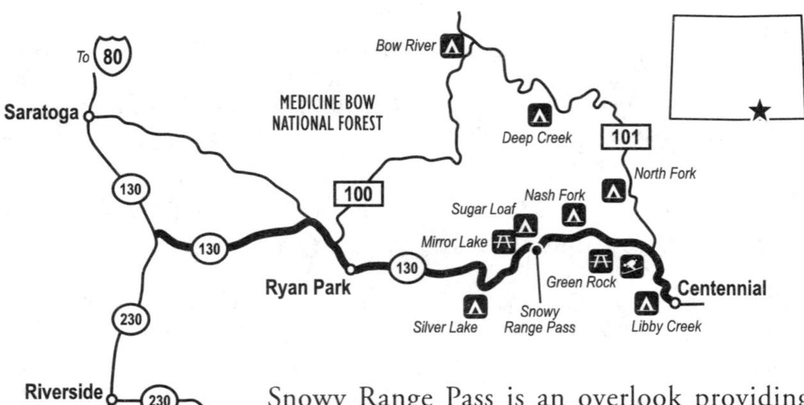

Snowy Range Pass is an overlook providing spectacular views of the surrounding mountains. Wildflowers display beautiful colors of pink and yellow in June and July. In autumn, stands of aspen paint the mountainsides with shimmering gold. This route was originally a wagon road used in the 1800s.

During winter months, much of the byway remains closed to automobiles but does provide access to excellent downhill and cross-country skiing. A downhill skiing area is located just five miles west of Centennial. There are over 300 miles of trails throughout the national forest, providing excellent cross-country skiing during winter and hiking during summer. A hiking trail at Lake Marie will lead you to the top of 12,013-foot Medicine Bow Peak. It's a three-mile hike with some steep climbs but the view from the top is worth the effort.

Visitors will find many lakes along the byway and throughout the national forest. Anglers will want to spend some time fishing for trout. Others may want to lay down a blanket and enjoy a picnic. Campgrounds can also be found on the shores of several lakes. If you're interested in pitching a tent or parking your RV, you'll find several campgrounds from which to choose. The national forest also permits dispersed camping nearly anywhere within the national forest. Check with the visitor center in Centennial for any restrictions.

Information: Medicine Bow National Forest, 2468 Jackson St, Laramie WY 82070 / 307-745-2300.

Lodging Invitation

Olde Depot Bed & Breakfast
201 N. 1st Street, Box 604
Riverside, WY 82325

Phone: 307-327-5277
Fax: 307-327-5230

Completely renovated train depot from the Saratoga Encampment Rail Road. Choose from three relaxing and comfortable rooms, all with private baths. A mixture of antique and replica furniture — 100 year old copper tub • Victorian clawfoot tub • jacuzzi spa tub — provides a unique theme for each room. A hot tub is also available for guests. Located in the Upper Platte River Valley between the Sierra Madre and Snowy Range Mountains. Only 5 miles from snowmobile & cross country ski trails. Only 100 yards to the Encampment River offering blue ribbon trout fishing.

Silver Moon Motel
412 E. Bridge St.
P.O. Box 929
Saratoga, WY 82331

Phone: 307-326-5974

A convenient location close to the main downtown area and the town's natural hot springs. All rooms at the Silver Moon Motel provide guests with color cable TV and phones. Only 20 minutes from the beautiful mountains where you will find winter cross country and snowmobile trails. Great fishing is only 1 block away in the North Platte River.

Snowy Mountain Lodge
P.O. Box 151
Centennial, WY 82055

Phone: 307-742-7669
Fax: 307-742-7669
Internet: www.snowfamilyranch.com

Located in the Medicine Bow National Forest, nestled between two mountain streams, the Snowy Mountain Lodge offers 15 rustic log cabins rich with 70 years of wild west history. The cabins vary in size and can accommodate one to 16 people. The summers offer an incredible outdoor experience with unrivaled scenery. 200 different varieties of wild flowers await your arrival as do the fish in the surrounding beaver ponds and streams. Other summer activities include hiking, rock climbing, mountain biking, or just plain old out the car window photography. In the winter, right outside our front door is the trail head of 280 miles of groomed snowmobile trails and pristine cross country ski trails. Just 2 miles down the road is a first class down hill ski resort. Guests are invited to the main lodge to warm up with a mug of hot cocoa by the roaring fire in the big stone fireplace and savor the delicacies of fine dining in the full service restaurant. Open year-round.

South Bighorn / Red Wall

South Bighorn / Red Wall is 13 miles northwest of Casper in central Wyoming. The 101-mile byway follows a series of Natrona County Roads that are a combination gravel and dirt roads. Although the roads are well maintained, a two-wheel drive, high-clearance vehicle is recommended. The byway is usually open May through November; portions may become impassable after periods of rain.

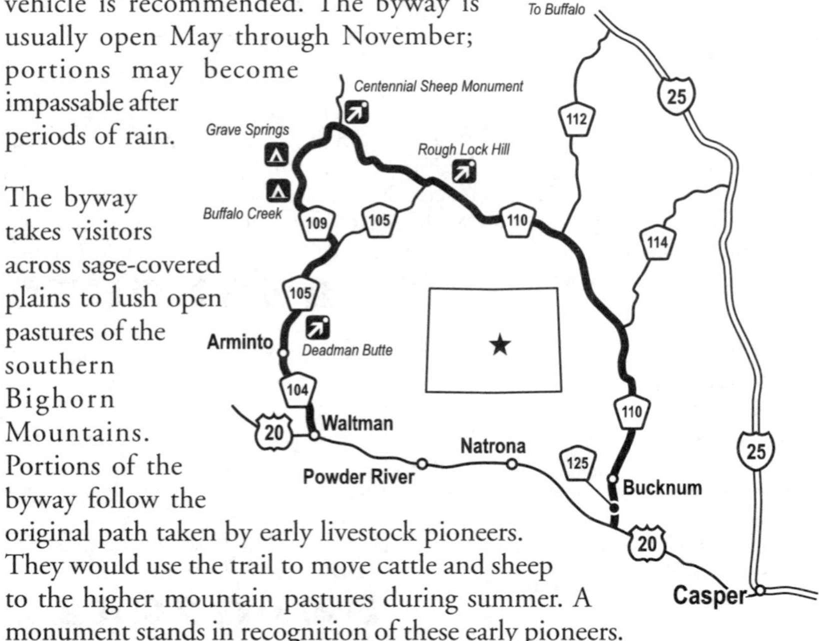

The byway takes visitors across sage-covered plains to lush open pastures of the southern Bighorn Mountains. Portions of the byway follow the original path taken by early livestock pioneers. They would use the trail to move cattle and sheep to the higher mountain pastures during summer. A monument stands in recognition of these early pioneers. Elk and mule deer are likely to be seen in these high mountain pastures.

Byway travelers are also treated to scenic views of the Bighorn Mountains rising to the north. As you descend from the higher elevations, you'll be traveling alongside a portion of the Red Wall. North of here is Hole-in-the-Wall and Outlaw Cave where Butch Cassidy and the Sundance Kid once hid out. If you decide you would like to hide out also, you'll find two BLM campgrounds with several sites. Picnic tables, fire rings, and pit toilets are provided but there is no drinking water.

Roughlock Hill sits 6,200 feet above sea level and provides scenic views of the surrounding countryside. Here pioneers would lock their wagon wheels with thick branches and skid down the steep rocky slope. If you look closely, you may see the evidence left behind.

Information: BLM-Casper Field Office, 1701 East E St, Casper WY 82601 / 307-261-7600.

Lodging Invitation

Royal Inn Motel	Phone:	307-234-3501
Aries Car Rental & Western Union	Fax:	307-234-7340
440 East "A" Street		
Casper, WY 82601		

The Royal Inn Motel offers travelers a convenient location in the business district of downtown Casper. Located in a well lighted quiet area — accommodations include 37 rooms, 3 with kitchenettes, and an outside swimming pool. Complimentary coffee in the morning. Nearby, guests will find theaters, banks, restaurants, airport, and post office. Only 15 minutes from Casper Mountain Ski Area. Reasonable rates. All major credit cards welcome. From I-25 travel south on Centre Street, turn left on "A" Street.

Wyoming Centennial

US FS

Wyoming Centennial is in northwest Wyoming. It begins in Dubois and ends in Pinedale, a distance of 161 miles. The byway follows US 26 and US 191, which are two-lane paved roads suitable for all vehicles. Delays are possible in winter, otherwise the byway is open year-round. The portion from Moran Junction to Moose is part of the John D. Rockefeller, Jr. Memorial Parkway.

Travelers can begin their scenic journey in Dubois and climb through the mountains to cross 9,658-foot Togwotee Pass. Reaching the pass results in spectacular views in all directions. From this mountain pass you'll continue through a mixed conifer forest, rising and descending through meadows and mountain valleys. You'll turn south in Moran Junction and follow the path dictated by the winding Snake River. The byway will then take you through Grand Teton National Park and Jackson Hole. Continuing southeasterly you'll drive through the canyon walls of Hoback Canyon with Hoback River accompanying you. After 161 miles through beautiful mountains and valleys, the byway ends in the community of Pinedale.

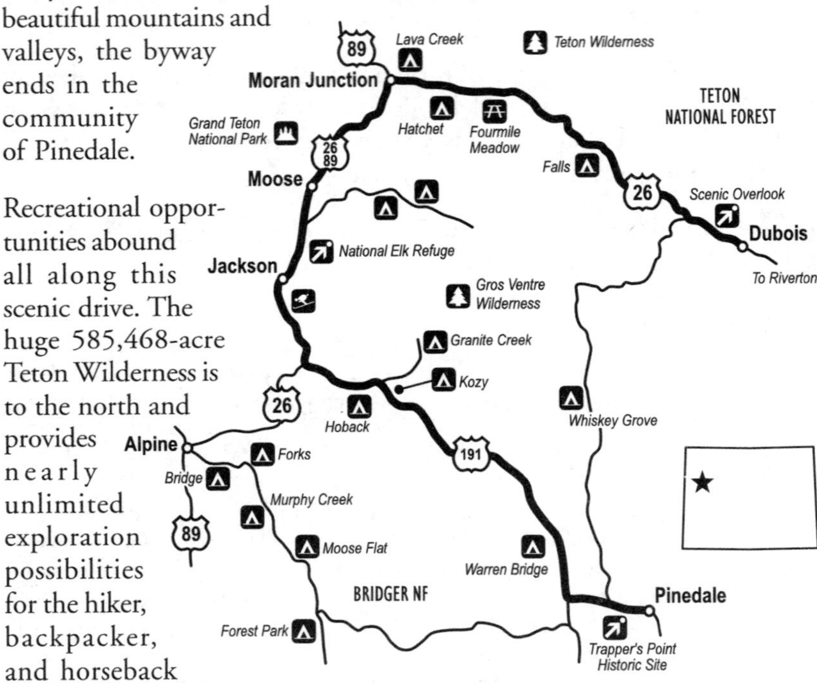

Recreational opportunities abound all along this scenic drive. The huge 585,468-acre Teton Wilderness is to the north and provides nearly unlimited exploration possibilities for the hiker, backpacker, and horseback rider. The 287,000-acre Gros Ventre Wilderness is embraced by the byway and also offers its own hiking opportunities. There are many public campgrounds situated along the banks of meandering streams and rivers or placid mountain lakes. Some offer short nature trails taking you among wildflowers or cascading waterfalls.

Information: Bridger-Teton National Forest, PO Box 1888, Jackson WY 83001 / 307-739-5500. Grand Teton National Park, PO Drawer 170, Moose WY 83012 / 307-739-3300.

Lodging Invitation

Dornan's Spur Ranch Cabins
10 Moose St.
P.O. Box 39
Moose, WY 83012

Phone: 307-733-2522
Fax: 307-733-3544
E-mail: spur@sisna.com
Internet: http://www.sisna.com/jackson/dornan/spur1.htm

Dornan's Spur Ranch Cabins is located just inside Grand Teton National Park next to the Snake River providing great views of the Teton Mountains. Accommodations include 8 one-bedroom and 4 two-bedroom housekeeping cabins with full kitchens. A grocery store, gift shop, wine shop, deli, sports shop and restaurant are all located on-site. Other services available include: scenic or whitewater float trips • sportswear and equipment shop for climbing, hiking, camping, and cross-country skiing • fishing tackle shop with guided fishing trips • rentals of mountain bikes and canoes. No pets—No TV's—No smoking.

Elk Refuge Inn
1755 N. Hwy. 89
P.O. Box 2834
Jackson, WY 83001

Phone: 800-544-3582
307-733-3582
Fax: 307-733-6531

Nestled in a scenic area 1 mile north of Jackson offering fabulous views of National Elk Refuge and Jackson Hole mountains. Accommodations include 23 modern rooms, 11 with kitchens and private balconies. Non-smoking and king rooms also available. All rooms have phones, cable TV, tub and shower. Facilities include: at door parking • winter plug-ins • horse corrals • and trailer parking. Near airport, skiing, golf courses, Teton and Yellowstone National Parks. Some pets allowed. Reasonable rates. For reservations call 800-544-3582. Your business is appreciated.

Lakeside Lodge Resort & Marina
Fremont Lake
P.O. Box 1819
Pinedale, WY 82941

Phone: 307-367-2221
Fax: 307-367-2221

Lakeside Lodge is located on Fremont Lake in the Wind River Mountains. The fifteen acre resort includes a marina, cabins, RV Park, and restaurant & lounge. The lake area offers a wide range of outdoor recreational activities for the entire family. A few of the activities guests can enjoy include: boating • fishing • skiing • hiking • wildlife observations • and golf nearby.

Pine Creek Ranch
#17 Bert Drive, Box 941
Pinedale, WY 82941

Phone: 307-367-2544
307-367-6887

For a special retreat, the Pine Creek Ranch offers a cozy cabin, built around 1900, on the bank of Pine Creek. The cabin has been completely restored and filled with antiques and western decor. Pine Creek Ranch offers a full kitchen, two baths, 4 bedrooms, large living area, fireplace, and peace & quiet. Abundant wildlife on property. Located just a moment from Pinedale, and a short distance from many recreational opportunities. Visa and MC accepted.

INDEX

D

E

F

Q, R

S